REDEEMED BY GOD - 1
Spiritual Life Principles
Associated with God's Word
3rd Edition

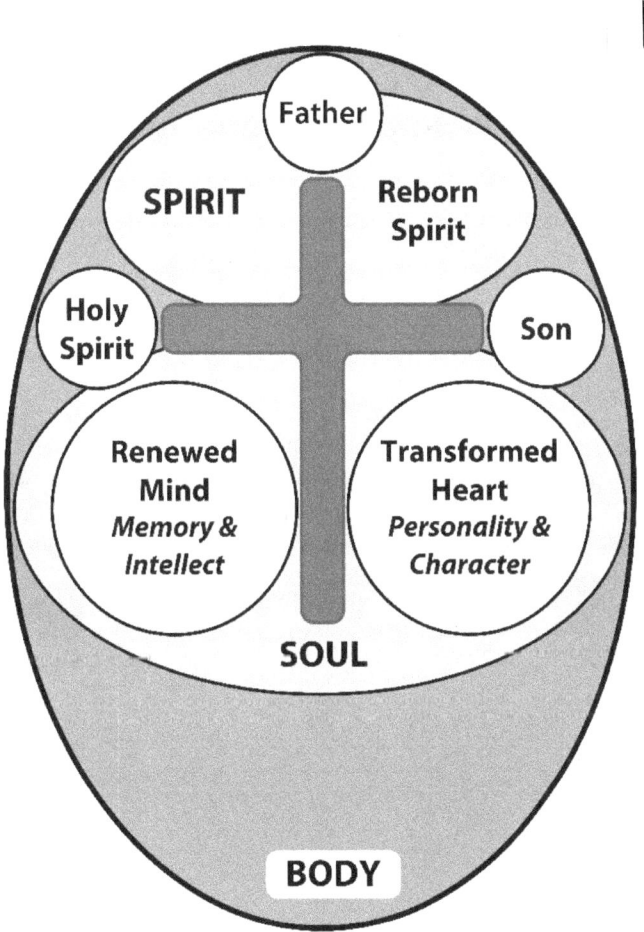

By
Douglas D. Reynolds, Ph.D.

ISBN: 978-1-960093-60-8   (Paperback)
ISBN: 978-1-960093-61-5   (eBook)

Scriptures taken from the NEW AMERICAN STANDARD BIBLE® Copyright © 1960, 1962, 1963, 1968, 1971, 1972, 1973, 1975, 1977, 1995, 2020 by the Lockman Foundation. Used with permission.

Book Ordering Information:
Atticus Publishing
548 Market St PMB 70756
San Francisco, CA 94104
(888) 208-9296
info@atticuspublishing.com
www.atticuspublishing.com

Printed in the United States of America

TITLE PAGE IMAGE

The apostle Paul stated in 1 Thessalonians 5:23 we are born with a spirit, soul and body. The outer ellipse in the title page image represents our physical body. Our body interacts with the physical world through our five physical senses of sight, hearing, touch, taste, and smell. The two inner ellipses in the outer ellipse of the body represent our spirit and soul. Our spirit gives life to our physical body and interacts with the spiritual realm where God exists. Our soul functions through our body and spirit as we interact with the physical world and the spiritual realm. Our spirit and soul are integrally linked. Our body dies and returns to dust when our spirit no longer can support physical life. Our spirit and soul continue in an eternal existence beyond physical death. They continue either in the kingdom of heaven in the presence of God, Jesus and the Holy Spirit or separated from Them in Hades (hell) before and in the lake of fire after the great white throne judgement.

Our soul is comprised of our mind and heart. Our mind is the seat of our memory and intellect. Our memory is the repository of information and experiences we have processed and assimilated throughout our life. Our intellect is the knowledge and wisdom we acquire from this information and these experiences. Our heart is the seat of our personality and character. Our personality is the organized pattern of behavioral characteristics that identify and define who we are. Our character defines the moral and ethical qualities of our personality.

Our soul possesses memory, acquires knowledge, experiences emotions, creates thoughts, forms habits, and initiates actions through our body and spirit. It develops as our mind and heart process and assimilate information they receive through our life experiences. It controls how we encounter, interpret and respond to new life experiences based on how it has processed and assimilated information it has received from prior life experiences.

The Bible teaches we relate to God as Father, Son and Holy Spirit. There are three eternal Persons within the Godhead even though there is one God. They each possess all the eternal attributes of God and interact with perfect agreement. However, they relate to and interact with us in distinct and unique ways. God, the Father, is our Creator and the One who is behind everything and to whom everyone in heaven and on earth is accountable. God's Son, Jesus, is our Lord and Savior. He is the One for and through whom all things have been created and are held together and through whom we approach God, the Father. The Holy Spirit, our Comforter and Helper, reveals the mind of God to us and makes our needs and requests known to God, the Father, through our prayers.

The Bible teaches we are born into this world with a sin nature that separates us from God. We are born spiritually dead because God's spirit is not present in us. However, the

Bible also teaches God loves us, desires to commune and fellowship with us, and is active in us through the Holy Spirit. The Holy Spirit makes us aware of sins in our life, leads us to repent of these sins, and creates a desire within us to enter a relationship with God. God has made this relationship possible through the sacrificial death and resurrection of Jesus. God extends His mercy and grace to us, and He makes known to us His desire to redeem and reconcile us to Himself through Jesus' death and resurrection. However, we must seek God's grace and forgiveness and acknowledge and repent of our sins to enter a reconciled relationship with Him through Jesus. God loves and forgives us, and He communes and fellowships with us when we approach Him through Jesus.

Jesus stated in John 14:6 we can only approach God, the Father, through Him. Therefore, being a good, moral and generous person independent of a relationship with God through Jesus does not gain us entrance into the kingdom of God while we are alive, nor does this gain us entrance into the kingdom of heaven after we die. God redeems and reconciles us to Himself through our faith and trust in and obedience to Jesus as a gift. This gift for us is free because we can do nothing to earn or obtain it independent of our relationship with God through Jesus. The Holy Spirit leads us to repent of our sins, profess with our mouth Jesus is Lord, and believe in our heart God raised Him from the dead to receive God's salvation through His gift of grace (Romans 10:9-10). This saves us from eternal separation from God, Jesus and the Holy Spirit after we die. We are spiritually reborn because God's Spirit along with Jesus and the Holy Spirit take up residence in us.

Paul instructed us in 1 Corinthians 3:10 - 15 to build our life on the foundation of Jesus. We begin building this foundation by reading and study God's word in the Bible. The Holy Spirit opens our mind to understand and internalize what we read and study in the Bible. Our mind is renewed as we internalize and assimilate the words Jesus spoke in the four Gospels, and the Holy Spirit enters our heart to transform our personality and character as our mind is renewed. We are transformed into the person God has created us to be as we continue to have faith in and trust Jesus and become obedient to the words He spoke in the four Gospels.

To the members of my family
my wife, Linda;
my son and daughter-in-law, John and Latricia, and son, Jeff (deceased);
my granddaughters, Janet, Jennifer and Ashlin;
my grandson, Jerry; and
my great grandchildren, Jered, Michael, Hailey,
Alex, Dustin, Ian, Mason and Jackson.

To the Rev. James "JD" Hilliard who reviewed the manuscript for this book and provided helpful guidance for its improvement.

TABLE OF CONTENTS

PREFACE

ACTIONS OF THE HOLY SPIRIT IN MY LIFE

God through the Holy Spirit indicated in 1982 He wanted me to write a book that addressed spiritual life principles associated with His word in the Bible. My initial response was why me? I am a Ph.D. mechanical engineer. I am not a pastor, Bible scholar or theologian. The Holy Spirit initiated a process when I committed to write this book that would enable and equip me to write and publish it. 2 Timothy 3:16-17 motivated me as I engaged in this process. Paul stated:

> "All Scripture is inspired by God and profitable for teaching, for reproof, for correction, for training in righteousness, so that the man of God may be adequate, equipped for every good work."

I again received God's call in 2000 for me to be one of His servants. He indicated He would reveal to me by my reading and studying the Bible and through the Holy Spirit an understanding of Scriptures related to the future. 2 Peter 1:20-21 provided significance to this understanding. Peter stated:

> "But know this first of all, that no prophecy of Scripture is a matter of one's own interpretation, for no prophecy was ever made by an act of human will, but men moved by the Holy Spirit spoke from God."

God indicated difficult days will arise in the future, and He wanted me to be a messenger who shares this understanding with others. He indicated He will be with and support those who trust and have faith in Jesus and obey His words. I believe the future God referred to in 2000 is now here.

The Holy Spirit has revealed to me through the Bible and life experiences the love God extends to us through Jesus and Him. He has helped me to understand the:

- Significance of the infinite sacrifice God made for us through the sacrificial death and resurrection of His Son, Jesus:
- Significance of the infinite sacrifice Jesus made through His death and shed blood on a cross so God, His Father, can redeem us;

- Importance of our receiving the redemption and reconciliation God extends to us through His grace and our faith and trust in and obedience to Jesus; and
- Significance of God's holiness in the context of His relationship with His creation and with us through Jesus.

God will execute His justice that is an extension of His holiness when we stand before and are judged by Jesus on the last day.

I initially wrote and published three books in response to the leadership of the Holy Spirit. My first book, *REDEEMED BY GOD, Our Relationship with God through His Son, Jesus Christ*, was published by Trafford Publishing in 2003. This book addressed the:

- The nature and character of God as Father, Son and Holy Spirit;
- The nature and character of Satan and sin;
- The nature of our creation as spirit, soul and body;
- Spiritual death we experience because of sin;
- Spiritual rebirth and life we receive from God by means of His grace extended to us through our faith and trust in and obedience to Jesus;
- Spiritual growth we experience through Bible study, prayer and a transformed heart;
- Spiritual gifts the Holy Spirit gives to us to enable and equip us to engage in ministry and service to others;
- Spiritual life principles that equip us to effectively address life challenges;
- The Christian Church through which we engage in ministry and service to others; and
- The seven-year tribulation through which God will execute His judgement on a fallen and rebellious world that has rejected Him, Jesus and the Holy Spirit.

The Holy Spirit led me in 2013 to revise and separate my original book into two books:

- *REDEEMED BY GOD - 1, Spiritual Growth and Life Principles Associated with the Gospel of Jesus*, and
- *REDEEMED BY GOD - 2, A Christian Perspective of the End Time and a New World Order.*

These books were published by Trafford Publishing in 2015. Discussion on the seven-year tribulation was placed in *REDEEMED BY GOD – 2, A Christian Perspective of the End Time and a New World Order* with discussions on the:

- Nature and character of God and Satan,

- Functions of our soul and spirit,

- Our relationship with God through our faith and trust in and obedience to Jesus, and

- Events associated with the establishment of a New World Order.

This book introduced cultural conflicts between secular humanism and Christianity, progressivism and conservatism, and socialism and capitalism. These conflicts and their consequences are evident today in the United States and other countries. They will lead to the formation of a New World Order. The topics covered in *REDEEMED BY GOD, Our Relationship with God through His Son, Jesus Christ* without material on the seven-year tribulation were revised and presented in *REDEEMED BY GOD – 1, Spiritual Growth and Life Principles Associated with the Gospel of Jesus.* Two subsequent revised editions of these two books were published by Trafford Publishing.

REDEEMED BY GOD – 1 and *REDEEMED BY GOD -2* were updated and re-released in 2020 as part of the three-book series with titles:

- *REDEEMED BY GOD – 1, Spiritual Life Principles Associated with God's Word*;

- *REDEEMED BY GOD – 2, Time of the End, Return of Jesus and a New World Order*; and

- *REDEEMED BY GOD – 3, God's Redemption through Jesus and His Plan for Eternity.*

The new releases of *REDEEMED BY GOD – 1* and *REDEEMED BY GOD – 2* contained revised materials presented in their prior releases. *REDEEMED BY GOD – 3* was condensed from *REDEEMED BY GOD – 2* and addressed the:

- Nature and character of God and Satan;

- Origin and nature of sin;

- Nature of our creation as spirit, soul and body;

- Functions of our soul and spirit;

- Our relationship with God through our faith and trust in and obedience to Jesus;

- God's future judgments of the unrighteous and righteous; and

- The destruction of the existing heaven and earth and the creation of a new heaven, earth and Jerusalem.

Revised 2nd editions of the above three *REDEEMED BY GOD* books were published in 2024.

My *REDEEMED BY GOD* books were written from an evangelical perspective of what I perceived the Bible was saying to and teaching me. My writing style as a Ph.D. mechanical engineer is that of a technical writer. Cultural influences on non-biblical topics in *REDEEMED BY GOD – 2* were addressed. This was not done in *REDEEMED BY GOD – 1* and *REDEEMED BY GOD - 3*.

My *REDEEMED BY GOD* books have been written for individuals who are struggling to cope with real life situations related to the cultural conflicts that are occurring in the world. Many are seeking a relationship with God through Jesus and the Holy Spirit to better equip themselves to address these conflicts and the life struggles they are creating. The revised 2nd edition releases of my *REDEEMED BY GOD* books are written for individuals who:

- Have entered a reconciled relationship with God through their faith and trust in and obedience to Jesus and want to grow and mature in this relationship through the presence of the Holy Spirit in their lives (*REDEEMED BY GOD – 1*);

- Have entered a reconciled relationship with God through their faith and trust in and obedience to Jesus and want to grow in their knowledge and understanding of events that will lead to the formation of a New World Order and the seven-year tribulation (*REDEEMED BY GOD – 2*); and

- Do not know God but who the Holy Spirit is nudging to seek and enter a redeemed relationship with Him through Jesus (*REDEEMED BY GOD -3*).

Bible scriptures are presented in these books to document that the spiritual life principle and precepts addressed in my books are from God. These Bible scriptures have been selected to aid in the spiritual growth of those who read my books.

SPIRITUAL ORIGIN OF TODAY'S CULTURAL CONFLICTS

The cultural conflicts addressed in *REDEEMED BY GOD - 2* are being discussed and framed today as a conflict between the progressive left and the conservative right. What is not being discussed is the spiritual origin of these conflicts. This origin is traced back to ancient secret societies that existed at the time of the Tower of Babel and after its fall described in Genesis 11:1-9. These secret societies opposed God and were led by illuminists who were the intellectual elite of their day. These illuminists were disciples of Lucifer and had as their objectives the:

- Absolute rule over the world,
- Elimination of private prosperity,
- Elimination of religions, and

- Elimination of nation-states.

These objectives after the death and resurrection of Jesus found their way into later anti-Christian secret societies that included the Luciferians, Rosicrucians and the Levellers. They eventually found their way into a secret society called the Illuminati.

The Illuminati controlled global movement was made popular by Adam Weishaupt during the latter part of the 18th century. The Illuminati wanted to establish a deistic, global and dictatorial government that will abolish:

- Governments of all nation-states;
- All private property;
- All inheritance rights;
- Patriotism to national causes;
- Social relationships within families,
- Sexual prohibition laws and moral codes; and
- Religious disciplines based on faith in a transcendent God, while promoting faith in nature, man and reason.

These objectives have been incorporated into the progressive left agenda that opposes the presence of God, Jesus and the Holy Spirit in our lives and culture.

SIGNIFICANCE OF GOD'S GRACE

I mention in my REDEEMED BY GOD books that we enter a redeemed relationship with God through our **faith** and **trust** in and **obedience** to Jesus. **Faith** is our strong belief in the **truth** of the Bible's discussions regarding our relationship with God and the roles Jesus and the Holy Spirit play in this relationship. **Trust** is our assured reliance on this **truth** and on God's and Jesus' ability to honor Their covenants and promises presented in the Bible. **Obedience** is our submission to the reality and requirements of this **truth** on our life and to God's laws and the words Jesus spoke in the four Gospels.

Paul stated in Ephesians 2:8 we are saved by God's **grace** through **faith**. God's **grace** is His conscious and deliberate extension of His love and good will to provide us with something we can neither earn nor provide for ourself. Paul stated God extends His **grace** to us as a gift, and he referred to this gift as being free in Romans 5:15-17. God extends His **grace** to and redeems us with no cost to us because we can do nothing to obtain it independent of His love for us, and so we cannot claim we are entitled to His grace because of actions we initiate. Paul continued in Ephesians 2:9 we cannot be redeemed by our own works independent of God's **grace**. He then stated in Ephesians 2:10 we become new creations by God in Christ Jesus to perform **good works** He has prepared beforehand for us to perform.

We are redeemed by God's **grace** when we profess with our mouth Jesus is Lord and believe in our heart God raised Him from the dead (Romans 10:8-10). The Holy Spirit then begins to reside in us, and we enter a bilateral relationship with God through Jesus and the presence of the Holy Spirit in our life. God, Jesus, the Holy Spirit and we have obligations in a relationship that results from our being redeemed by God's **grace**. We can **trust** God and Jesus to honor their covenants and promises regarding our relationship with Them that are presented in the Bible. We are to develop, grow and mature in our **faith** and **trust** in and **obedience** to Jesus with the assistance of the Holy Spirit in our relationship with God through Jesus.

Paul indicated in Romans 10:17 **faith** comes from hearing and proceeds from the words of Jesus. The Holy Spirit in our life facilitates the development and growth of our **faith** as we hear and are taught the words of Jesus in the four Gospels. These words, as we internalize them, facilitate the development and growth of our **faith** through a process that transforms our life by renewing our mind (Romans 12:2). Renewing our mind transforms our life choice from being defined and determined by our culture to being defined and determined by the words of Jesus.

Our **faith** and **trust** in and **obedience** to Jesus develop, grow and mature as we:

- Read, study and internalize God's word in the Bible (1 Peter 2:1–3);
- Incorporate the spiritual life principles associated with God's word in the Bible into our life (1 Timothy 4:13–16);
- Grow and mature in our relationship with God through Jesus and the presence of the Holy Spirit in our life (Philippians 2:12–13);
- **Obey** the words Jesus spoke in the four Gospels (John 14:15, 21, 23); and
- Do **good works** God has prepared for us to perform (Ephesians 2:10). The Holy Spirit, as we study and internalize the words of Jesus, equips us with unique supernatural spiritual gifts that enable us to perform **good works** God prepares for us to perform (Romans 12:4-8, 1 Corinthians 12:3-11, 28, and Ephesians 4:11-13).

We do **good works** because Jesus instructed us in Matthew 5:16:

> "Let your light shine before men in such a way that they may see your **good works**, and glorify your Father who is in heaven."

We do **good works** because Paul stated in Ephesians 2:10:

> "For we are [God's] workmanship, created in Christ Jesus for **good works**, which [He] prepared beforehand so that we would walk in them."

He affirmed in 2 Timothy 3:16–17 our understanding of the Bible enables and equips us to do the **good works** Jesus instructed and God has prepared for us to perform.

God through Jesus and the Holy Spirit draws us close to Himself to receive and grow in His love. The Holy Spirit motivates us to engage in the above activities to spiritually grow and mature in our relationship with God through Jesus. He enables us to love, minister to and serve others in Jesus' name. This equips us to perform **good works** out of love for God and others in **obedience** to Jesus with guidance from the Holy Spirit. God and Jesus bless and reward us when we engage in activities to spiritually grow and mature, and we perform **good works** Jesus instructs and God prepares for us to perform. However, we risk losing Their blessings and rewards when we fail to engage in activities to spiritually grow and mature, and we do none of the **good works** Jesus instructs and God prepares for us to perform after we have entered our relationship with Them (John 15:1–11).

GOOD WORKS

Our good works are fruit that proceeds from the vine of Jesus (John 15:1–6). They are activities God prepares for us to perform (Ephesian 2:10) to glorify Himself (Matthew 5:16). Good works are our response of love and obedience for receiving the gift of grace and redemption God extends to us through Jesus, and they are an integral part of our relationship with God through Jesus. They:

- Are our love-offerings to God that we extend to others (2 Timothy 2:15);
- Are performed to glorify God (Matthew 5:16);
- Are positions of leadership and service we perform in and through our local church (Ephesians 4:11-13);
- Are how we minister to and serve the needs of others (1 Peter 4:10).
- Are our witness to those who have not received Jesus as their Lord and Savior (Hebrews 13:2);
- Are our witness to fellow Christians (Colossians 3:16).
- Show we are God's workmanship, created in Christ Jesus to perform good works (Ephesians 2:10); and
- Reveal the presence of the Holy Spirit in our life (Matthew 5:14-16).

The Holy Spirits provides us with supernatural spiritual gifts that enable and equip us to perform our good works (Romans 12:4-8, 1 Corinthians 12:3-11, 28, and Ephesians 4:11-13). Paul instructed us in 1 Timothy 4:14-16:

> "Do not neglect the spiritual gift within you, which was bestowed on you through prophetic utterance with the laying on of hands by the presbytery. Take pains with these things; be absorbed in them that your progress will be evident to all. Pay close attention to yourself and to your teaching; persevere in these things, for as you do this you will ensure salvation both for yourself and for those who hear you."

Paul also instructed us in Titus 3:14:

> "Our people must also learn to engage in good deeds to meet pressing needs, so that they will not be unfruitful."

His reference to good deeds is the same as his reference to good works in previous Bible verses. We learn how to perform good works in and through our local church so we can bear fruit on Jesus' vine. We are taught how to perform our good works in our local church by individuals who know how to perform them.

KINGDOM OF GOD AND KINGDOM OF HEAVEN

The kingdom of God is a spiritual realm where God is everywhere present with His righteousness and holiness and where His rule is accepted and respected. The kingdom of heaven is included in the kingdom of God. Only individuals on earth who have been redeemed by and reconciled to God through their faith and trust in and obedience to Jesus are received into the kingdom of God on earth while they are alive. All others on earth are separated from God because of sin. Loving, ministering to and serving others while we are alive because we love and obey Jesus ensure our entrance into the kingdom of heaven after we die (2 Peter 1:5-11).

The kingdom of heaven is a spiritual realm where God is present with His righteousness and holiness and where His rule is accepted and respected. The kingdom of heaven is separated from the earth because the earth has been corrupted by sin. God's angles are present in the kingdom of heaven. The spirits and souls of individuals on earth who have been redeemed by and reconciled to God through Jesus before they die are also present there. These include all those throughout the ages who have obediently responded to God's call and been loyal to Him.

Jesus stated in Matthew 7:21-23:

> "Not everyone who says to Me, 'Lord, Lord,' will enter the kingdom of heaven, but he who does the will of My Father who is in heaven will enter. Many will say to Me on that day, 'Lord, did we not prophesy in Your name, and in Your name cast out demons, and in Your name perform many miracles?' And then I will declare to them, 'I never knew you; DEPART FROM ME, YOU WHO PRATICE LAWLESSNESS.'"

The Bible instructs us to spiritually grow and mature in our relationship with Jesus through the presence of the Holy Spirit in our life after we enter our relationship with Him through Jesus. Paul stated in Ephesians 2:10 that we become "[God's] workmanship, created in Christ Jesus" to perform good works He prepares for us to perform when we enter this relationship. We perform our good works when we share God's love and grace with others, and we serve and minister to them in Jesus's name. We are to perform our good works for God's glory, not for our benefit nor to satisfy our personal needs. Jesus may not allow us to enter the kingdom of heaven after we die when we did not perform our good works for God's glory while we were alive, or when we have not repented of intentional sin in our life and asked Him to forgive us while we were alive.

MEANING OF THE TERMS KINGDOM OF GOD AND KINGDOM OF HEAVEN IN THE FOUR GOSPELS

Parables of Jesus in the Gospel of Matthew refer to the kingdom of heaven. The same parables in the other Gospels refer to the kingdom of God. This may be because the Gospel of Matthew was written for a Jewish audience while the other Gospels were written for non-Jewish audiences. Saying and writing the word for God is a sin for Jews. The use and meaning of the kingdom of heaven and the kingdom of God are the same in the four Gospels.

OLD TESTAMENT SUPERSCRIPTS

Many of the New Testament scriptures presented throughout this book have Old Testament superscript references embedded in them. These references identify the Old Testament sources for the texts contained in the scriptures.

Douglas D. Reynolds, Ph.D.

CHAPTER 1
INTRODUCTION

"Jesus therefore was saying to those Jews who had believed Him, 'If you abide in My word, then you are truly disciples of Mine; and you shall know the truth, and the truth shall make you free." (John 8:31-32)

"All Scripture is inspired by God and profitable for teaching, for reproof, for correction, for training in righteousness; that the man of God may be adequate, equipped for every good work." (2 Timothy 3:16-17)

"But know this first of all, that no prophecy of Scripture is a matter of one's own interpretation, for no prophecy was ever made by an act of human will, but men moved by the Holy Spirit spoke from God." (2 Peter 1:20-21)

THIS BOOK

The information presented in this book will help you enter and grow in your relationship with God through Jesus and the presence of the Holy Spirit in your life. The Bible is God's love story to us. John stated in John 3:16:

"For God so loved the world, that He gave His only begotten Son, that whoever believes in Him should not perish, but have eternal life."

Paul stated in Romans 5:10:

"For if while we were enemies, we were reconciled to God through the death of His Son, much more, having been reconciled, we shall be saved by His life. While we were enemies of and separated from God because of sin, He extended His grace to us by sending His Son, Jesus, to die on a cross to redeem us and restore our broken relationship with Him."

We discover in the Bible God wants to give us spiritual life through Jesus. We are spiritually reborn, and the Holy Spirit takes up residence in us when we are reconciled to God through our faith in Jesus (Romans 6:28, Ephesians 2:8). God promises to be with us and never abandon us (Matthew 28:20). However, He requires us to grow in our knowledge of and internalize His word in the Bible through disciplined Bible study. Jesus stated in John 8:31-32:

> "If you continue in My word, then you are truly disciples of Mine; and you will know the truth, and the truth will make you free."

Jesus' word in the Bible must manifest itself through our personal, family, social and professional lives to be His disciple. His truth when studied and internalized gives us true freedom. It frees us from the eternal consequences of sin, fear and the paralyzing effects of fear, and all things that keep us in bondage to sin and separate us from God.

We often allow ourselves to be deprived of the best God desires for us when we approach Him through Jesus. Why? We may have never read and studied the Bible to learn God's promises and spiritual life principles. We may lack faith to act on them when we do know and understand them. God requires us to trust and believe in Him and Jesus when we enter our relationship with Him through Jesus. In Hebrews 11:6, the author stated:

> "And without faith it is impossible to please Him, for he who comes to God must believe that He is, and that He is a rewarder of those who seek Him."

God extends His grace through Jesus to us as a gift. We cannot earn, buy or bargain for it; we can only freely receive it through Jesus. However, we must trust God and have faith and believe in Him to receive the best He desires for us.

Paul stated in Philippians 2:12-13:

> "So then, my beloved, just as you have always obeyed, not as in my presence only, but now much more in my absence, work out your salvation with fear and trembling, for it is God who is at work in you, both to will and to work for His good pleasure."

God reconciles and redeems us through our faith in Jesus as a gift through His grace. Paul's statement to work out our salvation with fear and trembling appears to contradict the fact God's redemption through Jesus is a gift and his statement in Romans 5:15-16 this gift is free. Paul's statement must be received in the context of Peter's instruction in 1 Peter 2:1-2:

> "Therefore, putting aside all malice and all deceit and hypocrisy and envy and all slander, like newborn babes, long for the pure milk of the word, so that by it you may grow in respect to salvation, if you have tasted the kindness of the Lord."

We must begin activities to develop and grow in our relationship with Jesus as **Lord of our life** after we have received Him as our **Savior**.

There are two phases to the redemption and reconciliation we receive from God when we enter our relationship with Him through Jesus. First, God redeems us as a gift through His grace when we receive Jesus as our **Savior**. God facilitates this by His grace through the death and resurrection of Jesus. Second, we respond to God's gift of grace by accepting Jesus through faith as **Lord of our life**. This requires us to make Him ruler and master of all areas in our life. This begins a process through which we develop and grow in our ability to live a life of faith and trust in and obedience to God and Jesus. God and Jesus fascinate this process through the Holy Spirit in our life.

There will be struggles in our life as we engage in activities to develop and grow in our relationship with Jesus as Lord of our life. We will fail to make Jesus Lord in some areas in our life during this process. Our relationship with Him will be impaired when this occurs. However, Jesus will restore the impaired areas in our relationship with Him when we repent and submit these areas in our life to His lordship.

We develop our relationships with God, Jesus and the Holy Spirit through faithful and disciplined Bible study. This study is essential for us to:

- Learn and internalize God's spiritual life principles revealed to us in the Bible;
- Experience the resulting renewing of our mind and transforming of our heart through actions of the Holy Spirit in our life as we internalize these spiritual life principles; and
- Learn and take advantage of God's covenant and Jesus' promises available to us through our relationship with Them.

These equip us to live a life of obedience to God and Jesus more effectively and to make it possible for God to will and work for His good pleasure through us.

This book is a manual for Christian growth and living. I have written it from the perspective of a mechanical engineer, not a theologian. The organization and style of this book reflect this. It cannot be casually read. Focused and disciplined reading are required to fully understand and comprehend the information presented in the following chapters. Chapters 1 - 9 should be read sequentially. However, the remaining chapters can be read in any order. Information presented in this book has facilitated my growth into a more intimate relationship with God through Jesus.

There are six major sections in this book: Nature and Character of God (Chapters 2 - 7), Nature and Character of Man (Chapters 8 - 9), Spiritual Growth (Chapters 10 - 14), Spiritual Gifts (Chapters 15 - 17), Spiritual Life Principles (Chapters 18 - 22), and The Body of Christ (Chapters 23 and 24). Following is a brief synopsis of the six sections.

Nature and Character of God (Chapters 2 - 7): This section presents information regarding:

- The biblical concept of God as Father, Son (Jesus) and Holy Spirit being three distinct Persons who have distinct functions within the triune Godhead (the Trinity). Each has the same attributes of Deity, and each act with a unified purpose and temperament in executing God's plan for our redemption and reconciliation relative to Satan's introduction of sin into God's creation.
- Satan's introduction of sin into God's creation, the eternal conflict with God that resulted, and our subsequent separation from God because of sin.
- The activities of the Son (Jesus) and the Holy Spirit in implementing God's plan for our redemption and reconciliation.

Nature and Character of Man (Chapters 8 - 9): This section presents information regarding:

- The nature of our creation as spirit, soul and body, our being born into this world spiritual dead and its potential eternal consequences, and the importance of our spiritual rebirth in our relationship with God through Jesus.
- Functions of our soul and spirit and yearnings of and struggles within our soul.

Spiritual Growth (Chapters 10 - 14): This section presents information regarding:

- The washing and cleansing we receive through actions of the Holy Spirit and the significance of water baptism;
- The significance and meaning of grace and faith in our relationship with God and their relation to good works;
- Principles associated with prayer; and
- Spiritual growth that results in the renewal of our mind and transformation of our heart.

Spiritual Gifts (Chapters 15 - 17): This section presents information regarding:

- Spiritual ware fare;
- Gifts of the Holy Spirit - their definition, organization, and descriptions and how we discover, develop, and use our unique spiritual gifts; and
- The baptism of the Holy Spirit and speaking in tongues.

Spiritual Life Principles (Chapters 18 - 22): This section presents information regarding:

- Principles associated with effective money management;
- Principles associated with loving and forgiving others and resolution of anger;
- Principles associated with suffering;
- Principles associated with spiritual healing; and
- The Christian family, the relationships between husbands and wives and parents and children in the family, role of intimacy and sex in marriage, role of Jesus in the family, and divorce.

The Body of Christ (Chapters 23 - 24): Topics in this section include:

- Relationship God wants us to have with the Body of Christ, the Church, and how we can minister to and serve others through local churches; and
- Hope for life we have through our relationship with God through Jesus.

MY RELATIONSHIP WITH GOD THROUGH JESUS

God has revealed Himself to me as I have read and studied the Bible. The Holy Spirit has helped me to better understand God's promises and spiritual life principles in the Bible as I have sought God and moved into a more intimate relationship with Him through Jesus. The Holy Spirit has shown me the Bible is truth as I have studied and internalized the Scriptures. God reveals Himself to us in the Bible. He presents His covenants and promises that He is faithful to keep and His spiritual life principles that govern our life in the Bible.

I found the process of accepting Jesus into my life as Lord and Savior was simple and straight forward when I became a Christian as a teenager in 1961. I understood the redemption and reconciliation God extended to me through Jesus were gifts. However, the process of surrendering control of the core area of my life to God, learning His spiritual life principles, and developing the knowledge, wisdom and faith to apply them to my life has been a demanding lifelong process. God has revealed Himself to me as I have studied His word in the Bible and trusted and yielded control of my life to Him. I have grown to know His love is real, and I can trust Him with every aspect of my life. I understand how He desires to work in and through my life through the Holy Spirit. He has given me the ability to live a spirit-filled life and to reach out to others in love to witness about the presence of Jesus in my life.

I discovered God loved and accepted me as I was when I entered my relationship with Him through Jesus. I did not have to change and become someone different to come into His presence. This was a major freeing revelation to me. We are deceived into believing we are not good enough to come into God's presence. We believe we must change and transform our own life before He will accept us. We would never be able to approach God if this were true because it is impossible for us to transform ourself independent of the presence of the Holy Spirit in our life. The Bible first teaches God loves and accepts us as we are - warts and all. It then teaches He loves us too much to allow us to stay who we are. The Holy Spirit enters our life and begins the process of renewing our mind and transforming our heart as we give Him permission, making us into the person God has created us to be.

I have learned I have intrinsic value in God's eyes as I have grown in my relationship with Him through Jesus over the years. I have worth and value in and of myself that is independent of anything I may or may not do for God or for others. I have worth and value independent of what others may think of or how they may choose to relate to me. For that matter, the worth and value I have in God's eyes are independent of what I think of myself. I have learned I have worth and value solely because I am made in God's image. He wants His Spirit to dwell in me, and He has made an infinite sacrifice through His Son, Jesus, to redeem me and restore my broken relationship with Him. This understanding has been essential for the increased sense of healthy self-esteem and self-worth I have developed because of my relationship with God through Jesus.

God has never forced me to do anything I have not wanted to do. He has often been persistent in pursuing and leading me in directions He wanted me to go and in doing things He wanted me to do. However, the choices to obey or disobey Him have been mine. God has respected and accepted my choices even when they were contrary to what I perceived He wanted me to do. He has never complained, criticized or stopped loving me for making choices contrary to His will. However, He has never shielded or spared me from their consequences. One of the many mysteries of God's relationship with me is how He has been able to lead me in a positive and affirming manner to do those things He wanted me to do despite my initial refusals to do them.

UNIQUENESS OF THE BIBLE

The primary source of information for discussions presented in this book is the Bible. One of our main focuses in defining and developing our relationship with God must be reading and studying it because He reveals Himself in the Bible. We must answer four questions to our own satisfaction as we read and study the Bible.

- Is it God's word?
- Does it give evidence of being from God?
- Are the truths and principles recorded in it centuries ago relevant today?
- Are these truths and principles absolute and timeless, or do they change with time?

These questions must be satisfactorily resolved to develop a meaningful relationship with God through Jesus. How we resolve them determines the nature and character of this relationship.

According to Josh McDowell in his book, *A Ready Defense* (1990), three criteria must be met for the Bible to be considered as being from God. They are:

- The Bible must be transmitted to us accurately from the time it was originally written so we have an exact representation of what God said and did.
- The Bible must be correct when it deals with historical persons and events.
- Any revelation from God should be without scientific absurdities that would imply it came by mere human authorship.

Discussions relative to these questions have generated volumes of books. We will only briefly discuss them in the short space of this section. The information that will be presented was taken from two of Josh McDowell's books: *Evidence that Demands a Verdict* (1972) and *A Ready Defense* (1990).

The Bible is a unique book that was written over a period of around 1,500 years, a period of forty to sixty generations. The first books were written around 1410 B.C., and the last book was written sometime around 70-95 A.D. The Bible was written by more than forty authors who were separated from each other by hundreds of years and hundreds of miles. They included a political leader, fisherman, herdsman, military general, cupbearer, prime minister, doctor, king, tax collector, priest, prophet, and Rabbi. The Bible was written while the authors were in the wilderness, in a dungeon, in a prison, on an island, traveling, and in the rigors of a military campaign. It was written when Israel was in times of peace, war and exile. The moods of its authors ranged from deep sorrow and despair to heights of joy. The Bible was written on three continents (Asia, Africa, and Europe) and in three languages (Hebrew, Aramaic, and Greek). It includes hundreds of controversial topics. Yet all the authors wrote with harmony and continuity from its first book (Genesis) to its last book (Revelation). They wrote about the unfolding story of God's love for and relationship with His creation, His establishment of and relationship with the nation of Israel, and His redemption of men and women through His Son, Jesus. Paul stated in 2 Timothy 3:16-17:

> "All Scripture is inspired by God and profitable for teaching, for reproof, for correction, for training in righteousness; so that the man of God may be adequate, equipped for every good work."

Peter stated in 1 Peter 1:20-21:

> "But know this first of all, that no prophesy of Scripture is a matter of one's own interpretation, for no prophecy was ever made by an act of human will, but men moved by the Holy Spirit spoke from God."

The Bible was inspired by God and written under the inspiration of the Holy Spirit even though it was written by human authors.

The Bible contains 66 books that are divided into 39 books comprising the Old Testament and 27 books comprising the New Testament. The developments of the Old and New Testament canons are discussed in Appendix A. The Old Testament contains narratives of God's creation of the world and the introduction of sin into His creation. It describes God's establishment of and relationship with the nation of Israel through whom He was to send the Messiah to redeem His creation from sin. The New Testament records the birth, life, ministry, death and resurrection of Jesus, who was sent by God as the Messiah to redeem His creation. It describes the events associated with the birth and early growth of the Christian church and teaches us how we can know God and receive salvation, reconciliation, and life through Jesus.

Modern translations of the Bible are the work of dedicated teams of highly trained biblical scholars. These scholars have given these translations of the Bible to us by directly translating ancient manuscripts of the Bible written in their original languages of Hebrew, Aramaic and Greek. Large numbers of ancient Old and New Testament manuscripts exist that date back to around 200 B.C. for Old Testament manuscripts and to the first two centuries after the birth of Christ for New Testament manuscripts. These ancient manuscripts document and validate the accuracy of modern translations of the Bible in far greater detail than for any other ancient book. More information on Bible translations is given in Appendix A.

A consistent truth runs throughout the Bible that describes how God has dealt with the world in the past, is dealing with it today, and plans to deal with it in the future. The underlying theme of the Bible is the love God has for us and how He has acted in history to provide a means where our broken relationship with Him can be restored through His Son, Jesus. The Bible teaches how we can enter a relationship with God through Jesus and how we are to live in this relationship through the presence of the Holy Spirit. It teaches us the spiritual life principles necessary to live a life that is pleasing to God and by which we can receive the best He desires to give us.

There are many levels of truth in the Bible, and it is necessary to rely on the Holy Spirit to reveal them to us. It is impossible to probe its depths to obtain the knowledge and wisdom God wants to give us by relying on our own intellectual abilities. We learn by reading and studying the Bible, and we grow and mature in our faith by applying its spiritual life principles to our life as the Holy Spirit reveals them. We grow spiritually by applying the Scriptures to our life, living them, and discovering for ourself God is faithful to honors His covenants and promises.

The Bible is unique in its teachings concerning prophecy, history and personalities. It deals frankly with both the good and bad qualities and sins of its principal characters. It contains prophecies relating to individual nations, Israel, all the people of the earth, certain cities, and the coming of Jesus as the Messiah. The Bible contains a history of ancient civilizations and Israel that has been verified by archaeological discoveries and relevant ancient literature. The accuracy of this history exceeds that of all other major peoples and nations of the world.

Investigations by scientists relative to events associated with creation and other events recorded in the Bible indicate it does not violate scientific principles and laws even though it is not a scientific book. It supports and affirms their existence. Fred Heeren in his book *Show Me God* (1997) states the greatest astronomical discoveries of the 20th century point to an Intelligent Creator of the universe who exists outside of time and space. He indicates that of all:

> "... the ancient peoples, only the Hebrews got their cosmology right. While the rest of the world believed in a magical, eternal universe that gave birth to the gods, only they believed in an eternal, transcendent God who gave the universe its beginning."

Scientist ultimately discover the Genesis account of creation is true when they search for the cause of the beginning of the universe and life on earth. Science has shown there is no truth in Darwin's theory of evolution. Transitional species necessary to verify the theory of evolution have never been found. Scientists have discovered we live in a continually expanding universe using the Hubble space telescope. There had to be a first cause of the universe outside of the time and space to give it a beginning for this to be true.

Dr. Walter L. Bradley, material scientist and former head of the Mechanical Engineering Department at Texas A & M University, stated in Lee Strobel's book, *The Case for Faith* (2000):

> "I stand in awe of God because of what He has done through His creation. Only a rookie who knows nothing about science would say science takes away from faith. If you really study science, it will bring you closer to God."

More information on the relationship between the Bible and science can be obtained from: *The Fingerprint of God* (1989) by Hugh Ross and *A Scientific Approach to Christianity* (1990) and *A Scientific Approach to Biblical Mysteries* (1993) both by Robert W. Faid.

The Bible clearly meets the three criteria presented by Josh McDowell for it to be from God. It is God's word. It is timeless and given to us so we can know and understand the nature and character of God as Father, Son and Holy Spirit and the nature of the relationship He desires to have with us through Jesus. The Bible is just as valid in its application to our life today as it was to the lives of those for whom it was written. Archaeological discoveries and discoveries of ancient manuscripts indicate translations of the Bible we have today has been accurately transmitted to us from the languages in which it was originally written. Jesus stated in John 8:31-32 His word is truth. The Bible is God's primary means of communicating with us today. God reveals Himself to us in the Bible in a very personal way. He demonstrates His compassion and love for us and His desire to redeem and fellowship with us in it.

The Bible has been read by more people and published in more languages than any other book in history. The complete Bible has been translated into over 240 languages and dialects. One or more books of the Bible have been translated into over 740 additional languages and dialects. The Bible has survived over a period of 3,400 years. It has survived persecution and all attempts to destroy it. Many have tried to burn, ban and outlaw it; yet it has survived from around 1410 B.C. to the present day.

ORTHODOX BELIEFS OF THE CHRISTIAN FAITH

Orthodox beliefs of the Christian faith define the nature and character of our relationship with God through His Son, Jesus. They are supported by the Bible and creed statements handed down to us by the early church fathers. These beliefs are:

- The Bible is the inspired word of God. It is God's primary method of communicating with us today. It has been given to us by men who were inspired and led by the Holy Spirit when they wrote it.

- God is Trinity. There are three eternal persons within the Godhead, but there is only one God. God is Father, Son, and Holy Spirit. The Father, Son, and Holy Spirit each possess all the infinite attributes of God and respond to us in a manner that is internally consistent with the nature and character of the Godhead. They respond to us as one God; however, they each relate to us in ways that are unique to Their respective positions within the Godhead.

- God the Father created heaven and earth and everything visible and invisible in them. Everyone on earth and in heaven is accountable to the Father.

- Jesus is the Son of God. He is the One through whom and for whom all things have been created and in whom all things in creation are held together.

- Jesus was conceived in Mary by the Holy Spirit. Mary, the mother of Jesus, was a virgin when Jesus was conceived in her womb.

- Jesus was in every way tempted as we are tempted, yet He resisted all temptations and led a life without sin.

- Jesus was crucified and died. He was buried. He was raised from the dead on the third day after His death. He ascended into heaven where He is now seated with God the Father. Jesus experienced a literal death and resurrection. Like Jesus, we, too, will experience a literal death and resurrection.

- Jesus voluntarily accepted God's penalty of death for our sins. God accepted His death as a sufficient sacrifice for our sins when He died.

- The Holy Spirit is God in the world within us today. The Father and Son sent the Holy Spirit to make us aware of our sinful natures, to call us to repent for our sinful way of living, and to return to the Father through Jesus. The Holy Spirit opens our minds to receive and understand God's word in the Bible, and He intercedes to the Father on our behalf to make our needs and desires known to Him.

- The Church is the Body of Christ in the world today, and Jesus is its head.

- We are born into this world with a sin nature that separates us from God because of the original sin committed by Adam and Eve in the garden of Eden.

- We are redeemed by God's grace through our faith and trust in and obedience to Jesus. God forgives our sins, reconciles us to Himself, and receives us back into His presence when we repent of our sins and accept Jesus as our Lord and Savior.

- Jesus will return to earth and set up His 1,000-year kingdom at the end of the seven-year tribulation. The great white throne judgment will occur at the end of His kingdom. The existing earth and heaven will be destroyed, after which we will stand before the great white throne to be judged. Those whose names are written in the book of life will live throughout eternity with God, Jesus and the Holy Spirit in the new earth, heaven and Jerusalem God will create after this judgment. Those whose names are not written in the book of life will live throughout eternity separated from Them in the lake of fire.

- Those whose names are written in the book of life will stand before Jesus. He will examine the good works they have performed during their lives and what motivated them to perform them. Jesus will give them the reward they are to receive for performing their good works.

Knowledge of these orthodox beliefs of the Christian faith makes it easier for us to recognize misleading teachings within Christian churches and false doctrines associated with non-Christian cults. These cults often claim to be compatible with Christianity or falsely identify themselves as being Christian. However, they reject many or all the above orthodox beliefs. We can discern misleading teachings and false doctrines that are related to Christianity with greater certainty when we know and understand the underlying principles associated with these orthodox belie.

CHAPTER 2
NATURE AND CHARACTER OF GOD
FATHER, SON AND HOLY SPIRIT

"Thine, O LORD is the greatness and the power and the glory and the victory and the majesty, indeed everything that is in the heavens and the earth; Thine is the dominion, O LORD, and Thou dost exalt Thyself as head over all. Both riches and honor come from Thee, and Thou dost rule over all, and in Thy hand is power and might; and it lies in Thy hand to make great, and to strengthen everyone." (2 Chronicles 29:11-12)

"To you it was shown that you might know that the LORD, He is God; there is no other besides Him. Know therefore today, and take it to your heart, that the LORD, He is God in heaven above and on earth below; there is no other." (Deuteronomy 4:35, 39)

NATURE AND CHARACTER OF GOD (Chapters 2 - 7)

This section presents information regarding:

- The biblical presentation of God as Father, Son (Jesus) and Holy Spirit being three distinct Persons who have distinct functions within the triune Godhead (the Trinity). Each has the attributes of Deity, and They act with a unified purpose in executing God's plan for our redemption and reconciliation relative to Satan's introduction of sin into God's creation.
- Satan's introduction of sin into God's creation, the eternal conflict with God that resulted, and our separation from God because of sin.
- The activities of the Jesus and the Holy Spirit in implementing God's plan for our redemption and reconciliation.

TWO POSITIONS

What will the future hold for us? Does God exist? What is His nature and character and how will He interact with us if He does exist? People struggle with these questions.

Dose God exist? Some believe there is no transcendent God who created the universe, the world where we live and us. They believe we have evolved from an initial highly primitive state independent of any creative actions by God. They believe moral laws and ethical values are relative and are defined by individual beliefs and perceived cultural norms. They assume men and women are fundamentally good and can eventually resolve complex social and cultural problems independent of God. They believe we can establish a future world where we can ultimately live in peace.

Some believe God exists and created the universe, the world where we live and us. They believe He established spiritual principles and moral laws that govern our lives. They recognize we are born with a sinful nature that separates us from God and that requires a Savior to redeem and reconcile us to God. They understand we can only resolve complex social and cultural problems in the context of a redeemed relationship with God through his Son, Jesus.

NAMES OF GOD

Knowing another's name in Old Testament times was a privilege that offered special access to an individual whose name was known. God chose Israel to be His people. Therefore, He revealed Himself to them by several names that offer special insight into His nature and character.

Yahweh is the most important name for God in the Old Testament (*Nelson's Illustrated Bible Dictionary*, 1986). It means, *I am who I am*. The four-letter Hebrew word *YHWH* is the name by which God revealed Himself to Moses in the burning bush (Exodus 3:14). The name *Yahweh* expresses God is the infinite God, who is behind everything and to whom everyone in heaven and on earth is ultimately accountable. The *I am who I am* specifies nothing else defines who God is but God Himself. What God says and does defines who He is.

Jewish priests and leaders did not pronounce the sacred name *YHWH* during Old Testament times. They instead used other names that described various aspects of God's nature and character. These names are described below (H. L. Willington, *Willington's Guide to the Bible*, 1981):

> **Elohim** refers to God's power and might. This reference is used in Genesis 1:1 and Psalm 19:1. These verses refer to the creative activities of God.

Adonai refers to God as LORD and master over all His creation (Malachi 1:6). This name implies a master-servant relationship between God and man. God as master has a right to expect our obedience. We as servants have a right to expect God to provide for our needs.

The names *Elohim* and *Adonai* in the Bible refer to the creative power of God and the facts He is master of His creation and ruler over His kingdom. They imply we must obey and serve Him when we want to enter a relationship with Him. God covenants to provide for our needs when we are His servants.

Jehovah-Jireh refers to God as the LORD who provides (Genesis 22:13).

Jehovah-Nissi refers to God as the LORD my banner (Exodus 17:15).

Jehovah-Shalom refers to God as LORD is peace (Judges 6:24).

Jehovah-Sabaoth refers to God as LORD of host (Isaiah 6:1-3). This is a reference to God as captain of heaven's armies, who are composed of angels.

Jehovah-Maccaddeschcem refers to God as LORD thy sanctifier (Exodus 31:13). This is a reference to God's desire to set His people apart for special service.

Jehovah-Rohi refers to God as the LORD my shepherd (Psalm 23:1).

Jehovah-Tsidkenu refers to God as the LORD our righteousness (Jeremiah 23:6).

Jehovah-Shammah refers to God as the LORD who is present (Ezekiel 48:35).

Jehovah-Rapha refers to God as the L LORD our healer (Exodus 15:26).

The names of God in the Bible that have *Jehovah* as a prefix refer to the personal relationship God has with us. These names refer to the lordship of God relative to His creation and our lives. He is the LORD of hosts and commander of the angelic armies. He is the God who provides for us and goes before us to prepare our way. He is the God who brings peace to our lives and to the world. He is the God who is always present and who keeps us within His fold like a shepherd. He is the God who heals us, makes us righteous, and sets us apart to do His will and be in His service.

El Elyon refers to God as the strongest strong One (Genesis 14:17-20, Isaiah 14:13-14).

El Roi refers to God as the strong One who sees (Genesis 16:13).

El Shaddai refers to God as the breasted One (Genesis 17:1, Psalm 91:1). This speaks to the nurturing and protecting nature of God.

El Olam refers to God as the everlasting God (Isaiah 40:28-31).

The names of God in the Bible that have *El* as a prefix refer to the relationship God has with His creation. These names refer to the strength and power God has relative to His creation and us. They imply He is from everlasting to everlasting and the strong one relative to whom there is no one stronger. He is the one who sees everything there is to see. These names indicate God desires to nurture and protect those who serve Him.

NATURE OF GOD

The Eternal Nature of God

God is *eternal*. The nature and attributes of His character have no beginning and no end, and they will never change. The Old Testament declares the eternal nature of God. In one of the earliest books of the Bible, Elihu, one of Job's companions, stated in Job 36:26:

> "Behold, God is exalted, and we do not know Him; the number of His years is unsearchable."

The Psalms declare the eternal nature of God:

> "Before the mountains were born or You gave birth to the earth and the world, even from everlasting to everlasting, You are God." (Psalms 90:2)

> "But the lovingkindness of the LORD is from everlasting to everlasting on those who fear Him, and His righteousness to children's children, to those who keep His covenant and remember His precepts to do them." (Psalm 103:17-18)

"Forever, O LORD, Your word is settled in heaven. Your faithfulness continues throughout all generations; You established the earth, and it stands." (Psalms 119:89-90)

Isaiah stated in Isaiah 41:4:

"Who has performed and accomplished it, calling forth the generations from the beginning? 'I, the LORD, am the first, and with the last. I am He.'"

The New Testament declares the eternal nature of God. Paul stated in Romans 1:20:

"For since the creation of the world His invisible attributes, His eternal power and divine nature, have been clearly seen, being understood through what has been made, so that they are without excuse."

Peter stated in 1 Peter 1:24:

"For 'all flesh is like grass, and all its glory like the flower of grass. The grass withers, and the flower falls off, but the word of the LORD endures forever.' (Isaiah 40:6-8)" (Note: *Superscript Bible references denote the Old Testament source for the preceding Scripture.*)

In Hebrews 1:8-12, the writer stated:

"But of the Son He says, 'Your throne, O God, is forever and ever,
And the righteous scepter is the scepter of His kingdom.
You have loved righteousness and hated lawlessness,
Therefore God, Your God, has anointed You
With the oil of gladness above Your companion.' Psalms 45:6-7
And
'You, LORD, in the beginning laid the foundation of the earth,
And the heavens are the work of Your hands;
They will perish, but You remain;
And they all will become old like a garment,
And like a mantle You will roll them up,
Like a garment they will also be changed.
But You are the same,
And Your years will not come to an end.' Psalm 102:25-27"

God, Jesus and the Holy Spirit have eternal natures. In Hebrews 13:8 the author also stated, "Jesus Christ is the same yesterday and today and forever."

The Old and New Testaments confirm the eternal natures of God and Jesus. The Bible indicates the words They spoke will stand forever. Psalms 119:89-90 above indicates God's word is settled in heaven forever. Isaiah stated in Isaiah 40:8:

"The grass withers, the flower fades, but the word of our God stands forever."

Peter reaffirmed God's word endures forever. Jesus stated in Matthew 5:17-19:

"Do not think that I came to abolish the Law or the Prophets; I did not come to abolish but to fulfill. For truly I say to you, until heaven and earth pass away, not the smallest letter or stroke shall pass from the Law until all is accomplished. Whoever then annuls one of the least of these commandments, and teaches others to do the same, shall be called least in the kingdom of heaven; but whoever keeps and teaches them, he shall be called great in the kingdom of heaven."

God's word is the eternal standard by which we must live our life and form our character. God's word and commandments stand forever and will never change. This contrasts with cultural and social customs and laws which continually change.

Solomon stated in Ecclesiastes 3:11:

"He has made everything appropriate in its time. He has also set eternity in their heart, yet so that man will not find out the work which God has done from the beginning even to the end."

God has placed eternity in our heart. This leads us to engage in life activities and make life choices that have eternal consequences. These actions often require us to look outside ourself to obtain information necessary to make correct choices. We as Christians approach God through Jesus and the Holy Spirit to obtain this information. We may not initially understand why and how God desires to work in and through us. However, God reveals Himself to us through the Holy Spirt to give us the information we seek as we grow in our knowledge of and internalize God's word in the Bible.

The Sovereignty and Power of God

The Bible teaches God has dominion over the earth and the heavens. In 1 Chronicles 29:11-12, the writer stated:

> "Yours, O LORD, is the greatness and the power and the glory and the victory and the majesty, indeed everything that is in the heavens and the earth; Yours is the dominion, O LORD, and You exalt yourself as head over all. Both riches and honor come from You, and You rule over all, and Your hand is power and might; and it lies in Your hand to make great and to strengthen everyone."

There is only one God even though there may be many so-called gods. God stated Deuteronomy 32:39:

> "See now that I, I am He, and there is no god besides Me; it is I who put to death and give life. I have wounded, and it is I who heal; and there is no one who can deliver from My hand."

Moses stated in Deuteronomy:

> "To you it was shown that you might know that the LORD, He is God; there is no other besides Him. ... Know therefore today, and take it to your heart, that the LORD, He is God in heaven above and on earth below; there is no other." (Deuteronomy 4:35, 39)

> "Hear, O Israel! There is one God, the LORD!" (Deuteronomy 6:4)

> "For the LORD your God is the God of gods and the LORD of lords, the great, the mighty, and the awesome God who does not show partiality, nor take a bribe." (Deuteronomy 10:17)

God stated in Isaiah 46:9:

> "Remember the former things long past. For I am God, and there is no other; I am God, and there is no one like Me."

God is the Father of creation (Genesis 1:1, Revelation 4:11), Israel (Exodus 4:22-23, Jeremiah 31:9), Jesus (Matthew 3:16-17), and all who believe in Jesus (John 1:12-13, Romans 8:14).

The Spiritual Nature of God

God is a spiritual being. Jesus stated in John 4:24, "God is Spirit, and those who worship Him must worship in spirit and truth." God as a spiritual being:

- Creates (Genesis 1:1)
- Destroys (Genesis 19:24-25)
- Provides (Psalm 104:27-30)
- Promotes (Psalm 75:6-7)
- Cares (1 Peter 5:6-7)
- Heals (Deuteronomy 32:39)
- Hears (Psalm 94:9-10)
- Hates (Proverbs 6:16)
- Grieves (Genesis 6:6)
- Loves (John 3:16)

The Father is God (John 6:44-46, 1 Peter 1:2).

Jesus, the Son of God, is God (Matthew 1:23, John 1:14, John 20:1).

The Holy Spirit is God (Romans 8:12-16, Titus 3:4-7).

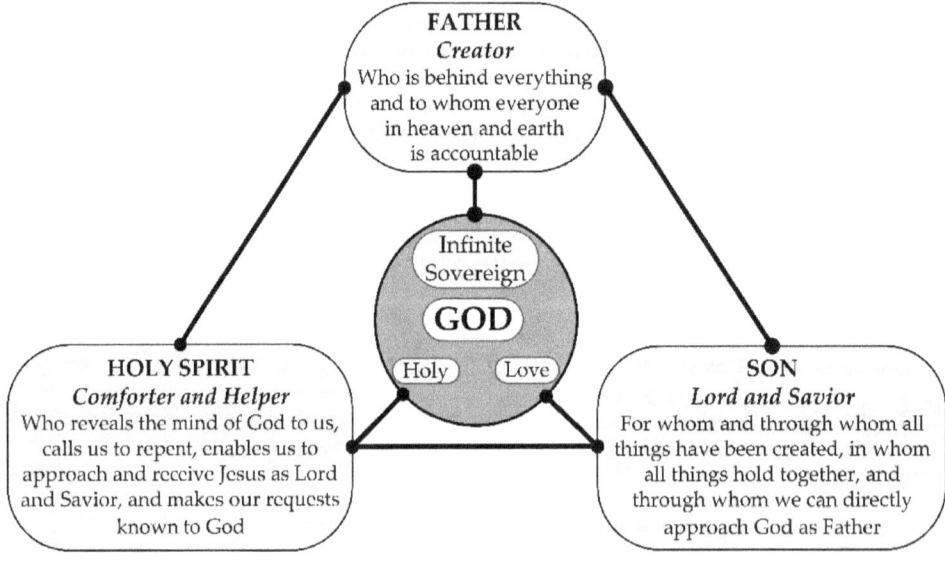

Figure 1

The Triune Nature of God

The Bible teaches there is one God (Deuteronomy 4:35, 4;39, 6:4, 10:17). However, there are three eternal Persons within the Godhead who interact with each other and us. God is Father, Son and Holy Spirit (Figure 1). Each Person within the Godhead possesses all the infinite and sovereign attributes of Deity. They each interact with us in ways that are unique to their positions within the Godhead. However, they all interact with us in a unified manner that is consistent with God's sovereignty and His attributes of holiness and love. The Bible refers to:

Jesus stated in John 14:16-17:

> "I will ask the Father, and He will give you another Helper, that He may be with you forever; that is the Spirit of Truth, whom the world cannot receive, because it does not behold Him or know Him, but you know Him because He abides with you, and will be in you."

He also taught in Matthew 28:19-20:

> "Go therefore and make disciples of all the nations, baptizing them in the name of the Father and the Son and the Holy Spirit, teaching them to observe all that I commanded you, and lo, I am with you always, even to the end of the age."

God the Father is the Creator of all things. He is the One who is behind everything and the one to whom everyone in all creation is accountable. Jesus, God's Son, is the One through and for whom all things have been created, in whom all things hold together, and through whom we can approach God the Father. The Holy Spirit is our Comforter and Helper. He is our Advocate before the Father and the One who reveals the mind of God to us. He calls us to repentance, enables us to approach and receive Jesus as Lord and Savior, and makes our requests known to God. The Holy Spirit opens our minds to receive and understand the God's word in the Bible.

The Bible teaches there is a hierarchy within the Godhead even though the Father, Son and Holy Spirit are God. Paul stated in 1 Corinthians 11:3; 15:28:

> "But I want you to understand that Christ is the head of every man, and the man is the head of a woman, and God is the head of Christ. ... When all things are subjected to Him, then the Son Himself also will be subjected to the One who subjected all things to Him, so that God may be all in all."

Jesus is God, but He was and is obedient to God the Father. He stated in John 5:30, 6:38, 14:28:

> "I can do nothing on My own initiative. As I hear, I judge; and My judgment is just, because I do not seek My own will, but the will of Him who sent me. ... For I have come down from heaven, not to do My own will, but the will of Him who sent Me. ... If you loved Me, you would have rejoiced, because I go to the Father; for the Father is greater than I."

Jesus stated the Holy Spirit proceeds from the Father (John 15:26) and was sent by the Father (John 14:6) and Him (John 15.26). The Holy Spirit was sent to glorify Jesus (John 16:14), bring to our remembrance all Jesus has taught us (John 14:26), and reveal the mind and thoughts of God as God wanted them revealed (1 Corinthians 2:11).

Paul stated regarding creation in 1 Corinthians 8:5-6:

> "For even if there are so-called gods whether in heaven or on earth, as indeed there are many gods and many lords, yet for us there is but one God, the Father, from whom are all things, and we exist for Him; and one Lord, Jesus Christ, by whom are all things, and we exist through Him."

All things come from God the Father through Jesus as Lord. We exist and live for God through Jesus. Paul continued in 1 Corinthians 12:3:

> "Therefore, I make known to you, that no one speaking by the Spirit of God says, 'Jesus is accursed'; and no one can say, 'Jesus is Lord,' except by the Holy Spirit."

In summary:

- We exist for the pleasure of God the Father through Jesus as our Lord;
- We can only come to God the Father through Jesus as our Savior; and
- The Holy Spirit enables us to approach and accept Jesus as our Lord and Savior.

CHARACTER OF GOD

Table 1 lists twenty-six attributes of God's character that are revealed in the Bible. These attributes are divided into three categories: God's infinite nature and sovereignty, His holiness and His love.

Table 1

GOD (FATHER, SON AND HOLY SPIRIT) IS:			
INFINITE	Sovereign	Self-existent	Self-sufficient
Eternal	Omnipresent	Omnipotent	Omniscient
Immutable	Inscrutable	Incomprehensible	Life
Holy	Wise	Righteous	Just
Truth	Light	Good	Impartial
Faithfull			
Love	Mercy	Gracious	Forgiving
Patient			

God's Infinite Nature and Sovereignty

God is infinite. God's stature, love, righteousness, truth, and all the other attributes of His character know no bounds. (1 Kings 8:27, 2 Chronicles 2,6, 6:18, Daniel 4:34-35)

God is sovereign. God exercises absolute authority over His creation. He does what He pleases and is accountable to no one. He makes His decisions and establishes the principles of His kingdom with assistance from no one. He acts in accordance with the other attributes of His character and never emphasizes one attribute at the expense of the others. For example, He never expresses love at the expense of justice, and He shows no partiality in expressing His love or in carrying out His justice. (Deuteronomy 32:39, Isaiah 40:10, 50:4-5, 61:1)

God is self-existent. God exists because He exists. He is not dependent on anything or anyone for His thoughts, will, power, or counsel. (Romans 11:33-34, Ephesians 1:5, Psalm 115:3, Psalm 33:10-11)

God is self-sufficient. God has never had in eternity past, nor can ever have in the ages to come, a single need for which His own divine nature has not already provided. (Psalm 50:10-12)

God is eternal. He has no beginning, and He will have no end. According to the Bible, His years are unsearchable, and He is from everlasting to everlasting. (Job 36:26, Psalm 90:2, Isaiah 40:8)

God is omniscient. God possesses all the knowledge and wisdom that ever has been or ever will be. He knows everything that has ever happened, is happening, or ever will happen. (Psalm 147:5, Hebrews 4:13)

God is omnipresent. God is everywhere present throughout all time and space. (Proverbs 15:3, Jeremiah 23:24, Hebrews 4:13)

God is omnipotent. God is all powerful and has the power and energy to do the total of all things. (Daniel 4:34-35, Matthew 19:26)

God is immutable. His nature and attributes and His relationship with His creation never change. He will never call anything back once He has spoken it into existence; it stands forever. What God has spoken through the Bible in ancient times is true, valid and powerful today. (Isaiah 40:8, Malachi 3:6, Hebrews 13:8, James 1:17)

God is inscrutable. It is not possible to understand the inexplicable and mysterious ways of God. For example: Why does a loving and caring God allow certain terrible tragedies to occur? (Romans 11:33)

God is incomprehensible. It is not possible to probe the depths of God's mind and completely know and understand all His wisdom and knowledge. It is possible to know and understand only what God reveals to us through the Bible with the help of Holy Spirit. (Ecclesiastes 3:11, Isaiah 55:8-9)

God is life. God is the only being who has life in and of Himself, and all life proceeds from Him. The Bible teaches it is possible to have true life only with the presence of God's indwelling Spirit. (Nehemiah 9:6, Job 33:4, Psalms 36:9, John 5:26)

God's Holiness

God is Holy. The most prominent attribute of God in the Bible is His holiness. Some suggest God's holiness is the attribute that ties all His other attributes together. God emphasizes His holiness by direct commands, objects, personal visions, and individual judgments. (Leviticus 19:2, Psalm 99:9, 1 Peter 1:15)

God is wise. God's wisdom is based on His omniscience. He can use His knowledge in a manner that is consistent with His love and holiness. (Psalm 136:5, 1 Timothy 1:17, Jude 1:25)

God is righteous. God will never do or cause anything that is wrong, evil or imperfect. He has and will never act in a malicious manner. He is the standard by which all moral and ethical standards are compared and judged. (Psalm 119:137, Psalm 145:17, John 7:18, Romans 3:26)

God is just. God will never do anything that is unfair in relation to any of His creation either in heaven or on earth. God executes His justice in accordance with His righteousness and is absolutely fair, even to those who stand in rebellion against Him. However, His righteousness demands He judge and expel from His presence all those in whom sin dwells. (Deuteronomy 32:4, Romans 3:26)

God is truth. All true knowledge and wisdom come only from God. Anything that opposes what God has revealed in the Bible is not truth. (2 Samuel 7:28, Isaiah 65:16, John 8:31-32)

God is light. God is the source and strength of all illumination. He is the source of all moral, mental and spiritual information and inspiration. (John 1:4-9, 1 Peter 2:9, 1 John 1:5-7, James 1:17)

God is good. This is the nature of God that disposes Him to be kind, cordial, benevolent and full of good will and compassion toward His creation and us. (Psalm 107:8, Romans 2:4)

God is impartial. God shows no partiality in measuring out His love or His justice. The standards of His righteousness apply equally to everyone. God does not establish one set of standards and laws for one group and a different set for another group. He treats everyone the same and shows no favors. All the attributes of His character apply equally to everyone. (Deuteronomy 10:17, Romans 2:11)

God is faithful. God can be trusted to keep His covenants and to follow through on the many promises He has given to us in the Bible. (Deuteronomy 7:9, 2 Timothy 2:13)

God's Love

God is love. God's love desires the temporal good and the eternal redemption of His creation. His love is extended in an unmerited fashion to everyone. It is given without any consideration of the merit or worth of those to whom it is extended. However, God loves us in a manner that is consistent with His holiness. His love for us will not violate the attributes of His righteousness and justice. (Romans 5:8, 1 John 4:16)

God is merciful. God's mercy seeks the temporal good in the earthly existence and the eternal salvation of all who have opposed His will, even at the cost of infinite self-sacrifice. Mercy is the aspect of God's love that causes Him to help those who either because of sin or of circumstances beyond their control have special needs. This help is selective in nature and undeserved. Mercy is the aspect of God's love that predisposes Him to withhold deserved punishment associated with sin. (Exodus 34:6, Psalm 103:8-17, 1 Timothy 1:13-16)

God is gracious. God's grace seeks to show undeserved favor and bestow undeserved position without regard to the merit or worth of those to whom it is extended and who receive it. Grace is the aspect of God's love that predisposes Him to redeem and reconcile us to Himself through the death and resurrection of His Son, Jesus. (Romans 3:24, Ephesians 2:8-9)

God is forgiving. Forgiveness is that aspect of God's love in which His mercy and grace are brought together through the shed blood of Jesus on a cross. God forgives our sins through Jesus' death and resurrection. (Matthew 9:2-5, Hebrews 10:17-22, James 5:15, 1 John 9:2-5)

God is patient. Patience is that aspect of God's love that predisposes Him to endure the actions of those in whom sin dwells and to withhold deserved eternal judgment. God is patient in His efforts to lead people to repentance. However, His attributes of righteousness and justice will ultimately lead Him to judge and eternally punish all in whom sin dwells and who do not repent and receive the gifts of His grace and redemption extended to them through Jesus. (Exodus 34:6, Romans 2:4, 2 Peter 3:9, 15, 2 Thessalonians 1:5-10)

THE LAWS OF GOD

God has given us laws that direct how we are to relate to Him and interact with others. The Bible refers to these laws as the Law of Moses. The ten commandments Moses received from God on Mount Sinai form the core of His laws that cover our relationships with Him and our parents and our interactions with others. They are (Deuteronomy 5:7-21):

- "You shall have no other gods before Me."
- "You shall not make for yourself an idol, or any likeness of what is in heaven above or on the earth beneath or in the water under the earth. You shall not worship them or serve them; for I, the LORD your God, am a jealous God, visiting the iniquity of the fathers on the children, and on the third and the fourth generations of those who hate Me, but showing loving kindness to thousands, to those who love Me and keep My commandments."
- "You shall not take the name of the LORD your God in vain, for the LORD will not leave him unpunished who takes His name in vain."
- "Observe the Sabbath day to keep it holy, as the LORD your God commanded you. Six days you shall labor and do all your work, but the seventh day is a Sabbath of the LORD your God; in it you shall not do any work, you or your son or your daughter or your male servant or your female servant or your ox or your donkey or any of your cattle or your sojourner who stays with you, so that your male servant and your female servant may rest as well as you."
- "Honor your father and your mother, as the LORD your God has commanded you, that your days may be prolonged, and that it may go well with you on the land which the LORD your God gives you."
- "You shall not murder."
- "You shall not commit adultery."
- "You shall not steal."
- "You shall not bear false witness against your neighbor."
- "You shall not covet your neighbor's wife, and you shall not desire your neighbor's house, his field or his male servant or his female servant, his ox or his donkey or anything that belongs to your neighbor."

Old Testament laws received by Moses in addition to the Ten Commandments are treated as extensions of the Ten Commandments. The Ten Commandments plus these laws form what is referred to as the Law. Jesus indicated in Matthew 5:18 that "not the smallest letter or stroke" shall be removed from the Law until heaven and earth pas away. Therefore, the Law defines and convicts us of sin.

Sexual sins associated with the commandment on adultery include:

- **Adultery** (Leviticus 20:10; Deuteronomy 22:13-22): Adultery is sexual contact between a man and woman, one or both who are married, but not to each other.
- **Fornicatio**n (Exodus 22:16-17; Deuteronomy 22:20-30): Formication is sexual contact between a man and woman neither of whom is married nor engaged to be married. A man and woman engaged to be married are not to have sexual contact until after they are married.
- **Homosexuality** (Leviticus 18:22, 20:13): Homosexuality is sexual contact between men and women of the same gender.
- **Incest** (Leviticus 20:11-12, 14; Deuteronomy 27:20, 22-23): Incest is sexual contact between parents and children of opposite gender, between brothers and sisters, and between aunts, uncles, nieces, nephews and cousins of opposite gender.
- **Bestiality** (Exodus 22:20; Leviticus 18:23, 20:15-16): Bestiality is sexual contact between a man or woman and an animal.
- **Exposing of Nakedness** (Leviticus 18:8-17, 20:17): Exposing of nakedness in a family is looking at the nude body of a family member of different gender other than a spouse. This includes viewing modern-day pornography.

Sin creates a barrier that separates us from God. The Bible teaches the Law cannot remove this barrier and redeem us from sin. It can only convict us of sin and condemn us to spiritual death and eternal separation from God, Jesus and the Holy Spirit.

GOD'S PRESENCE IN OUR LIFE

God has created us to worship and commune with Him. Those who believe God does not exist ignore the fact He does exist, and they attempt to escape from His presence. David wrote in Psalm 139:1-16:

"LORD, You have searched me and know me.
You understand my thought from afar.

You scrutinize my path and my lying down,
And are intimately acquainted with all my ways.
Even before there is a word on my tongue,
Behold, O LORD, You know it all.
You have enclosed me behind and before,
And laid Your hand upon me.
Such knowledge is too wonderful for me,
It is too high, I cannot attain to it.
Where can I go from Your Spirit?
Or where can I flee from Your presence?
If I ascend to heaven, You are there;
If I make my bed in Sheol, behold, You are there.
If I take the sings of the dawn,
If I dwell in the remotest part of the sea,
Even there Your hand will lead me,
And Your right hand will lay hold of me.
If I say, 'Surely the darkness will overwhelm me,
And the light around me will be night,'
Even the darkness is not dark to You,
And the night is as bright as the day.
Darkness and light are alike to You.
For You formed my inward parts;
You wove me in my mother's womb.
I will give thanks to You, for I am fearfully and wonderfully made;
Wonderful are Your works,
And my soul knows it very well.
My frame was not hidden from You,
When I was made in secret,
And skillfully wrought in the depths of the earth;
Your eyes have seen my unformed substance;
And in Your book were all written
The days that were ordained for me,
When as yet there was not one of them."

It is impossible to escape God's presence. He is everywhere we go to hide from Him. We cannot escape the fact God's laws govern the course of our life.

Two major precepts underlie our relationship with God through Jesus: God has created us with intrinsic worth and value, and He has given us a free will. We have worth and value by virtue of our relationship with God through Jesus because:

- God has created us in His own image and placed His Spirit within us (Genesis 1:26-27, 2:7; 1 John 4:13);

- God has made the conscious choice to love and forgive us, and His love and mercy are freely extended to us independent of anything we may or may not do to deserve them (John 3:16; Ephesians 2:8-9; 1 John 4:7-12); and

- God has made an infinite sacrifice for us in the death and resurrection of His Son, Jesus, through which He redeems us and heals and restores our broken relationship with Him (Romans 5:8; 1 John 4:13-16).

God has given us a free will in conjunction with our intrinsic worth and value. We can freely choose whether we will live according to His spiritual life principles and laws. We can choose to accept or ignore His presence in our life. God accepts and honors the choices we make. He never forces us to do anything we do not want to do. However, He holds us accountable for the choices we make and requires us to accept responsibility for the consequences of our choices.

We must accept responsibility for our decisions. Solomon stated in Proverbs 16:9, "The mind of man plans his way, but the LORD directs his steps." We must choose whether we will walk in the ways of God or go through life independent of Him. God will direct our steps according to His will once we have decided. He will not direct them according to our will. He desires to bring us into a reconciled relationship with Him through His Son, Jesus. We are promised we will succeed (Proverbs 16:3) when we submit our plans and related decisions to Him for His counsel and guidance and work to accomplish His will for our life. On the other hand, God will bring us to judgment (Proverbs 16:5) when we choose to pursue our life independent of Him. Solomon stated in Proverbs 19:21, "Many are the plans in a man's heart, but the counsel of the LORD, it will stand." God's counsel and will for His creation and our life will prevail irrespective of the desires and plans of our heart.

Dr. Charles Stanley in one of his In-Touch radio programs gave the following insights into the nature of God's will. He stated first there is God's sovereign will. This part of His will governs His overall relationship with His creation. It embodies all aspects of His nature and the attributes of His character. God will act in a manner consistent with His sovereign will as He corporately and individually relates to us.

Next, there is God's relational will. This is that aspect of His will that specifically addresses His individual relationships with us as nations, groups and individuals. There are three components to God's relational will: His intentional will, His permissive will and His immediate will. We will only discuss the aspect of God's relational will that addresses His relationship with us as individuals.

God's intentional will is associated with the reason He uniquely creates and brings us into this world. First and most important, God creates us to worship and fellowship with Him. David indicated in Psalm 139:1-16 God knows the days of our life before we live them. Therefore, He creates us for unique purposes in addition to worship and fellowship. Some are destined for greatness and activities that will influence multitudes while others are destined for obscurity and activities that will influence a few. We are significant and important to God regardless of why He creates and brings us into this world.

God does not force us to do anything we do not want to do. His permissive will gives us the freedom to accept, resist and reject His intentional will for our life. God creates us with a personality and related abilities and talents. They prepare us for specific occupations, ministries and other related activities when properly cultivated and developed. God establishes a preferred timeline for us to physically, emotionally and spiritually grow and mature and to develop our abilities and talents. He opens the doors to our occupations and leads us to participate in the ministries and other related activities for which He has prepared us when He determines we are ready. We can be obedient to God's intentional will for our life; we can resist it; and we can outright reject it. The choice is ours. God pursues us and initiates experiences designed to move us to accept His intentional will when we resist or reject it. However, He pursues us in a manner that never circumvents our right to accept, resist and reject His intentional will. One of the inscrutable mysteries of God's character is why He moves some to accept His intentional will while He allows others reject it.

We will suffer loss when we resist or reject God's intentional will for our life. We will miss or lose a blessing, an opportunity, a desired relationship, our sense of self-worth and self-esteem, etc. We may experience adversity, pain and suffering. Resisting or rejecting God's intentional will often results in a brokenness only He can heal and a barrenness only He can fill.

God will still work in and through us with the Holy Spirit when we initially resist or reject and later accept His intentional will for our life. He will work with us in a manner consistent with our life's circumstances at the time of our acceptance and bring healing to our life when necessary. God will begin to work His intentional will through us even though our initial rejection of it may have significantly altered the course of our life from what it might have been.

The final aspect of God's intentional will discussed by Charles Stanley is His immediate will. God's immediate will is associated with how He desires us to respond to life and relate to others daily. We daily respond to opportunities, decisions, experiences and others in a manner consistent with His spiritual life principles and laws when we are obedient to His immediate will. How we respond to God's immediate will helps define who we are and the true nature of our relationship with Him. It is characterized by our obedience to the Holy Spirit.

Understanding and being obedient to God's intentional will and being obedient to His immediate will for our life requires commitment and effort on our part. There are four activities we can undertake to learn and obey God's will for our life:

- The first and most important is to read and study the Bible on a regular basis. God reveals Himself to us in the Bible, and we can meet Him there. He explains how He wants us to interact with Him and others and live life in a positive and purposeful way. He presents His spiritual life principles and laws in the Bible that govern our life.

- We must learn to listen to and obey the Holy Spirit. We must give Him permission to come into the core area of our life to transform us into the person God wants us to be. He will open our mind to understand the Scriptures. He will reveal to us God's purpose and desires for our life. He will enable us to be the person God wants us to be and do the things God wants us to do.

- We must fellowship with mature Christians whose lives clearly reflect the presence of God, who have a clear understanding of the Bible, and who are willing to share this understanding with us. We must enter relationships with mature Christians through which we learn to apply God's spiritual life principles and laws to our life and spiritually grow.

- Finally, we must learn how to personally experience God in our life.

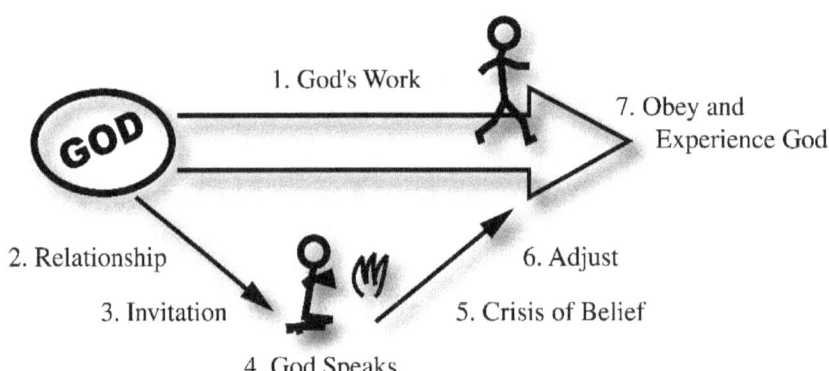

Figure 2

Henry Blackaby and Glaud King in their book, *Experiencing God* (1990), give us guidance in how to do this. They teach us (Figure 2):

1. God is always at work around us, and He desires to accomplish His work through us.

2. God pursues a continuing love relationship with us that is real and personal.

3. God invites us to become involved with Him in His work.

4. God speaks to us by the Holy Spirit through the Bible, prayer, circumstances and the church to reveal Himself, His purpose and His ways.

5. God's invitation for us to work with Him nearly always leads to a crisis of belief that requires both a faith response and a commitment to action.

6. We often must make major adjustments in our life to join God in what He is doing.

7. We come to personally know God by experience as we obey Him, and He accomplishes His work through us.

CHAPTER 3
NATURE AND CHARACTER OF GOD
SATAN AND SIN

"You are of your father the devil, and you want to do the desires of your father. He was a murderer from the beginning, and does not stand in the truth, because there is no truth in him. Whenever he speaks a lie, he speaks from his own nature, for he is a liar, and the father of lies. ... The thief comes only to steal, and kill, and destroy. " (John 8:44, 10:10)

NATURE AND CHARACTER OF SATAN

Many doubt the existence of Satan. They may believe there is something or someone who is a personification of evil in the world, but they believe there is no real spiritual being named Satan. The Bible teaches Satan exists (Ron Rhodes, *Angels Among Us*, 1994). He is mentioned in seven Old Testament books: Genesis, 1 Chronicles, Job, Psalms, Isaiah, Ezekiel and Zechariah. He is mentioned in nineteen of the twenty-seven books in the New Testament. He is mentioned by every New Testament writer:

- Matthew (Matthew 4:1)
- Mark (Mark 5:15)
- Luke (Luke 22:3)
- John (1 John 3:8)
- Paul (Romans 16:20)
- Peter (1 Peter 5:8)
- James (James 4:7)
- Jude (Jude 9)

He is mentioned by Jesus some twenty-five times in the Gospels. References are found in Matthew 4:10, Matthew 16:23, Matthew 25:41, Luke 10:18, John 8:44, and Luke 22:31. To deny the existence of Satan is to deny the validity of statements concerning his existence in the Bible and Jesus' own testimony.

God created three angels who had special positions when He created the heavens. One was Michael who is referred to as an archangel (Daniel 10:13, Jude 1:9). Another was Gabriel who is identified as a special messenger angel from the very presence of God (Daniel 9:21,

Luke 1:19). The third was Lucifer who some Bible scholars believe was given the special task of watching over the throne of God. Ezekiel presented a description of Lucifer, the son of dawn, in Ezekiel 28:12-17:

> "Again the word of the LORD came to me saying, 'Son of man, take up a lamentation over the king of Tyre, and say to him, 'Thus says the LORD God, you had the seal of perfection, full of wisdom and perfect in beauty. You were in Eden, the garden of God; every precious stone was your covering; the ruby, the topaz, and the diamond; the beryl, the onyx, and the jasper; the lapis lazuli, the turquoise, and the emerald; and the gold, the workmanship of your settings and sockets, was in you. On the day that you were created they were prepared. You were the anointed cherub who covers, and I placed you there. You were on the holy mountain of God; you walked in the midst of the stones of fire. You were blameless in your ways from the day you were created, until unrighteousness was found in you. By the abundance of your trade you were internally filled with violence, and you sinned; therefore I have cast you as profane from the mountain of God. And I have destroyed you, O covering Cherub, from the midst of the stones of fire. Your heart was lifted up because of your beauty; you corrupted your wisdom by reason of your splendor. I cast you to the ground; I put you before kings, that they may see you.'"

Lucifer was perhaps the most beautiful creature in heaven. He was the anointed cherub. A cherub is a special angelic being who magnifies the holiness and power of God and serves as a visible reminder of the majesty and glory of God and His abiding presence with His people. Some Bible scholars speculate Lucifer led the worship in heaven and had the special task of watching over the throne of God. However, pride entered his heart because of his beauty and position. He no longer wanted to worship and serve God; he wanted to be served and worshiped as God. Isaiah implied this in Isaiah 14:12-15:

> "How you have fallen from heaven, O star of the morning, son of the dawn! You have been cut down to the earth, you who have weakened the nations! But you said in your heart, 'I will ascend to heaven; I will raise my throne above the stars of God, and I will sit on the mount of assembly in the recess of the north. I will ascend above the heights of the clouds; I will make myself like the Most High.' Nevertheless you will be thrust down to Sheol, to the recesses of the pit."

Lucifer wanted to become independent of and take the place of God. Consequently, he and many of the angels in heaven rebelled with him against God. Lucifer and those angels who followed him were defeated and cast out of heaven. Jesus implied this when He stated in Luke 10:18, "I was watching Satan fall from heaven like lightning."

Lucifer's name was changed to Satan when he was cast out of heaven. It usually denotes a corresponding change in relationship with God when there is a name change in the Bible. Abram became Abraham, Sarai became Sarah, Jacob became Israel, Simon became Peter, and Saul became Paul. These name changes implied moving into a more favored and closer relationship with God. Satan's name change corresponded to his judgment and expulsion from the presence of God.

Satan is a created being (Ezekiel 28:12-17). He does not possess any of the sovereign and infinite attributes of God even though he possesses great power. His powers are limited by God. The Bible teaches Satan is a fallen angel who has been corrupted by sin.

The Bible teaches Satan is the god of this world (2 Corinthians 4:3-4) and the world is under his control (1 John 5:10). The following account is presented in Matthew 4:8-9 when Jesus was tempted by Satan after His forty days in the wilderness:

> "Again the devil took Him to a very high mountain and showed Him all the kingdoms of the world, and their glory; and he said to Him, 'All these things will I give You, if you fall down and worship me.' Then Jesus said to him, 'Begone, Satan! For it is written, 'You shall worship the Lord your God, and serve Him only.'"

Jesus did not dispute Satan's claim to dominion over the kingdoms of the world, but He rebuked and commanded him to depart. Satan is a trespasser who has dominion because men and women whose hearts have been darkened and blighted by sin have given it to him. He rules over the world because men and women choose to follow and serve him instead of God. God did not choose for Satan to have dominion over the earth, but He honored this transaction because Adam had authority to give him dominion. Many believe this is why God chose to become a man in the person Jesus. Adam had the authority to transfer dominion to Satan since he was initially given dominion (Genesis 1:28) over the earth. Therefore, only a man without sin could pay the required ransom to regain dominion from Satan (Matthew 20:28, 1 Timothy 2:6, Hebrews 9:15). This man was Jesus.

Table 2

THE ACTIVITIES OF SATAN INCLUDE

Imitates God	Sows tares among God's wheat
Instigates false doctrines	Perverts God's word
Hinders the work of God's servants	Blinds individuals to the truth
Resists the prayers of God's servants	of God's word
Accuses individuals before God	Steals God's word from the
Lays snares for individuals	hearts of individuals
Deceives individuals	Afflicts individuals
Prompts individuals to transgress the	Undermines the sanctity of the
Holiness of God	home

Satan works to undermine the works of God, destroy His kingdom, deny Him possession of those things that are rightfully His, and imitates God (Table 2). He has:

- A false trinity (Revelation 16:13),

- Synagogues (Revelation 2:9),

- Doctrines (1 Timothy 4:1-3),

- Mysteries (Revelation 2:24, 2 Thessalonians 2:7),

- A throne (Revelation 2:13),

- A kingdom (Luke 4:5-6),

- Worshipers (Revelation 13:4),

- Fallen angels (Revelation 12:7-8),

- Ministers (2 Corinthians 11:15),

- Miracles (2 Thessalonians 2:9-10),

- Sacrifices and fellowship (1 Corinthians 10:19-21), and

- Armies (Revelation 19:19).

In addition to imitating God, Satan:

- Sows tares among God's wheat (Matthew 13:24-30, 36-43);

- Instigates false doctrines (1 Timothy 4:1-3);

- Perverts God's word (Genesis 3:1-4, Matthew 4:6);
- Hinders the works of God's servants (1 Thessalonians 2:18);
- Resists the prayers of God's servants (Daniel 10:12-13);
- Blinds individuals to the truth (2 Corinthians 4:4);
- Steals God's word from human hearts (Matthew 13:19);
- Accuses Christians before God (Job 1:7-12, 2:3-6, Zechariah 3:1-4);
- Lays snares for individuals (2 Timothy 2:26);
- Tempts (Matthew 4:1, Ephesians 6:11);
- Afflicts (Job 2:7, Acts 10:38);
- Deceives (Revelations 12:9);
- Undermines the sanctity of the home (1 Corinthians 7:3-5); and
- Prompts both Christians and non-Christians to transgress against the holiness of God (1 Chronicles 21:1, John 13:2, Matthew 16:22-23, Acts 5:3).

Jesus stated Satan is a murderer and liar; he is a thief who comes to kill, steal and destroy (John 8:44, 10:10). Peter stated in 1 Peter 5:8:

> "Be of sober spirit, be on the alert. Your adversary, the devil, prowls about like a roaring lion, seeking someone to devour."

John stated in 1 John 3:8,

> "The one who practices sin is the devil; for the devil has sinned from the beginning."

Satan is the father of lies and master of deception. Paul stated in 2 Corinthians 4:3-4:

> "And even if our gospel is veiled, it is veiled to those who are perishing, whose case the god of this world has blinded the minds of the unbelieving so that they might not see the light of the gospel of the glory of Christ, who is the image of God."

He also indicated in 2 Corinthians 11:14-15 that Satan is an angel of light who disguises himself to lure by deception people away from God.

Satan has been defeated and judged through the redeeming work and shed blood of Jesus (John 12:21, John 16:11, 1 John 3:8). He has a lake of fire waiting for him (Revelation 20:10). Dominion is given back to us when the Holy Spirit resides in our heart (Acts 26:16-18, Colossians 1:13). We then have authority in the name of Jesus over Satan, and he must obey. John stated in 1 John 4:4:

> "You are from God little children, and have overcome them; because greater is He who is in you than he who is in the world."

James stated in James 4:2, "Submit therefore to God. Resist the devil and he will flee from you."

DOMINION VERSUS OWNERSHIP

God has ultimate dominion over and ownership of the heavens and earth. Ezra stated 1 Chronicles 29:11-12:

> "Thine, O LORD, is the greatness and the power and the glory and the victory and the majesty, indeed everything that is in the heavens and the earth; thine is the dominion, O LORD, and thou dost exalt thyself as head over all. Both riches and honor come from thee, and thou dost rule over all, and in thy hand is power and might; and it lies in thy hand to make great, and to strengthen everyone."

David stated in Psalm 24:1:

> "The earth is the LORD's, and all it contains, the world, and those who dwell in it."

The LORD stated in Deuteronomy 10:14

> "Behold, to the LORD your God belongs heaven and the highest heavens, the earth and all that is in it."

Leviticus 25:23 teaches God owns all land. Haggai 2:8 states God owns all gold and silver. Psalm 50:10-12 indicates all livestock belongs to God. The Bible teaches God is the creator and owner of all things in heaven and on earth. He did not transfer ownership even though He originally transferred dominion of His creation on earth to Adam. Therefore, Adam did not have the authority to transfer ownership even though he transferred dominion over the earth to Satan because of sin. Only God has this authority, and He has not given it to either man or Satan.

Dualism is often taught when addressing the conflict between God and Satan. It presumes God and Satan are equal: God representing good and Satan representing evil. The conflict between good and evil in the world is then portrayed as a conflict between God and Satan who are equally powerful. The Bible does not support this. Satan is an angelic being who was originally created to watch over the throne of God. He was cast out of heaven because of sin. His powers are defined and limited by God. The book of Job in the Old Testament indicates the pain and suffering with which Satan was allowed to afflicted Job were limited by God. God has placed boundaries on what Satan can and cannot do to us.

We intentionally or unintentionally serve Satan when we reject God and ignore His lordship over our life. As a result, sin reigns in our life, and Satan can exercise dominion over us. Satan is the god of this world, and he has dominion over it because mankind has rejected God's lordship over His creation. God has placed boundaries on the dominion Satan can exercise. The earth belongs to God even though Satan has been given dominion over it because of sin. Everything that happens in heaven and on earth occurs in a manner consistent with God's physical and spiritual laws.

NATURE AND CHARACTER OF SIN

Definition of Sin

There are two Greek words that can be used to define sin: *parabasis*, which means to overstep a forbidden line, and *hamartano*, which means to miss the mark. John stated in 1 John 3:4, "Everyone who practices sin also practices lawlessness; and sin is lawlessness." Paul stated in Romans 3:23, "For all have sinned and fall short of the glory of God." We sin when we disobey God's laws. We step over lines of acceptable behavior established by God into areas of behavior forbidden by Him when we sin. We miss the mark when we sin; we do not achieve the level of perfection necessary to enter God's presence to fellowship and commune with Him. We are all guilty of sin. As a result, we are separated from God in the absence of a saving relationship with Jesus.

Origin of Sin

Let us first examine the origin of sin in the universe. Biblical references in Ezekiel 28:11-19, Isaiah 14:12-15, Luke 10:18, 1 John 3:8, and Revelation 12:3-4 imply before creation there was a revolt against God in heaven that was led by Lucifer. This revolt is described in Ezekiel 28:11-19, Isaiah 14:12-15, and Revelation 12:3-4. The revolt was initiated when pride entered Lucifer, and he attempted to become like God. The Bible indicates this revolt introduced sin into God's creation even though it failed, and Lucifer was cast out of Heaven.

The Bible teaches sin originated on earth because of the disobedience of Adam and Eve. God stated they could eat any of the fruit in the garden except the fruit on the tree of the knowledge of good and evil when He created and placed them in the Garden of Eden. He indicated the moment they ate this fruit they would die (Genesis 1:26-30, 2:7-25). The account of the fall of Adam and Eve is presented in Genesis 3:1-7:

> "Now the serpent was more crafty than any beast of the field which the LORD God had made. And he said to the woman, 'Indeed, has God said, 'You shall not eat from any tree of the garden?' And the woman said to the serpent, 'From the fruit of the trees of the garden we may eat; but from the fruit of the tree which is in the middle of the garden, God has said, 'You shall not eat from it or touch it, lest you die.' And the serpent said to the woman, 'You surely shall not die; for God knows that in the day you eat from it your eyes will be opened, and you will be like God, knowing good and evil.' When the woman saw that the tree was good for food, and that it was a delight to the eyes, and that the tree was desirable to make one wise, she took from its fruit and ate; and she gave also to her husband with her, and he ate. Then the eyes of both of them were opened, and they knew that they were naked; and they sewed fig leaves together and made loin coverings."

This account indicates Eve was deceived by the serpent. It also indicates Adam was with her when she ate the forbidden fruit. God had given Adam and Eve dominion over all creatures on the earth, which included the serpent. Adam or Eve could have rebuked the serpent, and Satan who was a trespasser and had no legal authority or dominion on earth would have had to obey and leave. However, they did not do this. They instead disobeyed God and ate the forbidden fruit.

Sin can be defined as **a deliberate act of disobeying God's commandments based on deception**. Adam and Eve chose to disobey God because they did not believe He would hold them accountable and discipline them for their disobedience. This is the basis for our rejection of God's word today. We deliberately choose to ignore God and disobey His commandments because we do not believe He will hold us accountable for our acts of disobedience.

The Consequences of Sin

God's response to Adam's and Eve's disobedience is recorded in Genesis 3:14-19:

> "And the LORD God said to the serpent, 'Because you have done this, cursed are you more than all cattle, and more than every beast of the field; on your belly shall you go, and dust shall you eat all the days of your life; and I will put enmity between you and the woman, and between your seed and her seed; he shall bruise you on the head, and you shall bruise him on the heel.' To the woman He said, 'I will greatly multiply your pain in child birth, in pain you shall bring forth children; yet your desire shall be for your husband, and he shall rule over you.' Then to Adam He said, 'Because you have listened to the voice of your wife, and have eaten from the tree about which I commanded you, saying, 'You shall not eat from it; cursed is the ground because of you; in toil you shall eat of it all the days of your life. Both thorns and thistles it shall grow for you: and you shall eat the plants of the field; by the sweat of your face you shall eat bread, till you return to the ground, because from it you were taken; for you are dust, and to it you shall return.'''"

God's response to the introduction of sin into His creation was:

To Lucifer: He was cast out of heaven and became Satan. God told him he would be judged. This judgment occurred when Jesus shed His blood and died on a cross and was raised from the dead.

To men and women: Spiritual and physical death, pain and suffering entered the *world when Adam and Eve sinned. The Genesis account of creation implies God* originally created men and women to live forever in fellowship with Him. He breathed His Spirit into Adam and Eve, which enabled them to fellowship with Him, when He created them. God withdrew His Spirit from them when they sinned, and they spiritually died. As a result, they were no longer able to fellowship with God. Consequently, all men and women have been and are born into this world spiritually dead. God's Spirit does not dwell in them. God also told Adam and Eve they would physically die. God provided for their needs before they sinned, but they had to provide for their own needs after fellowship with Him was broken. This has been the case for all men and women since Adam and Eve. God initially shielded Adam and Eve from pain and suffering, but He indicated they and all men and women after them would experience pain and suffering.

To Nature: God created the earth a paradise where everything was in perfect harmony. The harmony was destroyed, and the paradise became a wilderness because of sin. The ground brought forth in abundance before sin entered the world. The ground brought forth weeds, thorns, thistles and barrenness in addition to the abundance it initially brought forth after sin entered the world.

Sin has both individual and global consequences. With respect to personal consequences:

Sin dooms our soul (Ezekiel 18:4). It separates us from God. As a result, God's Spirit does not dwell in us, we are spiritually dead, and our spirit and soul are not nurtured and supported by God.

Sin devours our intellect (1 Corinthians 2:14, Romans 8:5-8). We are unable to receive and understand the spiritual life principles of God gives to us in the Bible when Hiss Spirit does not dwell in us and nurture our spirit. As a result, our mind becomes controlled by the desires and teachings of the world, and we become hostile toward God.

Sin deceives and perverts our heart (Jeremiah 17:9, Mark 7:21-22). It causes evil thoughts, fornications, thefts, murders, adulteries, deeds of coveting and wickedness, deceit, sensuality, envy, slander, pride and foolishness to proceed from our heart.

Sin dulls our ears (Acts 28:27). It prevents us from hearing God's word when it is shared with us by others, and it prevents us from hearing God's voice when He quietly speaks to us through our spirit.

Sin darkens our eyes (Ephesians 4:18). It causes our soul to become darkened and blighted. We, therefore, are unable to experience God working in our individual life and see Him working in the lives of others and the world.

Sin diverts our feet (Isaiah 53:6). Sin causes us to rebel against God and entices us to do things that are offensive to Him and violate His commandments.

Sin defiles our tongue (Romans 3:13-14). Our mouth often speaks forth things that are unclean, profane and offensive to God because of sin, and it defiles our whole body.

Sin has created an infinite chasm that separates us from God (Figure 3). Sin prevents us from entering a relationship with Him. His light does not shine in our heart because of sin. Consequently, our heart becomes blighted and dark. Sin deceives us into believing we have freedom to do anything we desire when in fact this freedom leads to bondage and causes our joy to turn to sorrow and our peace to be replaced with turmoil. Sin leads us into activities that destroy lives and relationships and cause pain and suffering. Sin destroys our positive self-image and takes away from us the confidence God wants us to have in our ability to do the things He wants us to do. Sin takes us farther into disobedient acts than we initially plan to go, causes us to stay involved in them longer than we initially want to stay, and costs us more in terms of guilt, shame, pain and suffering than we initially expect to have to pay.

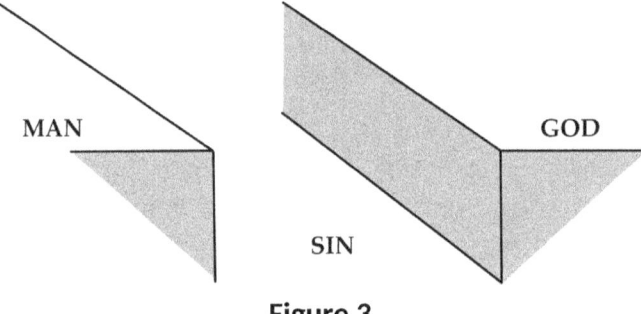

Figure 3

Sin has caused a fallenness to permeate God's original creation. He initially created everything to be perfect and in perfect harmony. However, sin has caused everything to become corrupt and imperfect. There are flaws in everything. These flaws are universal across time and human experiences and have caused disruptions in the harmony of God's original creation.

The fallenness of creation because of sin brings with it the potential for evil. Evil originated from Satan's rebellion against God in heaven and Adam and Eve disobeying God in the Garden of Eden. Evil lurks in the shadows and background of natural events and human affairs, looking for the right opportunities to spring forth. Evil is associated with actions and activities that give rise to sin and result in negative and hurtful consequences. Evil results in destruction through natural and man- made events and causes harm, injury and death. Evil perpetuates itself through the fallenness of creation and the fallen nature of people.

THE COMING JUDGMENT

Sin along with evil have existed in the world since the fall of Adam and Eve. The Bible teaches everyone who has ever been or will be born into this world is born into it with a sin nature. This sin nature separates us from God and predisposes us to disobedient, malicious and evil behavior. Genesis indicated God would send a Savior into the world who would be born from the seed of a woman and who will inflict a mortal wound to the head of the serpent who deceived Adam and Eve into disobeying God. Prophets in the Old Testament presented clues as to who this Savior would be. The New Testament teaches this promised Savior is Jesus, the Son of God.

Christianity has historically focused on the individual redemption and reconciliation extended to us by God's grace through our faith in Jesus. Our relationship with God is restored through this action, and we are spiritually reborn. More will be said about this in this book. However, sin and evil along with their effects and consequences continue to inflict pain, suffering and death. Satan remains the god of this world even though we are given authority over him through Jesus with respect to our individual life.

The Bible teaches God will judge the institutions and people of this world in addition to our promised individual redemption and reconciliation with Him through Jesus. He will then create a new heaven and earth in which there will be no sin, pain, suffering and death. Jesus will return to set up His earthly kingdom as part of this process. Satan, the fallen angles who have followed him, and those throughout history who have rejected God's grace extended to them through Jesus will be judged. They will be thrown into the lake of fire prepared for Satan and his angels.

CHAPTER 4
NATURE AND CHARACTER OF GOD
A CHOICE BETWEEN TWO KINGDOMS

"Do you not know that when you present yourselves to someone as slaves for obedience, you are slaves of the one who you obey, either of sin resulting in death, or of obedience resulting in righteousness? ... I am speaking in human terms because of the weakness of your flesh. For just as you presented your members as slaves to impurity and to lawlessness, resulting in further lawlessness, so now present your members as slaves to righteousness, resulting in sanctification. ... But now having been freed from sin and enslaved to God, you derive your benefit, resulting in sanctification, and the outcome, eternal life. For the wages of sin is death, but the free gift of God is eternal life in Christ Jesus our Lord." (Romans 6:16, 19, 22-23)

TWO KINGDOMS

The Bible teaches there are two spiritual kingdoms: the kingdom of God and the kingdom of Satan. We discussed the characters and natures of God and Satan in the previous two chapters. We now will examine the characteristics of their kingdoms. Table 3 lists some of the attributes of the kingdoms of God and Satan.

Table 3

THE KINGDOM OF GOD IS	THE KINGDOM OF SATAN IS:
Kingdom Characteristics	
a positive kingdom	a negative kingdom
a kingdom of light and truth	a kingdom of darkness built on lies a
kingdom of power	a kingdom of weakness.
a kingdom where holiness dwells	a kingdom where sin dwells
Relational Characteristics	
a place where there is:	**a place where there is:**
love	law
mercy	no mercy
forgiveness	only condemnation
grace	no grace
Eternal Characteristics	
a place of:	**a place of:**
faith	unbelief
agreement	disagreement
obedience	disobedience
righteousness	wickedness
sanctification	sin
eternal life	death
Emotional Characteristics	
a place of:	**a place of:**
honor	dishonor
glory	disgrace
peace	turmoil
joy	sorrow
hope	despair

KINGDOM CHARACTERISTICS

Kingdom of God

The kingdom of God is wherever God rules and reigns. Jesus stated in John 4:24:

> "God is spirit, and those who worship Him must worship in spirit and truth."

God's kingdom is a spiritual kingdom. Jesus indicated this in His statement to Pontius Pilot in John 18:36:

> "And Jesus answered, 'My kingdom is not of this world. If My kingdom were of this world, then My servants would be fighting, that I might not be delivered up to the Jews; but as it is, My kingdom is not of this realm.'"

God's kingdom has an actual throne (Isaiah 66:1, Psalm 11:4) and tabernacle (Hebrews 8:1-2) in heaven. Jesus stated in Luke 17:21, "the kingdom of God is in [our] midst." God's kingdom is a kingdom where the Spirit of God reigns, and men and women are in fellowship with God through the Holy Spirit. It is normal for us to interact and commune with God through Jesus.
The kingdom of God is a kingdom of light and truth. John stated in John 1:4-5, 9, 3:19-20, 4:24:

> "In Him was life, and the life was the light of men. And the light shines in the darkness, and the darkness did not comprehend it. ... There was the true light which, coming into the world, enlightens every man. ... This is the judgment, that the light is come into the world, and men loved the darkness rather than the light; for their deeds were evil. For everyone who does evil hates the light, and does not come to the light, lest his deed should be exposed. ... God is spirit, and those who worship Him must worship in spirit and truth."

Jesus stated in John 8:12 and 14:6:

> "I am the light of the world; he who follows Me shall not walk in the darkness, but shall have the light of life. ... I am the way, and the truth, and the life; no one comes to the Father but through Me."

Jesus taught His light brings life and His truth nourishes our minds. These facilitates our spiritual grow and impart God's knowledge and wisdom to us through the Holy Spirit.
Paul taught the kingdom of God is a kingdom of power. He stated in 1 Corinthians 2:4-5:

> "My message and my preaching were not in persuasive words of wisdom, but in demonstration of the Spirit and of power, that your faith should not rest on the wisdom of men, but on the power of God."

and in 1 Thessalonians 1:5:

> "Our gospel did not come to you in word only, but also in power and in the Holy Spirit and with full conviction."

Jesus added in Matthew 18:18-20:

> "Truly I say to you, whatever you shall bind on earth shall be bound in heaven; and whatever you lose on earth shall be loosed in heaven. Again I say to you that if two of you agree on earth about anything that they may ask, it shall be done for them by My Father who is in heaven. For where two or three have gathered together in My name, there I am in their midst."

We have power to accomplish things in God's kingdom through the Holy Spirit that are impossible without Him. We have authority in the name of Jesus to release His power through prayer to work on our behalf. Paul indicated our faith will be affirmed by the power of God working through us. This faith enables us to accomplish the intentional will of God for our life.

The kingdom of God is a kingdom where holiness dwells because God is holy. Righteousness is an expression of God's holiness because He is absolutely right and perfect. Justice is an expression of His holiness because He is absolutely fair and impartial in everything He does. Truth and faithfulness are expressions of God's holiness. However, the greatest expression of God's holiness is His love.

Kingdom of Satan

The kingdom of Satan is where Satan rules and reigns. The kingdom of Satan is a kingdom of darkness and lies. It is a kingdom built on deception where everything is negative, self is lord, and men and women do things only to please themselves.

The minds and hearts of men and women throughout the ages have become darkened and blighted because God's truth does not dwell in them. Human life has been drawn downward toward the earth instead of being drawn upward toward God. Their souls devoid of God's Spirit have become earth-minded and pleasure-seeking. The desires of the flesh, the envy and lust of the eyes and the desire to be in control manipulate the minds and hearts of men and women who are separated from God. They have fallen to earthly and pleasure-seeking lives.

This is referred to as the *fall of man*. Men and women separated from God live in darkness where there is no light and truth. As a result, Satan has deceived them, filled them with his lies, and assumed dominion of and established his kingdom in the world through them.

Covetousness, immorality, idolatry, drunkenness, homosexuality, adultery, fornication, jealousy, strife, and other negative qualities often characterize the lives of those who abandon God and become selfish and pleasure-seeking. These draw the vitality out of and deceive them into believing they are free to do as they please when in fact they become slaves to their own passions.

The kingdom of Satan is a kingdom of weakness because it is built on deception and lies. It can only maintain itself as long as it deceives and blinds men and women to the love, mercy, grace and forgiveness God desires to give them through Jesus. Satan's kingdom loses its control over them when they enter a reconciled relationship with God through Jesus.

The kingdom of Satan is a kingdom where sin dwells. John stated in 1 John 3:8:

> "The one who practices sin is the devil, for the devil has sinned from the beginning."

The kingdom of Satan is in constant rebellion against God. It seeks to deny God the possession of those things that are rightfully and legally His and rejects his right to be God.

RELATIONAL CHARACTERISTICS

Kingdom of God

Love abounds in the kingdom of God. The Bible teaches God expresses His love toward us through His grace, his unmerited favor. The essence of grace is mercy, and the true expression of mercy is forgiveness. Paul stated in Ephesians 2:4-9:

> "But God being rich in mercy, because of His great love with which He loved us, even when we were dead in our transgressions, made us alive together with Christ (by grace you have been saved), and raised us up with Him, and seated us with Him in the heavenly places, in Christ Jesus, in order that in the ages to come He might show the surpassing riches of His grace in kindness toward us in Christ Jesus. For by grace you have been saved through faith; and that not of yourselves, it is the gift of God; not as a result of works, that no one should boast."

Forgiveness is the visible manifestation of love and the expression of true holiness. Unforgiveness points to areas in our lives where there is unholiness. There is a corresponding lack of mercy, grace and love where there is unforgiveness. Paul taught:

> "And may the Lord cause you to increase and abound in love for one another, and for all men, just as we also do for you so that He may establish your hearts unblameable in holiness before our God and Father at the coming of our Lord Jesus with all the saints." (1 Thessalonians 3:12-13)

> "And be kind to one another, tenderhearted, forgiving each other, just as God in Christ has also forgiven you." (Ephesians 4:32)

Kingdom of Satan

Law must exist in the kingdom of Satan. The opposite of love is law. There of necessity must be law where there is no love. Paul stated in 1 Timothy 1:8-9:

> "But we know that the Law is good, if one uses it lawfully, realizing the fact that law is not made for a righteous man, but for those who are lawless and rebellious."

Laws are not meant for the righteous but for the rebellious and lawbreakers. There are no mercy, grace and forgiveness in Satan's kingdom because there is no love there. There is only condemnation. Satan is our accuser who continually accuses and berates us in an attempt to lead us into feelings of hopelessness and despair. He denies us the blessings God desires to give us through Jesus.

ETERNAL CHARACTERISTICS

Kingdom of God

We must have faith to enter fellowship with God through Jesus. We must believe God exists and Jesus is the Son of God, who died on a cross and was raised from the dead so we can be reconciled to God. In Hebrews 11:6, the author stated:

> "Without faith it is impossible to please Him, for He who comes to God must believe that He is, and that He is a rewarder of those who seek Him."

We accept and live according to God's spiritual life principles and laws through faith. Faith produces within us convictions that are beliefs we are willing to die for. Convictions result in obedience to God that is characterized by our willingness to live within His boundaries for acceptable behavior. Our faith in and obedience to God comes from the righteousness of Jesus that dwells within us. His righteousness results in sanctification that makes us holy and sets us apart to do God's work. Sanctification frees us from the eternal consequences of sin and results in eternal life.

Kingdom of Satan

The kingdom of Satan is a kingdom of unbelief. The Bible does not describe unbelief in the sense that we do not believe in something when it describes unbelief. Everyone believes in something when they have a philosophy that supports life. Unbelief here implies an absence of faith in God. The kingdom of Satan is a place where people reject God's word and His authority over their lives because it is a kingdom of unbelief. This rejection results in disobedience that is characterized by an unwillingness to live within boundaries of acceptable behavior established by God. Disobedience produces wickedness that results in sin. Sin separates us from God. Separation from God results in both spiritual and physical death. Faith in the kingdom of God produces agreement; agreement produces obedience; obedience produces righteousness; righteousness produces sanctification; and sanctification results in eternal life. Unbelief in the kingdom of Satan produces disagreement; disagreement produces disobedience; disobedience produces wickedness; wickedness produces sin; and sin results in death.

EMOTIONAL CHARACTERISTICS

Kingdom of God

The kingdom of God is a place of honor and glory where there are peace and joy (Romans 2:0-10, 14:17). The kingdom of God is a place where we have real freedom (Romans 8:21) and hope (Romans 5:3-5) because God can be trusted to keep His covenants and promises. He promised to redeem and reconcile us to Him through Jesus (Luke 12:32). Paul stated in Colossians 1:19-20:

> "For it was the Father's good pleasure for all the fullness to dwell in [Jesus], and through Him to reconcile all things to Himself, having made peace

through the blood of His cross; through Him, I say, whether things on earth or things in heaven."

God promises He will provide for our needs when we first seek His righteousness (Matthew 3:12-13).

Kingdom of Satan

The kingdom of Satan is a place of dishonor and disgrace. It is a place of constant turmoil and sorrow. There is neither peace nor joy in Satan's kingdom; there are only darkness and despair.

A CHOICE BETWEEN TWO KINGDOMS

The Bible teaches we are born into this world with a sin nature and initially have hearts where God's Spirit does not dwell. Four obstacles stand between God and us because of sin. They are:

- God's absolute holiness compared to our sinful natures separates us from Him (Romans 3:23).

- God's absolute justice requires we be punished for our sinful and rebellious natures. The punishment that He prescribed is death (Romans 6:23).

- We have denied God the right of lordship over our life and made ourself lord. As a result, we have transferred control of our lives to Satan who is the god and ruler of this world.

- We are born into this world spiritually dead because of sin. We are unable to understand and live according to God's spiritual life principles because His Spirit does not dwell in us.

These four obstacles are humanly insurmountable. God's love for us moved Him to establish a way to reconcile us to Himself. He did this by sending His Son, Jesus, into the world to die on a cross to give us spiritual life through Him. We now have a choice between two kingdoms. One is the kingdom of Satan, which results in eternal separation from God and death. The other is the kingdom of God, which we enter through Jesus, and in which we have fellowship with God and eternal life.

CHAPTER 5
NATURE AND CHARACTER OF GOD
JESUS - GOD INCARNATE IN MAN

"And Jesus cried out and said, 'He who believes in Me does not believe in Me, but in Him who sent Me. And he who beholds Me beholds the One who sent me. He who sees Me sees the One who sent Me. ... For I did not speak on My own initiative, but the Father Himself who sent Me has given Me commandment, what to say, and what to speak. And I know that His commandment is eternal life; therefore on things I speak, I speak just as the Father has told me." (John 12:44-45, 49-50)

"And He is the image of the invisible God, the firstborn of all creation. For in Him all things were created, both in the heavens and on earth, visible and invisible, whether thrones or dominions or rulers or authorities - all things have been created through Him and for Him. He is before all things, and in Him all things hold together. ... And although you were formerly alienated and hostile in mind, engaged in evil deeds, yet He has now reconciled you in His fleshly body through death, in order to present you before Him holy and blameless and beyond reproach - if indeed you continue in the faith firmly established and steadfast, and not moved away from the hope of the gospel that you have heard, which was proclaimed in all creation under heaven, and of which I, Paul, was made a minister." (Colossians 1:15-17, 21-23)

WHY WE NEED A SAVIOR

Humanly insurmountable obstacles exist between God and us because of sin and the fallenness sin has caused in the world. They are:

- The holiness of God compared to our sin natures;
- The debt of sin and God's holiness that requires death as a consequence;
- Obedience to self and Satan who is the god and ruler of this world; and

- Spiritual death associated with hearts devoid of the God's Spirit.

JESUS AND THE BIBLE

God's love and plan for the redemption of His creation through Jesus after the fall of Adam and Eve in the Garden of Eden are the central themes throughout the Bible. Events prophesied about Jesus' life in the Old Testament were fulfilled by Him during His life in the New Testament. Table 4 lists some of the major events in Jesus' life that were prophesied in the Old Testament and documented to have been fulfilled in the New Testament. Other prophesies are listed in Appendix B. According to Peter Stoner in his book, *Science Speaks: An Evaluation of Certain Christian Evidences* (1963), the probability the nine prophesies in the table that are preceded by an * could have been literally fulfilled by Jesus during His lifetime is 1 in 10^{17} (1 followed by 17 zeroes). 10^{17} silver dollars will cover the whole state of Texas to a depth of two feet. Imagine the probability of being able to pluck out one silver dollar that has been marked and randomly placed in that many silver dollars. This gives an indication of the reliability of Bible prophecies concerning events in the life, death and resurrection of Jesus.

Table 4

Events in Life	Old Testament Prophesies	Fulfilled in the New Testament
Born of a virgin	Isaiah 7:14	Matthew 1:23,25
*Born in Bethlehem	Micah 5.2	Matthew 2:1 Luke 2:4-7
Herod to massacre infants	Jeremiah 31:15	Matthew 2:16
Would heal people	Isaiah 53:4	Matthew 8:16-17
*To be preceded by a messenger	Isaiah 40:3 Malachi 3:1	Matthew 3:1-2 John 1:23, Mark 7:33-35
Would teach in parables	Isaiah 6:9-10	Matthew 13:10-15
Would be rejected	Psalm 69:8 Isaiah 53:3	John 1:11, 7:5
*To enter Jerusalem on a donkey	Zechariah 9:9	Mathew 21:4-5
*To be betrayed by a friend	Psalm 41:9, 55:12-14	Matthew 10:4, 26:49-50 John 13:21
*To be betrayed for 30 pieces of silver	Psalm 41:9, 55:12-14 Zechariah 11:12-13	Matthew 26:14-16, 21- 25

*Silver to be used to buy Potter's field	Zechariah 11:13	Matthew 27:7
To be forsaken by His disciples	Zechariah 13:7	Matthew 26:31
		Mark 14:27,50
*To be dumb before accusers	Isaiah 53:7	Matthew 27:12-19
To be wounded and bruised	Isaiah 53:5	Matthew 27:26
	Zachariah 13:6	
*Hands and feet to be pierced	Psalm 22:16	Luke 23:33
	Zechariah 12:10	John 20:25
*To be crucified between two thieves	Isaiah 53:12	Matthew 27:38
		Mark15:27-28
		Luke 22:37
Would rise from the dead	Psalm 16:10	Matthew 28:2-7
Would ascend into heaven	Psalm 24:7-10	Mark 16:19

JESUS - GOD'S AGENT OF REDEMPTION AND RECONCILIATION

The Bible teaches God's love for us moved Him to establish a means to redeem and reconcile us to Himself. He accomplished this in a manner consistent with His holiness and love. The Genesis account of the fall of Adam and Eve indicates God set into motion the means He would use to redeem and reconcile us to Himself immediately after the fall. He accomplished this by impregnating a virgin, named Mary, through an act of the Holy Spirit so His Son, Jesus, could be born into the world (Table 4).

Jesus stated in John 10:30), "I and the Father are One." John stated in John 1:1-3:

> "In the beginning was the Word, and the Word was with God, and the Word was God. He was in the beginning with God. All things came into being through Him, and apart from Him nothing came into being that has come into being."

Jesus is the Word who was with God in the beginning.

The Bible refers to Jesus as:

- God (Hebrews 1:8-9),
- The Son of God (Matthew 16:16),
- The Word (John 1:1),
- The King of kings and Lord of lords (1 Timothy 6:15),
- The Messiah (John 1:41), and

- The Savior (1 John 4:14).

These all attest to His deity. He is also referred to as:

- The Son of Man (Luke 9:22),
- The Son of David (Matthew 9:27), and

These attest to His humanity. Jesus referred to himself as:

- The bread of life (John 6:35),
- The light of the world (John 8:12),
- The door (John 10:9),
- The good shepherd (John 10:11, 14),
- The resurrection and life (John 11:25-26),
- The way, the truth, and the life (John 14:6), and
- The true vine (John 15:1-2).

These all point to the facts Jesus:

- Reestablished the kingdom of God on earth and in the hearts of men and women.
- Is the king of God's kingdom.
- Is the door through which everyone must pass to enter the kingdom of God.
- Is the true vine through which the Spirit of God passes to breathe spiritual life into the hearts of men and women to empower them to live according to the spiritual life principles and laws of God.

Paul stated in Colossians 1:15-17:

> "And [Jesus] is the image of the invisible God, the firstborn of all creation. For by Him all things were created, both in the heavens and on earth, visible and invisible, whether thrones or dominions or rulers or authorities - all things have been created by Him and for Him. And He is before all things, and in Him all things hold together."

Jesus is "the image of the invisible God," and all things in heaven and on earth have been created by and for Him. John stated in John 1:3 all things have come into being through

Jesus. He is "the firstborn of all creation," and all things in creation are held together in and by Him.

Jesus came into the world from the presence of God. He stated in John 6:38:

> "For I have come down from heaven, not to do My own will, but the will of Him who sent Me."

He came to reestablish the kingdom of God in the hearts of men and women. He stated in John 4:34,

> "My food is to do the will of Him who sent me, and to accomplish His work."

Jesus accomplished everything He did according to the will of and in a manner pleasing to God (Table 5).

Table 5

JESUS CAME TO:	
Do the will and accomplish the work of God	Be our Savior
Establish the kingdom of God on earth and in our hearts	Redeem us from the Law
Bring the light of God into the world	Cancel our certificate of debt for sin
Bear witness to the truth of God	Cleanse us of sin
Reveal the nature and character of God	Make us righteous before God
Call the world to repent	Reconcile us to God
Be a kinsman redeemer	Redeem us from sin
Fulfill the Law and the Prophets	Give us spiritual life
Establish a new covenant with God	Destroy the works of Satan
Be the mediator of this new covenant	Redeem us from Satan
Die for us on a cross	Become our high priest in heaven
Be a propitiation for our sins	Send the Holy Spirit into the world

The disobedience of the first Adam resulted in death and separation from God, but the perfect obedience of the last Adam, Jesus, resulted in eternal life and reconciliation with God (Romans 5:12-21, 1 Corinthians 15:20-22, 45). Jesus was a man with human attributes who was perfectly obedient to God. The Holy Spirit dwelt in Him without measure, enabling

Him to live according to the spiritual life principles and laws of God. Therefore, He exercised dominion over the earth, the flesh and Satan. He could say to:

- Storms be still (Matthew 8:23-27);
- The flesh stretches forth (Mark 3:1-5); and
- Demons come out (Luke 4:31-36).

Jesus came to reveal the nature and character of God and His kingdom as God wanted them revealed in His own person when He came into this world (John 1:9-18, 12:44-50). Jesus came:

- To call men and women to repent and return to God (Mark 1:14-15);
- As the Light to reveal the holiness of God and expose the wickedness that existed in the world (John 1:4-9, 3:19-21);
- To give us eternal life that no one can take from us (John 10:27-30);
- To judge and destroy the works of Satan (1 John 3:7-8); and
- To redeem us from sin and bondage to Satan (Romans 6:20-23).

Jesus came to bear witness to the truth of God, compared to the lies and deception of the devil. He told Pontius Pilate in John 18:37 when He was brought before him by the Jewish leaders:

> "You say correctly that I am a king. For this I have been born, and for this I have come into the world, to bear witness to the truth. Everyone who is of the truth hears My voice."

Jesus stated His truth results in freedom and eternal life whereas the deception and lies of Satan results in slavery and death (John 8:31-36, 51).

Jesus came to fulfill the Law and bring us out from under its curse (Romans 10:5-11). All the Law could do was bring slavery and death to those who lived by and were judged by it (Romans 3:10- 20). Jesus established a new covenant with us that was sealed by His blood shed on a cross when He fulfilled the Law by His death and resurrection. Jesus stated in Luke 22:20, "This cup which is poured out for you is the new covenant in My blood." In Hebrews 7:22, the author stated, "So much more also Jesus has become the guarantee of a better covenant." Jesus came to establish a new covenant that would bring us out from under the curse of the Law and into the presence of the redeeming love of God (Galatians 3:10-14).

Jesus came to be our savior (1 John 4:14, 1 Timothy 4:10). He came to die for us. In Hebrews 2:9, the author stated:

> "But we do see Him who has been made for a little while lower than angels, namely, Jesus, because of the suffering of death crowned with glory and honor, that by the grace of God He might taste death for everyone."

God's holiness requires the penalty of death for those guilty of sin. This means all humanity (Romans 3:10-17). The justifiable wrath of God is directed against sin. It is directed against us when sin dwells in us. However, God in His mercy established a sacrificial means whereby His wrath would be diverted from us and directed toward a single person who was willing to stand in our place. This person had to be acceptable to God, without sin, and willing to voluntarily die for our sins. This person was Jesus. He stated in John 10:17-18:

> "For this reason the Father loves Me, because I lay down My life that I may take it up again. No one has taken it away from Me, but I lay it down on My own initiative. I have authority to lay it down, and I have authority to take it up again. This commandment I receive from My Father."

The full wrath of God was directed against Jesus instead of us when Jesus hung and shed His blood on a cross. Jesus was a propitiation for our sins (Romans 3:23-25, 1 John 2:1-2); He stood in our place and accepted our death sentence for sin. Paul stated in Colossians 2:13-14:

> "And when you were dead in your transgressions and the uncircumcised of your flesh, He made you alive together with Him, having forgiven us all our transgressions, having canceled out the certificate of debt consisting of decrees against us and which was hostile to us; and He has taken it out of the way, having nailed it to the cross."

Jesus' blood shed on a cross was an acceptable sacrifice for God to cleanse us of sin because of His perfect holiness and obedience to God (1 John 1:7).

The Bible refers to Jesus as our redeemer. Jesus came to redeem us from sin, the Law and bondage to Satan. Jewish law in Leviticus 25:25:

> "If a fellow countryman of yours becomes so poor he has to sell part of his property, then his nearest kinsman is to come and buy back what his relative has sold."

A Jew and his property could only be redeemed by a kinsman who was a blood relative when he sold himself into slavery. Dominion of this world that was originally ours was transferred to Satan because of sin. We experience the effects of this transfer even though we may not actively serve him. God gave us the Law because of sin. The Bible teaches the Law only serves to expose our sinful natures in contrast with the holiness of God. It cannot save us from the eternal consequences of sin. We have come under its curse that results in death because we are unable to keep the Law. We are under bondage to sin, the Law and Satan without Jesus. It is impossible to free ourself from this bondage. The Bible teaches God initially created us to exercise dominion over the earth. However, Adam, transferred dominion to Satan when he disobeyed God and sinned. Therefore, only a man who could act as our kinsman redeemer could ransom back what Adam had been transferred. This man had to have authority to carry out the transaction and be able to pay the acceptable price of the ransom. The man who would pay the ransom had to be perfectly obedient to God and without sin because disobedience resulting in sin brought us into bondage to sin, the Law and Satan. Only God had these qualifications. It was necessary for a man without sin who would be perfectly obedient to God to be born into this world through the seed and womb of a woman. This man would pay the ransom for God to redeem fallen humanity and return dominion back to us. God accomplished this through His Son, Jesus. His death satisfied the justifiable wrath of God, and His perfect obedience to God resulted in His death being an acceptable ransom to redeem us from bondage to sin, the curse of the Law, and slavery to Satan when He died on the cross.

Jesus stated in Mark 20:45, "For even the Son of Man did not come to be served, but to serve, and to give His life a ransom for many." The Scriptures further teach:

> "For there is one God, and one mediator also between God and men, the man Christ Jesus, who gave Himself as a ransom for all, the testimony borne at the proper time." (1 Timothy 2:5-6)

> "Christ redeemed us from the curse of the Law, having become a curse for us - for it is written, 'cursed is everyone who hangs on a tree.'" (Galatians 3:13)

> "Since then the children share in flesh and blood, He Himself likewise also partook of the same, that through death He might render powerless him who had the power of death, that is the devil; and might deliver those who through fear were subject to slavery all their lives." (Hebrews 2:14-15)

Jesus said He was sending Paul to the Gentiles when He appeared to him on the Damascus road (Acts 26:18):

> "... to open their eyes so that they may turn from darkness to light and from the dominion of Satan to God, in order that they may receive forgiveness of sins and an inheritance among those who have been sanctified by faith in [Him]."

Therefore, our sins were forgiven, the Law was fulfilled, Satan was judged, and his control over us was ended through Jesus' death on a cross.

Jesus came to be the mediator of a new covenant that He established and sealed with His blood. In Hebrews 9:15-16, the author stated:

> "And for this reason He is the mediator of a new covenant, in order that since a death has taken place for the redemption of the transgressions that were committed under the first covenant, those who have been called may receive the promise of the eternal inheritance. For where a covenant is, there must of necessity be the death of the one who made it."

This covenant makes us righteous before God and enables us to receive God's love manifested through His mercy and grace (Romans 5:19, 1 Corinthians 5:21). It is a perfect covenant because Jesus is its mediator. He had to be acceptable to God and man for Him to be the mediator of this covenant. The only way for Him to accomplish this was to be God with all the attributes of God and to be a man with all the attributes of man but be without sin.

Jesus has become our high priest in heaven because He accepted God's required death penalty for sin though His death on a cross. In Hebrews 4:15, 7:23-27, the author stated:

> "For we do not have a high priest who cannot sympathize with our weaknesses, but one who has been tempted in all things as we are, yet without sin. ... The former priest, on the one hand, existed in greater numbers because they were prevented by death from continuing, but Jesus, on the other hand, because He abides forever, holds His priesthood permanently. Hence, also, He is able to save forever those who draw near to God through Him, since He always lives to make intercession for them. For it was fitting that we should have such a high priest, holy, innocent, undefiled, separated from sinners and exalted above the heavens; who does not need daily, like those high priest, to offer up sacrifices, first for his own sins, and then for the sins of the people, because this He did once for all when He offered up Himself."

Just as Jesus was God become man, He is now a man become God. He is a man in heaven who is the firstborn of a new creation (Romans 8:29, Colossians 1:18). He is our priest in heaven who is there to continually intercede for us before the Father. He knows and understands our weaknesses because He once was a man.

Jesus can save those who draw near to God through Him. He removed all the obstacles that stand between God and us. He destroyed the works of Satan and ended his dominion over us. He voluntarily endured the justifiable wrath of God against sin and died in our place. God no longer sees our sinful natures when we approach Him through Jesus; He sees us in the light of the righteousness of His Son. Paul stated in Romans 8:9-10:

> "However, you are not in the flesh but in the Spirit, if indeed the Spirit of God dwells in you. But if anyone does not have the Spirit of Christ, he does not belong to Him. And if Christ is in you, though the body is dead because of sin, yet the spirit is alive because of righteousness."

We are made spiritually alive and enabled to fellowship and commune with God when we come into Hiss presence through Jesus.

Finally, Jesus came to send the Holy Spirit into the world (John 14:16-17, 16:7). He promised His disciples He would not leave them orphans or defenseless. He said it was necessary for Him to return to His Father so He and His Father could send the Holy Spirit. Jesus promised He would send the Holy Spirit into the world to help them remember all He had taught them and to give them the ability to spread His gospel throughout the world. The Holy Spirit enabled the disciples to proclaim repentance for sin, preach the gospel of Jesus, witness to the presence of Jesus in their lives, and make disciples of others. The Holy Spirit enables us to do the same when we enter a relationship with God through Jesus and give Him permission to do so.

CHAPTER 6
NATURE AND CHARACTER OF GOD
JESUS - GOD'S ONLY PROVISION FOR SIN

"For there was a tabernacle prepared, the outer one, in which were the lamp stand and the table and the sacred bread; this is the holy place. And behind the second veil, there was a tabernacle which is called the Holy of Holies, having a golden altar of incense and the ark of the covenant covered on all sides with gold, in which was a golden jar holding the manna, and Aaron's rod which budded, and the tables of the covenant; and above it were the cherubim of glory over- shadowing the mercy seat; but of these things we cannot now speak in detaill. ... But when Christ appeared as a high priest of the good things to come, He entered through the greater and more perfect tabernacle, not made with hands, that is to say, not of this creation; and not through the blood of goats and calves, but through His own blood, He entered the holy place once for all, having obtained eternal redemption. For if the blood of goats and bulls and the ashes of a heifer sprinkling those who have been defiled, sanctify for the cleansing of the flesh, how much more will the blood of Christ, who through the eternal Spirit offered Himself without blemish to God, cleanse your conscience from dead works to serve the living God? ... And according to the Law, one may almost say, all things are cleansed with blood, and without shedding of blood there is no forgiveness. ... For Christ did not enter a holy place made with hands, a mere copy of the true one, but into heaven itself, now to appear in the presence of God for us; nor was it that He should offer Himself often, as the high priest enters the holy place year by year with blood not his own. Otherwise, He would have needed to suffer often since the foundation of the world; but now once at the consummation of the ages He has been manifested to put away sin by the sacrifice of Himself. And inasmuch as it is appointed for men to die once and after this comes Judgment, so Christ also, having been offered once to bear the sins of many, shall appear a second time for salvation without reference to sin, to those who eagerly await Him." (Hebrews 9:2-5, 11-14, 22, 24-28)

"There is therefore now no condemnation for those who are in Christ Jesus. For the law of the Spirit of life in Christ Jesus has set you free from the law of sin and of death. For what the Law could not do, weak as it was through the flesh, God did: sending His own Son in the likeness of sinful flesh and as an offering for sin, He condemned sin in the flesh, in order that the requirement of the Law might be fulfilled in us, who do not walk according to the flesh, but according to the Spirit. ... For all who are being led by the Spirit of God, these are sons of God. For you have not received a spirit of slavery leading to fear again, but you have received a spirit of adoption as sons by which we cry out, "Abba! Father!" The Spirit Himself bears witness with our spirit that we are children of God, and if children, heirs also, heirs of God and fellow heirs with Christ, if indeed we suffer with Him in order that we may also be glorified with Him." (Romans 8:1-4, 14-17)

JESUS IS OUR ONLY PROVISION FOR SIN

Jesus came to fulfill the Law and the Prophets, reconcile us to God, establish a new covenant between God and us, and redeemed us from sin and bondage to Satan. Sin:

- Stands between the holiness of God and us;
- Causes the wrath of God to be directed against us and require the penalty of death;
- Results in our being in bondage to Satan; and
- Has resulted in God's Spirit being withdrawn from us and our resulting spiritual death.

God removed these barriers by redeeming and reconciling us to Himself through the death and resurrection of Jesus.

Jesus is God's only provision for sin. Christianity is the only religion that addresses sin and its consequences. Other religions do not address the fallenness in the world caused by sin and the pain and suffering this fallenness causes. They are powerless to bring about positive changes in the lives of those who are in bondage to sin and free them from bondage to Satan. They are unable to bring about reconciliation and healing to broken relationships and conflicts between ethnic and religious groups and nations. They cannot reconcile us to God. Jesus is the only One who can address these conditions. He has reconciled us to and reestablished our broken relationship with God. He breathes spiritual life through the Holy Spirit into our spirit and soul. Jesus through the Holy Spirit affects positive changes in our life and enables us to live according to the spiritual life principles and laws of God.

JESUS WAS BORN OF A VIRGIN

Jesus' virgin birth is an orthodox belief of Christianity. Around 75 percent of Christians believe in Jesus' virgin birth. They believe Mary's seed was fertilized by the overshadowing of the Holy Spirit as described in Luke 1:26-35.

The Bible gives insights into the reality of the virgin birth of Jesus. We begin in the Genesis account of the fall of Adam and Eve to understand why the virgin birth was necessary. The events surrounding this fall and the introduction of sin into God's creation were discussed in Chapter 3. God judged Adam and Eve and placed His curse on the serpent (Genesis 3:14-19). He said to the serpent:

> "And I will put enmity between you and the woman and between your seed and her seed; He shall bruise you on the head and you shall bruise Him on the heel."

Bible scholars believe this verse implies the savior God would send was to enter this world through the seed of a woman by means of the natural birth process. Isaiah implied in Isaiah 7:14 Jesus was to be conceived in the womb of a virgin. He stated:

> "Therefore the LORD Himself will give you a sign: Behold, a virgin will be with child and bear a son, and she will call His name Emmanuel."

Emmanuel means *God with us*. Matthew stated in Matthew 1:18:

> "Now the birth of Jesus Christ was as follows: when His mother Mary had been betrothed to Joseph, before they came together she was found to be with child by the Holy Spirit."

Luke stated in Luke 1:26-35 that Gabriel said to Mary regarding Jesus:

> "He will be great and will be called the Son of the Most High; and the Lord God will give Him the throne of His father David; and He will reign over the house of Jacob forever; and His kingdom will have no end. The Holy Spirit will come upon you and the power of the Most High will overshadow you; and for that reason the holy offspring shall be called the Son of God."

The Bible confirms Jesus' virgin birth. This should be enough from a faith perspective, and it is for most of us. However, the question arises as to why the virgin birth of Jesus was necessary.

God is sovereign. He could have redeemed and reconciled us to Himself in any manner He chose. However, the Bible teaches God acts in ways compatible with the physical and spiritual laws He has established and the covenant relationships He has entered into with us. There are cases where He has performed miracles that transcend our understanding of these laws and relationships. However, He has never acted in a way that does harm to, opposes or invalidates them. This is true with the virgin birth.

The New Testament writers indicated there is a relationship between Adam and Jesus. Luke in his genealogy of Jesus (Luke 3:23-38) referred to Adam as the son of God. Gabriel in Luke 1:35 referred to Jesus as God. Paul stated in 1 Corinthians 15:22, 45:

> "For as in Adam all die, so also in Christ all will be made alive. ... So also it is written, 'The first man Adam becme a living soul. (Genesis 2:7) The last Adam became a life giving spirit.'"

Both Adam and Jesus are *sons* of God, the first through whom we experience death and the second through whom we can have eternal life. This relationship has significant implications.

The Genesis account of creation indicates Adam was created perfect and immortal (Genesis 1:26-28 and 2:4-25). He was created with a physical body into which God breathed His Spirit, after which he become a living soul. Adam was initially physically and spiritually alive. He could breathe and interact with the physical world where God placed him, and he could interact and fellowship with God (Genesis 3:8). Adam's immortality did not mean he could not die. However, it meant he would live forever in the absence of forces outside his body that could cause his death. This also implied children born to Adam and Eve would have also been immortal.

God perceived Adam needed a suitable helper. Therefore, He caused a deep sleep to fall upon him, removed one of his ribs from his side, and then formed Eve from this rib (Genesis 2:20-25). Adam said when God brought Eve to him:

> "This is now bone of my bones, and flesh of my flesh; she shall be called women, for she was taken out of man."

The symbolism associated with the biblical narrative of the creation of Adam and Eve has significant implications with respect to the virgin birth of Jesus. This narrative indicates:

- Adam and Eve had similar genetic makeups in their unfallen sinless state. They each had genetic makeups derived solely from Adam's original created body with the exception of the male and female characteristics God designed into each of their bodies.

- Adam possibly contained within his original created body both seeds necessary for procreation: the male sperm and the female ovum. God then separated these seeds, leaving in Adam the male sperm and transferring to Eve the female ovum when He formed Eve out of Adam. Therefore, all generations subsequent to Adam and Eve are descended from the original immortal male and female seeds that were initially in Adam. As a result, we are all descended from Adam.

- God created procreation to occur through the fertilization of the female seed (ovum) by the male seed (sperm) through normal sexual union within the covenant relation of marriage (Genesis 2:24-25, Matthew 19:4-6).

- Our bodies are conceived and then form through the joining together of the two seeds (sperm and ovum) from a man and woman while God Himself imparts to our body our spirit and soul. We become a living spirit and soul when this occurs. Our spirit and soul rightfully belong to and can only be redeemed by God because they are imparted to our body by Him.

God commanded Adam not to eat the fruit from the tree of the knowledge of good and evil (Genesis 2:17) when He placed him in the Garden of Eden. He told Adam he would die if he ate this forbidden fruit. Adam and Eve spiritually died after they disobeyed God and ate the forbidden fruit because God withdrew His Spirit and separated Himself from them. *Spiritual death is associated with separation from God.* God also stated in Genesis 3:19 Adam and Eve would also physically die because of their disobedience. Genesis 5:5 indicates Adam was 930 years old when he died a natural death. We can assume Eve also died a natural death at an advanced age.

It is reasonable to speculate God's judgement of and the subsequent curse He placed on Adam and Eve caused a change in their genetic makeup. Their physical immortality was replaced with their eventual physical death. This genetic change has resulted in the physical death of all subsequent generations after them.

Adam's and Eve's initial immortality was affirmed when God expelled them from the Garden of Eden (Genesis 3:22-24). He stated in Genesis 3:22:

> "Behold the man has become like one of Us, knowing good and evil, and now, lest he stretch out his hand, and take also from the tree of life, and eat, and live forever."

The potential for this to occur must have been disturbing to God because He did not complete His sentence. This statement implies fruit from the tree of life would have counteracted the genetic consequences of God's judgement and curse and given back to Adam and Eve and their descendants their physical immortality. However, this fruit would not change the spiritual consequence of God's judgement and curse. Adam and Eve and their descendants would have lived forever in a fallen sinful state separated from God. It would have been impossible for Him to redeem and reconcile fallen men and women to Himself, acting within the physical and spiritual laws He had established. He did not want this to occur. Therefore, God drove Adam and Eve from the Garden of Eden and prevented them and their descendants from returning. The Bible teaches God will redeem us and give back to us our immortality through Jesus by means of our spiritual rebirth and the resurrection of our body. We will eventually live forever in fellowship with God through Jesus.

Observations regarding God's judgment of Adam and Eve are:

- God said to Adam he would die because of his disobedience when He judged Adam and Eve (Genesis 3:19). Paul stated in Romans 5:12 physical death entered the world through Adam because of sin, and he stated in 1 Corinthians 15:22 in Adam we all die.

- God told Eve He would greatly increase her pain during childbirth (Genesis 3:16). He did not specifically state she would die; however, her eventual physical death can be implied from God's judgment of Adam.

- God promised a future redeemer would enter the world through Eve's seed (Genesus 3:14-15). He did not make this promise with respect to Adam's seed. Paul made a curious statement in 1 Timothy 2:15. He stated, "women shall be preserved through the bearing of children," possibly implying women contain in their seed the potential for immortality.

- Both Adam and Eve died natural deaths. All men and women from Adam and Eve to the present have physically died.

Observations concerning the effects of eating the forbidden fruit on Adam and Eve are:

- The effects of eating the forbidden fruit caused both Adam and Eve to lose their immortality and die. This could have been because of God's judgment, the effects of the forbidden fruit on their bodies, or both.

- God's judgement and curse caused a mutation to occur in Adam's seed (sperm) that destroyed its ability and the ability of all male seeds after Adam to transfer an immortal nature to future generations. This may not have had a similar effect on Eve's seed (ovum). Her seed and the seed of future women may not have completely lost their obility to transfer an immortal nature to future generations.

- The death nature of the sperm is transferred to the fertilized ovum when the sperm of a man fertilizes the ovum of a woman at conception, resulting in a child (either male or female) who will be mortal and ultimately die. Therefore, we all die through Adam.

- The potential may have existed for a woman's ovum to be fertilized by a sperm that did not carry with it the death nature associated with Adam's seed. The resulting child would be physically immortal if this were to occur. This does not mean the child could not be killed through external causes. However, it does mean that the child would be immortal and could live forever in the absence of such causes.

Jesus came to be our kinsman redeemer who redeems us from sin, the Law and bondage to Satan. He possessed all the human attributes that Adam possessed in his unfallen immortal state to accom plish this within physical and spiritual laws established by God. Jesus had an immortal body, was without sin, and was able to directly interact and fellowship with God, His Father. Jesus came directly from the presence of God and was born into this world with an immortal body to possess these attributes.

The seed in Mary's womb that possessed the potential for immortality had to be fertilized by a male seed that could produce an immortal child for Jesus to be born with an immortal body. We cannot presume the seeds of all women down through the ages have had or have the potential for immortality. However, we can presume Mary's seed did have this potential through natural or divine providence. However, Mary's seed could not be fertilized by a male seed descended from Adam. Therefore, the Holy Spirit came over Mary as Gabriel announced He would, and the immortal female seed in Mary's womb was fertilized by the immortal male seed from God. An immortal child who was to be named Jesus was then conceived in her womb.

Jesus was conceived in Mary with God as His father through the fertilization process of procreation He established when He created Adam and Eve. God then imparted the Spirit of His Son to this child who had been conceived in Mary's womb. God fulfilled His promise in Genesis 3:15 that a savior would be born into this world through the seed of a woman who would crush Satan's head. The creation narrative in Genesis 1-3 describes how God set into motion His process for the redemption of mankind from its fallen sinful state. He first created Adam who in his unfallen sinless state was created to be immortal and initially contained within his body both the immortal male and female *seeds* for procreation. God then formed Eve out of Adam, transferring to her the immortal female seed. He designed and fashioned her body to preserve this immortal seed through each successive generation until Mary, the mother of Jesus. Her seed was then fertilized by the overshadowing of the Most High through the Holy Spirit. We see in the act of the virgin birth the miracle of the supernatural combining with the natural. This produced in the stream of human life a child who was Jesus, the Son of God. Paul referred to Jesus as the last Adam who came to redeem and reconcile back to God the fallen descendants of the first Adam.

A more detailed and scientific discussion of the virgin birth of Jesus can be found in a series of papers written by Dr. Aurther C. Custance that are grouped together in a volume titled, Volume IV, *The Virgin Birth and the Incarnation*, (http://custance.org).

JESUS WAS CRUCIFIED

In Hebrews 9:8-10, the author stated:

> "After saying above, 'Sacrifices and offerings and whole burnt offerings and sacrifices for sin Thou hast not desired, nor hast Thou taken pleasure in them' (which are offered according to the Law), then He said, 'Behold, I have come to do Thy will.' He takes away the first in order to establish the second. By this will we have been sanctified through the offering of the body of Jesus once for all."

Jesus came into this world with an immortal body that contained His immortal Spirit. His body was conceived and formed by the uniting of the supernatural with the natural in the womb of Mary. Jesus could have lived forever had He chosen to do so. However, He came to do the will of His Father. Jesus came to offer Himself as a blood sacrifice to fulfill the requirements of the Law and establish a new covenant sealed with His blood to redeem and reconciled us to God. Our spirit and soul are redeemed through our spiritual rebirth and our body will be redeem through our future resurrection. The covenant relationship God established with Israel provides insight into the redemptive work He was to accomplish through Jesus. The covenant requirements of this relationship are described in Exodus, Leviticus and Deuteronomy in the Old Testament. God specified specific offerings and feasts the Israelites were to observe. They addressed issues related to sin in the lives of the Israelites and God's plan for redemption and pointed to Jesus' coming to redeem us.

The Day of Atonement was one of the feasts the Israelites were instructed to observe. God commanded Aaron, Israel's first high priest, to do the following on the Day of Atonement in Leviticus 16:5-15, 20-22:

> "And he shall take from the congregation of the sons of Israel two goats for a sin offering and one ram for a burnt offering. Then Aaron shall offer the bull for the sin offering which is for himself, that he may make atonement for

himself and for his household. And he shall take the two goats and present them before the LORD at the doorway of the tent of meeting. And Aaron shall cast lots for the two goats, one lot for the LORD and the other lot for the scapegoat. Then Aaron shall offer the goat on which the lot for the LORD fell, and make it a sin offering. But the goat on which the lot for the scapegoat fell, shall be presented alive before the LORD, to make atonement upon it, to send it into the wilderness as the scapegoat. Then Aaron shall offer the bull of the sin offering which is for himself, and make atonement for himself and for his household, and he shall slaughter the bull of the sin offering which is for himself. And he shall take a fire pan of coals of fire from upon the altar before the LORD, and two handfuls of finely ground sweet incense, and bring it inside the veil. And he shall put the incense on the fire before the LORD, that the cloud of incense may cover the mercy seat that is on the ark of the testimony, less he dies. Moreover, he shall take some of the blood of the bull and sprinkle it with his finger on the mercy seat on the east side; also in front of the mercy seat he shall sprinkle some of the blood with his finger seven times. Then he shall slaughter the goat of the sin offering which is for the people, and bring its blood inside the veil, and do with its blood as he did with the blood of the bull, and sprinkle it on the mercy seat and in front of the mercy seat. ... When he finishes atoning for the holy place, and the tent of meeting and the altar, he shall offer the live goat. Then Aaron shall lay both of his hands on the head of the live goat, and confess over it all the iniquities of the sons of Israel, and all their transgressions in regard to all their sins; and he shall lay them on the head of the goat and send it away into the wilderness by the hand of a man who stands in readiness. And the goat shall bear on itself all their iniquities to a solitary land; and he shall release the goat in the wilderness."

What God commanded Aaron to do on the Day of Atonement pointed to what Jesus was to accomplish when He was crucified on a cross. All of the Old Testament offerings and feasts that God commanded the Israelites to observe relating to sin pointed to and found their fulfillment in the suffering, death and resurrection of Jesus. The tabernacle and the Holy of Holies that God commanded Moses to build and where the ark of the covenant was placed was a copy of the perfect tabernacle that exists in heaven (Hebrews 9:1-14).

Manna eaten by the Israelites while they roamed in the wilderness after their exodus from Egypt, Aaron's rod that budded, and the tablets of the covenant (the ten commandments) were placed in the ark of the covenant. 364 days out of the year the seat on the ark was a seat of judgment. The manna represented our rejection of God's provisions for our physical needs. Aaron's rod represented our rejection of God's leadership and lordship over our lives. The tablets of the covenant represented our rejection of God's laws. All of these pointed to our rebellion against God and symbolized our sinful nature. God's response to this was death.

The blood of a slain lamb without blemish was spread over the seat of the ark of the covenant on the Day of Atonement, and it became the mercy seat of God. The three items in the ark of the covenant on this day symbolized the redemptive work God will accomplish through Jesus' blood. The manna represented Jesus coming as the bread of life whose food was to do the will of His Father. Aaron's rod which budded represented Jesus' death and resurrection through which we will be redeemed and reconciled to God. The tablets of the covenant represented Jesus coming to fulfill the requirements of the Law and establish a new covenant through which the power of sin will be destroyed. God saw the items in the ark of the covenant on the day of Atonement through the atoning blood of the slain lamb instead of seeing them as symbols of Israel's rebellion and disobedience. God sees us through the redeeming and atoning blood of Jesus because He carried it into the Holy of Holies in heaven and spread it over the mercy seat there.

The different acts Aaron was instructed to do on the Day of Atonement pointed to how God would deal with sin through Jesus. The crushing of the sweet incense represented the physical beatings Jesus was to receive at the hands of His captors (Isaiah 52:13 - 53:12). These beatings were so severe that His body was marred beyond recognition. Jesus endured the full savagery of sin directed toward Him from fallen humanity during these beatings, and He accepted the stroke of God's wrath directed against sin (Isaiah 53:8). Aaron was instructed to spread sweet incense over the fire to create a cloud that would preserve his life when he entered the Holy of Holies. God was satisfied when He saw Aaron through the cloud of incense that was a sweet smelling savor to Him and that represented the atoning work of Jesus toward us. Aaron was spared the stroke from God against sin. God was also satisfied when Jesus entered the Holy of Holies in heaven and voluntarily received the stroke of God's wrath against our sins (Isaiah 53:11). We no longer need to fear God's wrath against our sins when we approach Him through Jesus

Aaron was instructed to select two male goats that were without blemish. One was to be sacrificed to the LORD, and the other was to be the scapegoat. The goat that was to be sacrificed to the LORD was the sin offering. It was to be slain and its blood taken and spread over the mercy seat. This was the role Jesus took upon Himself as the guilt offering for sin. Isaiah 53:10 indicates:

> "But the LORD was pleased to crush Him, putting Him to grief; if He would render Himself as a guilt offering, He will see His offspring, He will prolong His days, and the good pleasure of the LORD will prosper in His hand."

Just as Aaron slew the lamb and took its blood and spread it upon the mercy seat in the Holy of Holies on earth, Jesus allowed Himself to be slain and then took His blood and spread it on the mercy seat in the Holy of Holies in heaven. He made a perfect atonement for our sins, past, present and future. God not only provided for a means of atoning for sin He provided for a means through which sin would be rooted out of and taken far away from us. David stated in Psalm 103:12:

> "As far as the east is from the west, so far has He removed our transgressions from us."

God accomplished this through the scapegoat. Aaron was instructed to lay his hands on the head of the scapegoat and transfer all the sins of Israel for that year to the scapegoat after the sin offering had been made. He was then instructed to send it into the wilderness. God transferred all the sins and effects of sins ever committed and to be committed by mankind to Jesus and sent Him from His presence after Jesus had taken and presented His blood as the guilt offering for sin into the Holy of Holies in heaven.

Jesus took upon Himself all sin and effects of sin when He underwent His trial and crucifixion on a cross. Paul stated in 2 Corinthians 5:21:

> "He made Him who knew no sin to be sin on our behalf, that we might become the righteousness of God in Him."

God indicated in Leviticus 4:32 the lamb to be slain for the sin offering was to be without blemish. Jesus was without sin when He was crucified. However, He willingly took upon Himself all sins throughout all time and became sin for us to redeem and reconcile us to His Father.

Jesus maintained all of the attributes of being God while being fully human when He took His blood into the Holy of Holies in heaven as a guilt offering for sin. God was satisfied when He received the blood of His Son as a guilt offer for our sins. Jesus became our scapegoat to take sin far away from us when God transferred all our sins to Him. We have been redeemed and reconciled by God and can now come into His presence as our Father as a result of Jesus' sacrificial death on a cross.

JESUS SUFFERED AND DIED

Jesus took upon Himself all rejection, oppression, afflictions, sickness, grief and iniquity for all mankind throughout all time when He became sin for us. He received the full stroke of God's wrath and judgment directed against all of the sins of fallen mankind while on a cross.

Jesus said, "It is finished. (John 19:30)" He released His Spirit to His Father and died when He had taken upon Himself all our sins and consequences of our sins on a cross and had completed everything He had come into this world to do to redeem and reconcile us to God.

Jesus could neither be killed nor die as God in heaven. However, He could offer Himself as the perfect blood sacrifice required by the Law for the redemption of fallen mankind as God become man. We cannot know the indescribable emotional and spiritual pain and suffering Jesus experienced when He who knew no sin was made to be sin on our behalf and His Father sent Him away from His presence for a moment in eternity.

Medical science offers a glimpse of the horrendous physical pain and suffering Jesus experienced when He offered Himself to be crucified. We tend to trivialize and downplay Jesus' pain and suffering in our discussions concerning His crucifixion and death. Information for the following discussion was obtained from Dr. Alexander Metherell's description of the physiological events associated with the death of Jesus in Lee Stroebel's book, *The Case for Christ* (1998).

Jesus stated in John 10:17-18:

> "For this reason the Father loves Me because I lay down my life that I may take it again. No one has taken it away from Me, but I lay it down on My own initiative. I have authority to lay it down, and I have authority to take it up again. This commandment I received from My Father."

He was perfectly obedient to His Father in all things, including His death on a cross. Two factors give eternal significance to Jesus sacrificing Himself for our sins:

- He was born into this world with an immortal body and could have lived forever had He chosen to do so. He did not have to die.

- He voluntarily offered Himself as a blood sacrifice for our redemption in obedience to the promise God made to redeem us. He chose to die even though He did not have to die, so we can be redeemed and reconciled to God.

The physical suffering and passion of Jesus began in the garden of Gethsemane. Jesus proceeded to Gethsemane on the Mount of Olives with Peter, James and John to pray after celebrating the Passover with His disciples. The account in Luke 22:39-46 indicates this was a time of great emotional agony for Jesus. So great was His agony that an angel from heaven was sent to strengthen Him. Jesus fully understood the horror that laid ahead for Him when He was to become our guilt offering for sin. Therefore, He fervently prayed:

"Father, if Thou art willing remove this cup from Me; yet not My will but
Thine be done."

Luke reported "His sweat became like drops of blood, falling down to the ground" while
Jesus prayed.

Bloody sweat is associated with the phenomenon of hematidrosis. This is a rare condition
when the tiny capillaries in the sweat glands rupture under extreme emotional stress,
mixing sweat with blood. This condition left Jesus physically weak and caused His skin to
become fragile and tender. This exacerbated the physical trauma Jesus was to experience
from His beatings and flogging.

Jesus was brought before Annas, Caiphas and the Sanhedrin after He was arrested
in the garden of Gethsemane (Luke 22:54-71, John 18:12-24, 28-40). He received His first
physical beatings from the palace guards who arrested Him when He refused to answer
questions from Caiphas. Jesus was blindfolded, spat upon, and beaten about His face and
head with fists during this encounter, resulting in contusions and lacerations on His head
and in His mouth.

Jesus was then taken before Herod and Pilot (Luke 23:1-25, John 18:28-40). Pilot ordered
Him to be scourged and then delivered Him to be crucified (Mark 15:15, Luke 23:24, John
19:1-16). He was stripped of His clothing, and His hands were tied to a post above His head.
A flagrum that consisted of several heavy leather thongs with embedded lead balls and
bone chips at the end of each thong was used for the scourging. The Roman soldier who
administered the scourging brought the flagrum down with full force again and again across
Jesus' shoulders, back and legs. It was customary for the soldier to administer thirty-nine
lashes. However, often more were administered. cccc The lead balls initially caused bruising
and deep contusions, and the combination of the lead balls and bone chips then cut into
the skin and subcutaneous tissues of the shoulders, back and legs. The heavy leather thongs
cut deeper into the subcutaneous tissues as the blows continued. They initially produce
an oozing of blood from capillaries and veins in the skin and then result in spurting arterial
bleeding from lacerated vessels in the underlying muscles. Jesus' shoulders, back and legs
were an unrecognizable mass of long strips of bleeding flesh when the scourging was finished.

The Roman soldiers removed Jesus from the post and place a crown of thorns on His head
that dug deep into His scalp after He had been scourged. They then proceeded to beat Him
about His face and head causing more contusions and lacerations (Mark 15:16-20, John 19:1-
3). Medical experts speculate the potentially large loss of blood and excruciating pain Jesus
experienced from His beatings and scourging eventually caused Him to go into hypovolemic
shock was caused by the significant loss of blood and resulting low blood pressure.

Jesus was taken to a place outside of Jerusalem called Golgotha to be crucified after
His beatings and scourging (John 19:17-30). His arms were stretched out on the cross beam

of a cross and spikes were driven through His wrists between the radius and carpal bones, crushing and severing the median nerves in both arms. This caused excruciating bursts of pain in both arms. A spike was then driven through Jesus' feet, damaging the peroneal nerve and branches of the medial and lateral plantar nerves, causing excruciating pain in both legs.

The primary cause of death from crucifixion is asphyxiation associated with the inability to properly breathe. The muscles in Jesus' chest and abdomen became fatigued and cramped because He hung from His arms. This allowed Him to draw air into His lungs, but not to exhale air from His lungs. Jesus had to push His body upwards to exhale. This allowed Him to exhale and take in another breath of air. His legs would then give way, and He would again slump back and hang from His arms. This motion resulted in excruciating pain in Jesus' arms and legs. The scraping of the mutilated flesh of His shoulders, back and legs on the rough cross during this motion added to His pain. This process would normally continue until the person being crucified could no longer push His body upwards, after which He would die of asphyxiation.

Medical experts believe Jesus died from a combination of hypovolemic shock and asphyxiation. The hypovolemic shock according to Dr. Metherell caused:

> "a sustained rapid heart rate that would have contributed to heart failure, resulting in the collection of fluid in the membrane around the heart, called pericardial effusion, and around the lungs, called pleural effusion." (*The Case for Christ*, 1998)

These fluids are clear and would appear as water to an untrained observer. The Roman soldier confirmed Jesus had died when he thrust his spear into Jesus' side, passing through His right lung into His heart. The fluids associated with the pericardial and pleural effusions came out first followed by blood when the soldier pulled out his spear. These fluids would appear as the water and blood reported by John in John 19:34.

The pictures we often see that depict Jesus hanging on the cross do not depict the horrendous physical beatings and suffering He experienced as He offered Himself as a sacrifice for our sins. Isaiah stated the physical beatings Jesus was to receive at the hands of His captors were to mar His body beyond recognition. The above discussion indicates this was presumably true. Most of us would not have been able to look at Jesus' body as it hung on the cross.

Jesus knew what He was to experience when He shed His blood as a sacrifice for our sins. However, He allowed Himself to be taken prisoner, beaten and crucified for us anyway. We cannot begin to comprehend the nature and depth of the love Jesus extended to us when He voluntarily died for our sins.

Jesus experienced what the Bible refers to as the second death, which is separation from God, when He died on the cross. God turned His back on Jesus and sent Him out of His presence for a brief moment in eternity when He became sin for us. Isaiah implied this in Isaiah 53:8:

> "By oppression and judgment He was taken away; and as for His generation, who considered that He was cut off out of the land of the living, for the transgressions of My people to whom the stroke was due?"

Jonah, who is an Old Testament type of Jesus, implied this in Jonah 2:2-9:

> "I called out of my distress to the LORD, and He answered me. I cried for help from the depth of Sheol; Thou didst hear my voice. For Thou hadst cast me into the deep, into the heart of the seas, and the current engulfed me. All Thy breakers and billows passed over me. So I said, 'I have been expelled from Thy sight. Nevertheless I will look again toward Thy holy temple.' Water encompassed me to the point of death. The great deep engulfed me. Weeds were wrapped around my head. I descended to the roots of the mountains. The earth with its bars was around me forever, but Thou hast brought up my life from the pit, O LORD My God. While I was fainting away, I remembered the LORD; and my prayer came to Thee, into Thy holy temple. Those who regard vain idols forsake their faithfulness, but I will sacrifice to Thee with the voice of thanksgiving. That which I have vowed I will pay. Salvation is from the LORD."

Jesus affirmed His relationship with Jonah in Matthew 12:39-40 when He responded to a request for a sign from the Scribes and Pharisees:

> "But He answered and said to them, 'An evil and adulterous generation craves for a sign; and yet no sign shall be given to it but the sign of Jonah the prophet; for just as Jonah was three days and three nights in the belly of the sea monster, [Jonah 1:17] so shall the Son of Man be three days and three nights in the heart of the earth.'"

The second death is implied in Isaiah's statement, "He was cut off out of the land of the living," and in Jonah's statement, "I have been expelled from Thy sight." We are spared the second death because Jesus has experienced it. God raised Him from the dead and gave Him dominion over everything on earth and in heaven because of His sacrifice and perfect obedience unto death (Matthew 28:18).

JESUS WENT TO HADES

The Bible teaches Jesus went to Hades after He had died. Luke indicated in Acts 2:30-32 that Peter stated to an assembled crowd at Pentecost:

> "And so, because he [David] was a prophet and knew that God had sworn to him with an oath to seat one of his descendents on His throne, [Psalm 132.11] he looked ahead and spoke of the resurrection of the Christ, that He was neither abandoned to Hades, nor did His flesh suffer decay." [Psalms 16:10]

Paul stated in Ephesians 4:8-10:

> "This is why it says, 'when He also ascended on high, He led captive a host of captives, and he gave gifts to men.' [Psalms 68:18] Now this expression, 'He ascended,' what does it mean except that He also had descended into the lower parts of the earth? He who descended is Himself also He who ascended far above all the heavens, so that He might fill all things."

Jesus' parable of the rich man and Lazarus in Luke 16:16–31 presented a description of Hades. It was a place that was divided into two regions. One region, referred to as Abraham's bosom, was a place of great comfort and rest. The righteous dead occupied this region. The other region, referred to as Hell, was a place of great torment and suffering. The wicked dead occupied this region. A great chasm separated the two regions that prevented occupants of one region from crossing over to the other region.

Peter stated in 1 Peter 3:18-20:

> "For Christ also died for sins once for all, the just for the unjust, so that He might bring us to God, having been put to death in the flesh, but made alive in the spirit; in which also He went and made proclamation to the spirits now in prison, who once were disobedient, when the patiencs of God kept waiting in the days of Noah, during the construction of the ark, in which a few, that is, eight persons, were brought safely through the water."

Peter indicated Jesus went to Hades after He was "made alive in the spirit" after His crucifixion, but before the resurrection of His physical body where He made a "proclamation to the spirits now in prison" there. It is reasonable to presume these imprisoned spirits were in the region of Hades referred to as Hell.

Jesus had dealt with many of the obstacles associated with sin that separate us from God when he went to Hades. He had redeemed us from sin, the Law and bondage to Satan. He had reconciled us to God and established a new covenant between God and us that was sealed with His blood. He had brought healing to us and become our high priest in heaven.

Jesus also decended to Hades to reclaim the authority Satan had usurped from Adam and Eve in the Garden of Eden. John stated in Revelation 1:17-18:

> "When I saw [Jesus] I fell at His feet like a dead man. And He placed His right hand on me, saying, 'Do not be afraid; I am the first and the last, and the living One; and I was dead, and behold, I am alive forevermore, and I have the keys of death and of Hades.'"

Jesus took the keys to death and Hades from Satan that were the symbol of His authority over death.

JESUS WAS RAISED FROM THE DEAD

Jesus was raised from the dead when He had dealt with sin and the consequences of sin and is now seated in heaven at the right hand of God. Paul stated in Ephesians 1:19-23:

> "These are in accordance with the working of the strength of [God's] might which He brought about in Christ, when He raised Him from the dead, and seated Him at His right hand in the heavenly places, far above all rule and authority and power and dominion, and every name that is named, not only in this age, but also in the one to come. And He put all things in subjection under His feet, and gave Him as head over all things to the church, which is His body, the fullness of Him who fills all in all."

Many today deny the reality of Jesus' resurrection. The chief priests and Jewish elders in Jerusalem conspired to spread the lie that His disciples came in the night and stole His body after His resurrection (Matthew 28:11-15). The Bible teaches after Jesus had been crucified, dead, buried and raised from the dead He appeared to:

- Mary Magdalene (Mark 16:9-11),
- Mary Magdalene and the other Mary (Matthew 28:1-10),
- Two disciples on the road to Emmaus (Mark 16:12, Luke 24:13-31),
- The apostles minus Thomas (Mark 16:14-18, Luke 24:36-48, John 20:19-23),

- The apostles including Thomas (John 20:24-30),

- Seven apostles at the Sea of Galilee (John 21:1-22),

- Peter, James and more than 500 brethren (1 Corinthians 15:5-7),

- The apostles (Acts 1:1-18), and

- Paul on the road to Damascus (Acts 9:3-8).

Zechariah in Zechariah 3:1-10 painted a very beautiful picture of the coronation that took place in heaven when Jesus returned to be seated at the right hand of God and assume dominion over His kingdom:

> "Then He showed me Joshua the high priest standing before the angel of the LORD, and Satan standing at His right hand to accuse him. And the LORD said to Satan, 'The LORD rebuke you, Satan! Indeed, the LORD who has chosen Jerusalem rebuke you! Is this not a brand plucked from the fire?' Now Joshua was clothed with filthy garments and standing before the angel. And He spoke and said to those who were standing before Him, saying, 'Remove the filthy garments from him.' Again He said to him, 'See, I have taken your children away from you and will clothe you with festal robes.' So they put a clean turban on his head and clothed him with garments, while the angel of the LORD was standing by. And the angel of the LORD admonished Joshua saying, 'Thus says the LORD of hosts, 'If you will walk in My ways, and if you will perform My service, then you will also govern My house and also have charge of My courts, and I will grant you free access among these who are standing here. Now listen, Joshua the high priest, you and your friends who are sitting in front of you - indeed they are men who are a symbol, for behold, I am going to bring in My servant the Branch. For behold, the stone that I have set before Joshua; on one stone are seven eyes. Behold, I will engrave an inscription on it,'' declares the LORD of Hosts, 'and I will remove the iniquity of the land in one day. In that day ' declares the LORD of Host, 'everyone of you will invite his neighbor to sit under his vine and under his fig tree.'"

Joshua is an Old Testament type of Jesus. Satan was finally and irrevocably judged and rebuked because of Jesus' suffering, death and resurrection. The filthy garments Joshua was wearing symbolized the filth and wretchedness of the sins Jesus had dealt with. The iniquity was taken from Joshua, and he was clothed with festal robes that were the symbol of Jesus' kingship. God has given all things into Jesus' hands because of His perfect obedience to Him. Peter stated in Acts 4:12:

"And there is salvation in no one else; for there is no other name under heaven that has been given among men, by which we must be saved."

Jesus was God incarnate in man in this world. He is now a man seated at the right hand of God and is the firstborn of a new creation who is in heaven to act as our mediator and high priest.

JESUS IS OUR HEALER AND REDEEMER

God will heal the hurting and broken areas in our spirit and soul and deliver us from the eternal consequences of sin through Jesus. Isaiah implied in Isaiah 53:5:

"But He was pierced through for our transgressions, He was crushed for our inequities; the chastening for our well-being fell upon Him, and by His scourging we are healed."

Peter affirmed in 1 Peter 2:21-24:

"For you have been called for this purpose, since Christ also suffered for you, leaving you an example for you to follow in His steps, who committed no sin, nor was any deceit found in His mouth; and while being reviled, He did not revile in return; while suffering, He uttered no threats, but kept entrusting Himself to Him who judges righteously; and He Himself bore our sins in His body on the cross, that we might die to sin and live to righteousness, for by His wounds you were healed."

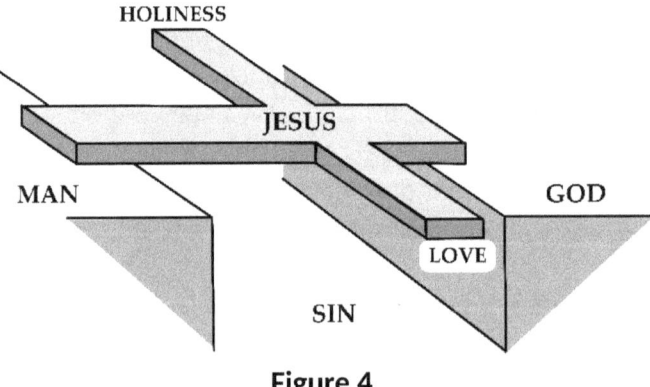

Figure 4

Only Jesus' cross can bridge the chasm of sin that separates us from God (Figure 4). God's justice and righteousness manifested through His holiness required the death penalty for our sins. His mercy and grace manifested through His love led Him to redeem and reconcile us to Himself through our faith in Jesus. The requirements of God's holiness and love are satisfied through Jesus' death and resurrection.

God established a new covenant with us through Jesus since He could not redeem us through the covenant of the Law He established with Israel through Moses. The Law can only convict us of sin and condemn us to death. The Law cannot:

- Free us from our bondage to sin and Satan;
- Justify us before God;
- Make us righteous and acceptable to God;
- Make us holy and enable us to come into God's presence;
- Sanctify us and set us apart for service to God; and
- Empowerus to live a life that is transformed by the Holy Spirit.

Only Jesus and the Holy Spirit living in and through us can accomplish these for us.

Jesus accomplished what the Law could not and cannot do. The tearing of the curtain to the Holy of Holies in the temple in Jerusalem after Jesus had been crucified (Matthew 27:50-53) symbolized it is no longer necessary for us to approach God through an earthly tabernacle. We have a new covenant with Him that enables us to directly approach Him. Jesus is the mediator of this covenant because He established and sealed it with His blood.

Paul stated in Romans 8:14-17:

> "For all who are being led by the Spirit of God, these are sons of God. For you have not received a spirit of slavery leading to fear again, but you have received a spirit of adoption as sons by which we cry out 'Abba Father!' The Spirit Himself testifies with our spirit that we are children of God, and if children, heirs also, heirs of God and fellow heirs with Christ, if indeed we suffer with Him so that we may also be glorified with Him."

He also stated in Colossians 1:19-22:

> "For it was the Father's good pleasure for all the fullness to dwell in Him, and through Him to reconcile all things to Himself, having made peace through the blood of His cross; through Him, I say, whether things on earth or things in heaven. And although you were formerly alienated and hostile in mind, engaged in evil deeds, yet He has now reconciled you in His fleshly body through death, in order to present you before Him holy and blameless and beyond reproach."

We become adopted children of God through Jesus and joint heirs of God with Him. God has redeemed and reconciled us to Himself through Jesus and sees us as blameless and beyond reproach through Him.

JESUS IS OUR ONLY WAY TO GOD

Many today believe Jesus was only a prophet and the most moral person and best moral teacher who ever lived. Jesus claimed to be more than these; He claimed to be the Son of God and to be God. Jesus stated to the Jews in John 8:58, "Before Abraham was born, I am." They picked up stones to stone Jesus for blasphemy because they understood the significance of His statement – He claimed to be God. Jesus stated in John 10:30, "I and the Father are One." He stated in John 10:38 "that you may know and understand that the Father is in Me, and I in the Father." Jesus left little doubt in the Gospels with respect to His understanding of who He is. He is the Son of God. He is God. He is our Lord and Savior.

Jesus stated we can only approach God through Him. He stated in John 14:6:

> "I am the way and the truth and the life. No one comes to the Father but through Me."

We must accept the truth of Jesus' statement because He is the Son of God. Many today inside and outside of Christianity believe there are many ways to approach and fellowship with God, and they believe Jesus is just one of them. Jesus was clear in His statement that He is the only way to God. He is the one through whom we all must come to fellowship with God our Father. Jesus stated in John 15:1-6:

> "I am the true vine, and My Father is the vine dresser. Every branch in Me that does not bear fruit, He takes away; and every branch that bears fruit, He prunes it so that it may bear more fruit. You are already clean because of the word which I have spoken to you. Abide in Me, and I in you. As the branch cannot bear fruit of itself unless it abides in the vine, so neither can you unless you abide in Me. I am the vine, you are the branches; he who abides in Me and I in him, he bears much fruit, for apart from Me you can do nothing. If anyone does not abide in Me, he is thrown away as a branch and dries up; and they gather them, and cast them into the fire and they are burned."

Jesus indicated:

- We are to grow, mature and bear fruit in our relationship with Him;
- We will not be able to do these independent of Him; and
- God will remove us from our relationship with Him when we fail to grow, mature and bear fruit in this relationship.

We bear fruit by:

- Reading, studying and internalizing God's word in the Bible;
- Ministering to and serving the needs of others in Jesus name; and
- Sharing the Gosple of Jesus with those to whom we minister and searve.

Jesus stated in Matthew 28:18-20:

> "All authority has been given to Me in heaven and on earth. Go therefore and make disciples of all the nations, baptizing them in the name of the Father and the Son and the Holy Spirit, teaching them to observe all that I commanded you, and lo, I am with you always, even to the end of the age."

God commissioned Adam and Eve to be fruitful by multiplying and subduing the earth after He created them. They failed when sin interred the world aftern they were decieved by Satan into disobeying God. Jesus commishenes us to go into the world to spread His gospel as His servants. We will succeed. The Holy Spirit enables and equips us to bear fruit as Jesus's servants when we perform this commission by baptising and teaching others to obscrve all He commanded us in the four Gospels.

CHAPTER 7
NATURE AND CHARACTER OF GOD
THE HOLY SPIRIT - GOD WITH US

"And I will ask the Father, and He will give you another Helper, that He may be with you forever; that is the Spirit of truth, whom the world cannot receive, because it does not behold Him or know Him, but you know Him because He abides with you and will be in you. ... But the Helper, the Holy Spirit, whom the Father will send in My name, He will teach you all things, and bring to your remembrance all that I have said to you. ... When the Helper comes, whom I will send to you from the Father, that is the Spirit of truth, who proceeds from the Father, He will testify about Me. ... But I tell you the truth, it is to your advantage that I go away; for if I do not go away, the Helper shall not come to you; but if I go, I will send Him to you. ... And He, when He comes, will convict the world concerning sin, and righteousness, and judgment; concerning sin, because I go to the Father, and you no longer behold Me; and concerning judgment, because the ruler of this world has been judged. I have many more things to say to you, but you cannot bear them now. But when He, the Spirit of truth, comes, He will guide you into all truth; for He will not speak on His own initiative, but whatever He hears He will speak; and He will disclose to you what is to come. He shall glorify Me; for He shall take of Mine, and shall disclose it to you. All things that the Father has are Mine; therefore I said that He takes of Mine, and will disclose it to you." (John 14:16-17, 26;15:26; 16:8-15)

"For to us God revealed them through the Spirit; for the Spirit searches all things, even the depths of God. For who among men knows the thoughts of a man except the spirit of the man, which is in him? Even so the thoughts of God no one knows except the Spirit of God. Now we have received, not the spirit of the world, but the Spirit who is from God, that we might know the things freely given to us by God, which things we also speak, not in words taught by human wisdom, but in those taught by the Spirit, combining spiritual thoughts with spiritual words." (1 Corinthians 2:10-13)

THE HOLY SPIRIT - GOD IN THE WORLD WITH US

Table 6

THE HOLY SPIRIT

In the Beginning:
Was active in creation

Relative to the Bible:
Inspired and spoke through the Scriptures

During Old Testament Times:
Enabled supernatural abilities
Enabled artistic skills
Gave strength and power Inspired prophecy
Mediated God's message

In the New Testament:
Glorifies Christ Searches all things
Empowers for spreading the gospel of Jesus
Calls ministers
Sends out workers
Forbids actions which are against the will of God
Administers His spiritual gifts

Relative to Salvation:
Convicts us of sin
Gives us the ability to call Jesus Lord
Makes us sons and daughters of God
Gives us life
Washes, sanctifies, and justifies us
Baptizes us into the Body of Christ
Regenerates us
Indwells us

In the Life of Christians:
Fills us with His presence

Helps us in our infirmities
Teaches us about all things
Intercedes to the Father for us
Strengthens our inner being
Enables us to walk in holiness

Jesus told His disciples it was to their advantage for Him to return to the Father when He knew it was time for Him to be crucified, so He could send the Holy Spirit. The Holy Spirit is the third person of the Trinity. Jesus said the Holy Spirit would proceed from the Father, and the Father and He would send the Holy Spirit. The Bible teaches Jesus is in heaven, seated at the right hand of God (Romans 8:34, Hebrews 8:1-2, 12:1-2), and the Holy Spirit is God in the world with us today. Table 6 shows activities and actions of the Holy Spirit during Old and New Testaments times and in our life today. Names given to the Holy Spirit that attest to His deity include:

- Spirit (Roman 8:9)
- Spirit of God (Romans 8:9)
- Spirit of our God (1 Corinthians 6:11)
- Spirit of the living God (2 Corinthians 3:3)
- Holy Spirit of God (Ephesians 4:30)
- Spirit of the Lord (Isaiah 61:1)
- Spirit of Jesus Christ (Philippians 1:19)
- Spirit of Christ (Romans 8:9)
- Spirit of His Son (Galatians 4:6)
- Spirit of grace (Hebrews 10:29)
- Helper, Comforter (John 16:7)

Names given to the Holy Spirit that identify His actions in our life include:

- Holy Spirit of promise (Ephesians 1:13-14)
- Spirit of life (Romans 8:2)
- Spirit of truth (John 14:16-17)

The Holy Spirit possesses all the infinite attributes of God and searches the depths and knows the mind and thoughts of God (1 Corinthians 2:10-13). The Holy Spirit:

- Has a will (1 Corinthians 12:11),
- Has a mind (Romans 8:27),
- Possesses knowledge (1 Corinthians 2:11, Romans 8:27), and
- Shows emotion, such as love (Romans 15:30), grief (Ephesians 4:30), and anger Hebrews 10:29-30).

The Holy Spirit can be:

- Lied to (Acts 5:3),
- Tested (Acts 5:9),
- Insulted (Hebrews 10:29),
- Resisted (Acts 7:51),
- Grieved (Ephesians 4:30), and
- Blasphemed against (Matthew 12:31-32).

The above point to the facts that the Holy Spirit possesses personality and is a spiritual being like God the Father and Jesus.

The Bible contains several symbols that are associated with the Holy Spirit. They include:

- Breath, Wind (John 3:8, 20:22, Acts 2:1-4) - symbolize life, power and mystery
- Dove (Matthew 3:16) - symbolizes peace, faithfulness and compassion
- Fire (Matthew 3:11) - symbolizes purification
- Oil (Luke 4:18, 2 Corinthians 1:21-22, 1 John 2:20) - symbolizes sanctification, anointing, setting apart, light and illumination
- Water (John 7:38-39) - symbolizes cleansing, washing and regeneration
- Seal, Pledge (2 Corinthians 1:21-22, Ephesians 1:13-14, 4:30) - Symbolize our guarantee as members of God's elect and heirs of His kingdom.

These point to actions of the Holy Spirit that bring us into a closer relationship with God as our Father.

Jesus told His disciples the Holy Spirit would dwell in them as their Helper and Comforter (John 14:16-17, 16:7). He told them the Holy Spirit would:

- Teach them all things and bring to their remembrance all He had said to them (John 14:26);
- Testify to and glorify Him (John 16:14);
- Convict the world concerning sin, righteousness and judgment (John 16:8-11);
- Lead them in all truth (John 16:13); and
- Take of what is His and disclose and give it to them (John 16:14-15).

The Holy Spirit performs these same actions with us when we become disciples of Jesus.

The Holy Spirit was present with God and Jesus in the beginning and was active with Them in the creation of the earth and man (Genesis 1:2). The Holy Spirit inspired and spoke through the Scriptures. Peter stated in 2 Peter 1:20-21:

> "But know this first of all, that no prophecy of Scripture is a matter of one's own interpretation, for no prophecy was ever made by an act of human will, but men moved by the Holy Spirit spoke from God."

The Holy Spirit was active during Old Testament times in restricted ways. He acted through prophets, ministers and selected leaders of Israel. The Holy Spirit during Old Testament times:

- Enabled supernatural abilities (Genesis 41:38-41),
- Enabled artistic skills (Exodus 31:2-5),
- Gave strength and power (Judges 3:9-11),
- Inspired prophecy (1 Samuel 19:20-24), and
- Mediated God's message (Micah 3:8-12).

The Holy Spirit became available to all of us when God and Jesus sent Him after Jesus had ascended into heaven to be with His Father. The Holy Spirit in the New Testament:

- Glorifies Jesus (John 16:13-14),
- Interceded for God's people (Romans 8:26-27),
- Empowers us for witnessing the Gospel of Jesus (Acts 1:7-8),

- Calls ministers (Acts 13:2-3),

- Sends out workers (Acts 13:2-3),

- Warns us of actions that are against the will of God (Acts 16:6-8), and

- Administers His spiritual gifts (Romans 12:4-8, 1 Corinthians 12:3-11, 28, Ephesians 4:11-13).

The Holy Spirit convicts us of sin (John 16:8-11), gives us the ability to call Jesus Lord (1 Corinthians 12:3), and helps us become children of God. Paul stated in Romans 8:14-17:

> "For all who are being led by the Spirit of God, these are sons of God. For you have not received a spirit of slavery leading to fear again, but you have received a spirit of adoption as sons by which we cry out, 'Abba! Father!' The Spirit Himself bears witness with our spirit that we are children of God, and if children, heirs also, heirs of God and fellow heirs with Christ, if indeed we suffer with Him in order that we may also be glorified with Him."

The Holy Spirit breathes spiritual life into our spirit and soul and baptizes us into the body of Christ. Jesus indicated in John 6:63:

> "It is the Spirit who gives life; the flesh profits nothing; the words that I have spoken are spirit and life."

Paul stated:

> "For by one Spirit we were all baptized into one body, whether Jews or Greeks, whether slaves or free, and we were all made to drink of one Spirit." (1 Corinthians 12:13)

> "Not that we are adequate in ourselves to consider anything as coming from ourselves, but our adequacy is from God, who also made us adequate as servants of a new covenant, not of the letter, but of the Spirit; for the letter kills, but the Spirit gives life." (2 Corinthians 3:5-6)

The Holy Spirit washes, sanctifies, justifies and regenerates us. Paul stated:

"And such were some of you; but you were washed, but you were sanctified, but you were justified in the name of the Lord Jesus Christ, and in the Spirit of our God." (1 Corinthians 6:11)

"But when the kindness of God our Savior and His love for mankind appeared, He saved us, not on the basis of deeds which we have done in righteousness, but according to His mercy, by the washing of regeneration and renewing by the Holy Spirit, whom He poured out upon us richly through Jesus Christ our Savior, that being justified by His grace we might be made heirs according to the hope of eternal life." (Titus 3:4-7)

The Holy Spirit dwells in us when we call Jesus Lord and are born into His kingdom. Paul stated in 1 Corinthians 3:16-17:

"Do you not know that you are a temple of God, and that the Spirit of God dwells in you? If any man destroys the temple of God, God will destroy him, for the temple of God is holy, and that is what you are."The Holy Spirit takes up residence in and works through us when we become a disciple of Jesus. Luke reported at Pentecost in Acts 2:4:

"And they [the apostles] were filled with the Holy Spirit and began to speak with other tongues, as the Spirit was giving them utterance."

The Holy Spirit gives us an understanding of the teachings of Jesus. Jesus stated in John 14:26:

"But the Helper, the Holy Spirit, whom the Father will send in My name, He will teach you all things, and bring to your remembrance all that I said to you."

John stated in 1 John 2:27:

"And as for you, the anointing which you receive from Him abides in you, and you have no need for anyone to teach you; but as His anointing teaches you about all things, and is true and is not a lie, and just as it has taught you, you abide in Him."

Paul stated in Romans 8:26-27 the Holy Spirit helps us in our infirmities and intercedes to God for us when we are unable to intercede for ourself. The Holy Spirit strengthens our inner being and enables us to walk in holiness. Paul stated in Ephesians 3:14-19:

"For this reason, I bow my knees before the Father, from whom every family in heaven and on earth derives its name, that He would grant you, according to the riches of His glory, to be strengthened with power through His Spirit in the inner man; so that Christ may dwell in your hearts through faith; and that you, being rooted and grounded in love, may be able to comprehend with all the saints what is the breadth and length and height and depth, and to know that love of Christ which surpasses knowledge, that you may be filled up to all the fullness of God."

The Holy Spirit perfects in us His fruits of love, joy, peace, patience, kindness, goodness, faithfulness, gentleness and self-control (Galatians 5:22-23). These are the good fruit Jesus referred to in Luke 6:43-45:

"For there is no good tree which produces bad fruit; nor, on the other hand, a bad tree which produces good fruit. For each tree is known by its own fruit. For men do not gather figs from thorns, nor do they pick grapes from a briar bush. The good man out of the good treasure of his heart brings forth what is good; and the evil man out of the evil treasure brings forth what is evil; for his mouth speaks from that which fills his heart."

The Bible teaches we should neither grieve the Holy Spirit nor quench His activities in our life (Ephesians 4:30, 1 Thessalonians 5:19). We should not ignore His indwelling, infringe upon His commands, and fail to follow His leading. We are further instructed to continually pray in the Spirit for all things and for the needs of all the saints (Ephesians 6:18, Jude 20-21). We are promised the Holy Spirit will intercede to the Father for us when we do these (Romans 8:26-27).

Jesus taught blaspheming against the Holy Spirit is the only unforgivable sin. He stated in Matthew 12:31-32:

"Therefore I say to you, any sin and blasphemy shall be forgiven men, but blasphemy against the Spirit shall not be forgiven. And whoever shall speak a word against the Son of Man, it shall be forgiven him; but whoever shall speak against the Holy Spirit, it shall not be forgiven him, either in this age, or in the age to come."

The Holy Spirit was sent into the world to testify to and glorify Jesus. He places the God-consciousness into our hearts and creates within us the desire and gives us the ability to call Jesus Lord. Sending the Holy Spirit into the world was God's final step in our redemption. The

Holy Spirit was sent to give us the power and ability to do what we cannot do for ourself. We stand in opposition to God's influence in our life when we reject the gentle wooing of the Holy Spirit to accept His grace and redemption through our faith in Jesus because we prefer darkness instead of light. Therefore, sin against the Holy Spirit is not a sin of ignorance; it is a sin of presumption against spiritual knowledge and light. It is not an isolated act; it is a habitual action and sin of character that is crystallized into action opposed to God. It is a sin of the heart. God says He has done all He can and will do to redeem and reconcile us to Himself when we reject the leading of the Holy Spirit to accept the salvation He extends to us through Jesus. He will not force us to do or accept anything against our will. We indicate we prefer darkness to light and death to life when we blaspheme against the Holy Spirit. There is no mercy, grace, and forgiveness for this; there is only judgment.

CHAPTER 8
NATURE AND CHARACTER OF MAN
SPIRITUAL DEATH, REBIRTH AND LIFE

"Unless one is born again, he cannot see the kingdom of God. ... Unless one is born of the water and the Spirit, he cannot enter into the kingdom of God. ... God is spirit and those who worship Him must worship in spirit and truth." (John 3:3, 5, 4:24)

"Unless you are converted and become like children, you shall not enter the kingdom of God." (Matthew 18:3)

"For the mind set on the flesh is death, but the mind set on the Spirit is life and peace, because the mind set on the flesh is hostile toward God; for it does not subject itself to the law of God, for it is not even able to do so." (Romans 8:6-7)

NATURE AND CHARACTER OF MAN (Chapters 8 - 9)

This section presents information regarding:

- The nature of our creation as spirit, soul and body; our being born into this world spiritual dead and its potential eternal consequences; and the importance of our spiritual rebirth in our relationship with God.
- Functions of our soul and spirit, the yearnings of our soul, and struggles within our soul.

UNDERSTANDING OUR CONDITION

Genesis 1 - 3 provides insight into our original relationship with God. Moses indicated God first created the heavens and earth. He then created a man and woman in His own image and likeness and placed them in the Garden of Eden. God breathed life into them, and they became living beings. The man's name was Adam, and the woman's name was Eve. Adam and Eve were the crown of God's creation. Everything in God's creation was in perfect harmony. Adam and Eve lived in harmony with God, each other and the environment around them. This harmony was contingent on their obedience to God and living within behavioral boundaries He established. There were no death, disease, discord and disasters in God's original creation, and there were no guilt, shame, pain and suffering. God commanded Adam and Eve to:

- Exercise dominion over the earth (Genesis 1:26);
- Be fruitful and multiply by bearing children, fill and subdue the earth, and rule over every living creature (Genesis 1:28);
- Dress, till and take care of the garden of Eden (Genesis 2:15); and
- Not eat the fruit from the tree of knowledge of good and evil in the garden of Eden (Genesis 2:17).

God placed His Spirit in Adam and Eve when He created them. They were spiritually alive because God's Spirit was present in them. God walked and communed with them daily in the garden of Eden (Genesis 3:8). He gave them freedom to choose how they would interact with Him, each other and the environment where He placed them (Genesis 2:16). However, He commanded them to live within the behavioral boundaries He established (Genesis 2:18).

Satan deceived Adam and Eve into believing they would become like God, knowing good and evil, when they ate the fruit from the tree of knowledge of good and evil (Genesis 3:1-7). Sin entered God's creation with their disobedience, and the harmony He established in His creation was destroyed. God withdrew His Spirit from Adam and Eve, and they spiritually died. Everyone since them has been and is born into this world spiritually dead because God's Spirit is not present in them. As a result, the minds and hearts of men and women have become hostile toward God without the intervention of Jesus. God placed a curse on Adam and Eve, the serpent and the earth because of their disobedience (Genesis 3:14-19). Sin caused spiritual and physical death, disease, discord and disasters to enter the world, and guilt, shame, pain and suffering entered the world with sin.

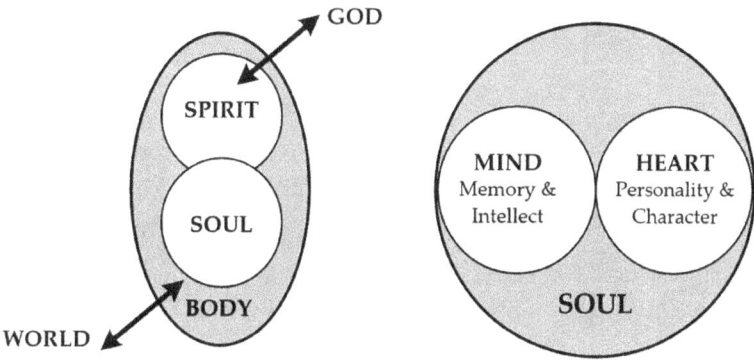

Figure 5

The consequences of Adam's and Eve's disobedience can be understood in terms of the nature of their and our creation. God created them with a spirit, soul and body (Figure 5). Moses stated in Genesis 2:7:

> "Then the LORD God formed man of dust from the ground, and breathed into his nostrils the breath of life; and man became a living being."

God formed Adam's body from the dust of the ground and breathed the breath of life into him. Adam was spiritually alive because God's Spirit was placed in him. Paul stated in 1 Thessalonians 5:23:

> "Now may the God of peace Himself sanctify you entirely; and may your spirit and soul and body be preserved complete, without blame at the coming of our Lord Jesus Christ."

He affirmed we are born with a spirit, soul and body. Adam and Eve interacted with their environment through their physical senses of sight, hearing, touch, smell and taste, and they interacted and communed with God in the spiritual realm through their spirit (Figure 5).

James stated in James 2:26 "the body without the spirit is dead." Our spirit resides in and functions through our body. It gives life to our body. Our spirit and soul function in and through our body while we are alive. They leave our body when it can no longer support physical life, and we die. Our body decays and returns to dust. Our spirit and soul continue in an eternal existence beyond death. They continue in the presence of God, Jesus and the Holy Spirit in the kingdom of heaven when we have been redeemed by and reconciled to God through Jesus. Our spirit and soul are separated from Them in Hades and eventually in the lake of fire when we have not sought and received the redemption and salvation God extends to us through Jesus.

Our soul and spirit have distinct functions. However, they are integrally linked. Jesus stated in Matthew 22:37-40:

> "'You shall love the Lord your God with all your heart, and with all your soul, and with all your mind.' (Deuteronomy 6:5) This is the great and foremost commandment. The second is like it, 'You shall love your neighbor as yourself.' (Leviticus 19:18) On these two commandments depend the whole Law and the Prophets."

His statement implied our soul is comprised of our mind and heart (Figure 5). Paul stated in 1 Corinthians 14:15:

> "What is the outcome then? I will pray with the spirit and I will pray with the mind also; I will sing with the spirit and I will sing with the mind also."

His statement implied our soul and spirit have distinct functions. God has created us with a body, spirit and soul. Our spirit resides in and functions through our body and gives it life. Our soul is linked with our spirit, and it controls the functions and actions of our body and spirit. **Our spirit is a body that resides in and gives life to our physical body. Our soul functions through our physical and spiritual bodies to enable us to interact with the physical world and the spiritual realm**.

Our soul is comprised of our mind and heart. Our mind is the seat of memory and intellect. Our memory is the repository of information and experiences we have processed and assimilated throughout our life. Our intellect is the knowledge and wisdom we have obtained from this information and these experiences. Our heart is the seat of our personality and character. Our personality is the organized pattern of behavioral characteristics that identify and define who we are. Our character defines the moral and ethical qualities of our personality.

Our soul controls the actions of our spirit and body. It is formed as we experience spiritual and physical life. It develops as it receives, processes and assimilates information from our spirit as we interact with God in the spiritual realm and from our five physical senses as we interact with the physical world. **Our soul develops and grows as our mind and heart process and assimilate information they receive from our life experiences. It controls how we encounter, interpret and respond to new life experiences based on how it has processed and assimilated information it has received from prior life experiences**.

Our spirit, soul and body develop as we encounter life. Our body develops and matures as we physically grow. It is the vessel through which our spirit interacts with God, others and the physical world. Our spirit and soul become the source and center of our conscience, insight and sensitivity and our creativity, inspiration and motivation as we spiritually and emotionally grow and mature.

Adam and Eve were spiritually alive before they disobeyed God and sinned. God's Spirit dwelt in them, and they fellowshipped with and were nurtured by His Spirit. Jesus stated in John 6:63:

> "It is the Spirit who gives life; the flesh profits nothing; the words that I have spoken to you are spirit and are life."

He affirmed God gave Adam and Eve spiritual life. God gives us spiritual life through Jesus and the Holy Spirit. We are spiritually alive when God's Spirit through the Holy Spirit dwells in us. Our soul is provided with the knowledge, wisdom and ability to bring our spirit and body into submission to the sovereign will and laws of God through the presence of the Holy Spirit. Our personality and character then develop in a manner pleasing to God, and they create within us the desire to live within the behavioral boundaries He has established.

SPIRITUAL DEATH

Adam and Eve were separated from and no longer able to commune with God when they disobeyed Him and sinned. God withdrew His Spirit from them, and they spiritually died (Figure 6). Spiritual death, which is associated with the absence of God's Spirit in our life, entered the world with sin.

Everyone who has been born since Adam and Eve has been born without God's Spirit. We have been born into this world spiritually dead. We have rejected God even though He reveals Himself to us in His creation. Our minds and hearts have become blighted and darkened as a result. Paul stated in Romans 1:20-23:

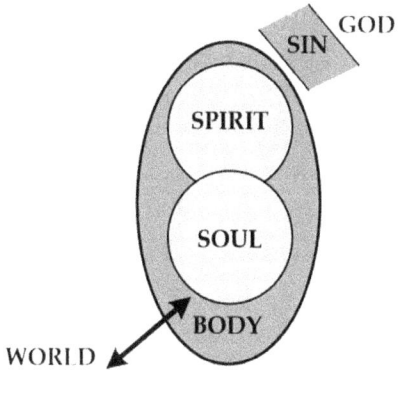

Figure 6

> "For since the creation of the world [God's] invisible attributes, His eternal power and divine nature, have been clearly seen, being understood through what has been made, so that they are without excuse. For even though they knew God, they did not honor Him as God, or give thanks; but they became futile in their speculations, and their foolish heart was darkened. Professing to be wise, they became fools, and exchanged the glory of the incorruptible God for an image in the form of corruptible man and of birds and four-footed animals and crawling creatures."

Our spirit and soul are not nurtured by God's Spirit through the Holy Spirit when we are spiritually dead. our soul does not receive the spiritual knowledge, wisdom and strength from the Holy Spirit necessary to equip us to live according to God's spiritual life principles and laws. We receive information only from the environment where we live and the world. Our mind and heart become controlled by the desires of our flesh and what the worlds teaches us is truth. Paul stated in Romans 8:5-8:

> "For those who are according to the flesh set their minds on the things of the flesh, but those who are according to the Spirit, the things of the Spirit. For the mind set on the flesh is death, but the mind set on the Spirit is life and peace, because the mind set on the flesh is hostile toward God; for it does not subject itself to the law of God, for it is not even able to do so; and those who are in the flesh cannot please God."

John stated in 1 John 2:15-16:

> "Do not love the world, nor the things in the world. If anyone loves the world, the love of the Father is not in him. For all that is in the world, the lust of the flesh and the lust of the eyes and the boastful pride of life, is not from the Father, but is from the world."

He indicated the thoughts and desires of our mind and heart when God's Spirit through the Holy Spirit does not live within us are controlled by:

- What we see and perceive with our eyes;
- What we perceive is necessary to satisfy the cravings of our body; and
- Our pride and desire to control our life.

These cause us to transgress God's behavioral boundaries and laws and make us hostile toward Him. This is our condition without Jesus.

Spiritual death has current and eternal consequences. We are separated from God when we are spiritually dead. This separation becomes an eternal separation when we physically die before we can be redeemed by and reconciled to God through our faith in Jesus. In Hebrews 9:27, the author stated, "And inasmuch as it is appointed for men to die once, and after this comes judgment."

SPIRITUAL REBIRTH AND LIFE

The Bible teaches God loves and desires to fellowship and commune with us. However, His Spirit must dwell in us through the Holy Spirit for us to fellowship and commune with Him. He has established the process through which He redeems and reconciles us to Himself. He extends His grace to and redeems us through our faith in Jesus.

Jesus indicated three actions must occur before God will redeem and reconcile us to Himself. He stated:

> "I tell you, no one can enter the kingdom of God without being born of water and spirit. What is born of the flesh is flesh and what is born of the Spirit is spirit." (John 3:5-6)

> Unless you are converted and become like children, you shall not enter the kingdom of God." (Matthew 18:3)

> "It is not those who are well who need a physician, but those who are sick. I have not come to call the righteous but sinners to repent." (Luke 5:31-32)

God is Spirit, and we must be spiritually reborn and made spiritually alive to fellowship and commune with Him. God's Spirit must dwell in us through the Holy Spirit for Him to redeem us. We must be converted - turn away from sine - and approach God with a childlike faith for Him to reconcile us to Himself. Finally, we must repent of our sins and seek God's forgiveness through Jesus before He will allow us to come into His presence. The first action represents what God has made possible through the blood Jesus shed on a cross and the Holy Spirit. The second and third actions represents responses we must make to receive God's forgiveness and His gift of salvation through Jesus.

God's Action toward Us

Jesus is our only way to God. He stated in John 14:6:

> "I am the way, and the truth, and the life; no one comes to the Father, but through Me."

Paul stated in Romans 3:23-24, 5:8-9:

> "For all have sinned and fall short of the glory of God, being justified as a gift by His grace through the redemption which is in Christ Jesus; whom God displayed publicly as a propitiation in His blood through faith. But God demonstrated His own love toward us, in that while we were yet sinners, Christ died for us. Much more then, having now been justified by His blood, we shall be saved from the wrath of God through Him."

We have all sinned and fall short of God's glory. Jesus stood in our place "as a propitiation in His blood" for our sins whose death God publicly displayed on a cross. We are justified by Jesus' blood because His death satisfied God's death penalty for our sins. Therefore, we no longer need to fear God's wrath directed toward us because of our sins. We must approach God through the cross of Jesus (Figure 7). Peter affirmed this in 1 Peter 1:3-5:

> "Blessed be the God and Father of our Lord Jesus Christ, who according to His great mercy has caused us to be born again to a living hope through the resurrection of Jesus Christ from the dead, to obtain an inheritance which is imperishable and undefiled and will not fade away, reserved in heaven for you, who are protected by the power of God through faith for a salvation ready to be revealed in the last time."

We are spiritually reborn through our faith in "the resurrection of Jesus Christ from the dead" and "protected by the power of God through faith."

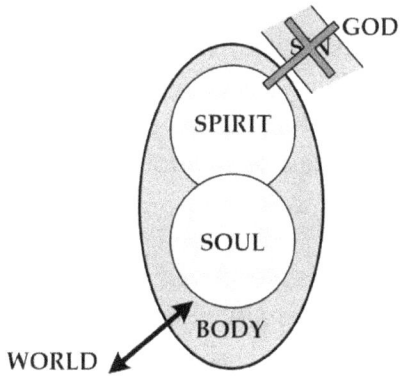

Figure 7

The Holy Spirit imparts spiritual life to us, and the blood of Jesus cleansed us of sin when we enter a reconciled relationship with God through faith in Jesus. Jesus stated in John 6:63, "It is the Spirit who gives life." John stated in 1 John 1:7:

> "But if we walk in the Light as [God] Himself is in the Light, we have fellowship with one another, and the blood of Jesus His Son cleanses us from all sin."

God's salvation is a gift extended to us through our faith in Jesus. Paul stated in Titus 3:47:

> "But when the kindness of God our Savior and His love for mankind appeared, He saved us, not on the basis of deeds which we have done in righteousness, but according to His mercy, by the washing of regeneration and renewing by the Holy Spirit, whom He poured out upon us richly through Jesus Christ our Savior, that being justified by His grace we might be made heirs according to the hope of eternal life."

God's salvation is not given to us based on deeds we have done in righteousness. It is a gift extended to us through His grace bestowed on us by His mercy.
Paul stated in Ephesians 2:8-10:

> "For by grace you have been saved through faith; and that not of yourselves, it is the gift of God; not as a result of works, so that no one may boast. For we are His workmanship, created in Christ Jesus for good works which God prepared beforehand so that we would walk in them."

He reaffirmed we are saved by God's grace extended to us through our faith in Jesus, not by our works of righteousness. However, Paul added we are "created in Christ Jesus" to perform "good works, which God prepared beforehand so that we would walk in them." We are expected to perform works of righteousness because of the redemption we receive from God even though these works alone will not redeem and reconcile us to God.

Paul instructed us in Romans 12:2:

> "Do not be conformed to this world, but be transformed by the renewing of your mind, that you may prove what the will of God is, that which is good and acceptable and perfect."

We are not to conform to the cultural and social customs of the world that are hostel toward God when we enter a relationship with Him through Jesus. We are to study God's word in the Bible, so the Holy Spirit can transform us by the renewing of our mind through our study of the Bible. Paul continued in Ephesians 4:20-24:

> "But you did not learn Christ in this way, if indeed you have heard Him and have been taught in Him, just as truth is in Jesus, that, in reference to your former manner of life, you lay aside the old self, which is being corrupted in accordance with the lusts of deceit, and that you be renewed in the spirit of your mind, and put on the new self, which in the likeness of God has been created in righteousness and holiness of the truth."

We will address the renewing of our mind through spiritual growth in Chapter 12.

Paul stated in Romans 8:14-17:

> "For all who being led by the Spirit of God, these are sons of God. For you have not received a spirit of slavery leading to fear again, but you have received a spirit of adoption as sons by which we cry out, "Abba Father!" The Spirit Himself testifies with our spirit that we are children of God, and if children, heirs also, heirs of God and fellow heirs with Christ, if indeed we suffer with Him so that we may also be glorified with Him."

We are received by God as adopted children when we enter a relationship with Him through faith in Jesus. We become His heirs and fellow heirs with Jesus and are "heirs according to the hope of eternal life" (Titus 3:47) through Jesus. We have an inheritance as God's heirs, "which is imperishable and undefiled and will not fade away" that is reserved for us in heaven (1 Peter 1:3-5).

God has taken the initiative to establish a process through which He can redeem and reconcile us to Himself. He sent His Son, Jesus, into the world to present His Word as He wanted it presented and to be a mediator of a new covenant. Jesus established and sealed this covenant by shedding His blood on a cross. This covenant fulfilled the covenant of the Law and provides the legal basis for God to redeem and reconcile us to Himself through our faith in Jesus. God has demonstrated His love for us and extended His mercy and grace to us through His Son's death. He has given us the freedom to choose how we will respond.

Our Response to God

We must do our part to receive God's gift of salvation in conjunction with Him doing His part. Jesus stated in Matthew 18:3 to enter the kingdom of God we must be converted and become like little children. The Greek word for *convert* is *strepho*, which means to twist, to turn around. The Greek word for *children* is *pardion*, which can also be translated *infants*. Jesus indicated we must turn away from our love of the world and turn toward Him to enter the kingdom of God. We must be spiritually reborn and become spiritual infants.

Peter stated in Acts 3:19:

> "Repent therefore and return, that your sins may be wiped away in order
> that times of refreshing may come from the presence of the Lord."

We must repent of our sins when we come to the Lord. Repentance is a heartfelt act of deep and painful regret and remorse for living a sinful life apart from God. Jesus stated in Luke 13:3, "I tell you, no, but unless you repent, you will all likewise perish." We will perish when we do not repent. However, Jesus stated in Luke 15:7:

> "There will be more joy in heaven over one sinner who repents, then over
> ninety-nine righteous persons who need no repentance."

Jesus accepts us as we are with the good and bad when we repent and approach Him to seek His forgiveness. This does not mean He approves of the bad things we have done. However, He forgives us and begins the process of transforming us into the person God wants us to be through the Holy Spirit. Many are deceived into believing God will never forgive them because they have done things that are so bad. This becomes an obstacle to their receiving the redemption He desires to extend to them through Jesus. God and Jesus will always forgive us when we sincerely repent of our sins and ask for Their forgiveness.

There are two specific encounters with Jesus in the New Testament that address the issue of acceptance and forgiveness. The first encounter was Jesus' encounter with a

Samaritan woman at a well, described in John 4:7-42. Jesus asked the woman where her husband was during their conversation. He did this knowing she had been married five times and the man with whom she was living was not her husband. Jesus still invited her to come to Him to receive "water springing up to eternal life." He did not tell the woman to get her life in order and then come to Him. He instead invited her to come to Him as she was with the implication He would transform her life through the presence of the Holy Spirit.

The second encounter was Jesus's encounter with a woman caught in the act of adultery described in John 8:3-11. The Scribes and Pharisees brought the woman to Jesus whom they had caught in the act of committing adultery. They attempting to entrap Him by stated the Law required her to be stoned to death and asked Him what He thought they should do. Jesus stated any accuser who was without sin should cast the first stone. They all dropped their stones and left when they heard this, leaving Jesus alone with the woman. Jesus then stated to her since her accusers had not condemned her neither did He condemn her. He commanded her to go her way and sin no more. Jesus did not command the woman to get her life in order and then return to Him to receive His forgiveness. He forgave her while she stood before Him guilty of committing adultery.

The women in these two encounters could have been men. They could be you and me today. Jesus does not tell us to go our way, get our lives in order, and then return to Him to receive forgiveness when we approach Him for forgiveness. Instead He accepts us as we are and forgives us, knowing we are guilty of sin.

Paul instructed us in Romans 10:9-10:

> "That if you confess with your mouth, 'Jesus as Lord,' and believe in your heart that God raised him from the dead, you shall be saved; for with the heart man believes, resulting in righteousness, and with the mouth he confesses, resulting in salvation."

Paul tells you what you must do when you have not accepted Jesus into your life and been reborn or when you are not sure Jesus is present in your life. You must first repent and ask for forgiveness of your sins. You must then confess with your mouth Jesus is Lord and believe in your heart God raised Him from the dead for your sins. You must receive and accept the reality of what He has accomplished for you when He shed His blood for you on His cross.

Following is a recommended prayer for receiving salvation through Jesus:

> "Father, I want to be born again. I want to have Your life-giving Spirit breathed back into my heart. I know I have done things that have been offensive to You and that have not been pleasing in Your sight. I ask You to forgive my sins and

cleanse me of all unrighteousness. Jesus, I acknowledge You as Lord, the Son of God, and I believe in my heart You were raised from the dead for my sins and for me. I invite You to come into my heart and live in and through me. Take my life, Jesus, and make me the person You want me to be. Thank you, Jesus, for hearing and answering my prayer, and thank you for the knowledge that You, along with the Father and Holy Spirit, are living in and through me. Thank you for breathing spiritual life back into me and for the knowledge that I have been born again by the Spirit of God. I will serve and love You the rest of my life."

The Holy Spirit washes us with the blood of Jesus and cleanses us of our sins when we repent (turn away from our old rebellious way of living) and accept what God has accomplished for us through Jesus on a cross, (1 Corinthians 6:11, Titus 3:5). We are reborn, and God's Spirit through the Holy Spirit takes up residence in and nurtures us. Paul stated in Romans 8:14-17:

> "For all who are being led by the Spirit of God, these are sons of God. For you have not received a spirit of slavery leading to fear again, but you have received a spirit of adoption as sons by which we cry out, "Abba! Father!" The Spirit Himself bears witness with our spirit that we are children of God, and if children, heirs also, heirs of God and fellow heirs with Christ, if indeed we suffer with Him in order that we may also be glorified with Him."

We become children of God when we receive and accept the redemption and reconciliation God extends to us through our faith in Jesus. The Holy Spirit regenerates our spirit and begins the process of renewing our mind and transforming our heart. Paul indicated when these occur in our life:

> "Therefore, if any man is in Christ, he is a new creature; the old things passed away; behold, new things have come." (2 Corinthians 5:17)

> "For this reason, I bow my knees before the Father, from whom every family in heaven and on earth derives its name, that He would grant you, according to the riches of His glory, to be strengthened with power through faith; and that you being rooted and grounded in love, may be able to comprehend with all the saints what is the breadth and length and height and depth, and to know the love of Christ which surpasses knowledge, that you may be filled up to all the fullness of God." (Ephesians 3:14-19)

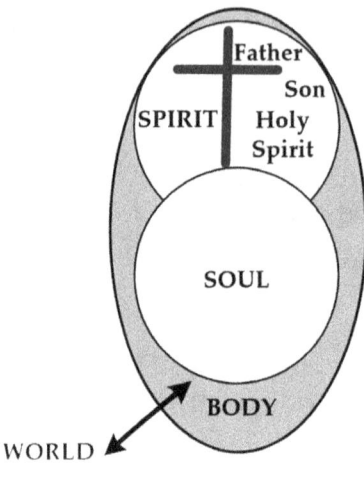

Figure 8

God (Father, Son and Holy Spirit) resides in us when we are spiritually reborn (Figure 8). Paul stated in 1 Corinthians 3:16:

> "Do you not know that you are a temple of God and that the Spirit of God dwells in you?"

We become a temple of God and a new creation in Christ when we are spiritually reborn. Our spirit and soul are energized and nurtured by the Holy Spirit. Paul stated in Galatians 2:20:

> "I have been crucified with Christ; and it is no longer I who live, but Christ lives in me; and the life which I now live in the flesh I live by faith in the Son of God, who loved me and gave Himself up for me."

God through the Holy Spirit calls us and enables us to respond to His call. God, Jesus and the Holy Spirit dwell in us after we come to God through our faith in Jesus. The Holy Spirit equips us to trust and obey God and Jesus in our relationship with Them. God reveals Himself to us through His word in the Bible and the presence of the Holy Spirit in our life. The Holy Spirit initiates and continues the process of transforming our heart through the renewing of our mind so we can discern God's will in our life (Romans 12:2) as we spiritually grow and mature.

CHAPTER 9
NATURE AND CHARACTER OF MAN
OUR SOUL AND SPIRIT

"You shall therefore impress these words of mine on your heart and on your soul; and you shall bind them as a sign on your hand and they shall be as frontals on your forehead. And you shall teach them to your sons, talking of them when you sit in your house and when you walk along the road and when you lie down and when you rise up. And you shall write them on the doorposts of your house and on your gates, so that your days and the days of your sons may be multiplied on the land which the LORD swore to your fathers to give them, as long as the heavens remain above the earth." (Deuteronomy 11:18-21)

"Do not fear those who kill the body but are unable to kill the soul; but rather fear Him who is able to destroy both soul and body in hell." (Matthew 10:28)

"But an hour is coming and now is, when the true worshipers shall worship the Father in spirit and truth, for such people the Father seeks to be His worshipers. God is spirit; and those who worship Him must worship in spirit and truth." (John 4:23-24)

OUR SOUL

Paul stated in 1 Thessalonians 5:23:

"Now may the God of peace Himself sanctify you entirely; and may your spirit and soul and body be preserved complete, without blame at the coming of our Lord Jesus Christ."

Our soul is an immaterial formless entity that is separable from our body that:

- Possesses memory
- Creates thoughts
- Acquires knowledge
- Forms habits
- Experiences emotions
- Initiates actions

Our soul, which is comprised of our mind and heart, instinctively moves us toward God. David stated in Psalm 139:13-16:

> "For You formed my inward parts;
> You wove me in my mother's womb.
> I will give thanks to You, for I am fearfully and wonderfully made;
> Wonderful are Your works,
> And my soul knows it very well. My frame was not hidden from You,
> When I was made in secret,
> And skillfully wrought in the depths of the earth;
> Your eyes have seen my unformed substance;
> And in Your book were written
> The days that were ordained for me,
> When as yet there was not one of them."

David implied in this Psalm our soul motivates us to be the person God has uniquely created us to be. It is our moral compass that leads and enables us to live life with dignity, integrity and humility when it is nurtured by God through the presence of the Holy Spirit.

THE STRUCTURE OF AND PROCESSES WITHIN OUR SOUL

Chapter 8 indicates our soul is comprised of our mind and heart - of memory, intellect, personality and character (Figure 5). Our soul governs how our spirit encounters, interprets and responds to life experiences through our body according to the way it assimilates and processes information it receives and experiences it encounters.

Chris Webb in his book, *The Fire of the Word: Meeting God on Holy Ground* (2011), presented the pictorial representation of our soul shown in Figure 9. The figure indicates our soul supports six actions and four processes. The six actions are senses, imagination, memory, reason, desires and drives. The four processes are perception, cognition, emotion and intention. Webb indicated the visual representation of the soul in Figure 9 was derived from ancient writings by Plato, Aristotle and the apostle Paul.

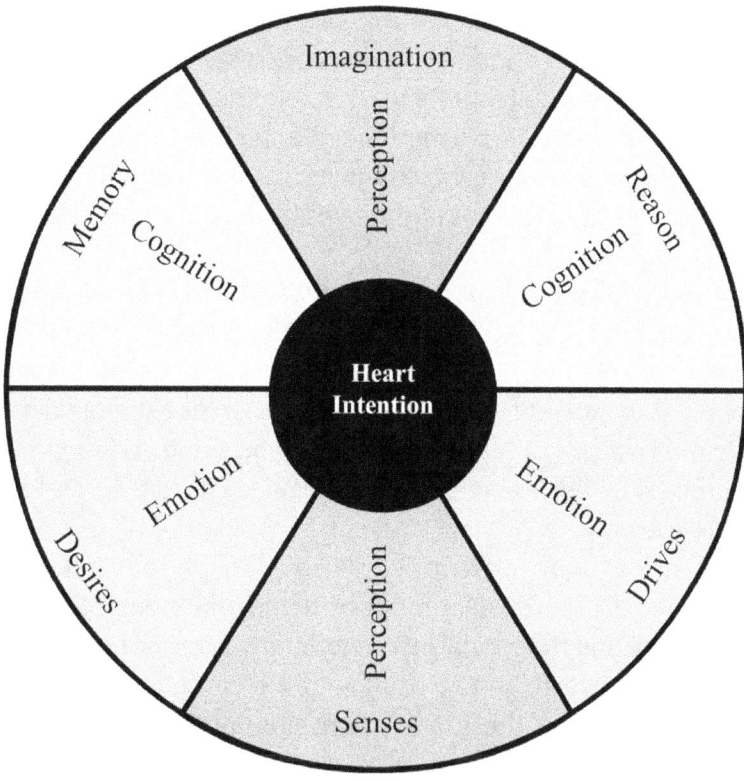

Figure 9

Inputs to our soul enter through the actions of *senses* and *imagination* in our mind. *Senses* receives information through our five physical senses (sight, hearing, touch, taste and smell) from the physical world and through our spirit from the spiritual realm. *Imagination* supplies supplemental information that further develops and embellishes information received into our mind. *Senses* and *imagination* allow us to receive information from God in the spiritual realm and from family, work and other environments where we are active in the physical world around us. *Senses* and *imagination* initiate the process of *perception*. *Perception* is the process through which we develop a coherent and unified awareness of the information we receive into our mind.

The actions of *memory* and *reason* interact in our mind to initiate the process of *cognition*. *Memory* is our repository of stored information received into our mind by *senses* and *imagination*. *Reason* is the action of our mind in which we assimilate and process this information in an orderly and systematic manner. *Cognition* is the process in our mind by which we acquire knowledge and gain insights and wisdom from this information. *Reason* and *cognition* combine to form *intellect*. The process of *cognition* facilitates the development of life skills. These skills enable us to engage in our life activities and challenges.

Desires and *drives* are actions within our heart. *Desires* are yearnings that predispose us to want to do certain activities and engage in specific tasks. *Drives* are strong urges that motivate and move us to do the activities and complete the tasks. *Desires* and *drives* initiate the process of *emotion* in our heart. *Emotion* is derived from the Latin words *emovere*, which means to disturb, and *movere*, which means to move. *Emotion* as it is used here is the process in our heart that motivates and moves us to act on information we process in our mind.

Our heart assimilates and processes outcomes from the processes of *perception*, *cognition* and *emotion* and initiates the process of *intention*. *Intention* is derived from the Latin word *intendere*, which means stretch, turn one's attention to. *Intention* as it is used here is the process that directs us to act in specific ways. It for example directs us to initiate a deliberate course of action, to form a new life habit, or to enter a new relationship. *Intention* is the process in our heart that directs us to stretch forth to engage in life's activities and challenges.

Figure 10 presents a more descriptive illustration of the actions and processes that occur within our soul. The development of this figure came to me in a dream. The emotional, psychological and functional interrelations between the actions and processes are complex. However, Figure 10 can be used with the preceding discussion to develop a more complete understanding of the interrelationships between the actions and processes shown in Figure 9

Figure 10 identifies additional processes that occur within and between our mind and heart. A *God and World Filter* is located between the symbol for the cognition process and the symbol for our personality and character. This filter can be referred to as the *God Site* in our soul. It performs an important function in the development of our personality and character. Its filter characteristics develop as we emotionally, psychologically and spiritually grow and mature. The development of the characteristics of this filter is influenced by two primary sources: God and the world. The filter characteristics most often are defined by God's laws and spiritual life principles when we live and grow up in an environment that affirms the existence of God and His presence in our life. The filter characteristics most often are defined by world and cultural norms and customs that may be hostile toward God when we live and grow up in an environment that denies His existence and may be hostile toward Him. The filter characteristics in many cases contain elements that are defined by both God and the world. This often results in struggles and conflicts within our soul that will be discussed later in this chapter.

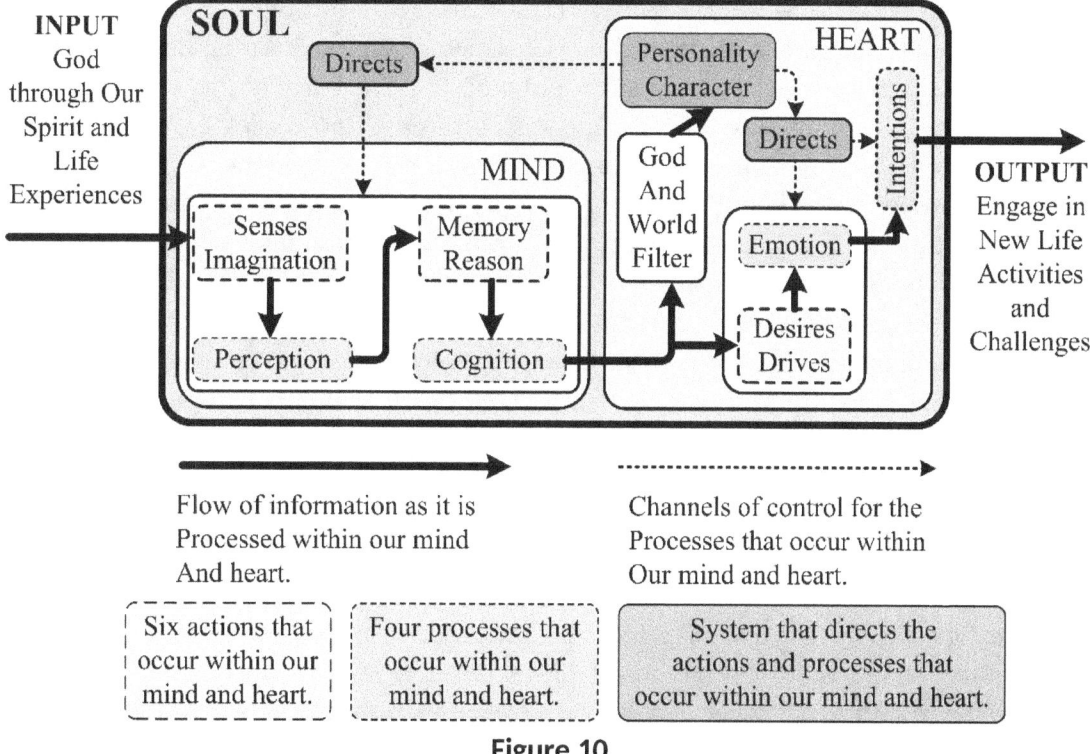

Figure 10

Figure 10 indicates our personality and character direct:

- The senses, imagination, memory and reason actions and the perception and cognition processes within our mind, and

- The desires and drives actions and the emotion and intention processes within our heart.

Outputs from the cognition process in our mind with their associated knowledge, insights and wisdom continually influence the development of our personality and character as we assimilate and process life experiences. These outputs are filtered and often modified by the *God and World Filter* before they affect the development of or initiate changes in our personality and character. The effects of this filtering process depend on whether the filter characteristics are defined by God or by the world. This influences whether we grow into a life and life activities that honor and are obedient to God or into a life and life activities that reject and may be hostile toward God.

The redemption and reconciliation we receive from God through Jesus are gifts. God (Father, Son and Holy Spirit) takes up residence in us when we enter a relationship with Him through Jesus. How this occurs is a mystery, but it occurs. The place of this residence is the *God and World Filter* in our heart (Figure 10). It becomes the *God Site* in our soul when God is present. He reaches out from here through the Holy Spirit to begin the healing process of hurting and broken areas in our spirit and soul (mind and heart) and to initiate processes that will facilitate the transformation of our personality and character necessary for us to become obedient to Him and Jesus.

God requires us to read, study and internalize His word in the Bible to grow and mature in our relationship with Him through Jesus and the Holy Spirit. He reveals Himself to us through the Holy Spirit as we enter and continue this process, and He continues His healing process within our spirit and soul. God's, Jesus' and the Holy Spirit's imprint on our mind becomes clearer and more focused, and Their presence in our heart becomes stronger and more active as we grow and mature in our relationship with them.

The Holy Spirit adapts our personality and character to be sensitive, responsive and obedient to God's and Jesus' presence in our life as we grow in our understanding of and continue to internalize God's word in the Bible. This focuses Their presence on the perception and cognition processes that renew our mind and inserts Their presence into the emotion and intention processes that transform our heart. Paul stated relative to these processes in Philippians 4:6-7:

> "Be anxious for nothing, but in everything by prayer and supplication with thanksgiving let your request be made known to God. And the peace of God, which surpasses all comprehension, will guard your hearts and your minds in Christ Jesus."

Paul continued regarding our relationship with God in Philippians 4:8-9:

> "Finally, brethren, whatever is true, whatever is honorable, whatever is right, whatever is pure, whatever is lovely, whatever is of good repute, if there is any excellence and if anything worthy of praise, dwell on these things. The things you have learned and received and heard and seen in me, practice these things, and the God of peace will be with you."

God through the Holy Spirit transforms the characteristics of the *God and World Filter* in our heart. This filter becomes the *God Site* in our heart when we initially grow up or live in an environment that rejects and is hostile toward God, and we later enter a reconciled relationship with Him through Jesus. The renewing and transforming processes described above will begin when this occurs. These processes can begin at any age or stage in our life.

OUR SOUL WHEN NURTURED BY GOD

Our soul is the seat of our conscience, insight and sensitivity. God designed our mind to be the repository of His spiritual knowledge, insights and wisdom. A God consciousness develops in the God Site in our heart that facilitates the transformation of our personality and character as we fellowship and grow in our relationship with God through Jesus. This is essential for Him to renew our mind and transform our heart. The Holy Spirit then opens our mind and heart to receive, understand and assimilate God's spiritual laws and principles that govern our life. We grow in our understanding of the kind of person God has created us to be and how He wants us to interact with and relate to Him, others and the world around us as we read, study and internalize His word in the Bible and enter into fellowship with other Christians. We learn our life is governed by these moral and spiritual laws and spiritual life principles, and the Holy Spirit creates within us the desire and gives us the ability to live according to them.

Our soul is also the seat of our creativity, inspiration and motivation. Our mind and heart process and assimilate information they receive from the spiritual realm of God and the physical world where we live, and they direct how we respond to this information. Life and meaning are given to ideas and beliefs that develop within our mind, and our heart inspires and motivates us to achieve tasks and to act on convictions that evolve from them.

Individuals whose minds and hearts are nurtured by the Holy Spirit:

- Experience the love, mercy, grace and forgiveness God gives to them through His Son, Jesus;

- Become sensitive to and reach out to and love others in the same way He reaches out to and loves them through Jesus.

- Are always able to approach life with a positive and balanced perspective;

- Have the energy, resiliency and motivation necessary to endure hardships and overcome obstacles they encounter;

- Develop insights into life and their relationship with God and others that are clearly inspired and motivated by the Holy Spirit;

- Radiate an enthusiasm for life that is contagious; and

- Have a zest for life that inspires and motivates others.

YEARNINGS WITHIN OUR SOUL

Our soul is created with built-in yearnings of the heart that drive us to move beyond ourself to seek meaning in life and our own distinct reality and destiny. Richard D. Grant and Andrea Wells Miller in their book, *Recovering Connections* (1993) and J. Keith Miller in his book, *The Secret Life of the Soul* (1997), indicate there are four basic yearnings of our soul. They are the yearning for:

- Perfect parenting,
- Perfect companionship,
- Perfect power and freedom, and
- Perfect meaning.

These yearnings begin at birth with our relationship with our parents. They progress to relationships with others, ultimately resulting in a relationship with God. They begin with our being dependent on our parents for meeting our physical, emotional and spiritual needs. We progress to where we want to be in control of our life, being dependent only on ourself for meeting these needs. We ultimately become dependent on God through Jesus and the Holy Spirit for meeting our needs. Yearnings of our soul that occur in infancy are characterized by our being selfish and self-centered and caring only about satisfying our own physical and emotional needs. We discover as we grow to adulthood true meaning in life is only achieved when we yield our life in obedience to God through Jesus and reach beyond ourself in selfless love to meet the legitimate needs of others.

Miller (The Secret Life of the Soul, 1997) indicated the above four yearnings can only be truly satisfied by God as Father, Son and Holy Spirit:

- Our yearning for a perfect parent is only satisfied when we enter an obedient and trusting relationship with God as Father.
- Our yearning for perfect companionship is only satisfied when we enter a surrendered relationship with Jesus within the fellowship and support of a local Christian community.
- Our yearning for perfect power and freedom is only satisfied when we invite the Holy Spirit into our life and allow Him to renew our mind and transform our heart.
- Our yearning for perfect meaning is only satisfied when our mind is renewed, our heart is transformed, and we seek and do God's will for our life.

Our personality develops the positive attributes God desires us to have and our moral and ethical values associated with our character become Christlike when our soul is nurtured by the Holy Spirit.

OUR SPIRIT WHEN NURTURED BY GOD

We will examine the functions of our spirit when we are spiritually alive, and our soul and spirit are nourished and nurtured by the Holy Spirit. Some functions are supported by the Bible while others are based on life experiences and observations (John and Paula Sandford, *Healing the Wounded Spirit*, 1985).

The first and most important function of our spirit is to worship God. Worship is our response to God's grace and His gift of redemption and reconciliation through our faith in Jesus. Paul stated in Romans 12:1:

> "I urge you therefore, brethren, by the mercies of God, to present your bodies a living and holy sacrifice, acceptable to God, which is your spiritual service and worship."

God has created us for His good pleasure to love and serve Him. Jesus stated in Mark 12:30 we are to love God with all our heart, mind, soul and strength. We are to focus our attention on, direct our affection toward, and use our talents for Him in everything we do. Jesus stated in John 4:23-24 we must worship God in spirit and truth. Real worship is a lifestyle through which we affirm the love we have for God. Everything we say and do in life must affirm His presence in our life and be done in a manner that brings Him glory and honor.

We approach God through corporate and private worship. Corporate worship is where we participate in singing and lifting praises, adoration and thanksgiving to God in fellowship with other Christians. Psalm 100:1-5 states:

> "Shout joyfully to the LORD, all the earth. Serve the LORD with gladness; come before Him with joyful singing. Know that the LORD Himself is God; it is He who has made us and not we ourselves; we are His people and the sheep of His pasture. Enter His gates with thanksgiving and His courts with praise. Give thanks to Him; bless His name. For the LORD is good; His loving kindness is everlasting and His faithfulness to all generations."

Corporate worship and fellowship are where we recognize God has created us and has facilitated our receiving all we possess. They are where we experience His love for use and receive strength to persevere.

Private worship and devotions are where we spend focused personal times with God. Our devotions are times when we approach Him through prayer and study His word in the Bible. We communicate with God through prayer, and He communicates with us through His word given to us in the Bible.

We receive knowledge of God's spiritual life principles that govern our life as we study His word in the Bible when we are spiritually alive. The Holy Spirit gives meaning and life to these principles and imprints them onto our mind and subconscious mind as we study and internalize them. We grow in our wisdom and insights related to these principles as we enter a deeper and more personal relationship with God through the guidance of the Holy Spirit. This enables us to incorporate them into our life more effectively.

God speaks to our mind and subconscious mind through the Holy Spirit, and we know He hears us when we speak to Him through prayer and lift our praises and adoration to Him in worship. Our soul is energized and receives strength from God through the Holy Spirit when we are spiritually alive. This enable us to engage life's challenges, endure its hardships and live a life that glorifies God and is built on the foundation of His spiritual life principles and laws.

Our spirit plays an important role in our interaction and communication with other persons. Our spirit reaches out through time and space to interact with others. We sense their presence, emotions and sensitivity with our spirit. Sometimes without any verbal communication our spirit senses an individual's acceptance or rejection. Our spirit empathizes with and tunes into another person's feelings and emotions. We often desire to interact with and develop a relationship with a person when our spirit resonates with that person's spirit. We avoid a person when our spirit is repulsed. We have a sensitivity toward others that lowers barriers and establishes channels of communication with them necessary to develop and grow lasting relationships when we are spiritually alive.

Our spirit gives us stamina and buoyancy to confront life's challenges and hardships. We have the stamina and buoyancy to confront life's challenges and hardships and persevere when we are spiritually alive. Proverbs 18:14 states, "The spirit of a man can endure his sickness, but a broken spirit who can bear?" We can persevere through challenging and difficult times when our spirit is nourished and strengthened by the Holy Spirit. We can work through and look beyond these times with eyes of faith to see and experience God working in our life to bring us into a closer and more intimate relationship with Him.

Our spirit becomes united with the spirit of our spouse in marriage. We become one flesh with our spouse in marriage. God stated in Genesis 2:24:

> "For this cause a man shall leave his father and his mother and shall cleave to his wife; and they shall become one flesh."

Jesus reaffirmed this in Mark 10:6-8 where he stated:

> "But from the beginning of creation, God made them male and female. For this cause a man shall leave his father and mother and the two shall become one flesh; consequently they are no longer two, but one flesh."

The Bible implies marriage is consummated in the sexual union between a husband and wife. Paul implied this in 1 Corinthians 6:16-18:

> "Or do you not know that the one who joins himself to a harlot is one body with her? For [Jesus] says, 'The two will become one flesh." But the one who joins himself to the Lord is one spirit with Him. Flee immorality. Every other sin that a man commits is outside the body, but the immoral man sins against his own body.'"

God has created marriage to be a holy and sacred covenant relationship between a husband and wife. It is the most intimate and sacred of all human covenants. Marriage is a relationship where all the functions of our spirit are active.

The spirits of a husband and wife resonant with each other when their spirits are alive and nourished by the Holy Spirit. Weaknesses and shortcomings of one are accepted and buoyed up by the strengths of the other. A husband and wife nurture and help each other, and they work to meet and satisfy each other's needs. They find their completeness in each other, and the most holy and sacred form of this completeness is manifested as they unselfishly give themselves to each other in sexual union. A husband and wife affirm each other's right to develop unique identities within the context of their marriage relationship as they experience life together. However, they develop these identities in the context of becoming one in spirit and developing a unified identity in their marriage that is formed through shared experiences.

STRUGGLES WITHIN OUR SOUL

God creates and brings each one of us into this world for specific purposes, and He has established behavioral boundaries. He gives us the freedom to choose if we will live according to the purposes for which He has created us and within the behavioral boundaries He has established. Our mind and heart will develop under the guidance of and be nurtured by the Holy Spirit when we choose to live according to God's will through Jesus. Our soul will be in communication with God through our spirit. However, this does not always occur in our life.

The Bible indicates our soul is a battleground in our life between good and evil, righteousness and unrighteousness, and obedience and disobedience. Our soul is where we decide we will live a life of dignity, integrity and humility in obedience to God through Jesus or a life of disobedience to God where we seek those things the world says we are entitled. How we resolve the struggles within our soul determines whether our life will be controlled by:

- The presence and guidance of God through the Holy Spirit, or
- Our desire to be in control and seek those things the world indicates are important.

The choices we make will affect our ability to find true meaning and purpose in life and to develop a healthy sense of self-esteem and self-worth.

The development and growth of our soul is influenced by our needs to:

- Be nurtured and supported (perfect parenting);
- Seek and enter into relationships with others (perfect companionship);
- Achieve success and status in life (perfect power and freedom); and
- Find purpose in life and develop self-esteem and self-worth (perfect meaning).

The development and growth of our soul occurs in a fallen world that has been corrupted by sin and where we are in conflict with our sin nature. Our sin nature predisposes us to be hostile toward God and to seek what the world says is true and important.

We seek to satisfy the four yearnings of our soul in a hostile environment. In this environment:

- We sometimes do not have perfect parents as a child. Our parents may not give us the affection, support and nurturing we need. There are those who are emotionally, physically and sexually abused as children by their parents or other adults.

- We do not enter perfect relationships. We enter relationships where we are teased, tormented, rejected, used, manipulated, abused, molested, and assaulted. We enter personal, business and marriage relationships that fail.

- We do not make wise decisions in our quest for success and status in life. We make decisions that compromise our character and integrity. Just as we may become victims of others in their pursuit for success and status, we may make decisions and institute actions that victimize others. We experience disappointment and failure in our quest for success and status.

- Problems and failures we experience in our attempts to satisfy the first three yearnings of our soul can cause us to lose purpose and meaning in our life and leave us with a sense of a lack of self-esteem and self-worth. Our life can be devastated by negative experiences and appear to be out-of-control.

Consequences associated with not addressing our failures to satisfy the yearnings of our soul result in wounds within our soul and spirit. These wounds can derail God's purpose for our life and His desired development of our personality and character.

We can become angry at and shut God out of our life when we experience serious wounds within our soul and spirit. This separates us from God, and the continued development of our personality and character occurs in a manner that shields us from being wounded again. This intensifies struggles that occur within our soul.

Thoughts and voices occur within our mind when our soul processes the battles, struggles and conflicts that occur within it. These come from three sources:

- **The spiritual realm of God through angels and the Holy Spirit.** Thoughts/voices that originate from the spiritual realm of God direct us toward God who desires to heal our emotional and spiritual wounds. They affirm our value, dignity and worth in the eyes of God, and they encourage us to seek a life that is acceptable and pleasing to Him. They lead us to accept and receive the love, mercy, grace and forgiveness God extends to us through Jesus. They encourage us to give the Holy Spirit permission to enter our life to heal our emotional and spiritual wounds and to begin or continue the processes of renewing our mind and transforming our heart.

- **The spiritual realm of Satan through demonic sources.** Thoughts/voices that originate from the spiritual realm of Satan accuse and condemn us and work to draw us away from and make us hostile toward God. They attempt to shame us and take away our sense of value, dignity and worth. They create within us a sense that we are stupid, careless, worthless, etc. They imply we deserve the failures and bad and devastating experiences that have occurred in our life. They seek to drive us into a state of hopelessness and despair.

- **Our own mind.** Thoughts/voices that originate in our own mind and subconscious mind represent our perception of the state of our life. They reflect our concerns, fears, dreams, desires, plans, etc. They also reflect our emotional response to the thoughts/voices that come from the spiritual realms of God and Satan. How we process these thoughts/voices will either enhance our sense of self-worth and dignity or draw us into a deeper sense of hopelessness and despair.

The affirming thoughts/voices in our mind from the spiritual realm of God are ignored or repressed when our personality and character develop independent of God. The shaming and condemning thoughts/voices from the spiritual realm of Satan then become dominant, and the thoughts/voice originating within our own mind often condemn and shame us.

Thoughts/voices originating in our mind that condemn and shame us can occur whether we have entered a relationship with God through Jesus. This is certain to occur when we reject Jesus' claim on our life and are separated from God. However, it can occur when we invite Jesus into our life but do not give the Holy Spirit permission to perform His renewing and transforming processes. The Holy Spirit will not begin these processes in our soul until we give Him permission. The nurturing presence of God in our life is impaired when we fail to give the Holy Spirit permission to function within our soul.

Miller (*The Secret Life of the Soul*, 1997) indicated we enter activities directed at quieting and escaping the shaming and condemning thoughts/voices that exist in our mind when our personality and character develop independent of God. This leads us into compulsive and addictive behaviors. We may become overachievers and workaholics, hoping to find purpose and meaning in life and escape these thoughts/voices. We may become addicted to alcohol, drugs, pornography and sex because of their nagging presence. We ultimately discover these behaviors do not afford us any relief or escape. We experience a greater sense of hopelessness and despair as we enter further into these behaviors.

There are several potential negative consequences on our life when we allow our personality and character to develop independent of God.

- Spiritual communication with God is seriously impaired or cut off. As a result, our soul is unable to receive spiritual information from and to be nurtured by the Holy Spirit. Paul stated in 1 Corinthians 2:14:

  "But a nature man does not accept the things of the Spirit of God; for they are foolishness to him and he cannot understand them, because they are spiritually appraised."

We become controlled by our interaction with the world when we take control of our life away from God, Jesus and the Holy Spirit. We become self-reliant and hostile toward God instead of developing a dependent, nurturing and loving relationship with Him.

- We are blind to God's absolute moral and spiritual laws that govern our life. The safeguards He has given us to keep our life in harmony with Him, others, ourself and the world are inoperable; they are dormant. Consequently, our life becomes controlled by our physical desires and appetites and by what the world says is important rather than by what God says is important. This increases our independence from and hostility toward God.

- We tend to become manipulative and controlling in nature and to relate to others in a way that can cause them to be apprehensive and defensive. We are unable to be compassionate and sensitive to others because we are unable to experience God's love and compassion. This results in the erection of barriers that impede the development of meaningful and trusting relationships.

- We are overcome and discouraged by hardships and crises in our life. We lack the stamina and buoyancy necessary to effectively confront them in a positive manner. They become devastating and destructive, particularly when we cannot see through or beyond them to the better times that will lie ahead. At a minimum, they become events that result in the development of a negative and defeated attitude. In more serious situations, they result in serious emotional and spiritual problems.

The beautiful story that runs throughout the Bible is God is loving, caring and patient. He continually reaches out to us with an invitation to come to Him through Jesus. God will remain in the background as long as we want to be in control of our life and allow our personality and character to develop independent of Him. He will permit us to sink deeper into hopelessness and despair until we ultimately give up and surrender to and seek Him. The voice of the Holy Spirit will quietly and gently break through the shaming and condemning thoughts/voices in our mind at this point to affirm God loves, forgives and desires to enter a loving, healing and nurturing relationship with us though His Son, Jesus.

We can begin to approach God on a more intimate bases through a process knowns as *Lectio Divina*. This process that is traditionally used in Catholicism to read and study the Bible can be used by anyone. It has four steps:

Read God's word in the Bible with reverance and the inspiration of the Holy Spirit;

Meditate by focusing our thoughts on what we have read;

Pray over the relevance of what we have read to our life; and
Contemplate on how we plan to apply what we have read to our life.

When we surrender and yield ourself to God through our faith in Jesus:

- The Holy Spirit will:

  1. Enter our life and initiate processes that result in healing of our soul and spirit, renewal of our mind, and transformation of our heart, and

  2. Facilitate the growth of the positive personality attributes and Christlike character God has created within us.

- The dominant thoughts/voices in our mind will be those from the spiritual realm of God. They will:

  1. Affirm our value, dignity and worth in the eyes of God,

  2. Affirm our relationship with God through our faith in Jesus,

  3. Encourage us to live a life that is built on the foundation of God's spiritual life principle revealed to us in the Bible, and

  4. Transform the thoughts/voices that originate in our mind and subconscious mind to be compatible with the thoughts/voices we receive from the spiritual realm of God.

- We will develop and grow in our ability to live a life of faith and trust in and obedience to God through our faith and trust in and obedience to Jesus.

- Our soul will commune with and be nurtured and strengthen by God through actions of the Holy Spirit in our life.

- We will find true meaning and purpose in and for our life and experience true freedom and joy.

CHAPTER 10
SPIRITUAL GROWTH
WASHING, CLEANSING AND BAPTISM

> "Since therefore brethren, we have confidence to enter the holy place by the blood of Jesus, by a new and living way which He inaugurated for us through the veil, that is, His flesh, and since we have a great priest over the house of God, let us draw near with a sincere heart in full assurance of faith, having our hearts sprinkled clean from an evil conscience and our bodies washed with pure water." (Hebrews 10:19-20)

> "And now why do you delay? Arise, and be baptized, and wash away your sins, calling on His name." (Acts 22:16)

SPIRITUAL GROWTH (Chapters 10 - 14)

This section presents information regarding:

- The washing and cleansing we receive through actions of the Holy Spirit and the significance of water baptism;
- The significance of grace and faith in our relationship with God;
- Principles associated with prayer; and
- Spiritual growth that results in the renewal of our mind and transformation of our heart.

WASHING OF REGENERATION

Paul stated in Titus 3:4-7:

> "But when the kindness of God our Savior and His love for mankind appeared, He saved us, not on the basis of deeds which we have done in righteousness, but according to His mercy, by the washing of regeneration and renewing by

the Holy Spirit, whom He poured out upon us richly through Jesus Christ our Savior, that being justified by His grace we might be made heirs according to the hope of eternal life."

The Greek word for *regeneration* is *paliggenesia*, which can be translated spiritual rebirth. Being saved by the *washing of regeneration* is associated with our spiritual rebirth when we accept Jesus as our Lord and Savior, and God's Spirit dwells in us.

In Hebrews 9:22, the author stated:

"And according to the Law, one may almost say, all things are cleansed with blood, and without shedding blood there is no forgiveness."

The agent of our washing is the blood of Jesus. Paul stated in Ephesians 1:7:

"In [Christ] we have redemption through His blood, the forgiveness of our trespasses, according to the riches of His grace."

We are redeemed and receive forgiveness of our sins through the blood of Jesus. John stated in 1 John 1:6-7:

"If we say that we have fellowship with Him and yet walk in the darkness, we lie and do not practice the truth; but if we walk in the light as He Himself is in the light, we have fellowship with one another, and the blood of Jesus His Son cleanses us from all sin."

The Holy Spirit washes and cleanses us with the blood of Jesus when He enters our life, resulting in our pardon and release from the power of sin. Our sins are purged and rooted out of and taken away from us. This is consistent with Jesus' dual role as the sacrificial lamb (by His death He atones for our sin) and the scapegoat (He purges us of sin and takes it far away from us).

Paul stated in Romans 5:9:

"Much more now being justified by His blood, we shall be saved from the wrath of God through Him."

We are rendered innocent before God when we are washed in and cleansed by the blood of Jesus. He no longer sees our sin natures. He instead sees us as we are in the light and image of Jesus. We enter a new legal relationship with God through Jesus when we are justified. We are judged to be innocent because of Jesus' death and resurrection. We, therefore, no longer must fear the eternal consequences of God's judgment against our sins because our names are written in the book of life (Revelation 20:12, 15, 21:17).

In Hebrews 9:13-14, 13:12, the author stated:

> "For if the blood of goats and bulls and the ashes of a heifer sprinkling those who have been defiled, sanctify for the cleansing of the flesh, how much more will the blood of Christ, who through the eternal Spirit offered Himself without blemish to God, cleanse your conscience from dead works to serve the living God. ... Therefore, Jesus also, that He might sanctify the people through His own blood, suffered outside the gate."

We are made holy when we are sanctified through the blood of Jesus. Our conscience is cleansed "from dead works to serve the living God." We are then set apart to be in service to God and to minister to others in the name of Jesus.

Paul stated in Romans 5:19:

> "For as through the one man's disobedience the many were made sinners, even so through the obedience of the One the many will be made righteous."

The righteousness that is in us is not our righteousness; it is the righteousness of Jesus. In the spiritual realm, our character becomes equal to His, and we can enter the very presence of God.

WATER BAPTISM

Role of Baptism in the Life of a Christian

Peter instructed in Acts 2:38 to repent and be baptized in the name of Jesus for the forgiveness of our sins. The Greek word for baptism is *baptizo*, which means to make whelmed. To make *whelmed* is to submerge. Water baptism is a New Testament experience that began with the ministry of John the Baptist. There is no Old Testament ceremonial law that required the immersion of the whole body following repentance and that pictured spiritual regeneration, a death to sin, and a resurrection to new life as baptism is pictured in the New Testament.

There are two misconceptions that are commonly associated with water baptism:

- One cannot be saved and admitted into the kingdom of God without baptism.
- Baptism is of little importance to the Christian experience.

Repentance and a profession of faith by accepting Jesus as Lord and Savior always preceded baptism in all New Testament instances of water baptism. Baptism is a public profession of the occurrence of these events in the life of the believer. Baptism does not save us. We are saved by faith in Jesus and what He accomplished for us on the cross. Baptism is an act of righteousness, and it is a good work. Paul taught we are not saved by acts of righteousness (Titus 3:4-7) or by good works (Ephesians 2:8-10). We are instructed in the New Testament we need only to believe God raised from the dead and profess with our mouths Jesus is Lord to set the events associated with our salvation (spiritual rebirth and washing in and cleansing by the blood of Jesus) into motion. The Bible teaches the usual order of events in the life of the believer is:

- He hears the Word preached.
- He believes the Word.
- He repents and turns to the Lord.
- He is spiritually reborn.
- He makes a public profession of faith.
- He is baptized.
- He then enters full church membership.

The New Testament teaches us literal water baptism is a necessary part of our Christian experience. Peter and other apostles in Acts commanded believers to be baptized. Jesus set the example for us by being baptized by John the Baptist (Matthew 3:13-17), and He commanded the disciples in Matthew 28:18-20:

> "All authority has been given to Me in heaven and on earth. Go therefore and make disciples of all the nations, baptizing them in the name of the Father and the Son and the Holy Spirit, teaching them to observe all that I commanded you; and lo, I am with you always, even to the end of the age."

Water baptism is a very important and central event in our walk with Jesus even though we are not saved by it.

Baptism in the Early Church

Baptism was a central event in the life of a Christian in the early church. An individual was enrolled into the catechumenate, which was the ranks of those preparing for baptism, when he professed faith in Jesus (Gangel & Wilhoit, *The Christian Educator's Handbook on Spiritual*

Formation, 1994). The period of preparation ranged from a few weeks to three years. The preparation during the shorter period began on Ash Wednesday and went through Lent with baptism occurring on Easter. The Scriptures were read and interpreted to the initiates during this time. They were given instruction in Christian character, and all aspects of their lives were examined with respect to their new relationship with Jesus. The initiates gave a profession of their faith at the end of their preparation before the church when they were baptized and withstood a public scrutiny of both their character and conduct. Baptism in the early church followed the initiates' profession of faith, and it initiated them into full membership in the church. Baptism in the early church was the culmination of the conversion process and the spiritual rebirth and resocialization of the believer.

The early church practiced total bodily immersion for water baptism. Some of the earliest recorded instructions of the church for water baptism are contained in the *Didache* or *Teaching of the Lord to the Gentiles through the Twelve Apostles* (Lane, *Harper's Concise Book of Christian Faith*, 1984):

> "You should baptize in this way. Having recited all these things, baptize in the name of the Father and of the Son and of the Holy Spirit in running water. But if you have no running water, use other water and if you cannot use cold water, use warm. If you have neither, then pour water on the head three times in the name of the Father and of the Son and of the Holy Spirit (Didache 7)."

The instructions were to totally immerse an individual in running water when possible. A pool or other similar body of water could be used when this was not possible. Water could be poured on the head of the individual being baptized when neither were present. Baptism by pouring or sprinkling became the preferred method of baptism with the total transition to infant baptism by the sixth century and particularly in arid regions or in regions where water was scarce.

The early church believed an individual received the gift of the Holy Spirit at the time of baptism (Gangel & Wilhoit, *The Christian Educator's Handbook on Spiritual Formation*, 1994). Two scriptural references justified this belief. First, is the fact the Holy Spirit descended upon Jesus as a dove when He was baptized in the Jordan River by John the Baptist (Matthew 3:13-17). The second scripture is found in Acts 2:38 where Peter stated to those who asked what they must do to be saved:

> "Repent, and let each of you be baptized in the name of Jesus for the forgiveness of your sins; and you shall receive the gift of the Holy Spirit."

Infant Baptism

Infant baptism began in the fourth century and became universal in the Christian church by the sixth century (Gangel & Wilhoit, *The Christian Educator's Handbook on Spiritual Formation*, 1994). With the transition from adult baptism to infant baptism came a corresponding change in the emphasis of baptism. The profession of faith was associated with the faith of the one being baptized with adult baptism. In infant baptism, the profession of faith was associated with the church's faith. The early church believed an infant received the gift of the Holy Spirit when it was baptized when it switched to infant baptism. The church further believed this secured the infant's soul for salvation should it die before it could grow and mature to the point where it could make its own profession of faith. The church then became responsible to spiritually nurture a child that was baptized with the transition to infant baptism. The child grew in its faith and understanding of its spiritual relationship with God the church had initiated it into at infancy as it grew and matured within the church.

Baptism in the Modern Church

The role baptism plays in the life of a Christian in modern times is often little understood. Sometimes it is misunderstood. Young parents often want to have their infants baptized because of tradition even though they may not be active in a Christian church nor fully understand the spiritual significance of water baptism.

Different Christian traditions have different specific beliefs with respect to water baptism. Some traditions believe an individual must be totally immersed during water baptism, while others believe an individual may have water poured over or sprinkled on their head during baptism. Some traditions accept either immersion or pouring or sprinkling. Some traditions accept infant baptism, while others do not.

Those traditions that do not accept infant baptism believe individuals must be old enough to accept Jesus as their Lord and Savior for themselves and to make a public profession of faith in Jesus before the church when they are baptized. Baptism then precedes their being accepted as full members into the church.

Those traditions that do practice infant baptism believe the church and the parents of the infant being baptized make a corporate profession of faith. The church and the parents commit to nurture and raise the child in a Christian environment where it can grow and mature in its understanding of its relationship with God through Jesus. The child when he/she is old enough goes through a period of formal training when he/she is taught spiritual precepts associated with his/her relationship with God through Jesus. The child decides at the end of this training whether he/she desires to accept the relationship with God through

Jesus his/her parents and the church initiated him/her into at infancy. The child is then accepted into full membership when he/she accepts this relationship and makes his/her own public profession of faith in Jesus before the church.

Water baptism in the modern church is an important and central event in the life of a Christian. John Wesley gave us an understanding of the importance of water baptism when he stated:

> "In baptism we are cleansed of the guilt of original sin; initiated into the covenant with God; admitted into the church; made an heir of the divine kingdom; and spiritually regenerated (Wesley, A Treatise on Baptism)."

Baptism becomes a public and outward sign of an inward transformation that takes place in the life of a Christian.

Paul taught:

> "Or do you not know that all of us who have been baptized into Christ have been baptized into His death? Therefore we have been buried with Him through baptism into death, in order that as Christ was raised from the dead through the glory of the Father, so we too might walk in newness of life." (Romans 6:3-4)

> "For in Him all the fullness of Deity dwells in bodily form, and in Him you have been made complete, and He is the head over all rule and authority; and in Him you were also circumcised with a circumcision made without hands, in the removal of the body of the flesh by the circumcision of Christ; having been buried with Him in baptism, in which you were also raised up with him through faith in the working of God, who raised Him from the dead." (Colossians 2:9-12)

The Greek word for *buried* is *sunthapto*, which means to enter company with, to assimilate spiritually. The Greek word for *raised* is *sunegeiro*, which means to rouse from death in company with. We are symbolically buried with Jesus into His death when we are baptized in order that, as Jesus was raised from the dead, we too might be raised and walk with Him in newness of life. We experience "a circumcision made without hands, in the removal of the body of the flesh by the circumcision of Christ." We are then clothed with Christ (Galatians 3:27) and become a new creature with old things passed away (2 Corinthians 5:17). We begin the process through baptism where we are continually "being renewed to a true knowledge according to the image of the One who created [us] (Colossians 3:10)."

THE HOLY SPIRIT

The early church believed an individual did not receive the gift of the Holy Spirit until he was baptized. Today we believe we receive the gift of the Holy Spirit when we repent, accept Jesus as our Lord and Savior, and are spiritually reborn. A justification for this belief can be found in Acts 10:44-48:

> "While Peter was still speaking these words, the Holy Spirit fell upon all those who were listening to the message. And all the circumcised believers who had come with Peter were amazed, because the gift of the Holy Spirit had been poured out upon the Gentiles also. For they were hearing them speaking with tongues and exalting God. Then Peter answered, "Surely no one can refuse the water for these to be baptized who have received the Holy Spirit just as we did, can he?" And he ordered them to be baptized in the name of Jesus Christ."

This encounter was the first time the Gentiles had received the gift of the Holy Spirit. This event was a sign to the Apostles salvation and the gift of the Holy Spirit were available to the Gentiles, as well as for the Jews. In this case, the Holy Spirit was received by the Gentiles before they were baptized. Today we believe we receive the Holy Spirit when we profess with our mouth Jesus is Lord and believe in our heart He was raised from the dead for our sins. This is the point at which we are spiritually reborn.

The Holy Spirit is active in all phases of our salvation, spiritual rebirth and spiritual growth. The Holy Spirit:

- Convicts us of sin (John 16:8-11) and calls us to repentance;
- Gives us the ability to come to Jesus and call Him Lord (1 Corinthians 12:3);
- Breathes spiritual life back into us when we accept Jesus as our Lord and Savior (John 6:63);
- Washes, sanctifies and justifies us (1 Corinthians 6:11);
- Regenerates our soul (Titus 3:4-7);
- Baptizes us into the Body of Christ (1 Corinthians 12:13); and
- Gives us the ability to become children of God (Romans 8:14-17).

CHAPTER 11
SPIRITUAL GROWTH
GRACE, FAITH AND GOOD WORKS

"But as many as received Him, to them He gave the right to become children of God, even to those who believe in His name, who were born not of blood, nor of the will of the flesh, nor of the will of man, but of God." (John 1:12-13)

"For by grace you have been saved through faith and that not of yourselves. It is the gift of God; not as a result of works, so that no one may boast. For we are His workmanship, created in Christ Jesus for good works, which God prepared beforehand so that we would walk in them." Ephesians 2:8-10)

"But we are not those who shrink back to destruction, but of those who have faith to the preserving of the soul. Now faith is the assurance of things hoped for, the conviction of things not seen. For by it the men of old gained approval. By faith we understand that the worlds were prepared by the word of God, so that what is seen was not made out of things which are visible. ... And without faith it is impossible to please Him, for he who comes to God must believe that He is, and that He is a rewarder of those who seek Him. ... Therefore, since we have so great a cloud of witnesses surrounding us, let us also lay aside every encumbrance and the sin which so easily entangles us, and let us run with endurance the race that is set before us, fixing our eyes on Jesus, the author and perfecter of faith, who for the joy set before Him endured the cross, despising the shame, and has sat down at the right hand of the throne of God." (Hebrews 10:39-11:3, 6, 12:1-2)

OUR RELATIONSHIP WITH GOD THROUGH OUR FAITH IN JESUS

We can gain insight into our relationship with God through our faith in Jesus by understanding the relation between God's grace and our faith. The Bible defines God's grace as His extending to us His undeserved favor and position. His favor is His redemption and salvation given to us through our faith in Jesus. His position is His reconciliation and adoption of us as His children though the death and resurrection of Jesus. We have received God's favor and position as an undeserved gift. Paul addressed this in Romans 3:22-28, 5:1-2:

> "But now apart from the Law the righteousness of God has been manifested, being witnessed by the Law and the Prophets, even the righteousness of God through faith in Jesus for all those who believe; for there is no distinction; for all have sinned and fall short of the glory of God; being justified as a gift by His grace through the redemption which is in Christ Jesus; whom God displayed publicly as a propitiation in His blood through faith. This was to demonstrate His righteousness, because in the forbearance of God He passed over the sins previously committed; for the demonstration, I say, of His righteousness as at the present time, that He might be just and the justifier of the one who has faith in Jesus. Where then is boasting? It is excluded. By what kind of law? Of works? No, but by the law of faith. For we maintain that a man is justified by faith apart from works of the Law. ... Therefore having been justified by faith, we have peace with God through our Lord Jesus Christ, through whom also we have obtained our introduction by faith into this grace in which we stand, and we exult in the hope of the glory of God."

Being *justified* means to be *judged* not guilty by God. This is a gift of His grace that allows us to enter an undeserved relationship with Him through our faith in Jesus. The essence of grace is mercy, and the true expression of mercy is forgiveness. Therefore, God extends His love, grace and mercy to us by forgiving our sins and redeeming us when we receive and accept the salvation He extends to us through Jesus.

The Bible teaches we can only receive the *action* of God's grace as a gift by accepting it as an *action* of our faith in Jesus (Figure 11). We cannot earn or buy His grace through *actions* we initiate. We demonstrate our faith by believing in and trusting God, appropriating for ourself His salvation through Jesus, and yielding ourself to His authority over our life by believing and obeying His Word revealed to us by Jesus. *Grace* defines God's attitude toward and relationship with us through Jesus. *Faith* defines our attitude toward and relationship with God through Jesus. Therefore, Jesus is the conduit through which God extends His *grace* to us and we show our *faith* to God.

GOD'S RESPONS TO US

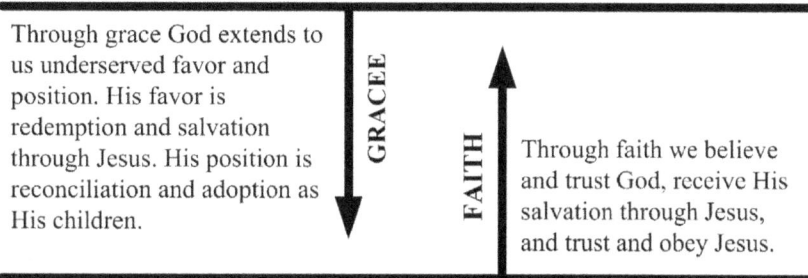

Through grace God extends to us underserved favor and position. His favor is redemption and salvation through Jesus. His position is reconciliation and adoption as His children.

GRACEE

FAITH

Through faith we believe and trust God, receive His salvation through Jesus, and trust and obey Jesus.

OUR RESPONS TO GOD

Figure 11

GRACE

Grace - God's Attitude toward Us

Grace defines God's attitude toward us through Jesus. He expects us to approach Him with gratitude and humility regarding the infinite sacrifice He and Jesus made to reconcile and restore our broken relationship with Him. These expectations are like the ones God conveyed to the Israelites in Deuteronomy 8:1-2, 5-6, 10-20 before they entered the land He had promised them:

> "All the commandments that I am commanding you today, you shall be careful to do, that you may live and multiply, and go in and possess the land which the LORD swore to give to your forefathers. You shall remember all the way which the LORD your God has led you in the wilderness these forty years, that He might humble you, testing you, to know what was in your heart, whether you would keep His commandments or not. ... Thus you are to know in your heart that the LORD your God was disciplining you just as a man disciplines his son. Therefore, you shall keep the commandments of the LORD your God, to walk in His ways and to fear Him. ... When you have eaten and are satisfied, you shall bless the LORD your God for the good land which He has given you. Beware lest you forget the LORD your God by not keeping His commandments and His ordinances and His statutes which I am commanding you today; lest, when you have eaten and are satisfied, and have built good houses and lived in them, and when your herds and your flocks multiply, and your silver and gold multiply, and all that you have multiplies, then your heart becomes proud, and you forget the LORD your

God who brought you out from the land of Egypt, out of the house of slavery. He led you through the great and terrible wilderness, with its fiery serpents and scorpions and thirsty ground where there was no water; He brought water for you out of the rock of flint. In the wilderness He fed you manna which your fathers did not know, that He might humble you and that He might test you, to do good for you in the end. Otherwise, you may say in your heart, 'My power and the strength of my hand made me this wealth.' But you shall remember the LORD your God, for it is He who is giving you power to make wealth, that He may confirm His covenant which He swore to your fathers, as it is this day. And it shall come about if you ever forget the LORD your God, and go after other gods and serve them and worship them, I testify against you today that you shall surely perish. Like the nations that the LORD makes to perish before you, so you shall perish; because you would not listen to the voice of the LORD your God."

God required the Israelites to obey His commandments, walk in His ways, and fear Him. He encouraged them to never forget what He had done for and given them in the wilderness and to continue to bless and thank Him for the prosperity He would give them when they entered the land, He had promised them.

God's statements describe several key aspects of His attitude toward us today even though they were given to an ancient people thousands of years ago. God:

- Is faithful to honor His covenants and promises with us.
- Expects us to keep His commandments, obey His statutes, and live within boundaries He has established for our life.
- Expects us to bless, thank and give Him credit for what He has accomplished for and gives to us.
- Will test us to determine the true attitudes of our heart.
- Will discipline us when we do not keep His commandments, disobey His statutes, and fail to live within the boundaries He has established for our life.
- Will humble us when we become proud and arrogant.
- Works to transform us into the persons He desires us to be when He tests, disciplines and humbles us.
- Will walk with us when we look to Him for help and support; He will prepare the way for us when we go through difficult and troubled times.

- Will chastise and discipline us when we take credit for the things He has done for and given to us. He will oppose us when we become proud and believe we can accomplish these things through our own efforts independent of Him.

Paul stated in Romans 8:5-8:

> "For those who are according to the flesh set their minds on the things of the flesh, but those who are according to the Spirit, the things of the Spirit. For the mind set on the flesh is death, but the mind set on the Spirit is life and peace, because the mind set on the flesh is hostile toward God; for it does not subject itself to the law of God, for it is not even able to do so, and those who are in the flesh cannot please God."

We believe we do not need God in our life when we live according to the flesh. This leads to pride that results in death. We recognize the presence of God's grace in our life when His Spirit dwells in us. This results in gratitude and humility that leads to life and peace. Paul indicated it is impossible to please God when we are controlled by the desires of our flesh. James stated in James 4:6:

> "But He gives us a greater grace. Therefore it says, 'God is opposed to the proud, but gives grace to the humble. '"

God extends grace to the humble. Our humility is displayed by our entering an obedient relationship with God and genuine, honest and unselfish relationships with others. Humble persons focus more on God and others than on themselves.

Humility begins by fearing God. Solomon taught in Proverbs 15:33, "The fear of the LORD is the instruction for wisdom, and before honor comes humility." This fear is not associated with being afraid of God. Rather it is born out of an acceptance of and respect for the position and power God has as Creator and Father. It develops as we accept and positively respond to the testing and disciplining God gives us as He transforms us into the person He wants us to be.

Humility develops as we learn from Jesus' relationships with God and others in the Bible. It grows when we acknowledge and accept the lordship of Jesus over our life and realize the needs of others are sometimes greater and more important than our needs. Humility does not produce pride as it develops. Rather, it produces gratitude, compassion, kindness, gentleness and patience. It creates within us the desire to believe in, trust and obey Jesus and to love, forgive and help others.

The Proverbs and Psalms teach us:

"When pride comes, then comes dishonor,
But with the humble is wisdom." (Proverbs 11:2)

"The reward of humility and the fear of the LORD Are riches, honor and life."
(Proverbs 22:4)

"He leads the humble in justice,
And He teaches the humble His way." (Psalms 25:9)

God has chosen to redeem and reconcile us to Himself through His grace rather than through our works of righteousness. Our works, independent of God, produce self-reliance and pride. Pride makes us hostile toward and separates us from God. God extends His grace to us as an undeserved gift when we humble ourself, acknowledge our sins, repent, and accept His salvation through Jesus. Paul affirmed the difference between the Law and God's grace in Romans 5:20-21:

"The Law came in so that the transgressions would increase; but where sin increased, grace abounded all the more, so that, as sin reigned in death, even so grace would reign through righteousness to eternal life through Jesus Christ our Lord."

Grace - God's Relationship with Us

Grace defines God's relationship with us through Jesus. Paul stated in Romans 5:1-2, 8-10:

"Therefore, having been justified by faith, we have peace with God through our Lord Jesus Christ, through whom also we have obtained our introduction by faith into this grace in which we stand; and we exult in hope of the glory of God. ... But God demonstrated His own love toward us, in that while we were yet sinners, Christ died for us. Much more then, having now been justified by His blood, we shall be saved from the wrath of God through Him. For if while we were enemies we were reconciled to God through the death of His Son, much more, having been reconciled, we shall be saved by His life."

God has judged us to be innocent of sin. He has justified and redeemed us through the sacrificial death of Jesus and the shedding of His blood on a cross. This is God's action of grace extended to us through Jesus. We are then justified by our action of faith in Jesus in response to His grace. We secure our redemption by and reconciliation with God through our faith and trust in and obedience to Jesus.

Following are examples of how God's grace works in and through our life.

God enables us through His grace to enter a relationship with Him where He communicates with us through the Bible, and we communicate with Him through worship and prayer. God desires to fellowship with us. He walked daily with Adam and Eve in the Garden of Eden before they sinned and fellowship with Him was broken. God has reestablished His relationship with us through Jesus and the Holy Spirit. He communicates His commandments and life principles to us through His Word in the Bible. The Holy Spirit renews our mind as we study and internalize His Word. God listens and responds to us as we worship Him. Worship is our focused response to God's love that permeates everything we say and do in our life. It includes public and corporate adoration and praise and private devotions and prayer. Through corporate worship, we lift our praises, adoration and thanksgiving to God and acknowledge we are His. We talk to and bring our desires, concerns and needs to Him through prayer. God's word given to us in the Bible is His primary means of communicating with us. Prayer is our primary means of communicating with Him.

God enables us through His grace to accept ourself and be secure in our uniqueness. We discover God accepts us as we are when we enter a relationship with Him through Jesus. He loves us for the individual we are, not as we or others think we ought to be. This is the foundation of any real relationship with God and others. God's love and acceptance give us the ability to accept ourself. However, this may be difficult for those who have hurting and broken areas in their life. God will heal these areas when we give the Holy Spirit permission to enter, redeem and heal them. God wants to renew our mind and transform our heart, molding us into the person He has created us to be, even though He accepts us as we are. He accomplishes this through the Holy Spirit who opens our mind to understand and internalize God's word as we study the Bible and facilitates our spiritual growth.

God enables us through His grace to maintain a proper perspective on life during our good and bad times. God's grace extended through the Holy Spirit enable us to respond to good and bad life experiences with balance and purpose. We respond to afflictions and poverty with hope and to blessings and prosperity with humility. God wants us to give to and share with others from the blessings and prosperity He extends to us and to support and encourage them in their afflictions and poverty. God through the Holy Spirit comforts and supports us in our times of need, and He expects us to do the same for others in their times of need. Peter stated in 1 Peter 5:10:

> "And after you have suffered for a little while, the God of all grace, who called
> you to His eternal glory in Christ, will Himself perfect, confirm, strengthen
> and establish you."

God's grace gives our afflictions and poverty meaning and hop and our blessings and prosperity direction and purpose.

God equips us through His grace to do what He calls us to do. Jesus stated in John 15:4-5:

> "Abide in Me, and I in you. As the branch cannot bear fruit of itself unless it
> abides in the vine, so neither can you unless you abide in Me. I am the vine,
> you are the branches; he who abides in Me and I in him, he bears much fruit,
> for apart from Me you can do nothing."

Jesus through the Holy Spirit equips us to do what God calls us to do. He is clear in His statement that we can do nothing apart from Him. However, we can accomplish much through Him. Paul stated in 2 Corinthians 9:10-11:

> "Now He who supplies seed to the sower and bread for food will supply and
> multiply your seed for sowing and increase the harvest of your righteousness;
> you will be enriched in everything for all liberality, which through us is
> producing thanksgiving to God."

God will equip us for what He calls us to do, and He will multiply the harvest of our labor.

God works in us through His grace and our weaknesses. Paul stated in 2 Corinthians 12:9:

> "Concerning this I implored the Lord three times that it might leave me. And
> He has said to me, 'My grace is sufficient for you, for power is perfected in
> weakness.' Most gladly, therefore, I will rather boast abort my weakness, so
> that the power of Christ may dwell in me."

Jesus indicated His power is perfected in us through our weaknesses. God wants to be first in our life, and He wants us to trust Him to meet our needs. The Proverbs and Psalms teach:

> "Every word of God is tested; He is a shield to those who take refuge in Him."
> (Proverbs 30:5)

"The LORD is my strength and my shield; My heart trusts in Him, and I am helped; therefore my heart exults, and with my song I shall thank Him." (Psalms 28:7)

God knows we become proud when we succeed in life without Him. This pride makes us hostile toward and separates us from Him. Therefore, He chooses to work in us through our weaknesses. Humility develops when we trust God to meet our needs. He then becomes our shield and strength through Jesus and the Holy Spirit. Jesus stated in Matthew 19:26, "With people this is impossible, but with God all things are possible." Paul stated in Philippians 4:13, "I can do all things through Him who strengthens me."

God enables us through His grace to accept, develop and use our spiritual gifts. The Holy Spirit takes up residence in us when we receive God's grace through Jesus (John 14). Paul stated in 1 Corinthians 3:16, "Do you not know that you are a temple of God, and that the Spirit of God dwells in you?" He continued in Romans 12:6-8:

> "Since we have gifts that differ according to the grace given to us, each of us is to exercise them according to the proportion of his faith; if service, in his serving; or he who teaches, in his teaching; or he who exhorts, in his exhortation; he who gives, with liberality; he who leads, with diligence; he who shows mercy, with cheerfulness."

We have been given spiritual gifts that differ according to the grace God has given us. Our spiritual gifts are given to and developed in us by the Holy Spirit. Peter instructed in 1 Peter 4:10 -11:

> "As each one has received a special gift, employ it in serving one another as good stewards of the manifold grace of God. Whoever speaks, is to do so as one who is speaking the utterances of God; whoever serves is to do so as one who is serving by the strength which God supplies; so that in all things God may be glorified through Jesus Christ, to whom belongs the glory and dominion forever and ever. Amen."

We are to employ our spiritual gifts "as good stewards of the manifold grace of God" given to us. Spiritual gifts are discussed in more detail in Chapter 15 through 17.

God enables us through His grace to receive His assistance in our life. God wants us to surrender our life to Him, so He can transform us into the person He has created us to be. He wants us to surrender the broken and wounded areas in our life and the areas that are blighted by sin to Him, so He can cleanse and heal them and free us from the pain, suffering and bondage they create in our life. Jesus invited us in Matthew 11:28-30:

> "Come to Me, all who are weary and heavy-laden, and I will give you rest. Take My yoke upon you, and learn from Me, for I am gentle and humble in heart; and you shall find rest for your souls. For My yoke is easy, and My load is light."

Jesus stated He is "gentle and humble in heart;" His "yoke is easy;" and His "load is light." We will find rest for our soul when we, who are hurting, depressed, lonely, desperate, etc., yoke ourself to Jesus. He will come into and comfort, heal, strengthen and empower us. He will meet our needs. James stated in James 1:17:

> "Every good thing is given and every perfect gift is from above, coming down from the Father of lights, with whom there is no variation, or shifting shadow."

All good things and perfect gifts come from God through our faith in Jesus.

Types of Grace

God through grace:

- Calls us to repent and enter a relationship with Him through Jesus;
- Allows us to respond to His call to repent and accept the salvation He extends to us through Jesus; and
- Enters a relationship with us through Jesus and the Holy Spirit in which He empowers us to do good works and participate in ministries and service to others.

John Wesley identified these three phases of God's grace as prevenient grace, justifying grace and sanctifying grace.

Prevenient grace: John Wesley indicated God extends His love toward to call us to repentance and reconciliation in our unsaved state. Jesus stated in John 6:44-45:

"No one can come to Me unless the Father who sent Me draws him; and I will raise him up on the last day. It is written in the prophets, 'And they shall all be taught of God.' (Isaiah 54:13) Everyone who has heard and learned from the Father, comes to Me."

God shields and prevents us from entering greater sin through His prevenient grace. One of the inscrutable mysteries of God is why He shields and protects some and not others. God through the Holy Spirit touches our life in special and mysterious ways to call us to repentance through His prevenient grace.

Justifying grace: We experience God's justifying grace when we respond to the leading of the Holy Spirit to repent and enter a reconciled relationship with Him through Jesus. Paul stated in Romans 3:21-25:

> "But now apart from the Law the righteousness of God has been manifested being witnessed by the Law and the Prophets, even the righteousness of God through faith in Jesus Christ for all those who believe; for there is no distinction; for all have sinned and fall short of the glory of God, being justified as a gift by His grace through the redemption which is in Christ Jesus; whom God displayed publicly as a propitiation in His blood through faith."

We are justified by God's gift of grace and the redemption and reconciliation we receive from Him through our faith in Jesus. He judges us to be innocent of our sins because Jesus, who took our place on our cross, paid the required death penalty for them when He publicly shed His blood on His cross and died.

Sanctifying grace: We are set apart for a sacred purpose and religious use through God's grace. Paul stated in 1 Thessalonians 5:23:

> "Now may the God of peace Himself sanctify you entirely; and may your spirit and soul and body by preserved complete, without blame at the coming of our Lord Jesus Christ."

The Holy Spirit begins His process of setting us apart and preparing us for ministry and service to others after we enter a reconciled relationship with God through Jesus. Paul instructed us in Romans 12:2:

"And do not be conformed to this world, but be transformed by the renewing of your mind, so that you may prove what the will of God is, that which is good and acceptable and perfect "

God sanctifies us by transforming us into the person He has created us to be as our mind is renewed by the Holy Spirit. Peter indicated in 1 Peter 2:1-3 the Holy Spirit accomplishes this thorough:

"Therefore, putting aside all malice and all deceit and hypocrisy and envy and all slander, like newborn babies, long for the pure milk of the word, so that by it you may grow in respect to salvation, if you have tasted the kindness of the Lord."

Our mind is renewed as we study and internalize God's word in the Bible. Paul stated why God sanctifies us through His grace and our faith in Jesus in Ephesians 2:8-10:

"For by grace you have been saved through faith; and that not of yourselves, it is the gift of God; not as a result of works, so that no one may boast. For we are His workmanship, created in Christ Jesus for good works, which God prepared beforehand so that we would walk in them."

We are sanctified by God to accomplish the "good works, which [He] prepared beforehand so that we would walk in them.

Grace - Our Inheritance through Jesus

We have an inheritance that is imperishable and undefiled and that will not pass away through God's grace. Peter stated in 1 Peter 1:3-5:

"Blessed be the God and Father of our Lord Jesus Christ, who according to His great mercy has caused us to be born again to a living hope through the resurrection of Jesus Christ from the dead, to obtain an inheritance which is imperishable and undefiled and will not fade away, reserved in heaven for you, who are protected by the power of God through faith for a salvation ready to be revealed in the last time."

We are "protected by the power of God through faith" for an eternal salvation that will "be revealed to us in the last time," and we have an inheritance that is reserved for us in heaven. We must know to whom we are an heir to understand what our inheritance is. Paul stated in Romans 8:16-17:

> "The Spirit Himself bears witness with our spirit that we are children of God, and if children, heirs also, heirs of God and fellow heirs with Christ, if indeed we suffer with Him in order that we may also be glorified with Him."

We become children of God through our faith in Jesus. We become "heirs of God and fellow heirs with Christ as a result." Jesus stated in Matthew 25:34:

> "Then the King will say to those on His right, 'Come, you who are blessed of My Father, inherit the kingdom prepared for you from the foundation of the world."

Jesus is the King in this verse, and we are joint heirs with Him. We will "inherit the kingdom prepared for [us] from the foundation of the world" as joint heirs. This kingdom is the kingdom of heaven (Matthew 25:1). In the kingdom of heaven, our inheritance includes:

- Salvation (Hebrews 1:14),
- Eternal life (Mark 10:17),
- The covenants and promises of God given to us in the Scriptures (Hebrews 6:13-14), and
- The resurrection kingdom that will come into existence at the second coming of Jesus (Revelation 21:5-7).

FAITH

Faith - Our Relationship with God

Faith defines our relationship with God through Jesus. The Greek word for *faith* is *pistis*, which is translated as the power to induce to believe, the conviction or trust regarding the truth of something. We believe God exists, is the creator and ruler over all things, and is the provider and giver of salvation through Jesus when we have faith in Him. We believe Jesus is the Son of God through whom we are reconciled to and enter our relationship with God. Faith requires trust, and trust implies our willingness to follow the One in whom we have faith. We have faith in God when we:

- Believe He is who He says He is, has done what He claims He has done, and will do what He has promised to do;
- Believe He has redeemed and reconciled us to Himself through Jesus; and
- Yield ourself to His authority and obey Him. Paul stated in Romans 10:8-10:

> "But what does it say? 'The word is near you, in your mouth and in your heart' (Deuteronomy 30:14) - that is, the word of faith which we are preaching, that if you confess with your mouth Jesus as Lord, and believe in your heart that God raised Him from the dead, you will be saved; for with the heart a person believes, resulting in righteousness, and with the mouth he confesses, resulting in salvation."

The Holy Spirit initiates in us the desire and gives us ability to believe in and trust Jesus. We believe with our heart when we approach God through Jesus, resulting in righteousness, and confess with our month Jesus as Lord, securing our salvation.

Faith - Our Attitude toward God

Faith defines our attitude toward God. In Hebrews 11:1, the author states:

> "Now faith is the assurance of things hoped for, the conviction of things not seen."

Hebrews states *faith is*; it occurs in the present and is not needed for what has already occurred. Faith gives us hope for what we expect to receive in the future.

Two types of *things* are implied in Hebrews 11:1: *things hoped for* and *things not seen*. The Greek word for *things* is *pragma*, which means that which is or exists. The *things hoped for* are things that exist and can be perceived and experienced in the physical realm. Things *not seen* also exist. However, they exist in a realm we cannot perceive with our physical senses. In Hebrews 11:3, the author stated where the *things not seen* are from:

> "By faith we understand that the worlds were prepared by the word of God, so that what is seen was not made of things which were visible."

Paul further stated in Romans 4:17 God "calls into being that which does not exist." Therefore, the *things not seen* are from the spiritual realm of God. This implies the *things hoped for* are made from things that cannot be perceived with our physical senses and that come from the spiritual realm of God.

Faith gives us the ability to see beyond the physical realm where we live into the spiritual realm of God. Paul stated in 2 Corinthians 4:17-18, 5:7:

> "For the momentary light affliction is producing for us an eternal weight of glory far beyond all comparison, while we look not at the things which are seen, but at the things that are not seen; for the things that are seen are temporal, but the things that are not seen are eternal. For we walk by faith, not by sight."

We should never use our feelings, emotions and perceptions of life experiences to interpret how God is working in and through our life. Our relationship with Him through Jesus is not based on feelings, emotions and perceptions. It is secured by the covenant relationship we have with God through Jesus and undergirded by the solid foundation of His spiritual principles and laws presented in the Bible. Paul indicated things we perceive and events we experience are temporary; they will cease to exist.

God will replace them with things from His spiritual realm. We must look beyond the physical realm into God's spiritual realm with faith to understand how He desires to work in and through us.

Life becomes depressing when we focus only on adverse events in our life. We must look beyond and approach them with faith and hope God will give us *things not seen* that we need to respond to them. We walk by faith not by sight when we do this.

The writer of Hebrews stated, "faith is the assurance of *things hoped for.*" The Greek word for *assurance* is *hupostatis*, which means confidence, firm trust. This gives us insight into the nature of hope. There is no confidence in hope without faith. Hope has no reality in itself; it is only real when faith is added to it. We hope for things when we do not have them with the expectation we will receive them. Faith gives reality to what we hope to receive.

The writer of Hebrews continued, "[faith is] the conviction of things not seen." The Greek word for *conviction* is *elegchose*, which means evidence, that by which invisible things are proven. Faith then is the evidence of the existence of *things not seen* until we physically receive them. We believe the things we expect to receive from God will come from things that exist in His spiritual realm when we walk by faith.

Faith - It Comes from God's Word

Faith develops as we grow in our understand of and act on God's word in the Bible. Paul stated in Romans 10:17, "So faith comes from hearing, and hearing from the word of Christ." He continued in 2 Timothy 3:14-15:

> "You, however, continue in the things you have learned and become convinced of, knowing from whom you have learned them; and that from childhood you have known the sacred writings which are able to give you the wisdom that leads to salvation through faith which is in Christ Jesus."

Our faith formation begins by reading and studying the Bible. It continues as we hear God's word preached and taught and witness it work with power in the lives of those who have internalized and acted on it. For our faith to develop and grow we must:

- Read and study the Bible. The Bible is where we obtain our knowledge and understanding of our covenant relationship with God through Jesus, the promises He has given us, and how we can act on them. It is where we learn about God's spiritual life principles and how He wants us to live by them.

- Hear the words of God in the Bible preached and taught and witness how they have worked and are working with power in the lives of those who have read, heard and acted on them.

- Internalize God's words in the Bible and act on them to discover they are true and will work for, in and through us with power.

Paul stated in Romans 10:17 faith proceeds from the words of Christ. Faith develops in us the ability to trust and obey God. We can substitute the *word of Christ* for the word *faith* in Hebrews 11:1:

> "[The word of Christ] is the assurance of things hoped for, the conviction of things not seen."

The words Jesus spoke produce *faith* that gives *hope* substance in our life. Faith develops in us as we witness Jesus' words work in the lives of others and experience them work in our life. This gives us confidence the things not seen from the spiritual realm of God will be given to us as needed.

Faith - It Comes by Focusing on Jesus

In Hebrews 12:1-2, the author stated:

> "Therefore, since we have so great a cloud of witnesses surrounding us, let us also lay aside every encumbrance and the sin which so easily entangles us, and let us run with endurance the race that is before us, fixing our eyes on Jesus, the author and perfecter of faith, who for the joy set before Him endured the cross, despising the shame, and has sat down at the right hand of the throne of God."

Jesus is the author and perfecter of our faith. He must be the object of our faith. Matthew gives us an understanding of what it means to focus on Jesus as the object of our faith in Matthew 14:22-31:

> "And immediately [Jesus] made the disciples get into the boat, and go ahead of Him to the other side, while He sent the multitudes away. And after He had sent the multitudes away, He went up to the mountain by Himself to pray; and when it was evening, He was there alone. But the boat was already many stadia away from the land, battered by the waves; for the wind was contrary. And in the fourth watch of the night He came to them, walking on the sea. And when the disciples saw Him walking on the sea, they were frightened, saying, 'It is a ghost!' And they cried out for fear. But immediately Jesus spoke to them, saying, 'Take courage, it is I; do not be afraid.' And Peter answered Him and said, 'Lord, if it is You, command me to come to You on the water.' And He said, 'Come!' And Peter got out of the boat, and walked on the water and came toward Jesus. But seeing the wind, he became afraid, and beginning to sink, he cried out, saying, 'Lord, save me!' And immediately Jesus stretched out His hand and took hold of him, and said to him, 'O you of little faith, why did you doubt?'"

Peter's actions were based on his faith in Jesus. They demonstrated two types of faith in this relationship: initial faith and sustaining faith. Peter's initial faith was seen in his getting out of the boat and walking on the water toward Jesus. He took his eyes off Him as he approached Jesus, looked at the high waves, and became afraid. His initial faith faded, and he began to sink. Peter did not exercise sustaining faith even though he demonstrated initial faith. However, Jesus reached out His hand and took hold of Peter when he cried out to Jesus to save him.

This story indicates we must focus on Jesus as the author of our faith as it develops and grows. Peter could get out of the boat and walk on the water toward Jesus because he trusted and had faith in Him. This demonstrated initial faith. We begin new life experiences with Jesus because we initially have faith in and trust Him. We have initial faith in Jesus. However, we soon discover our new experiences with Him contain difficult and troubled times. Like Peter, we too may take our eyes off Jesus during these times and begin to falter and have difficulty exercising sustaining faith to carry us through these times. Sustaining faith develops as we read and study the Bible, hear God's word and words of Jesus preached and taught, and discover for ourself God and Jesus can be trusted to sustain us through these times. We can reach out to Jesus for help when our initial faith begins to falter. He will reach out to take hold of us as He did with Peter and gently pull us toward Him. Jesus will walk with us as we develop sustaining faith through both good and troubled times.

THE RELATION BETWEEN GRACE, FAITH AND GOOD WORKS

Grace and faith are the foundation of our relationship with God through Jesus. God extends His redemption and reconciliation to us through His grace in this relationship. He requires us to enter the good works He calls us to enter through our faith in Jesus in this relationship. Good works are the ministries and service to others God calls us to enter in Jesus' name.

Many who understand the significance of grace and faith in our relationship with God through Jesus do not understand the significance of good works in this relationship. Two scripture verses help us understand the relation between grace, faith and good works. The first is Ephesians 2:8-10, where Paul stated:

> "For by grace you have been saved through faith and that not of yourselves. It is the gift of God; not because of works, so that no one may boast. For we are His workmanship, created in Christ Jesus for good works, which God prepared beforehand so that we would walk in them."

The second is James 2:14-26 where James stated:

> "What use is it my brethren, if a man says he has faith, but he has no works? Can that faith save him? If a brother or sister is without clothing and in need of daily food, and one of you says to them, 'Go in peace, be warmed and be filled,' and yet you do not give them what is necessary for their body, what use is that? Even so faith, if it has no works, is dead, being by itself. But someone may well say, 'You have faith, and I have works; show me your faith without works, and I will show you my faith by my works.' You believe that

God is one. You do well; the demons also believe, and shudder. But are you willing to recognize, you foolish fellow, that faith without works is useless? Was not Abraham our father justified by works, when he offered up Isaac his son on the altar? You see that a man is justified by works, and not by faith alone. And in the same way was not Rahab the harlot also justified by works, when she received the messengers and sent them out by another way? For just as the body without the spirit is dead, so also faith without works is dead."

There are two types of works referred to in these scripture verses. The first type of words are works referred to in Ephesians 2:8 we use to justify ourself to God. Paul indicated these works will never justify us to God. The second type of works referred to in Ephesians 2:10 are "good works, which God prepared beforehand so that we would walk in them." It is reasonable to belief the works referred to in James 2:17-26 are the same as the good works referred to in Ephesians 2:10.

Paul indicated in Ephesians 2:8 we can only be justified by God's grace through our faith in Jesus. James and Paul taught our faith in Jesus must be confirmed by our love for, trust in and obedience to Him. Our faith must motivate us to perform the good works God has prepared beforehand for us to perform. James stated our faith becomes useless and dies when we do not enter these good works. Our relationship with God is impaired when we do not live a life of faith and trust in and obedience to Jesus and our faith does not motivate us to enter the good works the Holy Spirit calls us to enter.

CHAPTER 12
SPIRITUAL GROWTH
RENEWAL OF OUR MIND AND SPIRITUAL GROWTH

"Therefore, putting aside all malice and all guilt and hypocrisy and envy and all slander, like newborn babes, long for the pure milk of the word, that by it you may grow in respect to salvation, if you have tasted the kindness of the Lord." (1 Peter 2:1-3)

"And I, brethren, could not speak to you as to spiritual men, but as to men of flesh, as to babes in Christ. I gave you milk to drink, not solid food; for you were not yet able to receive it. Indeed, even now you are not yet able, for you are still fleshly. For since there is jealousy and strife among you, are you not fleshly, and are you not walking like mere men?" (1 Corinthians 3:1-3)

"For though by this time you ought to be teachers, you have need again for someone to teach you the elementary principles of the oracles of God, and you have come to need milk and not solid food. For everyone who partakes only of milk is not accustomed to the word of righteousness, for he is a babe. But solid food is for the mature, who because of practice have their senses trained to discern good and evil." (Hebrews 5:12-14)

"As a result, we are no longer to be children, tossed here and there by waves, and carried about by every wind of doctrine, by the trickery of men, by craftiness in deceitful scheming; but speaking the truth in love, we are to grow up in all aspects into Him, who is the head, even Christ, from whom the whole body, being fitted and held together by that which every joint supplies, according to the proper working of each individual part, causes the growth of the body for the building up of itself in love." (Ephesians 4:14-16)

RENEWAL OF OUR MIND

Paul urged us in Romans 12:1-2:

> "I urge you therefore, brethren, by the mercies of God, to present your bodies a living and holy sacrifice, acceptable to God, which is your spiritual service of worship. And do not be conformed to this world, but be transformed by the renewing of your mind, that you may prove what the will of God is, that which is good and acceptable and perfect."

He continued in 2 Corinthians 4:16:

> "Therefore, we do not lose heart, but though our outer man is decaying, yet our inner man is being renewed day by day."

Cultural norms and customs that conflict with God's word should not define who we are. We must permit the Holy Spirit to transform *our inner man* through the transformation of our heart by the renewing of our mind. Our spirit is made alive by the Holy Spirit when we are spiritually reborn. Our mind is then energized, and we receive knowledge from the Holy Spirit essential for our spiritual growth. This knowledge is hidden from us when we are spiritually dead. It is revealed to us when we study the Bible and enter mentoring and discipling relationships with other Christians. Our mind is renewed, and the Holy Spirit facilitates the transformation of our heart as we internalize this knowledge, recreating us into a new person who trusts and has faith in and is obedient to Jesus.

We renew our mind by disciplined Bible study through which we replace what the world teaches us with what God reveals to us in the Bible. The results of our study are enhanced as the Holy Spirit opens our mind to receive, understand and internalize the knowledge we obtain from the Bible. The Holy Spirit then facilitates the transformation of our heart as we assimilate this knowledge.

SPIRITUAL GROWTH

We experience spiritual growth as our mind is renewed and our heart is transformed. Negative personality traits take on a more positive nature as we spiritually grow and incorporate God's word in the Bible into our life. Our personality begins to exhibit the positive traits desired by God as we become a new person through Jesus.

Spiritual growth that results from a renewed mind and transformed heart is intentional. It requires a dedication of time and effort, a willingness to set aside selfish self-interests, and a commitment to trust and obey God. We must study and internalize God's word in the Bible, worship God, and engage in fellowship with other Christians to grow spiritually and mature. In addition, we must participate in Christian ministry and service to others. Paul instructed us to do all of these under the supervision and authority of a local Christian church.

Rick Warren in his book, *The Purpose Driven Church* (1995), presented six basic principles associated with spiritual growth.

Spiritual growth is intentional. It requires commitment and effort. People grow from spiritual infancy to spiritual adulthood because they want to and are willing to put in the time and effort necessary to facilitate their spiritual growth.

Spiritual growth can be experienced by everyone. Spiritual growth is not something reserved for a select few. Any Christian can grow from spiritual infancy to spiritual adulthood when they are willing to develop habits necessary to facilitate their spiritual growth.

Spiritual growth is a process that takes time. Spiritual growth is a process that involves study, life experiences, discipleship and on-the-job training. Spiritual growth occurs best in an environment that supports and encourages it. This environment exists in fellowship with other Christians in a local Christian church.

Spiritual maturity is demonstrated more by behavior than by beliefs. Spiritual maturity is displayed by Christian conduct and Christlike character. Increased biblical knowledge alone is not sufficient to develop spiritual maturity. Growth in all areas of Christian knowledge, perspectives, convictions, life skills and character are essential for the development of spiritual maturity.

Christians need relationships to grow spiritually and develop spiritual maturity. We grow through relationships with parents, family members, friends, teachers, business associates, etc. in other areas of our life. We grow spiritually and develop spiritual maturity through relationships with other Christians.

It takes a variety of spiritual experiences with God to grow spiritually and develop spiritual maturity. Spiritual growth and maturity develop through our emotional, experiential and relational experiences with God through Jesus. Genuine spiritual growth and maturity develops when we:

- Have a heart that worships and praises God;

- Build and enjoy relationships with other Christians;

- Use our talents and spiritual gifts in ministries and service to others; and

- Share our faith with Christians and non-Christians.

We spiritual mature along with our spiritual growth as we enter and perform the "good works, which God prepared beforehand so that we would walk in them" (Ephesians 2:10). This enhances our ability to apply what we learn through the renewing of our mind by the Holy Spirit as we study and internalize God's word in the Bible. Spiritual growth without the corresponding development of spiritual maturity often produces Christians with judgmental attitudes and spiritual pride.

Like newborn babies as infants in Christ we are required to study God's word in the Bible after we enter our relationship with Him through Jesus. Peter stated in 1 Peter 2:1-3:

> "Therefore, putting aside all malice and all deceit and hypocrisy and envy and all slander, like newborn babies, long for the pure milk of the word, so that by it you may grow in respect to salvation, if you have tasted the kindness of the Lord."

Our spiritual growth begins with our feeding on the on "the pure milk of the word" of God by studying the Bible. Paul emphasized this in 1 Corinthians 3:1-3:

> "And I, brethren, could not speak to you as to spiritual men, but as to men of flesh, as to infants in Christ. I gave you milk to drink, not solid food; for you were not yet able to receive it. Indeed, even now you are not yet able, for you are still fleshy."

We grow to spiritual maturity by internalizing "the elementary principles of the oracles of God" when we feed on "the pure milk of the word" as stated in Hebrews 5:11-13:

> "Concerning [Christ] we have much to say, and it is hard to explain, since you have become dull of hearing. For though by this time you ought to be teachers, you have need again for someone to teach you the elementary principles of the oracles of God, and you have come to need milk and not solid food. For everyone who partakes only of milk is not accustomed to the word of righteousness, for he is an infant. But solid food is for the mature, who because of practice have their senses trained to discern good and evil."

Solid food from the Bible is for the spiritually mature who, "because of practice have their senses trained to discern good and evil." It equips them to engage in the good works God has prepared for them.

God requires us to spiritually grow and mature when we enter our relationship with Him through Jesus. We are to study, internalize and assimilate the solid food in the Bible. Spiritual growth, like physical and emotional growth, progresses through the four stages of infancy, childhood, adolescence and adulthood. The characteristics of each stage can be summarized with a two-word phrase: infancy - *feed me*, childhood - *teach me*, adolescence - *guide me*, and adulthood - *use me*.

Spiritual Infancy: We have little knowledge of "the elementary principles of the oracles of God" presented in the Bible during spiritual infancy. Therefore, God does not expect us to have this knowledge during spiritual infancy nor does He hold us accountable for our disobedience to Him and Jesus because we lack this knowledge. The development of our understanding of the Bible and our spiritual growth is influenced by the knowledge and integrity of Christians with whom we fellowship as spiritual infants. Therefore, we must be in an environment where we can be fed the pure milk of God's word and be protected from influences that will draw us away from God and Jesus as we begin our spiritual growth. This environment is present in a Christian church where we are taught God's unaltered word from the Bible and hear His word preached from the pulpit.

Spiritual Childhood: We enter spiritual childhood as we continue to feed on the pure milk of God's word in the Bible and begin to incorporate its precepts into our life. We grow in our knowledge and understanding of "the elementary principles of the oracles of God" during spiritual childhood. We develop spiritual perspectives and life skills as we study the Bible and observe how spiritually mature Christians have incorporate biblical precepts into their lives. We often do not develop the spiritual maturity necessary to engage in the good works God has prepared for us even though we grow spiritually during spiritual childhood.

Spiritual Adolescence: We enter spiritual adolescence as our spiritual growth continues. This is often a difficult, troubled and rebellious time during our spiritual growth. We discover our desires and lifestyle conflict with our knowledge of God's word, and we must make changes in our life as we move closer to God through Jesus. These changes are often difficult to make and require we enter mentoring relationships with mature Christians we trust and with whom we can share sensitive and personal life issues. Our knowledge of God's word and related spiritual perspectives become convictions that form our character as we work through and make these life changes. We discover God's word is true and God is faithful to honor His word. We begin to develop spiritual maturity necessary to equip us for the good works God has prepared for us as we progress through spiritual adolescence.

Spiritual Adulthood: We enter spiritual adulthood as we spiritually grow and develop spiritual maturity. These are lifelong processes that progress as we feed on and digest the solid food of God's word in the Bible. We become spiritual adults as we through "practice have [our] senses trained to discern good and evil." We are then equipped to engage in the good works God has prepared for us.

SPIRITUAL GROWTH THROUGH BIBLE STUDY

Rick Warren indicated there are five areas of development that are associated with spiritual growth (*The Purpose Driven Church*, 1995): biblical knowledge; Christian perspectives, life skills, convictions and Christlike character. All of these are developed in the context of our relationships with other mature Christians in a local Christian church. The importance of biblical knowledge will be discussed in this and the following section.

Spiritual growth begins with Bible study. Bible study is one of God's primary means of renewing our minds. Paul stated in Colossians 3:9-10:

> "Do not lie to one another, since you laid aside the old self with its evil practices, and having put on the new self who is being renewed to a true knowledge according to the image of the One who created him."

Studying is one of the major methods of acquiring knowledge. The true knowledge referred to by Paul is from God, and we obtain His knowledge from the Bible. The Bible is God's primary means of communicating with us. *God will not reveal any information (either through normal or supernatural means) to us that is different from or contradicts what He has already revealed in the Bible.*

A major problem associated with Christianity today is biblical illiteracy. Many Christians are deprived of the blessings God desires to give them, and they often live in bondage to anxieties and fears because they do not know God's spiritual life principles in the Bible. Many individuals become snared by cults or are seduced by false or distorted doctrines in the Christian church because they are biblically illiterate. Jesus stated in John 8:32 "and you will know the truth, and the truth will make you free." We must study, learn and understand the spiritual life principles contained in the Bible when we want to avoid being deceived by false or distorted doctrines and receive the blessings God desires to give us

Richard Foster in his book, *Celebration of Discipline* (1988), indicated there are four steps to effective Bible study: repetition, concentration, comprehension and reflection.

Repetition: Repetition even without understanding causes our mind to move in specific directions that form habits. Repetition is essential for memorization. Our mind becomes trained by being repeatedly exposed to specific stimuli. The habits that are formed are positive and uplifting when the stimuli embody love, caring, compassion, etc. They are negative and destructive when the stimuli embody selfishness, lust, pride, etc. Repetition is essential for us to learn and memorize Bible passages.

Concentration: Concentration is essential for effective learning. Learning is enhanced when we concentrate on what we study. Concentration focuses our mind on what we study. Therefore, we must be in a quiet environment free of distractions to effectively concentrate and focus our mind on materials we study.

Comprehension: Comprehension occurs when we focus and center on what we study. Comprehension associated with God's word in the Bible occurs when the Holy Spirit open our mind to understand what we study in the Bible. Repetition and concentration are learning habits we can develop independent of the Holy Spirit. However, we must rely on the Holy Spirit to open our mind to receive and comprehend God's word when we study the Bible.

Reflection: Reflection helps us internalize, add reality to, and determine the significance of what we have studied and learned. It enables us to determine how what we have studied and learned applies to us. The Holy Spirit through reflection enables us to comprehend how the spiritual life principles in the Bible apply to our life.

Following are suggestions for studying the Bible:

- Read the Bible as part of personal devotions for enjoyment. Read the complete Bible in a systematic manner to obtain a general overview of its contents. Begin with the New Testament and then read the Old Testament. The New Testament is the fulfillment of the Old Testament. However, it is usually easier to start with reading the New Testament and then the Old Testament when reading the Bible for the first time.

- Read the Bible again for comprehension. This can be accomplished by selecting specific books of the Bible for in-depth study. Bible apps and the Internet can be used to conduct topical studies associated with Bible passages.

- Use Bible commentaries and books written by recognized authorities to obtain a better understanding of specific books or topics being studied.

- Get involved in a Bible study through a local Christian church or fellowship group. This can be a study associated with specific books in the Bible or a study of the whole Bible prepared by one of the major church denominations or by recognized nondenominational sources.

- Enter a mentoring or discipling relationship with a mature Christian you trust. A one-on-one relationship with an individual who can help you relate biblical principles to personal life issues is essential for spiritual growth. Men should be mentored or discipled by men, and women should be mentored or discipled by women.

- Establish a plan as to how you will accomplish an in-depth study of the Bible. Seek assistance from your mentor or discipling partner when necessary.

- In-depth study requires discipline. Select the scripture topic, book of the Bible, scripture verses, etc. you want to study. Select a specific time to study each day and select a place with no distractions or interruptions. Make sure reference materials, such as different Bible translations, Bible commentaries, Bible concordances and lexicons, and other related books are accessible.

- Learn how to outline sections of the Bible and to keep a journal of your impressions, thoughts and interpretations associated with the material you study. Do not be afraid to mark up your Bible by underlining meaningful verses and writing notes in the margins of your Bible. Memorize important and meaningful Bible verses. These are essential for increasing your ability to comprehend what you read and study and to reflect on the application and significance of what you study to your life.

- In addition to formal Bible studies and mentoring relationships in which you may be involved, enter dialogue with others who may be struggling to understand the Bible. Enter dialogue with individuals who have a mature understanding of the Bible. These encounters are important in testing and expanding your understanding of the Bible and specific biblical principles.

Bible study requires focus, concentration and dedication. It involves study of Bible commentaries and other books written by authors that give in-depth information relative to spiritual principles contained in the Bible. We must enter discipling relationships with nature Christians to resolve issues associated with spiritual principles we do not fully understand.

REASONS FOR BIBLE STUDY

Why is Bible study important? Howard and William Hendricks in their book, *Living by the Book* (1991), indicated Bible study is essential for us to spiritual grow and mature and to be spiritually effective in our life. They indicated there are three words that address the truth in 1 Peter 2.1-3 on page 167: attitude, appetite and aim.

Attitude: Our attitude toward Bible study must be to continually feed on the pure milk of the word to sustain our spiritual life.

Appetite: We must develop an appetite for the pure milk of the word to spiritually grow and mature through disciplined Bible study.

Aim: We must understand the aim of feeding on the milk of the word through Bible study is to grow in respect to salvation and developing a greater awareness of the presence of God in our life as He reveals Himself to us in His word.

Hebrews 5:11-14 implies a process occurs for many of us when we study the Bible. We feed on the pure milk of the word in the Bible through Bible study. We begin to spiritually grow and apply what we have studied in and learned from the Bible to our life, and our senses to discern good and evil begin to develop. However, many of us develop a learning disability at this point in our spiritual growth; we become dull of hearing and slow to learn. Our spiritual growth slows to a point where we are unable to feed on the solid food of the word of righteousness. We must then have someone explain to us again "the elementary principles of the oracles of God."

We most likely have strayed from studying the Bible when this occurs. Howard and William Hendricks indicated there are six reasons why people stray from disciplined Bible study (*Living by the Book*, 1991):

- We believe the Bible is archaic and out-of-date. We believe it neither applies nor works for us today; it lacks relevance to real life issues.

- We do not know how to effectively study the Bible. We become frustrated when we attempt to read and understand the Bible because we lack the basic skills to study it.

- We feel we are just laypersons. We are not seminary graduates. Therefore, we cannot be expected to understand the Bible; it is a book to be read and studied only by professionals.

- We do not have time. Our lives are so cluttered with other activities we do not have the time or energy to study the Bible. Studying the Bible has a low priority in our lives.

- We have our doubts about the accuracy of the Bible. We question its credibility, reliability and authority. We do not believe we can ever really determine or understand its meaning.

- We just cannot seem to make Bible study interesting. It is difficult to get excited about developing spiritual insights into God's word. Bible study is perceived as being boring and not worth our attention.

We must begin our spiritual growth with disciplined Bible study. Paul stated in 2 Timothy 3:16-17:

> "All Scripture is inspired by God and profitable for teaching, for reproof, for correction, for training in righteousness; that the man [and woman] of God may be adequate, equipped for every good work."

The whole Bible is inspired by God, and it is essential "for teaching, for reproof, for correction, for training in righteousness." The Bible teaches and reveals to us the spiritual principles of God as He wants them revealed. These are essential for us to properly structure our thinking in relation to spiritual matters and to ensure we correctly understand spiritual truths. The Bible rebukes us when we go astray and sin. It corrects us when we process spiritual information incorrectly and we receive false and misleading spiritual information. The Bible trains us in areas of righteous living and enables us to conform to God's will for our life. The Bible gives us positive guidelines on how to properly live life when it convicts, rebukes and corrects us for sin in our life. These functions of the Bible adequately equip us to engage in the good works to which God calls us.

Paul indicated in 1 Timothy 4:12-16:

> "Let no one look down on your youthfulness, but rather in speech, conduct, love, faith and purity, show yourself an example of those who believe. Until I come, give attention to the public reading of Scripture, to exhortation and teaching. Do not neglect the spiritual gift within you, which was bestowed upon you through prophetic utterance with the laying on of hands by the presbytery. Take pains with these things; be absorbed in them, so that your progress may be evident to all. Pay close attention to yourself and to your teaching; persevere in these things; for as you do this you will ensure salvation both for yourself and for those who hear you."

Paul continued in Ephesians 4:14-16:

> "As a result, we are no longer to be children, tossed here and there by waves, and carried about by every wind of doctrine, by the trickery of men, by craftiness in deceitful scheming; but speaking the truth in love, we are to grow up in all aspects into Him, who is the head, even Christ, from whom the whole body, being fitted and held together by that which every joint supplies, according to the proper working of each individual part, causes the growth of the body for the building up of itself in love."

We are instructed to publicly read, exhort and teach God's word in the Bible and to publicly display our spiritual growth to others. Why? God through Jesus and the Holy Spirit becomes our anchor in a world that opposes and wants to separate us from Him. We move closer to God as we spiritually grow and mature through assimilating and applying His word in the Bible to our life. God reveals Himself to us and presents His commandments, spiritual life principles and doctrines that govern our life in the Bible. He wants us to introduce Him to and share this information with others in return. We develop into spiritual adults as we publicly share His word in the Bible with others. God builds us up in His love as we read, exhort and teach His Word to others and equips local churches through us to engage in His good works.

BIBLE STUDY ALONE IS NOT ENOUGH

Bible study alone will not facilitate the development of our spiritual maturity. We must combine our knowledge of God's word in the Bible with Christian perspectives, life skills and convictions and Christlike character to develop into spiritually mature spiritual adults (*The Purpose Driven Church*, 1995). These characteristics develop in an environment with other Christians in a local Christian church. Knowledge of the Bible without the corresponding development of these characteristics often produces spiritual pride.

Christian Perspectives: Perspectives are our understanding of things because we see them from a larger frame of reference. Christian perspectives help us to see how God's word is interrelated with our life. The words understanding, wisdom and discernment are associated with Christian perspectives in the Bible. Christian perspectives answer the why questions associated with life. Following are four benefits of learning to see life issues from God's perspective:

- Christian perspectives cause us to love God more. The better we understand God's word, the more we love Him and want to fellowship with, praise and worship Him.

- Christian perspectives help us to resist temptation. They help us to realize long-term consequences of sin outweigh any short-term pleasure sin may provide us. We often follow our inclinations to disobey God's commandments and ignore His spiritual life principles when we lack Christian perspectives.

- Christian perspectives help us to properly handle trials. They help us to see God working in our life through our life experiences. This includes both good and bad experiences.

- Christian perspectives protect us from error. They help us see our life through God's eyes. They give our life the solid foundation of the absolute truths of God's word in the Bible.

We must grow in our understanding of God's perspectives as they relate to work, money, pleasure, suffering, good and evil, relationships, etc. as we grow to spiritual adults.

Christian Skills: Skills are abilities to do things with ease and accuracy. Christian skills are the *how-to-do* steps associated with spiritual growth. They represent our ability to transfer knowledge of biblical principles learned through Bible studies to practical applications associated with living and ministry. Christian skills can never be learned in isolation. They can only be learned through relationships with other Christians. They are most often learned as we receive on-the-job training from other Christians when we participate in service and ministry to others through our local church.

Christian Convictions: Convictions are strong beliefs related to our values, commitments and motivations. They are beliefs we are willing to die for. Christian convictions develop from our knowledge of God's word in the Bible, our perspectives of why God's word applies to our life, and our skills that enable us to apply God's word to our life. They motivate us to do what we must do to spiritual grow and lead us to make the commitments of time and effort necessary for our spiritual growth. According to Rick Warren (*The Purpose Driven Church*, 1995), knowing what to do (knowledge), why to do it (perspective), and how to do it (skill) are all worthless when we lack the conviction to motivate us to do it. We will never reach the level of commitment necessary for us to be an effective witness for Jesus to others when we lack Christian convictions. Christian convictions usually evolve through our relationships with other Christians even though they can be taught in sermons, classes, seminars etc. They are contagious. We develop Christian convictions by being around others who already have them. They develop as we witness God's word in the Bible work with power in the lives of other Christians and then experience it work with power in our life.

Christlike Character: The development of Christlike character is the goal of spiritual growth. The development of Christlike character is our most important task because it is the only thing we can take with us after death into eternity. Christlike character develops through life experiences. It develops as we allow the Holy Spirit to enter the core area of our life to unite our biblical knowledge with our Christian perspectives, life skills and convictions in a manner that transforms us into the person God desires us to be.

IMPORTANCE AND CHARACTERISTICS OF CHRISTIAN FELLOWSHIP

God does not want us to remain alone or isolated when we enter our relationship with Him through Jesus. He wants us to engage in fellowship with other Christians through a local Christian church. Fellowship with other Christians is essential to:

- Increase our knowledge of God's word in the Bible and grow in our relationship with God through Jesus and the Holy Spirit;
- Provide a protective, nurturing and caring environment where we can spiritually grow and mature;
- Provide mentoring and discipling relationships with mature Christians in which we can develop our and aid others to develop their Christian perspectives, life skills and convictions and Christlike character; and
- Provide an environment in and through which we can engage in the good works God has prepared for us.

Paul instructed us in Colossians 3:12-17:

> "And so, as those who have been chosen of God, holy and beloved, put on a heart of compassion, kindness, humility, gentleness and patience; bearing with one another, and forgiving each other, whoever has a complaint against anyone; just as the Lord forgave you, so also should you. And beyond all these things put on love, which is the perfect bond of unity. And let the peace of Christ rule in your hearts, to which indeed you were called in one body; and be thankful. Let the word of Christ richly dwell within you, with all wisdom teaching and admonishing one another with psalms and hymns and spiritual songs, singing with thankfulness in your hearts to God. And whatever you do in word or deed, do all in the name of the Lord Jesus, giving thanks through Him to God the Father."

Christen fellowship is essential for us to spiritually grow in our relationship with God through Jesus. It is to be characterized by:

- Compassion, kindness, humility, gentleness and patience while bearing with and forgiving one anther;
- Love which is the perfect bond of unity and the peace of Christ which units us in one body; and
- Teaching one another the words of Jesus and admonishing one another with psalms, hymns and spiritual songs with thankfulness in our hearts to God.

We are to do these in the name of the Jesus, giving thanks through Him to God the Father. Paul also instructed us in 1 Thessalonians 5:12-14:

> "But we request of you, brethren, that you appreciate those who diligently labor among you, and have charge over you in the Lord and give you instruction, and that you esteem them very highly in love because of their work. Live in peace with one another. And we urge you, brethren, admonish the unruly, encourage the fainthearted, help the weak, be patient with all men."

We are to within our fellowship:

- Appreciate and honor those who are called by God to work among us and be obedient to those who have authority over and teach us God's word in the Bible; and
- Live in peace with one another, admonish the unruly, encourage the fainthearted, help the weak and be patient with all men.

The fellowship described by Paul in Colossians and 1 Thessalonians will provides a nurturing and protective environment where we can spiritually grow and mature and be trained to engage in the good works God has prepared for us.

IMPORTANCE OF OBEDIENCE TO JESUS IN OUR SPIRITUAL GROWTH

God expects us to trust, honor and obey Jesus as we spiritually grow and mature. The Psalms and Proverbs describe the benefits of our trusting, honoring and obeying Him. Psalm 91 states:

"He who dwells in the shelter of the Most High will abide in the shadow of the Almighty. I will say to the LORD, 'My refuge and my fortress, My God, in whom I trust!' For it is He who delivers you from the snare of the trapper, and from the deadly pestilence. He will cover you with His pinions, and under His wings you may seek refuge; His faithfulness is a shield and bulwark."

"You will not be afraid of the terror by night or of the arrow that flies by day; of the pestilence that stalks in darkness, or of the destruction that lays waste at noon. A thousand may fall at your side, and ten thousand at your right hand; but it shall not approach you. You will only look on with your eyes and see the recompense of the wicked. For you have made the LORD, my refuge, even the Most High, your dwelling place. No evil will befall you, nor will any plague come near your tent."

"For He will give His angels charge concerning you, to guard you in all your ways. They will bear you up in their hands, lest you strike your foot against a stone. You will tread upon the lion and cobra, the young lion and the serpent you will trample down."

"Because he has loved Me, therefore I will deliver him; I will set him securely on high, because he has known My name. He will call upon Me, and I will answer him; I will be with him in trouble; I will rescue him, and honor him. With a long life I will satisfy him, and let him behold My salvation."

The Psalmist instructed us to make God our refuge and fortress and to trust and draw our strength from Him in times of adversity. God does not guarantee we will never experience adversities in our life. However, He promises to give us the ability and strength to persevere through and overcome our adversities when we take refuge in Him through Jesus and the Holy Spirit. He will walk with and guide us through our adversities. Knowing, claiming and resting on God's promises is our shield in times of trouble and temptation. He will give His angels charge over us during these times, and they will lift us up and guard us. God will:

- Deliver us from evil when we acknowledge, love and honor Him;
- Lift us up and rescue us in times of adversity;
- Honor us; and
- Let us behold His salvation and give us a long life when we seek, trust and obey Him.

Proverbs 3:1-12 states:

> "My son do not forget my teaching, but let your heart keep my commandments; for length of days and years of life, and peace they will add to you. Do not let kindness and truth leave you; bind them around your neck, write them on the tablet of your heart. So you will find favor and good repute in the sight of God and man. Trust in the LORD with all your heart, and do not lean on your own understanding. In all your ways acknowledge Him, and He will make your paths straight. Do not be wise in your own eyes; fear the LORD and turn away from evil. It will be healing to your body, and refreshment to your bones. Honor the LORD from your wealth, and from the first of all your produce; so your barns will be filled with plenty, and your vats will overflow with new wine. My son, do not reject the discipline of the LORD or loathe His reproof, for whom the LORD loves He reproves, even as a father, the son in whom he delights."

God will make our paths straight and exalt us when we acknowledge, trust and depend on Him. He promises healing and refreshment for our bodies when we:

- Turn away from evil,
- Honor Him, and
- Do not trust in our own knowledge but trust His wisdom.

God assures us of prosperity when we honor and give Him the first fruits of all our labors.

God instructs us to obey Him, not forget His teachings, keep His commandments, and not let truth to depart from us in Proverbs 3. He promises "the length of days and years of our lives and peace will be added to" us when we incorporate His teachings into our life and obey Him. God wants us to prosper, experience peace and joy, be healthy, and have our days be long. However, we must obey, trust and have faith in Him to receive these blessings. We often believe God is unfaithful when we find ourself living in poverty; not experiencing peace, joy and good health; and not receiving God's blessings. God is faithful to keep His promises, and He wants us to receive the blessings He desires to give us. However, we often do not receive God's blessings because our life is not in harmony with Him, we prefer to trust in ourself instead of in Him, and we do not know and obey His word in the Bible. God requires we have faith in, trust and obey Him to receive the grace and blessings He extends to us through Jesus and the Holy Spirit. This is the only way pride in and dependency on ourself can be overcome and we can spiritually grow and mature into spiritual adults.

JESUS IS THE FOUNDATION OF OUR LIFE

Jesus stated at the end of His sermon on the mount in Matthew 7:24-25:

> "Therefore, everyone who hears these words of Mine, and acts upon them, may be compared to a wise man, who built his house upon the rock. And the rain descended, and the floods came, and the winds blew, and burst against that house; and yet it did not fall, for it had been founded upon the rock."

Jesus stated we will be a wise person who builds his house upon *the rock* when we hear and act on His words. He referred to the foundation of our life as being *the rock* instead of being just *a rock*. The possible meaning of *the rock* can be found in Deuteronomy 32:3-4 where Moses stated in a song:

> "For I proclaim the name of the LORD;
> Ascribing greatness to our God!
> The Rock! His work is perfect,
> For all His ways are just;
> A God of faithfulness and without injustice,
> Righteous and upright is He."

Moses used the words "*the Rock*" to refer to God. Jesus' use of the words "*the Rock*" was a possible reference to Himself as God. Jesus indicated we will be able to stand firm because our life will be built upon the foundation of His words when we experience adversity, affliction, persecution and suffering.

Paul stated in 1 Corinthians 3:9-15:

> "For we are God's fellow workers; you are God's field, God's building. According to the grace of God which was given to me, like a wise master builder I laid a foundation, and another is building on it. But each man must be careful how he builds on it. For no man can lay a foundation other than the one which is laid, which is Jesus Christ. Now if any man builds on the foundation with gold, silver, precious stones, wood, hay, straw, each man's work will become evident; for the day will show it because it is to be revealed with fire, and the fire itself will test the quality of each man's work. If any man's work is burned up, he will suffer loss; but he himself will be saved, yet so as through fire."

Jesus is the foundation of our life on which we continue to build as we spiritually grow and mature in our faith and perform the good works God has prepared and places before us. The quality of our works is revealed by our life choices and actions. These works will be revealed and tested by fire as they are examined by Jesus when we stand before Him on the last day. Some works will be accepted and remain, while others will be rejected and burned up. We will suffer loss for those works that are burned up, but we will not lose our salvation.

Jesus affirmed the importance of Him being the foundation of our life on which we continue to build when He stated in John 15:1-6:

> "I am the true vine, and My Father is the vine dresser. Every branch in Me that does not bear fruit, He takes away; and every branch that bears fruit, He prunes it so that it may bear more fruit. You are already clean because of the word which I have spoken to you. Abide in Me, and I in you. As the branch cannot bear fruit of itself unless it abides in the vine, so neither can you unless you abide in Me. I am the vine, you are the branches; he who abides in Me and I in him, he bears much fruit, for apart from Me you can do nothing. If anyone does not abide in Me, he is thrown away as a branch and dries up; and they gather them, and cast them into the fire and they are burned."

Jesus indicated:

- We are to grow, mature and bear fruit in our relationship with Him;
- We will not be able to do these independent of our relationship with Him; and
- God will remove us from our relationship with Him when we fail to grow, mature and bear fruit in this relationship.

Jesus' warning is often overlooked or ignored, but it is consistent with similar warnings He gave us in His parables of the talents in Mathew 25:14-30 and Luke 19:12-27. Jesus affirmed God will enable and equip us to bear more fruit as we grow and mature in our relationship with Him.

Peter stated in 2 Peter 1:5-11:

> "Now for this very reason also, applying all diligence, in your faith supply moral excellence, and in your moral excellence, knowledge; and in your knowledge, self-control, and in your self-control, perseverance, and in your perseverance, godliness; and in your godliness, brotherly kindness, and in your brotherly kindness, love. For if these qualities are yours and are increasing, they render you neither useless nor unfruitful in the true

knowledge of our Lord Jesus Christ. For he who lacks these qualities is blind or shortsighted, having forgotten his purification from his former sins. Therefore, brethren, be all the more diligent to make certain about His calling and choosing you; for as long as you practice these things, you will never stumble; for in this way the entrance into the eternal kingdom of our Lord and Savior Jesus Christ will be abundantly supplied to you."

Peter's progression results from God's pruning. This pruning transforms our faith into genuine love we are to share with and extend to others without expecting something in return. Peter indicated:

- Faith and trust in God, Jesus and the Holy Spirit precede and result in moral excellence;
- Moral excellence facilitates the acquisition of spiritual knowledge;
- Spiritual knowledge enables self-control;
- Self-control facilitates perseverance;
- Perseverance results in godliness;
- Godliness leads to brotherly kindness; and
- Brotherly kindness results in genuine love.

This progression enables and equips us to be fruitful as we spiritually grow, mature and engage in the good works God has prepared for us to perform. It assures our entrance into Jesus' eternal kingdom.

CHAPTER 13
SPIRITUAL GROWTH
PRAYER

"Truly I say to you, whoever says to this mountain, "Be taken up and cast into the sea," and does not doubt in his heart, but believes that what he says is going to happen, it shall be granted him. Therefore I say to you all things for which you pray and ask, believe that you have received them, and they shall be granted you." (Mark 11:23-24)

"Truly, truly, I say to you, he who believes in Me, the works that I do shall he do also; and greater works than these shall he do; because I go to the Father. And whatever you ask in My name, that will I do, that the Father may be glorified in the Son. If you ask Me anything in My name, I will do it." (John 14:12-14)

"If you abide in Me, and My words abide in you, ask whatever you will, and it shall be done for you." (John 15:7)

REASONS FOR PRAYER

God reveals Himself to and communicates His commandments, spiritual life principles and doctrines to us through the Bible; prayer is our way of communicating our thoughts, needs and desires to Him. We pray because it is a normal part of our relationship with God through Jesus and the Holy Spirit. Old Testament patriarchs, prophets, priests and national leaders of Israel continually prayed to God. Jesus continually prayed to His Father while He lived on earth. The disciples and other early church leaders consistently prayed to God. Prayer has always been an integral part of the life of individual Christians and the Christian church throughout history.

Prayer within the framework of our relationship with God through Jesus gives us direct access to Him through the Holy Spirit. James stated in James 1:5, "But if any of you lack wisdom, let him ask of God, who gives to all men generously and without reproach, and it will be given to him." We approach God through the Holy Spirit when we pray, and He never turns us away nor disappoints us.

Prayer is the cornerstone of our faith in God we develop through Jesus. Jude stated in Jude 20-21:

> "But you, beloved, building yourselves up on your most holy faith; praying in the Holy Spirit; keep yourselves in the love of God, waiting anxiously for the mercy of our Lord Jesus Christ to eternal life."

Jesus stated in Matthew 7:7-8:

> "Ask, and it shall be given to you; seek, and you shall find; knock, and it shall be opened to you. For everyone who asks receives, and he who seeks finds, and to him who knocks it shall be opened."

Asking, seeking and pursuing are actions that affirm our faith and trust in and obedience to Jesus. We will receive what we request, find what we seek, and have opened to us what we pursue when these actions are supported by prayer. They build up the foundation of our faith as we grow in our relationship with God through Jesus. Paul stated regarding our spiritual growth in Colossians 1:9-12:

> "For this reason also, since the day we heard of it, we have not ceased to pray for you and to ask that you may be filled with the knowledge of His will in all spiritual wisdom and understanding, so that you may walk in a manner worthy of the Lord, to please Him in all respects, bearing fruit in every good work and increasing in the knowledge of God; strengthened with all power, according to His glorious might, for the attaining of all steadfastness and patience; joyously giving thanks to the Father, who has qualified us to share in the inheritance of the saints in light."

Prayer brings healing to sick bodies, results in the forgiveness of sins, and restores our relationships with God and others. James taught in James 5:14-16:

> "Is anyone among you sick? Let him call for the elders of the church, and let them pray over him, anointing him with oil in the name of the Lord; and the prayer offered in faith will restore the one who is sick, and the Lord will raise him up, and if he has committed sins, they will be forgiven him. Therefore, confess your sins to one another, and pray for one another, so that you may be healed. The effective prayer of a righteous man can accomplish much."

Prayer prepares us for ministry and service to others, opens doors for the spreading of God's word, and prepares and sends out Christian workers. Paul requested in Colossians 4:2-4:

"Devote yourselves to prayer, keeping alert in it with an attitude of thanksgiving; praying at the same time for us as well, that God may open up to us a door for the word, so that we may speak forth the mystery of Christ, for which I have also been imprisoned; in order that I may make it clear in the way I ought to speak."

Luke stated in Acts 12:2-3:

"And while they were ministering to the Lord and fasting, the Holy Spirit said, 'Set apart for Me Barnabas and Saul for the work to which I have called them.' Then, when they had fasted and prayed and laid their hands on them, they sent them away."

All ministries and service to others must be undergirded with prayer. Jesus instructed His disciples in Matthew 9:37-38:

"The harvest is plentiful, but the workers are few. Therefore beseech the Lord of the harvest to send out workers into His harvest."

Prayer strengthens us in our conflict with Satan. Paul instructed in 2 Thessalonians 3:1-3:

"Finally, brethren, pray for us that the word of the Lord may spread rapidly and be glorified, just as it did also with you; and that we may be delivered from perverse and evil men; for not all have faith."

He stated in Ephesians 6:11-12, 18:

"Put on the full armor of God, so that you will be able to stand against the schemes of the devil. For our struggle is not against flesh and blood, but against the rulers, against the powers, against the world forces of this darkness, against the spiritual forces of wickedness in the heavenly places. … With all prayer and petition pray at all times in the Spirit, and with this in view, be on the alert with all perseverance and petition for all the saints."

Satan is a powerful, intelligent and well organized angelic being who has an army of fallen angels (demonic spirits) who work with him in his spiritual conflict against us and the church. We are promised we will prevail against him when we stand firm in our relationship with God through Jesus and seek His assistance through the Holy Spirit with prayer. Jesus promised in Matthew 16:18 the gates of hell shall not prevail against the church.

The peace of God guards our hearts and minds in Christ Jesus through prayer. Paul stated in Philippians 4:6-7:

> "Be anxious for nothing, but in everything by prayer and supplication with thanksgiving let your requests be made known to God. And the peace of God, which surpasses all comprehension, shall guard your hearts and your minds in Christ Jesus."

We are to be anxious for nothing and to bring everything (our joys, sorrows, disappointments, victories, defeats, needs, desires, expectations, etc.) to God in prayer with thankful hearts. God will comfort and give us a peace that will surpass anything we can comprehend or expect in response. This peace will guard our soul, our heart and mind, in difficult and happy times.

Paul indicated in Philippians 4:13 he could do all things through Christ who strengthened him. He undergirded everything he did with personal prayer and through the prayers of the saints in the churches he started. The Bible teaches we can do impossible things with God and these impossible things are initiated by our interaction with God through prayer. Prayer needs to proceed, support and undergird everything we individually and corporately do as a church. Paul stated in 2 Thessalonians 1:11-12:

> "To this end also we pray for you always our God may count you worthy of your calling, and fulfill every desire for goodness and the work of faith with power; in order that the name of our Lord Jesus may be glorified in you, and you in Him, according to the grace of our God and the Lord Jesus Christ."

Jesus will be glorified, and our works of faith will be empowered by God through the Holy Spirit when prayer undergird everything we do in the Jesus' name.

PRINCIPLES FOR EFFECTIVE PRAYER

We must approach God with respect and humility. We can directly approach God through prayer because of the relationship we have with Him through Jesus. We must approach God with respect and humility when we come to Him in prayer. Jesus stated in Luke 18:10-14:

> "Two men went up into the temple to pray, one a Pharisee, and the other a tax-gatherer. The Pharisee stood and was praying thus to himself, 'God, I thank Thee that I am not like other people: swindlers, unjust, adulterers, or even like this tax-gatherer. I fast twice a week; I pay tithes of all that I get.' But the tax-gatherer, standing some distance away, was even unwilling to lift his eyes to heaven, but was beating his breast, saying, 'God, be merciful to me, the sinner!' I tell you, this man went down to his house justified rather than the other; for everyone who exalts himself shall be humbled, but he who humbles himself shall be exalted."

We must have a sense of the infinite and sovereign nature of God. He still is our creator and in absolute control of His creation even though we have the right to come into His presence through Jesus. We are accountable to Him; He is not accountable to us.

God will respond to our prayers as He chooses. Approaching God in the manner He prescribes in the Bible does not guarantee He will respond to us in ways we ask or desire. We must rely on God's wisdom as to how He chooses to respond to us when we come to Him in prayer. God will not allow us to place Him in a box or force Him to respond to us in a particular manner because we have correctly prayed to Him. God's wisdom is infinite, and He knows the outcome of every possible response He can make to our prayers. We must trust Him to make the correct and best responses to us. Sometimes He will deny requests we have made and respond to us in ways that are different from what we have asked because He knows His response is better.

We must pray according to God's word in the Bible. Our mind must be renewed, and our heart transformed by actions of the Holy Spirit for our prayers to be effective. James stated in James 4:3:

> "You ask and do not receive, because you ask with wrong motives, so that you may spend it on your pleasures."

We must pray according to God's word in the Bible. John affirmed in 1 John 5:14-15:

> "And this is the confidence which we have before Him, that, if we ask anything according to His will, He hears us. And if we know that He hears us in whatever we ask, we know that we have the request which we asked of Him."

We grow in our knowledge and understanding of God's will as we grow in our knowledge and understanding of His word in the Bible. The Holy Spirit renews our mind, transforms our heart, and brings our life into harmony with God's will through this grow.

We must believe our prayers will make an effective and noticeable difference when we pray. Jesus and His disciples prayed with an expectation God would respond to their prayers. We must trust God will respond to our prayers in a manner consistent with His will, which may sometimes not be precisely what we pray for. We must trust God knows what is best when He responds to our prayers. Ending our prayers with "if it be Your will" must never characterized the attitudes of Jesus and His disciples when they prayed. The disciples approached God with faith their prayers would be effective and make a noticeable difference. This attitude must characterize us when we pray.

We must trust and obey Jesus for our prayers to be effective. These are essential for effective prayer just as faith and obedience are essential in all other aspects of our relationship with God through Jesus. Jesus promised in John 15:7-8:

> "If you abide in Me and My words abide in you, ask whatever you wish, and it will be done for you. My Father is glorified by this, that you bear much fruit, and so prove to be My disciples."

John reaffirmed this in 1 John 3:21-22:

> "Beloved, if our heart does not condemn us, we have confidence before God; and whatever we ask we receive from Him, because we keep His commandments and do those things that are pleasing to Him."

We must forgive those who have offended us. We must forgive those who have who have offended us for our prayers to be effective. Jesus stated in Mark 11:25-26:

> "Whenever you stand praying, forgive, it you have anything against anyone, so that your Father who is in heaven will also forgive you your transgressions. But if you do not forgive, neither will your Father who is in heaven forgive your transgressions."

We must boldly approach God in prayer with confidence. In Hebrews 4:16, the author stated:

"Let us therefore draw near with confidence to the throne of grace, that we may receive mercy and find grace in time of need."

The Greek word for *confidence* is *parrhesia*, which can be translated as boldness of speech, frankness, bluntness. We are instructed to approach God openly and boldly and with confidence when we approach Him in prayer. He expects us to be frank and open with Him about how we feel in our heart and what we desire. We do not need to be timid or tentative when we approach God.

We must be persistent in our prayers. God expects us to be persistent in our prayers. Jesus affirmed this in the parable of a widow in Luke 18:1-7 who persistently implored a local judge to give her protection. The judge was not initially inclined to grant the widow's request. However, he eventually granted her request because she kept returning to his courtroom seeking protection. God may sometimes test the sincerity of our prayers through our persistence before He will respond.

Some believe repeatedly approaching God concerning prayer requests demonstrates a lack of faith. The Bible does not support this view. We must rely on the Holy Spirit to lead us how we should pray about specific prayer requests. Praying about a specific prayer request only once does not always indicate strong faith, nor does repeatedly praying about the request indicate a lack of faith. We should pray as we are led by the Holy Spirit to pray.

Our prayers should be simple and to the point. Jesus taught in Matthew 6:7-8:

"And when you are praying, do not use meaningless repetition, as the Gentiles do, for they suppose that they will be heard for their many words. Therefore do not be like them; for your Father knows what you need, before you ask Him."

We do not need to be skilled in how we pray when we pray. God knows our needs before we ask Him. However, we must make our requests through prayer before He will respond. We develop a better understanding of our prayer needs as we formulate the words for our prayers. This may often be part of God's response to our prayers through the Holy Spirit. Jesus told us not to use vain repetitions when we pray. Vain repetitions, using skilled prayer methods and vocabularies, do not move God to respond to our prayers. Prayers spoken with faith and an expectation He hears us and will respond move Him to respond.

We may sometimes need to seek agreement with other Christians when we pray. Jesus stated in Matthew 18:19-20:

"Again I say to you, that if two of you agree on earth about anything that they may ask, it shall be done for them by My Father who is in heaven. For where two or three have gathered together in My name, there I am in their midst."

Sometimes when we pray, for our prayers to be effective, we must seek agreement with other Christians with respect to our prayer requests. This can be done with individuals or a group. Jesus stated when we agree with respect to what we are requesting, our "Father who is in heaven" will grant our requests. There are two reasons why this is important:

- God expects us to be specific with respect to the requests we bring to him in prayer. We may not know what we should pray concerning a specific situation. We can personally pray for guidance or enter dialogue with fellow Christians concerning how we should pray. Often consensus will be reached concerning what specific requests should be brought to God in prayer after these discussions. Consensus will usually represent what God desires us to pray for when the discussion was a prayerful one where the guidance of the Holy Spirit was sought. God's requirement for agreement will then have been met when we corporately bring this prayer to God. He will grant the requests.

- There are cases when the power a single individual can release through prayer is insufficient to effectively address the situation for which this individual is praying. These cases can be associated with requesting healing for critical illnesses, dealing with serious individual or family problems, engaging in spiritual conflicts or warfare with demonic forces, initiating new or undergirding existing ministries and church programs, etc. It may be necessary to enter prayerful dialogue with fellow Christians to seek consensus on how and what should be prayed for these situations. The seriousness and intensity of a situation and the extended time period over which prayer must be offered to be effective may require both consensus and several individuals being in prayer together about the same situation either over an extended period of time or at the same time. This may be necessary to release enough prayer power in the spiritual realm of God to facilitate action, movement, or change with respect to the issue for which prayer is being offered.

We must never forget our covenant relationship with God through Jesus. This permeates every aspect of our relationship with God through Jesus. We can come into His presence because of Jesus' death and resurrection. Jesus is our mediator and high priest in heaven who continually makes intercession to the Father for us. Therefore, we must pray to God, the Father, through Jesus, the Son, with the assistance of the Holy Spirit when we pray. Jesus affirmed in John 14:12-14:

"Truly, truly, I say to you, he who believes in Me, the works that I do, he will do also; and greater works than these he will do; because I go to the Father. Whatever you ask in My name, that will I do, so that the Father may be glorified in the Son. If you ask Me anything in My name, I will do it. If you love Me, you will keep My Commandments."

MODEL FOR PRAYER

Jesus gave us a model for prayer in the Lord's prayer. He taught to pray in Matthew 6:9-14:

> "Our Father who is in heaven,
> Hallowed be Your name.
> Your kingdom come.
> Your will be done,
> On earth as it is in heaven.
> Give us this day our daily bread.
> And forgive us our debts, as we also have forgiven our debtors.
> And do not lead us into temptation, but deliver us from evil.
> For Thine is the kingdom, and the power, and the
> glory, forever. Amen."

The elements of prayer that are found in the Lord's prayer are:

Our Father - implies a personal relationship with God.

who art in heaven - implies a faith relationship with God in heaven.

Hallowed be Your name. - implies worship and adoration of God.

Your kingdom come. - implies hope and expectation God's kingdom will be established in our hearts.

Your will be done, on earth as it is in heaven. - implies submission to the will of God in our life.

Give us this day our daily bread. - implies petitioning God for our daily needs.

And forgive us our debts - implies confession and repentance of our sins.

as we also have forgiven our debtors. - implies compassion toward and forgiveness of those who have offended and hurt us.

And do not lead us into temptation but deliver us from evil. - implies the necessity of and our dependence on the presence of God in our life to live a life that is pleasing to Him and that keeps us away from evil.

For Thine is the kingdom, and the power, and the glory, forever. - implies acknowledgment of the sovereignty of God over our lives and His creation.

The Lord's prayer models our attitudes toward and the relationships we should have with God and others when we pray. We should approach God with the expectation He will hear and respond to us even though we should approach Him with an awareness of His majesty and sovereignty.

TYPES OF PRAYERS

Most of us pray instinctively when we pray. We are guided by our perception of our own needs and the needs of others and by our understanding of local, regional and world events. However, we discover our prayers are a combination of different types of individual prayers that can be divided into two groups when we examine our prayers:

- Prayers that are associated with our personal relationship with God, and
- Prayers that are associated with our involvement with others and Christian service.

These two groups can be further subdivided into different types of individual prayers that can be identified from personal observations concerning prayer and from insights gained from Richard Foster's book, *Prayer, Finding the Heart's True Home* (1992). Regarding our personal relationship with God, our prayers can be subdivided into:

- Prayer of adoration
- Prayer of the heart
- Prayer of examination
- Prayer of repentance
- Prayer of relinquishment
- Prayer of submission

Regarding our involvement with Christian service to others, our prayers can be subdivided into:

- Prayer of guidance
- Prayer of forgiveness
- Prayer of supplication
- Prayer of intercession,
- Prayer of healing
- Prayer of authority
- Prayer of deliverance
- Prayer of protection
- Prayer of rest

The types of prayer listed above are not meant to be rigid classifications into which all prayers must be grouped. They are designed to be general guides to help understand the nature of the prayers most of us instinctively pray and to assist in more effectively forming and framing our prayers when we pray.

Prayer of adoration: The prayer of adoration is a prayer in which we recognize God's sovereignty and control over His creation and our lives. It is a prayer in which we worship, honor, magnify and glorify God. It is a prayer in which we acknowledge God's right to be God and we stand in awe and adore the beauty of His creation. The Psalms are a good source of prayers of adoration.

Prayer of the heart: The prayer of the heart is a special form of the prayer of adoration. It is a prayer in which we become overwhelmed by the love God extends to us through Jesus and we communicate our heartfelt love and appreciation toward Him. It is a prayer in which we acknowledge the special position we have with Him through Jesus, and we express our love and appreciation both toward God as Father and His Son, Jesus, for the infinite self-sacrifice both made to secure our redemption and salvation. Again, the Psalms are a good source for prayers of the heart.

Prayer of examination: The prayer of examination is a prayer in which we search the depths of our heart concerning our personal relationship with God through Jesus. It is a prayer in which we examine those areas of our life that need to be transformed and renewed to allow us to move into a closer relationship with God through Jesus. It is a prayer in which we identify specific areas of our life that:

- Are blighted by sin and must be brought to God in prayers of repentance and
- We must relinquish control of and surrender to God in prayers of relinquishment.

The prayer of examination is undertaken with the guidance and revealing light of the Holy Spirit.

Prayer of repentance: The prayer of repentance is a prayer in which we bring to God specific areas of our life that are blighted by sin. It is a prayer in which we identify specific things we have done that have been offensive to God and transgressed His laws and for which we seek and receive His forgiveness.

Prayer of relinquishment: The prayer of relinquishment is a prayer in which we transfer control of specific areas of our life to God. This transfer is necessary before God can bring healing to areas of our life that need healing and before He can renew and transform specific areas of our life that must be renewed and transformed so we can move into a closer relationship with Him through Jesus.

Prayer of submission: The prayer of submission is a prayer in which we submit to God's authority and control over our life. It is a prayer in which we commit to allow God to use our life and possessions as He chooses to spread of His Word, establish His kingdom in the world, and build up the body of Christ, the Church. It is a prayer in which we ask the Holy Spirit to reveal to us the spiritual gifts He has given to us, and we commit to develop and use these gifts to build up our local church. This prayer entails committing our life to God for Christian service and ministry. For some this may mean committing their life to full-time Christian service as a pastor or other type of full-time Christian worker. For others this may mean committing their life to God for use in Christian service as He chooses in their family, local Christian church, profession, community, etc.

Prayer of guidance: This is a prayer that should precede any type of prayer or activity that is directed toward others or toward Christian service. This is a searching prayer in which we seek God's guidance and His intentional will for our life. This is a prayer in which we seek God's knowledge, wisdom and direction relative to actions He desires us to take concerning prayer or other Christian activities. Knowledge is associated with knowing what God desires us to do, and wisdom is associated with knowing how we are to accomplish what He desires us to do in a loving, understanding, sensitive, caring and uplifting manner.

Prayer of forgiveness: The prayer of forgiveness is a prayer in which we forgive others for wrongs they have intentionally or unintentionally directed toward us. It is a prayer in which we give up our right to seek vengeance or retribution for these wrongs, and we seek the restoration and healing of broken or injured relationships these wrongs have caused. It is also a prayer in which we seek to address the wrongs we have inflicted on others, and we seek the restoration and healing of relationships we are responsible for breaking or injuring. The prayer of forgiveness should precede any other prayer or activity that is associated with our involvement with others in which there are broken or injured relationships.

Prayer of supplication: The prayer of supplication is a prayer in which we ask God for things we need or desire. Prayers of supplication can be associated with:

- Special knowledge and wisdom we are seeking,

- Specific or general guidance we are seeking for our life,

- Specific needs or desires we may have,

- Spiritual, emotional or physical healing we may need,

- Healing of broken or injured relationships,

- Help to achieve specific objectives or goals,

- Strength to overcome specific obstacles, or

- Any other request we desire to bring to God.

Prayer of intercession: The prayer of intercession is a prayer we make on behalf of others. We can make the same requests that are associated with prayers of supplication, the difference being - we make these requests for others. Prayers of guidance should precede prayers of intercession. We should be in continual contact with the Holy Spirit when we pray to ensure we pray for the right things. Having a sense of compassion and empathy for individuals we pray for is a sign we are to pray for them. In prayers of intercession, we must pray for individuals as persons who are loved by God.

Prayer of healing: The prayer of healing is a special form of the prayer of supplication or intercession in which we seek the spiritual, emotional and physical healing of the individual for whom we are praying. Healing was one of Jesus' special ministries during His time on carth, and He expects us, as representatives of His church, to be involved in this type of prayer ministry. We must be aware of the fact God can and does use many forms of healing when we pray for healing of ourself or others. He can supernaturally and instantaneously heal someone for whom we pray. However, this happens for only a small percentage of these individuals for whom we pray. God often chooses to use normal healing methods, which include counseling, surgery and taking prescribed medications. Our prayers assist in and often speed up the healing process in these cases. They accomplish what cannot be accomplished through normal medical and other related treatments. We must pray in conjunction with the individual seeking proper professional medical treatment when necessary for prayers of healing for an individual.

Prayer of authority: The prayer of authority is a prayer in which we speak directly to a situation rather than about or for the situation. It is a prayer in which we claim authority over or control of the situation for which we are praying, and we speak directly to the situation, rather than about the situation. Jesus instructed His disciples to speak directly to the mountain - "whoever says to this mountain, 'Be taken up … ' " when He instructed them relative to praying to the mountain in Mark 11:23-24. Peter did not pray about the man's paralysis when he addressed the crippled man in Acts 3:1-7. He instead looked straight at the man and commanded him, "In the name of Jesus Christ of Nazareth, walk." Peter then grabbed the man's hand to help him up, and the man was instantaneously healed and walked. Jesus gave us the authority to use His name to bring about healing and deliverance from bondage. We can use His name in the context of prayer (In the name of Jesus, we pray …), or we can use His name in the context of a command (In the name of Jesus, walk.). The prayer of authority must be used with great compassion and spiritual discernment under the guidance of the Holy Spirit. The prayer of guidance and spiritual discernment from the Holy Spirit must precede the prayer of authority. The prayer of authority can easily become a presumptuous prayer that can do much harm when we do not trust in and are not sensitive to the guidance and leading of the Holy Spirit. The prayer of authority can be used to facilitate the Holy Spirit working directly to bring about an instantaneous action, for example instantaneous healing, when used with compassion and spiritual discernment. The man Peter commanded to walk was instantaneously healed and walked. Sensitivity and caution must be exercised when the prayer of authority is used to bring healing to an individual.

Prayer of deliverance: The prayer of deliverance is a special form of the prayer of authority. It is used to free an individual from the control of or harassment from demonic spirits. This prayer is used with individuals who have been involved in cults or with occult practices and who have come under some form of demonic control or influence in their life as a result. Principles associated with the prayer of authority apply to the prayer of deliverance. Jesus has given us authority in His name to come against Satan and the demonic spirits who follow him. Demotic spirits must obey when we command them to leave and stop harassing an individual in Jesus' name. Paul was harassed in Philippi by a young girl who was possessed by a demon spirit of divination (Acts 16:16-18). Paul confronted the demonic spirit in the young girl after several days and said, "I command you in the name of Jesus Christ to come out of her." The demon spirit departed the girl. The prayer of deliverance is also used to free individuals from serious and chronic addictions. Individuals should not get involved with prayers of deliverance unless they are spiritually mature, have a well-developed knowledge of the principles of spiritual warfare, and are extremely sensitive and obedient to the guidance and leading of the Holy Spirit.

Prayer of protection: The prayer of protection is used in conjunction with our involvement in spiritual warfare. Paul indicated in Ephesians 6:12 as Christians we continually war:

> "against the rulers, against the powers, against the world forces of this darkness, against the spiritual forces of wickedness in the heavenly places."

It is often necessary for us to pray the prayer of protection to seek relief from these spiritual forces of darkness. We claim the healing and protection that comes from covering ourselves with the blood of Jesus with this prayer, and we petition God to send His angels from heaven to guard and protect us from demonic forces that harass us.

Prayer of rest: Continual involvement in Christian ministry and service can be exhausting and drain us of spiritual, emotional and physical strength. As a result, it is often necessary to use the prayer of rest to enter God's rest. We ask God in this prayer through the Holy Spirit to come into our life to regenerate us and replace the spiritual, emotional and physical strength we have lost. God shields us from adversities and conflicts, protects us from attacks from demonic forces, and allows us to receive His direction and guidance when we pray the prayer of rest so we can again engage in Christian ministry and service refreshed and rejuvenated. Jesus often departed from the crowds that continually surrounded Him and went to lonely and isolated places to pray to His Father. These were times of replenishment, remaining in touch with God, and seeking God's guidance and direction. We must follow Jesus' example and allow for times of replenishment and regeneration in our life if we are to succeed in God's work.

Several of the individual types of prayers discussed above are generally grouped together to form overall prayers. Below are some examples of the grouping of individual prayers:

Worship:	Prayers of adoration, examination and repentance
Introspection and self-examination:	Prayers of examination, repentance, relinquishment, and submission
Supplication and intercession:	Prayers of guidance, forgiveness, supplication, intercession and healing
Spiritual warfare:	Prayers of guidance, forgiveness, authority, deliverance, and protection
Revitalization and regeneration:	Prayers of adoration, the heart, examination, repentance, relinquishment, submission and rest

Prayers of adoration and sometimes prayers of the heart precede our prayers.

OBSTACLES TO EFFECTIVE PRAYER

We can determine we are praying correctly by whether our prayers are answered. God will respond to us when we pray and answer our prayers when we enter a faithful and obedient relationship with Him through Jesus. There is usually an obstacle or block somewhere when our prayers are not answered. Following are some obstacles to effective prayer.

Lack of faith and obedience: Two major obstacles to effective prayer are a lack of faith and obedience. In Hebrews 4:2, 6, the author stated:

> "For indeed we have had good news preached to us, just as they also; but the word they heard did not profit them, because it was not united with faith in those who heard. … Since therefore it remains for some to enter it, and those who formerly had good news preached to them failed to enter because of disobedience."

We can understand and experience God's word on two levels: intellectual and faith. Many of us hear God's word and embrace it because intellectually it makes sense; it is logical. God's word helps us to understand and gain a perspective of life unobtainable by other means. However, the writer of Hebrews indicated God's word must be combined with biblical faith and obedience for it to profit us. Expanding this to prayer, James stated in James 1:5-6:

> "But if any of you lack wisdom, let him ask of God, who gives to all men generously and without reproach, and it will be given him. But let him ask in faith without any doubting, for the one who doubts is like the surf of the sea driven and tossed by the wind."

God will not respond to our prayers when we do not believe He will answer them. James indicated we will be tossed about by the whims of the world when we doubt God's desire and ability to answer our prayers. God is our anchor and Jesus is the rock which supports our life when we have faith. Our life has no anchor and foundation when we lack faith. As a result, we often find ourself tossed about by the events for which we pray. The only remedy for this is to repent, turn to God, and begin the process of establishing or reestablishing a relationship with Him through Jesus.

In Hebrews 4:6, the author stated God requires obedience along with faith. He stated in Hebrews 2:18:

"And to who did He swear that they should not enter His rest, but to those who were disobedient."

Jesus stated in John 15:7:

"If you abide in Me, and My words abide in you, ask whatever you wish, and it shall be done for you."

John indicated in 1 John 3:21-22:

"Beloved, if our heart does not condemn us, we have confidence before God; and whatever we ask we receive from Him, because we keep His commandments and do the things that are pleasing in His sight."

We must give up our life of sin when we approach God through Jesus in a trusting and obedient relationship. We sometimes think we can come to God and have the best of two worlds. We mistakenly believe we can have one foot in the kingdom of God and with the other foot allow Satan to have a foothold in our life by transgressing God's laws. Jesus stated in Matthew 6:24:

"No one can serve two masters; for either he will hate the one and love the other, or he will hold to one and despise the other. You cannot serve God and mammon."

Paul stated in 1 Corinthians 10:21:

"You cannot drink the cup of the Lord and the cup of demons; you cannot partake of the table of the Lord and the table of demons."

James taught in James 1:7-8:

"For let not the man expect that he will receive anything from the Lord, being a double-minded man, unstable in his ways."

We cannot lead a double life by serving two masters. We cannot pretend to trust and be obedient to God, while at the same time we willfully transgress His laws. James indicated we cannot expect to receive anything from God through prayer when we are double-minded and have a double loyalty: one to God and the other to the world. Some of the most miserable and troubled individuals are those who attempt to be loyal and obedient to God, while at the same time, they willfully violate His laws. These individuals will have no stability or rest in their lives until they realize they must truly repent and turn to God through Jesus. They must completely step into His kingdom and allow the Holy Spirit to control their lives and direct their walk with the Lord.

Failure to make our needs known to God: We can pray and God will respond to our request when we live in God's kingdom, are obedient to His commandments, and pray and ask according to His word. We sometimes live in spiritual poverty despite this. James taught in James 4:3:

> "You do not have because you do not ask. You ask and do not receive, because you ask with wrong motives, so you can spend it on your pleasures."

We are physically and spiritually poor because we do not ask God to meet our basic needs. We will not receive anything from God when we do not ask. We may be deceived into believing God will not listen to our prayers, or we may be afraid to come to Him in prayer. We may believe our prayer requests are insignificant compared to the needs of others and keep silent. We may believe we are to work problems out for ourself. Whatever the reason, we often do not receive because we do not come to God in prayer and ask. The Bible teaches everything we bring before God in prayer is significant and important to Him. We should never be afraid to approach God in prayer, and we should hold nothing back when we do come to Him in prayer.

Praying with wrong motives: James stated in James 4:3 we will not receive what we request from God in prayer when we ask with wrong motives. God will not respond to our prayers when they center around satisfying our needs in a manner that is incompatible with our relationship with Him through Jesus.

Failure to give God the credit for what He gives to and does for us: God wants us to acknowledge He is the One who responds to our prayers. James stated in James 1:17:

> "Every good thing bestowed and every perfect gift is from above, coming down from the Father of lights, with whom there is no variation, or shifting shadow."

God responds to our prayers because He wants to direct our life to Him through Jesus. He gives us what we request because He wants to edify and build us up in His love; He wants to edify and build us up in Jesus. He gives us what we request so we can give Him the glory, honor and praise for responding to our prayers. We can use His responses to our prayers as a witness to others that illuminates how a loving Father desires to interact with His children.

We cannot take credit for what God gives to and does for us and expect Him to continue to respond to our prayers. God will cease to respond to our prayers when our eyes turn away from Him as the source of all good things from above and turn toward ourself as the source of the things God gives to does for us.

Lack of harmony within our family: An obstacle to effective prayer can result from a lack of harmony within our family. Peter stated in 1 Peter 3:7:

> "You husbands likewise, live with your wives in an understanding way, as with a weaker vessel, since she is a woman; and grant her honor as a fellow heir of the grace of life, so that your prayers may not be hindered."

Harmonious relations within a family are essential to an unhindered relationship with God through Jesus. A husband and wife who are sensitive to each other, who have established a loving relationship based on biblical principles, and whose spirits are united with each other in Jesus can release faith and power through prayer. Therefore, Satan works to cause discord within families and destroy marriages. The faith and power released by the prayers of the individual family members are hindered when there is discord and a lack of harmony within the family. This is because there is a lack of agreement in many cases. Jesus stated:

> "Again, I say to you, that if two of you agree on earth about anything that they may ask, it shall be done for them by my Father who is in heaven."

No better and more powerful relationship exists in the spiritual realm than a husband and wife who agree on what they are praying for.

Lack of forgiveness: Jesus stated in Mark 11:25-26:

> "And whenever you stand praying, forgive, if you have anything against anyone; so that your Father also who is in heaven may forgive you your transgressions. But if you do not forgive, neither will your Father who is in heaven forgive your transgressions."

One of the major causes of emotional problems in individuals is unresolved anger and hostility toward others. Retaining hatred, anger and bitterness associated with wrongs others have committed against us affects our ability to develop meaningful and trusting relationships. This also results in a barrier between God and us that affects our prayer life. Jesus stated in Matthew 5:22-24:

"But I say to you that everyone who is angry with his brother shall be guilty before the court; and whoever says to his brother, 'You good-for-nothing,' shall be guilty before the supreme court; and whoever says, 'You fool,' shall be guilty enough to go into the fiery hell. Therefore if you are presenting your offering at the altar, and there remember that your brother has something against you, leave your offering there before the altar and go; first be reconciled to your brother, and then come and present your offering."

We must right broken relationship before we come to God in prayer. We must seek forgiveness and make restitution when required when we were the one doing the offending, and we must forgive when we have been the one who was offended. Jesus implied this is required for God to forgive our transgressions and for us to develop an effective and meaningful prayer life with Him.

UNANSWERED PRAYER

We may believe there are no obstacles or barriers between God and us when we pray. We have faith and believe God will answer our prayers. Jesus' words abide in us, and with the help of the Holy Spirit, we are doing our best to keep His commandments and lead a life that is pleasing to Him. We have no unresolved unforgiveness in our life, and we have harmonious relations within our family and with others. Yet somehow our prayers seem to go unanswered. There are several possible reasons for this.

The timing is not right. It may be God is saying now is not the time to respond; there are other issues that must be addressed and resolved before He will give us what we are requesting. We must exercise faith and patiently wait for God's timing when this is the case.

We may need more prayer support. The issue for which we are praying may require agreement and prayer support from other Christians. Our praying alone may not be adequate. We must invite other Christians to participate with us in prayer when this is the case.

We may need to assume responsibility for our prayer request. We often attempt to pass onto God through prayer responsibilities we must assume relative to our prayer requests. God will not assume this responsibility. He expects us to make appropriate decisions in response to His response to our prayer requests. He will then guide our steps. Proverbs 16:9 states, "The mind of man plans his way, but the Lord directs his steps." We must pray for guidance regarding a decision we must make when we lack clarity regarding the decision. We must then trust God to direct our steps in a manner consistent with His will for us once we have received the requested information and decided what we will do.

We may not be specific enough in our prayers. We should examine our prayers to determine if we are being specific enough in what we are requesting. We sometimes pray in vague generalities, using a shotgun approach to present God with several general requests. We may believe He will certainly respond to some of our requests. We can then believe some responses are from God when something positive occurs regarding our requests even though this may not be the case. On the other hand, we can believe we are not important enough for God to respond when nothing occurs. This kind of lukewarm faith is offensive to God (Revelations 3:14-22). God will not respond to our prayer requests when this is our attitude when we come to Him in prayer. We must be specific in what we request from God when we pray. We may be tempted to reply we lack proper knowledge to do this. However, Jesus stated in Luke 11:9-10:

> "And I say to you, ask, and it shall be given to you; seek, and you shall find; knock, and it shall be open to you. For everyone who asks, receives; and he who seeks, finds; and to him who knocks, it shall be open."

James stated in James 1:5:

> "But if any of you lacks wisdom, let him ask of God, who gives to all men generously and without reproach, and it will be given him."

God knows we may sometimes lack specific knowledge with respect to what we should pray for in a situation. We are instructed to ask for knowledge with the assurance it will be given to us when we lack knowledge. God will be faithful and respond. Depending on the situation, He may give us the knowledge by impressing specific thoughts in our mind. He may give us a specific understanding of a scripture we read in the Bible. He may direct someone to us or us to someone who understands the situation for which we are praying. We can then accurately ask God for what we need with the assurance He will respond once we have the requests knowledge.

God may require us to act first with respect to a prayer request. We may need to first act on specific parts of our prayer request before God will respond when we request His help. We must pray for guidance as to what He will do and what He expects us to do when this is the case. We must then in faith begin doing what God expects from us before He will respond.

We may need to release control of certain issues related to our prayer request to God. God expects us to release control of the situations surrounding our prayer request to Him when we pray. He must be in control. He must be free to determine the timing events related to our prayer request will occur. He must open the doors for us to walk through.

Our faith response requires us to trust Him and follow His leadership. God will often remain silent when we attempt to maintain control of situations surrounding our prayer request. He will not interfere with our actions when we believe we know and understand more about these situations than He does. He will continue to let us do our own thing. God will respond to our prayer request only when we totally release control of the situations surrounding it to Him.

We may have to first address some spiritual issues in our life before God will respond to our prayer requests. We may sense something in our life that is difficult to identify is preventing us from entering a closer relationship with God through Jesus. This also hinders our prayer life. This often can be traced to some form of spiritual or demonic presence in our life. This presence can occur because of past participation in a cult and dabbling in occult practices. It can sometimes be traced to traumatic life experiences where extreme fear or a life-shattering event allowed a demonic presence to enter our life. We must pray the prayer of guidance to identify these life experiences for which we may need spiritual healing and deliverance when this occurs. We must first pray prayers of healing once they have been identified. We must also pray prayers of deliverance to remove the spiritual obstacles and control that are preventing us from entering a closer relationship and prayer life with God through Jesus when necessary. It may be necessary to seek and receive the help of a spiritually mature and trained Christian counselor when we have difficulty identifying past events that have resulted in spiritual control in our life and in being freed from this control once they have been identified.

God may be saying no to our prayer request. A perceived lack of response to a specific prayer request may be God's way of answering no. As was mentioned earlier, we must trust God's wisdom concerning how He chooses to respond to our prayer requests when we pray. We must understand God may choose to respond in a manner different than what we request or expect. He will do so in a manner we know He is present and has heard our request when He answers no to a specific prayer request. We must then request the Holy Spirit to give us discernment and understanding regarding why God has chosen to respond to our prayer request the way He has. We may also need to pray for guidance concerning how to change our prayer request to be more in line with God's desired response.

THE PRAYER OF JABEZ

There is an obscure prayer in 1 Chronicles that gives significant insight into how God desires to interact with us through prayer (Bruce Wilkinson, *The Prayer of Jabez*, 2000). Ezra in 1 Chronicles 4:9-10 wrote:

"Jabez was more honorable than his brothers, and his mother named him Jabez saying, 'Because I bore him with pain.' Now Jabez called on the God of Israel, saying, 'Oh that You would bless me indeed, and enlarge my borders, and that Your hand might be with me, and that You would keep me from harm that it may not pain me!' And God granted him what he requested."

This verse implies Jabez had major obstacles to overcome in his life because his mother had borne him with much pain. However, it also implies Jabez was able to overcome these obstacles with God's help and prosper because he prayed a prayer of faith to God.

Jabez requested God to:

Bless him indeed. The *indeed* at the end of Jabez's request to bless him was like adding an exclamation point to the end of his request. Jabez did not ask God to bless him in just ordinary ways; he asked God to favor and bless him in magnanimous ways. Jabez's request implied he left it up to God to determine what His blessings would be and the how, when, where and why associated with the His blessings.

Enlarge his borders. Jabez asked God to increase the boundaries of his property and his influence. He asked God to prosper him so he could be a more effective and influential vessel through whom God could work to reach out to and touch others in a more magnanimous way.

Be with him. Jabez realized he would need God's presence in his life along with His knowledge, wisdom and strength to support and sustain him in shouldering the responsibilities and carrying out the activities that would result from God blessing him and enlarging his borders.

Keep him from harm so it would not cause him problems. Great success brings with it increased difficulties and the potential for failure. Jabez knew the best way to address these difficulties and the potential for failure was to ask God to equip him to confront them more effectively. He realized this would only occur when he had faith in and trusted God to walk with and support him when confronting them.

God in His relationship with us though Jesus wants to bless and walk and commune with us. He desires to increase our prosperity and influence so we can be a more effective witness to His presence in our life. He wants to shield us from harm. God wants us to enter an obedient and trusting relationship with Him through our faith and trust in and obedience to Jesus to accomplish these.

Jesus taught in John 14 the true sign of our love for Him is our willingness to keep His commandments. He promised He, the Father and Holy Spirit will dwell in us when we do this. Jesus further promised in John 15:7:

> "If you abide in Me, and My words abide in you, ask whatever you wish, and it will be done for you."

God's granting Jabez's prayer requests affirms this.
James stated in James 4:2-3:

> "… You do not have because you do not ask. You ask and do not receive, because you ask with wrong motives, so that you may spend it on your pleasures."

We must bring our requests to God in prayer before He will respond, and we must approach Him with humility and right motives. God desires to bless us, walk and commune with us, enable us to increase our prosperity and influence, and keep us from harm. His response to Jabez's prayer teaches these are not presumptuous or selfish requests. They are legitimate when we humbly approach God with right motives.

CHAPTER 14
SPIRITUAL GROWTH
TRANSFORMED LIVES

"You will know them by their fruits. Grapes are not gathered from thorn bushes, nor figs from thistles, are they? Even so, every good tree bears good fruit; but the bad tree bears bad fruit. A good tree cannot produce bad fruit, nor can a bad tree produce good fruit. Every tree that does not bear good fruit is cut down and thrown into the fire. So then, you will know them by their fruits." (Matthew 7:16-20)

"For there is no good tree which produces bad fruit; nor, on the other hand, a bad tree which produces good fruit. For each tree is known by its own fruit. For men do not gather figs from thorns, nor do they pick grapes from a briar bush. The good man out of the good treasure of his heart brings forth what is good; and the evil man out of the evil treasure brings forth what is evil; for his mouth speaks from that which fills his heart." (Luke 6:43-45)

TRANSFORMATION OF OUR HEART

The Holy Spirit gives us spiritual life and opens our mind to receive, understand and assimilate God's word through Bible study, Christian fellowship and prayer. He facilitates our understanding of God's spiritual life principles and laws and enables us to live a life of faith and trust in and obedience to Jesus. The Holy Spirit facilitates a transformation of our heart that results in a restructuring of our personality and character as our mind is renewed. These actions give meaning to Paul's statement in 2 Corinthians 5:17:

"Therefore, if anyone is in Christ, he is a new creature, the old things passed away; behold, new things have come."

Jesus indicated evil thoughts proceed from our heat. He stated in Mark 7:20-22:

"That which proceeds out of the man, that is what defiles the man. For from within, out of the heart of men, proceed the evil thoughts, fornications, thefts, murders, adulteries, deeds of coveting and wickedness, as well as deceit, sensuality, envy, slander, pride and foolishness."

Paul further identified evil that proceeds from our heart in Romans 1:28-32, 1 Corinthians 6:9-10, Galatians 5:19-21, and Ephesians 5:5. It includes:

unrighteousness, wickedness, evil, envy, deceit, covetousness, slander, murder, strife, malice, immorality, impurity, sensuality, idolatry, sorcery, jealousy, outbursts of anger, disputes, dissensions, factions, drunkenness, carousing, fornication, adultery, homosexuality and pride.

He indicated individuals from whom these evil proceeds are:

gossips, slanderers, thieves, swindlers, revilers, haters of God, insolent, arrogant, boastful, inventors of evil, disobedient to parents, without understanding, untrustworthy, unloving and unmerciful.

The evil Paul identified results from sin that proceeds from an unregenerated mind and an unrepentant heart. It develops into a personality and character independent of God.

God works through a heart submitted to the transforming influence of the Holy Spirit and a mind committed to trusting Him and obeying Jesus. We must turn away from a life that violate God's commandments and separates us from Him to enter to a life of faith and trust in and obedience to Jesus. Paul stated in Romans 6:16:

"Do you not know that when you present yourselves to someone as slaves for obedience, you are slaves of the one whom you obey, either of sin resulting in death, or of obedience resulting in righteousness."

We must permit the Holy Spirit to enter our life to develop within us a personality and character formed through our trust in and obedience to God and Jesus.

We often find ourself experiencing the frustration Paul experienced when we enter a relationship with God through Jesus. Paul stated in Romans 7:15:

"For that which I am doing, I do not understand; for I am not practicing what I would like to do, but I am doing the very thing I hate."

God knows we will continue to sin and violate His commandments. This is why He sent His Son to die on a cross for us. He expects us to approach Him as the sinners we are and to allow Him through the Holy Spirit to make us new creatures in Christ. He will enable us through the Holy Spirit to do what we cannot do by ourself.

God accepts and responds to us as we are. He initiates and continues processes in our life through the Holy Spirit that transforms us from within. Changes occur within our heart that transform our personality and character. Changes occur within our mind that lead us to have faith and trust in and to obey Jesus. God responds to us in our pain and joy, successes and failures, and sadness and happiness. The changes He initiates in our life through the Holy Spirit transform us into the person He desires us to be. They result in a regenerated spirit, renewed mind and transformed heart (Figure 12).

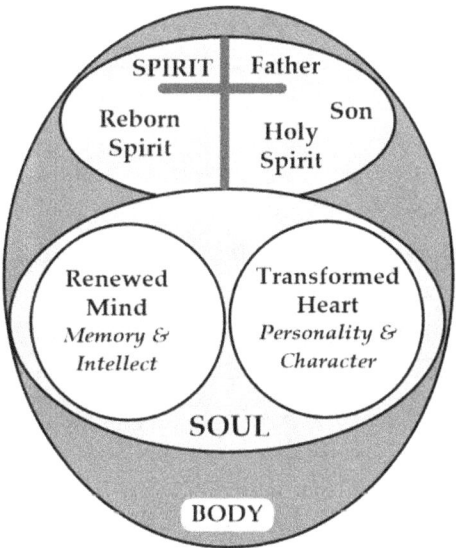

Figure 12

God expects us to trust and obey Him when we repent and enter a relationship with Him through Jesus. The extent to which we trust and obey Him determines how He will respond to us in our relationship with Him. God will always extend His love, mercy and grace to us. These are gifts He extends to us through Jesus. However, the greater our trust in and obedience to Him the more of Himself He will reveal to us and the greater the blessings He will extend to us.

Peter and the writer of Hebrews gave us some warnings regarding our relationship with God through Jesus. Peter stated 2 Peter 2:20-22:

> "For if after they have escaped the defilements of the world by the knowledge of the Lord and Savior Jesus Christ, they are again entangled in them and are overcome, the last state has become worse for them than the first. For it would be better for them not to have known the way of righteousness, than having known it, to turn away from the holy commandment delivered to them. It has happened to them according to the true proverb, 'A dog returns to its own vomit,' and, 'A sow, after washing, returns to wallowing in the mire.'"

Being tempted by sin will not cease after we enter a relationship with God through Jesus. Areas in our life that have previously been blighted by sin will seek to draw us back into a life of disobedience to and rebellion against God. Peter warns the state of sin we are draw back into after we have escaped through Jesus will be worse than our initial state. We see this in individuals who have been freed from addictions. The state of addiction they fall back into after they have been freed is often worse than the state from which they were freed.

In Hebrews 6:4-6, 10:26-31, the author stated:

> "For in the case of those who have once been enlightened and have tasted of the heavenly gift and have been made partakers of the Holy Spirit, and have tasted the good word of God and the powers of the age to come, and then have fallen away, it is impossible to renew them again to repentance, since they again crucify to themselves the Son of God, and put Him to open shame. ... For if we go on sinning willfully after receiving the knowledge of the truth, there no longer remains a sacrifice for sins, but a certain terrifying expectation of judgment, and the fury of a fire which will consume the adversaries. Anyone who has set aside the Law of Moses dies without mercy on the testimony of two or three witnesses. How much severer punishment do you think he will deserve who has trampled underfoot the Son of God, and has regarded as unclean the blood of the covenant by which he was sanctified, and has insulted the Spirit of grace? For we know Him who said, 'Vengeance is Mine, I will repay.' And again, 'The Lord will judge His people.' It is a terrifying thing to fall into the hands of the living God."

The writer of Hebrews addressed extreme cases where individuals who are drawn back into or continue in intentional habitual sins after they have entered a relationship with God through Jesus. God will forgive sins that occur because we yield to temptations when we repent and seek his forgiveness. However, the writer indicates we will face judgement when we intentionally turn away from God or continue in intentional habitual sin after we have entered and grown in our relationship with God.

John was instructed to write in Revelations 3:19-21 where Jesus stated:

> "Those whom I love, I reprove and discipline; be zealous therefore, and repent. Behold, I stand at the door and knock; if anyone hears My voice and opens the door, I will come in to him, and will dine with him, and he with Me. He who overcomes, I will grant to him to sit down with Me on My throne, as I also overcame and sat down with My Father on His throne."

Jesus indicated he will reprove and discipline us when we stray from Him because He loves us. He instructed us to repent when He does this. Jesus stands at the door of our heart and knocks. We have to open the door and invite Him in. He promises to come into our life when we open the door and invite Him in.

OUR TONGUE - A REFLECTION OF OUR HEART

The words we speak reflect what is in our heart. Jesus stated in Luke 6:45:

> "The good man out of the good treasure of his heart brings forth what is good; and the evil man out of the evil treasure brings forth what is evil; for his mouth speaks from that which fills his heart."

He stated in Mark 7:18-23 it is not what goes into the mouth that makes a person unclean and profane; it is what comes out of his mouth that defiles him. He stated in Matthew 12:37, "For by your words you will be justified, and by your words you will be condemned." The words we speak justify us when we receive and accept the redemption and reconciliation God extends to us through Jesus. They condemn us when we reject the redemption He extends to us.

Words we speak have power. They can build people up or tear them down. They can bring healing and health back to sick minds and bodies or bring sickness and even death to previously healthy minds and bodies. They can bring happiness, joy and freedom or sadness, despair and bondage. Paul stated in Ephesians 4:29, 5:4:

> "Let no unwholesome word proceed from your mouth, but only such a word as is good for edification according to the need of the moment, that it may give grace to those who hear. ... And there must be no filthiness and silly talk, or coarse jesting, which are not fitting, but rather giving of thanks."

We should never use profanity, speak unkindly to others, or say things that attack their character. Our words should edify and build up the faith of those with whom we speak.

James stated in James 1:26:

"If anyone thinks himself to be religious, and yet does not bridle his tongue, this man's religion is worthless."

He continued in James 3:1-12:

"Let not many of you become teachers, my brethren, knowing that as such we shall incur a stricter judgment. For we all stumble in many ways. If anyone does not stumble in what he says, he is a perfect man, able to bridle the whole body as well. Now if we put the bits into the horses' mouths so that they may obey us, we direct their entire bodies as well. Behold, the ships also, though they are so great and are driven by strong winds, are still directed by a very small rudder, wherever the inclination of the pilot desires. So also the tongue is a small part of the body, and yet it boasts of great things. Behold, how great a forest is set aflame by such a small fire! And the tongue is a fire, the very world of iniquity; the tongue is set among our members as that which defiles the entire body, and sets on fire the course of our life, and is set on fire by hell. For every species of beast and birds, of reptiles and creatures of the sea, is tamed, and has been tamed by the human race. But no one can tame the tongue; it is a restless evil and full of deadly poison. With it we bless our Lord and Father; and with it we curse men, who have been made in the likeness of God; from the same mouth come both blessing and cursing. My brethren, these things ought not to be this way. Does a fountain send out from the same opening both fresh and bitter water? Can a fig tree, my brethren, produce olives, or a vine produce figs? Neither can salt water produce fresh."

Our tongue controls and directs the course of our life even though it is a small part of our body. Examples of this can be seen by observing others. Individuals who are healthy, have healthy and positive attitudes, and are trusted and successful generally reflect these characteristics in the words they speak. Individuals who are negative, have negative and unhealthy attitudes, and are not trusted and unsuccessful generally reflect these characteristics in the word they speak.

The Proverbs teach us:

> "A man will be satisfied with good by the fruit of his words, and the deeds of a man's hands will return to him. ... There is one who speaks rashly like the thrust of a sword, but the tongue of the wise brings healing. Truthful lips will be established forever, but a lying tongue is only for a moment. ... From the fruit of a man's mouth he enjoys good, but the desire of the treacherous is violence. The one who guards his mouth preserves his life; the one who opens wide his lips comes to ruin." (Proverbs 12:14, 18-19, 13:2-3)

> "He who has a crooked mind finds no good, and he who is perverted in his language falls into evil." (Proverbs 17:20)

> "With the fruit of a man's mouth his stomach will be satisfied; he will be satisfied with the product of his lips. Death and life are in the power of the tongue, and those who love it will eat its fruit." (Proverbs 18:20-21)

> "He who guards his mouth and his tongue, guards his soul from troubles." (Proverbs 21:23)

Proverbs 16:23-24 states:

> "The heart of the wise teaches his mouth, and adds persuasiveness to his lips. Pleasant words are a honeycomb, sweet to the soul and healing to the bones."

This Proverb teaches we control what we say from our heart. This is consistent with what Jesus taught. The only way righteousness can proceed from our heart is to have God's Spirit and spiritual life breathed back into us. The Holy Spirit accomplishes this through Jesus.

We believe we must be in control. We must know what to say and do and when to say and do it. We must discipline ourself to do those things that are acceptable and pleasing to God and others. We can accomplish these actions only when the Spirit of God through the Holy Spirit dwells in us and guides them. The words we speak will be persuasive, and people will listen. They will be pleasant, sweet to the soul, and bring healing to us and others. Psalm 37:30-32 states:

> "The mouth of the righteous utters wisdom, and his tongue speaks justice. The law of his God is in his heart; his steps do not slip."

FRUIT OF THE SPIRIT - PROOF OF A TRANSFORMED LIFE

God regenerates our spirit, renews our mind, and transforms our heart when He dwells in us through the Holy Spirit. We become a new creation as we yield ourself in obedience to God through Jesus. This process occurs over a lifetime and requires commitment, perseverance and effort on our part. God patiently works in our life through the Holy Spirit to transform us into the person He desires us to be. Jesus stated we will be known by the fruits of our life and these fruits will proceed from our heart.

They are planted and grow in our soul. Paul indicated in Galatians 5:22-26:

> "But the fruit of the Spirit is love, joy, peace, patience, kindness, goodness, faithfulness, gentleness, self-control; against such things there is no law. Now those who belong to Christ Jesus have crucified the flesh with its passions and desires. If we live by the Spirit, let us also walk by the Spirit."

The fruit of the Spirit manifests itself in us when we crucify the passions and desires of our flesh in Christ Jesus. The Holy Spirit takes evil desires away from us and replaces them with His fruit. He works in and through us as we grow spiritually and mature in our understanding of God's word in the Bible and apply it to our life. We then develop within ourself "love, joy, peace, patience, kindness, goodness, faithfulness, gentleness and self-control."

The order of the fruit of the Spirit is important. It begins with God's love and ends with our self- control. His love in us grows through our relationship with Him through Jesus. Joy, peace, patience, kindness, goodness, faithfulness and gentleness develop through this relationship. These then lead to our self-control.

We may attempt to begin our relationship with God through our self-control, attempting to develop the fruit of the Spirit in us through our effort. We want to be in control instead of allowing God to be control when we do this. We soon discover this does not work. We must first receive God's love and forgiveness through Jesus and invite His Spirit through the Holy Spirit to dwell in us to develop the fruit of the Spirit. This enables us to love because God loves us, and the fruit of the Spirit then develops in us through His love.

Jesus stated in John 8:31-32:

> "If you continue in My word, then you are disciples of Mine; and you will know the truth, and the truth will make you free."

Discipleship requires Bible study, Christian fellowship and prayer. Seeds of the fruit of the Spirit are planted in our heart through these disciplines and grow to maturity. The fruit of the Spirit as it grows in and proceeds from our heart produces the freedom Jesus referred to and gives us the ability to live and prosper as His disciples.

God has shown us His love through His Son, Jesus. He enables us to receive and experience it through the Holy Spirit. God's love regenerates, renews and transforms our life. It produces in our heart a personality and character that develop from the fruit of the Spirit and transforms us into the person God wants us to be. Paul stated this love is so strong nothing in all creation will be able to take it away from us in Romans 8:35-39:

> "Who shall separate us from the love of Christ? Shall tribulation, or distress, or persecution, or famine, or nakedness, or peril, or sword? Just as it is written, 'For Thy sake we are being put to death all day long; we were considered as sheep to be slaughtered.' But I am convinced that neither death, nor life, nor angels, nor principalities, nor things present, nor things to come, nor powers, nor height, nor depth, nor any other created thing, shall be able to separate us from the love of God, which is in Christ Jesus our Lord."

CHAPTER 15
SPIRITUAL GIFTS
SPIRITUAL WARFARE AND THE FULL ARMOR OF GOD

"Finally, be strong in the Lord, and in the strength of His might. Put on the full armor of God, that you may be able to stand firm against the schemes of the devil. For our struggle is not against flesh and blood, but against the rulers, against the powers, against the world forces of this darkness, against the spiritual forces of wickedness in the heavenly places. Therefore, take up the full armor of God, that you may be able to resist in the evil day, and having done everything, to stand firm. Stand firm therefore, having girded your loins with truth, and having put on the breastplate of righteousness, and having shod your feet with the preparation of the gospel of peace; in addition to all, taking up the shield of faith with which you will be able to extinguish all the flaming missiles of the evil one. And take the helmet of salvation, and the sword of the Spirit, which is the word of God. With all prayer and petition pray at all times in the Spirit, and with this in view, be on the alert with all perseverance and petition for all the saints." (Ephesians 6:10-18)

SPIRITUAL GIFTS (Chapters 15 - 17)

This section presents information regarding:

- Spiritual warfare;
- Gifts of the Holy Spirit - their definition, organization, and descriptions and how we discover, develop, and use our unique spiritual gifts; and
- The baptism of the Holy Spirit and speaking in tongues

SPIRITUAL WARFARE

We are involved in spiritual warfare as Christians. Paul stated we must stand firm against the spiritual (or demonic) forces who follow Satan and who use deception to work through individuals who reject God and Jesus. These individuals operate to remove God and Jesus from our personal lives and from local, regional and world affairs. The spiritual forces of Satan attempt to deceive and harass us and to gain control over our minds and hearts (our souls).

Satan accomplishes his objectives through a hierarchy of demonic forces. Paul divided this hierarchy into rulers, powers, world forces of this darkness, and spiritual forces of wickedness.

Rulers: Rulers are spiritual forces of Satan who exert influence and control over specific geographic areas and regions. These can be small areas, such as a village, town or small region within a large region. They can be larger regions, such as a large city or a region within a country. They can be a larger region, such as a country or continent. Rulers work to exclude God and Jesus from the geographic areas and regions over which they have control and to keep people who live there in bondage to Satan.

Powers: Powers influence and control people. Therefore, they are spiritual forces of Satan who exert influence on and work through:

- Individuals in local, regional and world executive, legislative and judicial governmental bodies,
- The leadership of businesses and corporations, public and private organizations, and religious groups and organizations,
- Schools, colleges and universities; and
- Cults.

They use this influence to accomplish Satan's objectives.

World forces of this darkness: World forces of this darkness are spiritual forces of Satan who work in the lives of individuals to oppose the influence of God through the Holy Spirit in their lives. They are lying spirits who blind "the minds of unbelievers, so they cannot see the light of the gospel of the glory of Christ, who is the image of God" (2 Corinthians 4:3-4).

Spiritual forces of wickedness: Spiritual forces of wickedness are spiritual forces of Satan who work to lure by deception individuals into activities that transgress the laws, statutes and ordinances of God. They are demonic spirits who create within us desires to satisfy "the lusts of the flesh and the lust of the eyes and the boastful pride of life" (1 John 2:16).

The spiritual forces of Satan work with him to:

- Keep us in bondage to Satan.
- Cause suffering and generate conflicts throughout the world.
- Encourage us to oppose God and transgress His laws, statutes and ordinances.
- Keep us in spiritual bondage through sin in our life.
- Blind us to the necessity of and prevent us from receiving salvation through Jesus.
- Pull us back into a life of sin after we have received Jesus as Lord and Savior.
- Keep us from looking toward God as the supplier of all good things.
- Cause us to take our eyes off Jesus, who is our source of authority and power.
- Neutralize our witness to the presence of Jesus in our life.
- Defeat us in our service and ministry to others.

They directly and indirectly assault us through:

- Local, regional and world leaders;
- Religious leaders who deny the lordship of Jesus and leaders of cults;
- Instructors, teachers and professors;
- Family members, close friends, coworkers and general acquaintances;
- Life situations and conflicts;
- Business, corporate and government actions; and
- Any other means that may be open to them.

These assaults can result in sickness, affliction, persecution, poverty, loss of job, loss of income, or any other adversity. Concerning the suffering these may cause, Peter stated in 1 Peter 5:8-9:

> "Be of sober spirit, be on the alert. Your adversary, the devil, prowls about like a roaring lion, seeking someone to devour. But resist him, firm in your faith, knowing that the same experiences of suffering are being accomplished by your brethren who are in the world."

We are members of God's army in our conflict against the demonic forces of Satan, and Jesus is our leader. Paul stated in Ephesians 1:22:

> "And He [God] put all things in subjection under His feet, and gave Him as head over all things to the church, which is His body, the fullness of Him fills all in all."

Jesus has authority over us as Christians, and He has authority over Satan and his demonic forces. The power and glory of Jesus is manifested in and through us as Christians, and He has given us authority to use His name. Therefore, Satan and those who follow him must obey when we come against them in Jesus' name. John stated in 1 John 4:4:

> "You are from God, little children, and have overcome them, because greater is He who is in you than he who is in the world."

FULL ARMOR OF GOD

We must prepare ourselves to be victorious in our conflicts with Satan and his demonic forces. Paul used the metaphor of Roman armor to teach us how to prepare for spiritual conflict. He stated we are to put on the "full armor of God" (Ephesians 6:11-18). Table 7 list the elements of the full armor of God. The Roman armor that Paul referred to was intended for close-in, hand-to-hand fighting and was effective in protecting the wearer only when he directly faced and confronted the enemy.

Table 7

FULL ARMOR OF GOD

PROTECTION OF THE SOUL
Helmet of Salvation - Protects the mind
Breastplate of Righteousness - Protects the heart
PREPARATION FOR ACTION IN SPIRITUAL REALM
Loins Girded with Truth - Applying God's word
in the Bible to every part of our life
Feet Shod with the Gospel of Peace - Knowing and
understanding God's word in the Bible

PROTECTION AGAINST ASSAULTS FROM SPIRITUAL REALM
Shield of Faith **-** Repels assaults from the spiritual realm
OFFENSIVE WEAPONS IN THE SPIRITUAL REALM
Sword of the Spirit **-** God's word in the Bible
Prayers for the Saints **-** Continual communication with God

---

Helmet of salvation and breastplate of righteousness: These are the piece of the full armor of God that protect and guard our heart and mind (our soul). Paul stated in Philippians 4:6-9:

> "Be anxious for nothing, but in everything by prayer and supplication with thanksgiving let your request be made known to God. And the peace of God which surpasses all comprehension, shall guard your hearts and your minds in Christ Jesus. Finally, brethren, whatever is true, whatever is honorable, whatever is right, whatever is pure, whatever is lovely, whatever is of good repute, if anything worthy of praise, let your mind dwell on these things. The things you have learned and received and heard and seen in me, practice these things; and the God of peace shall be with you."

The helmet of salvation protects our mind, and the breastplate of righteousness protects our heart. Together, they protect and guard our soul. Peter stated in Acts 4:12 there is salvation in no one else but Jesus, and Paul stated in 2 Corinthians 5:21 the righteousness that is in us is the righteousness of Jesus. In addition to Jesus doing His part to protect and guard our mind and heart, we must do our part. Our mind must dwell on things that are true, honorable, right, pure, lovely, of good repute, excellent and worthy of praise. We must keep our mind free of things that will defile it and pull us back into the sinful and disobedient life from which God has freed us through Jesus. We must give the Holy Spirit permission to enter our life and carry out His transforming process for the righteousness of Jesus to dwell and grow in our heart, and we must obey Jesus' words.

Loins girded with truth: This is the first piece of the full armor of God mentioned by Paul. The truth he referred to is the truth found in the Bible. This truth equips us for ministry and service to God. The dress for men during Jesus' day usually included:

- A tunic-coat or ketonet, which was a long close-fitting inner garment,

- A cloak or mantle, which was a large, loose-fitting garment worn over the Ketonet for warmth or appearance, and
- A girdle, which was usually two to six inches wide, made either of cloth or leather, and worn around the Ketonet.

A man prepared himself for action or service by pulling the Ketonet and cloak when he wore one up around his loins and tied them in place with the girdle to give him adequate freedom of movement. Girded loins were a symbol of readiness for action or service.

The same symbol applies to activities in the spiritual realm. Jesus stated in John 8:31-32:

> "If you abide in My word, then you are truly disciples of Mine; and you shall know the truth and the truth shall make you free."

The freedom Jesus referred to is freedom from the eternal consequences of sin, bondage to Satan, spiritual death, guilt and depression, and anything else that would keep us from effectively engaging in Christian service or spiritual conflicts. This freedom allows us to place our eyes firmly on Jesus as our savior and our source of power and authority. This equips us for uninhibited action and service. Jesus stated the only way to obtain this freedom is to know His truth, and the only way to know His truth is to know and apply God's word in the Bible to our life. Having our loins girded with truth involves being obedient to God by applying the Scriptures to and living them through our life. The better we know and the more we live God's word in and through our life, the greater our freedom and effectiveness in ministry and service to Him and others and the greater our ability to prevail in spiritual conflicts.

Feet shod with the preparation of the gospel of peace: This is the second piece of the full armor of God that equips us for ministry and service to God. This preparation is directly related to our knowledge and understanding of God's word in the Bible. Feet shod with the preparation of gospel of peace equip us for action and conflict in the spiritual realm. We wear shoes to facilitate effective movement and keep our feet comfortable and in good health. Our feet often become sore, and we experience difficulty walking when we allow our shoes to wear out and become ineffective in protecting them. It is the same in the spiritual realm. We become more effectively equipped for ministry and service to God as we grow in our knowledge and understanding of the Bible. The greater our knowledge and understanding of the Scriptures, the greater our ability to maneuver in the spiritual realm when engaged in spiritual conflict. Spiritual forces that stand against us can often out maneuver and defeat us when we lack knowledge of the Scriptures.

The shield of faith: This is the third piece of the full armor of God that equips us for ministry and service to God. The shield of faith enables us to "extinguish all the flaming missiles of Satan. It is directly associated with God's word. Paul stated in Romans 10:17, "So faith comes from hearing, and hearing by the word of Christ." Faith comes from studying and hearing God's word preached and witnessing it work in the lives of other Christians. For faith to develop and grow, we must:

- Be a part of a local Christian church,
- Read and study the Bible,
- Hear the Bible discussed and preached,
- Witness biblical principles and laws work in the lives of other Christians, and
- Experience these principles and laws work in our own life.

In the spiritual realm, properly covered feet and girded loins prepare us for effective service and ministry and enable us to effectively engage in spiritual conflict. However, only faith allows us to repel and extinguish all the flaming missiles that Satan throws at us. These missiles come toward us in the form of problems, sickness, adversity, affliction, persecution, etc. Faith that comes from studying, hearing and internalizing God's word in the Bible will enable us to stand firm against and repel all these missiles.

Sword of the Spirit: This is the only piece of the full armor of God that is a divinely powerful offensive weapon in the spiritual realm. The sword of the Spirit is God's word in the Bible. Paul stated in 2 Corinthians 10:3-4:

> "For though we walk in the flesh, we do not war according to the flesh, for the weapons of our warfare are not of the flesh, but divinely powerful, for the destruction of fortresses."

The only divinely powerful weapons at our disposal in spiritual conflicts are God's word and prayer. The only way to effectively use any offensive weapon is to know and understand how to use it and then practice using it. To prevail against Satan and his demonic forces, we must:

- Know and understand our covenant rights with God through Jesus.
- Know and believe Satan has already been judged and defeated and we have authority over him in the name of Jesus.
- Know how to use the power and authority we have through God's word in the name of Jesus.

- Know how to implement the Scriptures as we live in the kingdom of God and participate in ministries to which God calls us.
- Know how to use the power and authority we have been given in the name of Jesus in spiritual conflicts.

Prayer: Some may argue prayer is technically not part of the full armor of God. However, prayer is a divinely powerful offensive weapon in the spiritual realm. Paul commanded us to always be in continual communication with God through praying for the needs of others and ourselves.

Paul taught by using the metaphor of clothing ourselves with Roman armor how we can effectively prepare and equip ourselves to engage and prevail in spiritual conflicts with Satan and his demonic forces. These center around our being part of a local Christian church where we can study and grow in our understanding of the Bible, participate in Christian fellowship, and engage God through prayer. The extent to which we do these determines:

- The spiritual freedom we have through Jesus,
- Our ability to effectively participate in ministries and service to God and others,
- Our ability to effectively engage in spiritual conflicts, and
- The degree to which God reveals Himself to us and gives to us those things He desires us to have.

CHAPTER 16
SPIRITUAL GIFTS
DEFINITION AND USE OF SPIRITUAL GIFTS

"For just as we have many members in one body and all the members do not have the same function, so we, who are many, are one body in Christ, and individually members one of another. And since we have gifts that differ according to the grace given to us, let each exercise them accordingly: if prophecy, according to the proportion of his faith; if service, in his serving; or he who teaches, in his teaching; or he who exhorts, in his exhortation; he who gives, with liberality; he who leads with diligence; he who shows mercy, with cheerfulness." (Romans 12:4-8)

"Therefore, I make known to you, that no one speaking by the Spirit of God says, "Jesus is accursed"; and no one can say, "Jesus is Lord," except by the Holy Spirit. Now there are varieties of gifts, but the same Spirit. And there are varieties of ministries, and the same Lord. And there are varieties of effects, but the same God who works all things in all persons. But to each one is given the manifestation of the Spirit for the common good. For one is given the word of wisdom through the Spirit, and to another the word of knowledge according to the same Spirit; to another faith by the same Spirit, and to another gifts of healing by the same Spirit, and to another the effecting of miracles, and to another prophecy, and to another the distinguishing of spirits, to another various kinds of tongues, and to another the interpretation of tongues. But one and the same Spirit works all things, distributing to each individually just as He wills. ... And God has appointed in the church, first apostles, second prophets, third teachers, then miracles, then gifts of healing, helps, administrations, various kinds of tongues." (1 Corinthians 12:3-11, 28)

"And He gave some as apostles, and some as prophets, and some as evangelists, and some as pastors and teachers, for the equipping of the saints for the work of service, to the building up of the body of Christ; until we all attain to the unity of the faith, and of the knowledge of the Son of God, to a mature man, to the measure of the stature which belongs to the fullness of Christ." (Ephesians 4:11-13)

DEFINITION OF SPIRITUAL GIFTS

God expects us to do good works and enter ministries and service to Him and others when we enter a relationship with Him through Jesus and grow to spiritual maturity. These works, ministries and service will be administered and accomplished through the Body of Christ, the Church. They will be accomplished through local churches. God provides us with the means to do what He calls us to do when He calls us to do good works and enter ministries and service. Paul stated in 2 Corinthians 3:5-6:

"Not that we are adequate in ourselves to consider anything as coming from ourselves, but our adequacy is from God, who also made us adequate as servants of a new covenant, not of the letter, but of the Spirit; for the letter kills, but the Spirit gives life."

God enables us to serve by giving us spiritual gifts.

We need to distinguish between the *gift of the Holy Spirit* and *gifts of the Holy Spirit* (spiritual gifts). Peter stated in Acts 2:38 we receive the *gift of the Holy Spirit* when we enter a reconciled relationship with God through our faith in Jesus. This occurs when we accept Jesus as our Lord and Savior, and the Holy Spirit takes up residence in us. Paul asked in 1 Corinthians 3:16:

"Do you not know that you are a temple of God, and that the Spirit of God dwells in you?"

Gifts of the Holy Spirit are spiritual gifts the Holy Spirit gives to us to build up the Body of Christ, the Church. This enables and prepares members of local churches to participate in ministries and service to God and others. *Spiritual gifts are channels of power through which the Holy Spirit works in and through our life to accomplish the ministries God desires to perform through us as disciples of Jesus.*

Psalms 139:13-16 states:

> "For You formed my inward parts;
> You wove me in my mother's womb.
> I will give thanks to You, for I am fearfully and wonderfully made;
> Wonderful are Your works,
> And my soul knows it very well.
> My frame was not hidden from You,
> When I was made in secret,
> And skillfully wrought in the depths of the earth;
> Your eyes have seen my unformed substance;
> And in Your book were all written
> The days that were ordained for me,
> When as yet there was not one of them."

These Psalms teach the foundations for our personality attributes, human talents and life skills that will develop as we physically and emotionally grow and mature are imparted to us at birth. Also imparted to us at birth are the spiritual gifts God will equip us through the Holy Spirit to use in ministry and service to others should we choose to enter a reconciled relationship with Him through Jesus. Our human talents and life skills develop under our control as we physically and emotionally grow and mature. Our spiritual gifts become active in our life and develop under the guidance of the Holy Spirit as we spiritually grow and mature in our relationship with God through our faith in Jesus.

Spiritual gifts are divine supernatural abilities given to Christians by the Holy Spirit to equip them to do good works and participate in ministries and service to God and others through a local church. They are:

- Administered by and through a local church,
- Given for the purpose of building up the local church, and
- Given so the local church can be equipped to minister to the community and region it serves and to the world.

Our unique spiritual gifts are revealed to us by and developed in us under the guidance of the Holy Spirit to equip us to perform the good works God has prepared beforehand for us to enter. Paul stated in 1 Corinthians 14:32:

> "And the spirits of prophets are subject to the prophets; for God is not a God of confusion but of peace, as in all the churches of the saints."

The Holy Spirit works in and through us in cooperation with our human spirit.

ORGANIZATION OF SPIRITUAL GIFTS

Information on the organization of spiritual gifts in the church is given by Paul in 1 Corinthians 12:4-6:

> "Now there are varieties of gifts, but the same Spirit. And there are varieties of ministries, and the same Lord. And there are varieties of effects, but the same God who works all things in all persons."

There are three categories of spiritual gifts. The first category is varieties of gifts. This comes from the Greek word *charisma*, which is translated a miraculous faculty, a spiritual endowment. The second category is varieties of ministries. This comes from the Greek word *diakonia*, which can be translated service. The third category is variety of effects. This comes from the Greek word *energema*, which can be translated operations, workings. *Energema* is derived from the Greek word *energo*, which can be translated to be mighty in or powerful.

Paul provided a complete list of the spiritual gifts in Romans 12:4-8, 1 Corinthians 12:3-11, 28, and Ephesians 4:11-13. There is no consensus as to how this list should be divided into categories of varieties of gifts, ministries and effects. However, a suggested grouping of the list of spiritual gifts given to us by Paul is given in Table 8.

Table 8

Motivational Gifts Gifts (*charisma*)	Operation (or Manifestation) of the Holy Spirit (*energema*)	Ministries (*diakonia*)
		Ephesians 4:11-13
Romans 12:4-8	1 Corinthians 12:3-11	1 Corinthians 12:28
prophecy	word of wisdom	apostles
service	word of knowledge	prophets
teaching	faith	evangelist
exhortation	gifts of healing	pastors
giving	effecting miracles	teachers
leading	prophecy	ministries of miracles
(administration)	distinguishing of spirits	ministries of healing
showing mercy	various kinds of tongues	ministries of helps
	interpretation of tongues	(service ministries
		of administration
		ministries of various
		kinds of tongues

Variety of Gifts

Varieties of gifts (*charisma*) are spiritual gifts that equip us for specific areas of ministry and service within a local church to which God calls and the Holy Spirit equips us to participate. Varieties of gifts are often called motivational gifts. Everyone is given a core cluster of motivational gifts by God. The cluster normally consists of two or three spiritual gifts where one gift is more dominant than the others. Our motivational spiritual gifts:

- Represent inherent tendencies and specific capabilities God creates within us at birth; and
- Identify areas of ministry and service within a local church to which God calls and the Holy Spirit equips us to participate.

Varieties of Operations of the Holy Spirit

Varieties of operations of the Holy Spirit *(energema)* refer to the supernatural operations of the Holy Spirit that work within and through each of us in union with our human spirit. Operations of the Holy Spirit are:

- Administered by the Holy Spirit for the common good of all in a local church;
- Distributed by the Holy Spirit to each person as He wills; and
- Designed to elevate our interaction with God through the Holy Spirit from purely intellectual and emotional levels to a supernatural spiritual level.

They are spiritual gifts the Holy Spirit uses through our motivational gifts to equip us to participate in the areas of ministry and service we are called by God to participate in our local church. They are used in union with our human spirit to enable us to more effectively:

- Participate in the areas of ministry and service to which God calls us;
- Interact with the spiritual realm in a manner specified by and acceptable to God;
- Communicate with and receive information from God through the Holy Spirit; and
- Effectively enter spiritual conflicts with divinely powerful spiritual weapons.

Varieties of Ministries

Varieties of ministries *(diakonia)* are channels of ministry and service available to us within our local church through which we apply our motivational gifts. They are often referred to as gifts of ministry that are used to build up and equip a local church for ministry and service. This enables the church to minister to and serve its local community and the world. Gifts of office described in Ephesians 4:11-12 (apostles, prophets, evangelists, pastors and teachers) are used to train, equip and motivate members of a local church to participate in specific areas of ministry and service to which they may be called. Other gifts in this group (gifts of miracles, healing, helps, administrations and various kinds of tongues) are used to nurture and support the members of a local church, organize and coordinate the programs and ministries of the church, and enable the church to be in ministry and service to persons inside and outside of the church. Depending on our cluster of motivational gifts, God calls each of us to specific areas of ministry and service. We may be called to participate in more than one area of ministry and service, but we usually have one predominant ministry or service to which God calls us.

Relation between the Varieties of Gifts, Operations and Ministries

There is no consensus as to how the categories of spiritual gifts relate to one another. The following is suggested. Activities of the Holy Spirit in our life that proceed from our motivational gifts work through our gifts of ministry. Supernatural operations of the Holy Spirit function in conjunction with our motivational gifts through our gifts of ministry to produce specific results in our ministries. This explanation is consistent with Paul's discussion on the organization of spiritual gifts in 1 Corinthians 12:7-11. The following relation is suggested by this explanation:

[Motivational Gifts + Operations of the Holy Spirit] -> Ministries -> Results

The Holy Spirits gives each one of us as Christians a specific and unique cluster of spiritual gifts. He gives us specific motivational gifts and calls us to specific areas of ministry and service. Paul instructed us to earnestly desire and seek our specific spiritual gifts and ministries. We must humbly receive and accept the spiritual gifts the Holy Spirit chooses to give us and enter and participate in the ministries and service to which the Holy Spirit calls us. God expects us to develop our unique cluster of spiritual gifts through Bible study, fellowship and prayer after we have sought and discovered them. We are then to use them in His service through our local church. We must be sensitive and obedient to the leadership of the Holy Spirit in receiving, developing and using those operations of the Holy Spirit He chooses to use through us to more effectively equip us for ministry and service.

PRINCIPLES ASSOCIATED WITH SPIRITUAL GIFTS

With respect to the distribution of spiritual gifts, the following principles apply (Kinghorn and Gustafson, *Discovering and Using Your Spiritual Gifts*, 1987):

- God imparts the gifts of the Holy Spirit by His divine grace. Spiritual gifts cannot be requested or earned by human merit.

- Spiritual gifts are distributed according to God's discretion. They are never distributed according to our own demands or desires. The Holy Spirit distributes spiritual gifts within a local church as He chooses.

- Every Christian has a unique cluster of spiritual gifts. However, there may be some Christians who have not discovered their spiritual gifts, choose not to use their spiritual gifts when they discover them, or misuse their spiritual gifts.

- No Christian has all the spiritual gifts. Paul affirmed this in 1 Corinthians 12. Different clusters of spiritual gifts are given to individuals within a local church who then are expected to work together in unity to build up the church in Christ.

- God gives spiritual gifts to train and equip members of a local church for ministries and service to themselves, the community they serve, and the world. God never gives spiritual gifts for the purpose of exalting specific individuals within a local church. We are expected to use our spiritual gifts in ministries and service so Jesus can be glorified in and through us.

With respect to the use of spiritual gifts in a local church, the following principles apply (Kinghorn and Gustafson, *Discovering and Using Your Spiritual Gifts*, 1987):

- Spiritual gifts should flow naturally out of our relationship with Jesus. They are never taught or imparted from one individual to another. They are never contrived, coerced, or manipulated. There are no prescribed formulas or procedures for receiving them.

- Spiritual gifts should be used for the benefit of others and to help them grow spiritually. They should be unpretentious. They should never draw attention to ourself or be used in a manner that makes others feel uncomfortable or embarrassed. Spiritual gifts should always be used to facilitate moving into a reconciled relationship with God through Jesus and discovering one's own spiritual gifts.

- Spiritual gifts should draw Christians together in unity. They should never be used in a manner that divides a local church.

- Spiritual gifts should receive a balanced emphasis in the life of a local church. They should never be perceived as an end in themselves, but rather be used to an end. They should be used to train, equip and enable persons for ministries and service. With respect to the life of a church, emphasis on spiritual gifts and their use should be balanced with emphases on prayer, evangelism, missions, stewardship, etc.

- Spiritual gifts should always function from an inner motive of love. They work in unity to build up and edify a local church when they are properly fitted together in love.

- Spiritual gifts and the fruit of the Spirit (Ephesians 5:22-23) should develop and work together in our life. Spiritual gifts are channels of power through which the Holy Spirit works in our life to equip us for ministries and service. The development of the fruit of the Spirit in our life represents the development of high moral character and our quality of life. The discovery, development and use of our spiritual gifts equip us for ministries and service and to enter spiritual warfare with divinely powerful spiritual weapons. The development of the fruit of the Spirit in our life is a measure of our growth to spiritual maturity and adulthood.

DESCRIPTIONS OF SPIRITUAL GIFTS

Motivational Gifts

Prophecy: Prophecy is the ability to accurately present God's word with clarity, forthrightness and insight. Prophecies are generally messages, warnings, exhortations and revelations that are derived from an understanding of the Bible under the inspiration and leadership of the Holy Spirit. They can be directed toward the spiritual life and purity of a local church or the Body of Christ, the Church, in general.

Service: Service is the ability in a task-oriented manner to meet the temporal needs of others and render loving and caring assistance to others; it is also the ability to give practical assistance to individuals, thus relieving them to perform even greater or other services to others.

Teaching: Teaching is the ability to understand and clarify the truths received from God in the Bible and communicate God's word contained in the Bible to others in a manner they understand.

Exhortation: Exhortation is the ability to call forth the best that is within others in an understanding, encouraging and uplifting manner. An exhorter can motivate other Christians to move into a deeper faith in and dedication to Jesus and cause an individual or individuals to move from a particular problem to a resolution to the problem.

Giving: Giving is the ability to discern and understand the material and financial needs of others and then meet these needs in a magnanimous manner. God prospers those individuals who have and use the gift of giving so they can give even more.

Leading (Administration): Administration is the ability to provide leadership and direction in administration and organizational matters. The gift of leading implies the ability to recognize and focus the spiritual gifts and abilities of others into coordinated plans of action.

Showing Mercy: Showing mercy is the ability to discern and understand the spiritual, emotional and physical needs of others and then move to meet these needs with empathy, respect and honesty.

Operations of the Holy Spirit

Word of Wisdom: A word of wisdom is a supernatural insight and perspective, which enables one to sense divine direction and act in an appropriate manner relative to a specific situation or problem. A word of wisdom generally works interactively with a word of knowledge and spiritual discernment.

Word of Knowledge: A word of knowledge is a supernaturally revealed fact relative to a situation or person that is essential to continuing the process of moving to resolution of a problem or problems associated with the situation or person. A word of knowledge can also be a supernatural revelation associated with God's will relative to a specific situation.

Faith: Faith as a manifestation or operation of the Holy Spirit transcends the normal faith the Bible instructs us to have in God. It is the supernatural ability to believe in God without doubt, enabling an individual to move in directions, initiate actions, or participate in ministries to which God calls him/her.

Gifts of healing: Gifts of healing as a manifestation or operation of the Holy Spirit refers to supernatural healing without human aid. Gifts of healing extend to healing of the human spirit, soul and body. They can be associated with deliverance from addictions and spiritual bondage, emotional healing and physical healing. Gifts of healing may include divinely assisted applications of normal medical treatments.

Effecting miracles: Effecting miracles are actions which supernaturally intervene and counteract earthly or evil forces in a manner that supersedes known natural laws. Effecting miracles often work in conjunction with the manifestations of faith and gifts of healing.

Prophecy: Prophecy as a manifestation or operation of the Holy Spirit is a supernatural proclamation of God's word in a language known to the speaker that is inspired by the Holy Spirit and not by human intellect. Prophecy as a manifestation or operation of the Holy Spirit will never contradict or be different from what God has already revealed in the Bible.

Distinguishing of spirits: Distinguishing of spirits is the supernatural ability to distinguish between actions and activities that are associated with divine, human, or satanic sources. It is the ability to discern the presence of demonic spirits in an area and whether a specific teaching or counsel is divinely, humanly, or demonically inspired.

Various kinds of tongues: Various kinds of tongues are the ability to speak in a language not known to the speaker. The language can be a language that exists in the world, can be revived from some past culture, or can be a heavenly language. Speaking in tongues is an action where the Holy Spirit speaks directly through the human spirit of the speaker. Various kinds of tongues can be prophetic utterances, or they can be utterances that praise and glorify Jesus. The Holy Spirit as with prophecy will never reveal anything through various kinds of tongues that contradicts or is different from what God has already revealed in the Bible.

Interpretation of tongues: Interpretation of tongues is the supernatural ability to reveal the meaning of a message publicly spoken in tongues. The interpretation of tongues is associated with the Holy Spirit speaking directly through the human spirit of the interpreter in a language known to the interpreter and those who hear the massage publicly spoken in tongues. Normally, the individual who interprets a message in tongues does not understand the tongue language he/she interprets.

Ministries

Apostles: Apostles can communicate the Gospel of Jesus across cultural and linguistic barriers and plant new Christian churches in areas where there is no knowledge of the Christian Gospel. The office of apostle is thought to have ended with the death of the last apostle of Jesus. Missionaries are often considered to be modern-day apostles.

Prophets: Prophets are spiritually mature individuals who have a special, divinely focused message to the church or to the world. Prophets are uniquely gifted individuals who have the motivational gift of prophecy.

Evangelists: Evangelists can present the Gospel of Jesus to uncommitted individuals in a manner that leads them to accept Jesus as their Lord and Savior. Evangelists usually have the motivational gift of prophecy.

Pastors: Pastors can shepherd or lead and nurture, care for and teach a body of Christian believers.

Teachers: Teachers can understand and communicate biblical principles and the Christian faith to others in manners that make their truths clear.

Ministries of miracles: The ministry of miracles is performed by those individuals in whom the Holy Spirit works His manifestation of effecting miracles and the gifts of healing. Usually the ministry of miracles and ministries associated with gifts of healing work together.

Ministries of healing: Healing ministries are usually undertaken by spiritually mature individuals who have the motivational gift of showing mercy and who have been called by the Holy Spirit to facilitate healing of the human spirit, soul and body. Healing ministries generally involve individuals who are:

- Sensitive to the spiritual, emotional and physical needs of other individuals;
- Sensitive to the leading and guiding of the Holy Spirit;
- Understand and know how to use prayers of healing, authority and deliverance; and
- Understand and know how to use the supernatural manifestations or operations of the Holy Spirit. Healing can be accomplished:
- Supernaturally through the proper uses of prayer and spiritual gifts,
- Normally through the proper application of medical treatment, counseling and medication, or
- Through a combination of the proper uses of prayer and spiritual gifts and the proper application of medical treatment, counseling and medication.

Ministries of helps: Ministries of helps are normally undertaken by those individuals who have the motivational gift of service.

Ministries of administration: Ministries of administrations are normally undertaken by those individuals who have the motivational gift of leading.

Ministries of various kinds of tongues: Ministries of various kinds of tongues are normally undertaken by those individuals who have the manifestations or operations of the Holy Spirit of various kinds of tongues and interpretation of tongues. This ministry involves the speaking in tongues and the interpretation of tongues in public meetings and services. More will be said about this in the next chapter.

DISCOVERING OUR SPIRITUAL GIFTS

The Bible instructs us to desire, seek, not neglect and use our spiritual gifts to serve one another. Following are reasons why we should desire and seek our spiritual gifts (Kinghorn and Gustafson, *Discovering and Using Your Spiritual Gifts*, 1987):

- Helps us to determine and understand God's will for our life's vocation and our ministries within a local church. Identifying our spiritual gifts gives our life direction and helps us to understand what God wants us to do with our life both in our church and the secular community where we live.

- Mobilizes a local church for Christ's ministries. We have all been given spiritual gifts according to God's grace in us, and as a result, we are ministers of Christ. Identifying our spiritual gifts enables us to determine where we should plug into the life and ministry of our church. Paul instructed us in 1 Corinthians 12 to always honor each other's gifts. Some will be given highly visible gifts, such as prophecy, teaching, exhortation, speaking in tongues, etc., whereas others will be given inconspicuous gifts, such as serving, giving, showing mercy, etc. Paul indicated all spiritual gifts are essential for a healthy and active church.

- Assists us in establishing priorities for study, growth and ministry within a local church. To effectively grow, a church must establish strategic plans to determine areas it must develop, directions it must go, commitments it must make concerning its resources, and ministries it desires to enter. A local church must know in what areas various individuals should develop and into what ministries they should enter. Churches should enter those ministries and areas of service where they are uniquely gifted.

- Gives everyone in a local church a healthy sense of self-acceptance and self-worth. It is edifying to know each one of us is uniquely gifted for service to God.

- Enables everyone to receive support and assistance from others within a local church. We all benefit and are supported as everyone uses their specific spiritual gifts in the life and ministries of the church.

- Fosters unity among the members of a local church. We have all been given spiritual gifts as members of the body of Christ. Therefore, we all have unique contributions to make to the life and ministries of our church. We grow in our love for each other and our ability to function with others as we use our spiritual gifts.

Following are six principles associated with discovering your spiritual gifts (Kinghorn and Gustafson, *Discovering and Using Your Spiritual Gifts*, 1987):

- Open yourself to God as a channel for His use. You must seek your spiritual gifts along with the giver of the gifts, God. You must seek them with pure and honest motives and the intent to enter ministries and service to God through Jesus. You must submit to God's authority and leading in your life and accept His choice of spiritual gifts for you.

- Examine your natural desires for service and ministries. You should pay close attention to your hungers, longings, dreams, hopes, desires and aspirations. Keeping these things in balance, you should look to doing those things you enjoy doing. Examine those gifts that seem to be naturally appealing and desirable to you.

- Identify those areas of need you feel are important in the life of your church. There are needs that underlie each of the spiritual gifts. Quite often areas of need you identify as important are areas where you should be involved. Identify those areas of greatest perceived needs. These will often point you to specific spiritual gifts.

- Evaluate the results of your efforts to be involved in specific areas of ministry. Identify areas where you have been affirmed and received little positive affirmation, where doors have been naturally opened and closed, and where opportunities have normally and naturally developed and have been closed off. These point to specific ministries where God may desire you to participate.

- Obey the written Word of God in the Bible. God commands you to be good stewards over those resources and opportunities He entrusts to your care. Before you will be given opportunities in great things, you must prove your faithfulness in small things. The development of your relationship with God through Jesus is a process that occurs over a long period of time. God will reveal your spiritual gifts to you as He determines you are ready to receive and use them. Be sensitive as you study the Bible to those areas you readily understand. Trust the leading of the Holy Spirit to act upon what you know and understand because this will lead you in the directions God wants you to go.

- Listen to the response and counsel of other mature Christians. Quite often they will see and perceive things in you that you do not. You normally discover your spiritual gifts in a community of Christians. Others may see and identify specific spiritual gifts you have before you do. Also, others may confirm specific spiritual gifts you have already identified. Learn to rely on and receive what others give to you in service and ministries because this will help you develop your spiritual gifts as you learn how to serve and minister to others.

You can use the Spiritual Gifts Inventory located in Appendix C at the end of this book to help begin the process of identifying your specific clusters of spiritual gifts and ministries.

DEVELOPING OUR SPIRITUAL GIFTS

In Hebrews 5:14, the author stated:

> "But solid food is for the mature, who because of practice have their senses trained to discern good and evil."

We develop and learn how to use our spiritual gifts:

- In an environment of Christian fellowship in a local Christian church;
- Through the study of the Bible;
- By developing a clear understanding of our covenant relationship with God through Jesus and the role the Holy Spirit plays in this relationship;
- As we develop a relationship with God through prayer;
- As we become sensitive and obedient to the leading of the Holy Spirit;
- As we become accountable to and develop relationships with spiritually mature Christians whom God places in authority over us; and
- Through the tutelage and guidance of mature Christians who enter mentoring and teaching relationships with us.

We develop and learn how to use our spiritual gifts by employing them in ministries and service in and through our local church. We begin in small areas with proper instruction and supervision. We start to move out on our own under the guidance of the Holy Spirit as we continue to grow and develop our spiritual gifts. We engage in ministries and areas of service with greater responsibilities until we grow to maturity and have our "senses trained to discern good and evil."

CHAPTER 17
SPIRITUAL GIFTS
BAPTISM WITH THE HOLY SPIRIT

"Then He opened their minds to understand the Scriptures and He said to them, 'Thus it is written, that the Christ should suffer and rise again from the dead the third day; and that repentance for forgiveness of sins should be proclaimed in His name to all the nations, beginning from Jerusalem. You are witnesses of these things. And behold, I am sending forth the promise of My Father upon you; but you are to stay in the city until you are clothed with power from on high.'" (Luke 24:45-49)

"And gathering them together, He commanded them not to leave Jerusalem, but to wait for what the Father had promised, 'Which,' He said, 'you heard from Me; for John baptized with water, but you shall be baptized with the Holy Spirit not many days from now.' And so when they had come together, they were asking Him, saying, 'Lord, is it at this time You are restoring the kingdom to Israel?' He said to them, 'It is not for you to know times or epochs which the Father has fixed by His own authority; but you shall receive power when the Holy Spirit has come upon you; and you shall be My witnesses both in Jerusalem and in all Judea and Samaria and even to the remotest part of the earth.'" (Acts 1:4-8)

"And when the day of Pentecost had come, they were all together in one place. And suddenly there came from heaven a noise like a violent, rushing wind and it filled the whole house where they were sitting. And there appeared to them tongues as of fire distributing themselves and they rested on each one of them. And they were all filled with the Holy Spirit and began to speak with other tongues, as the Spirit was giving them utterance. And when this sound occurred, the multitude came together and were bewildered, because they were each one hearing them speak in his own language." (Acts 2:1-6)

GIFT OF VARIOUS KINDS OF TONGUES

Defining, describing, discovering and developing our unique cluster of spiritual gifts were addressed in the previous chapter. Two of the operations (or manifestations) of the Holy Spirit are various kinds of tongues and interpretation of tongues, and one of the ministries of the Holy Spirit is the ministry of various kinds of tongues. These operations (or manifestations) and related ministry of the Holy Spirit are not well understood in many mainline protestant churches. Confusion and often controversy are associated with these spiritual gifts of the Holy Spirit as a result.

From the preceding chapter:

> Various kinds of tongues are defined as the supernatural ability to speak in a language not known to the speaker. The language can be a language that exists in the world, can be revived from some past culture, or can be a heavenly language. Speaking in tongues is an action where the Holy Spirit speaks directly through the human spirit of the speaker. Various kinds of tongues can be prophetic utterances, or they can be utterances that praise and glorify Jesus.

Receiving the gift of speaking in tongues is normally referred to as receiving the *baptism with the Holy Spirit*. This is different from and should not be confused with receiving the *gift of the Holy Spirit* when we accept Jesus as our Lord and Savior. This spiritual gift when received enables the Holy Spirit to work in and through us in a unique manner. He is also fully present in the lives of those who do not receive this spiritual gift to work in and through them as He wills.

BIBLICAL ACCOUNTS OF SPEAKING IN TONGUES

Bible accounts in Acts associated with the baptism with the Holy Spirit and the gift of speaking in tongues will first be examined. The Bible teaches the disciples had two experiences associated with receiving the Holy Spirit. The first is described in John 20:21-22:

> "Jesus therefore said to them again, 'Peace be with you; as the Father has sent Me, I also send you. And when He had said this, He breathed on them and said to them, 'Receive the Holy Spirit.'"

This occurred after Jesus was raised from the dead but before He ascended into heaven. It involved His breathing on the disciples and enabling them to receive the Holy Spirit. The disciples were the first to be spiritually reborn by receiving the gift of the Holy Spirit. After this, Jesus instructed them in Luke 24:48-49 and in Acts 1:4-8 to wait in Jerusalem until they were "clothed with power from on high." He told them they would be "baptized with the Holy Spirit" and "receive power when the Holy Spirit had come upon" them. This occurred at Pentecost after Jesus had ascended into heaven.

The Greek word for the "power" that Jesus said His disciples would receive at Pentecost is *dunamis*, which is translated miraculous power with the implication the disciples were to be workers of miracles. The same Greek word *dunamis* was used to describe the power of the Holy Spirit Jesus returned to Galilee with after His forty days in the wilderness (Luke 4:1-13) and the same power He had when He healed the sick (Luke 5:17) and commanded demons to come out of persons who were possessed (Luke 4:36). The power the disciples received at Pentecost was the power the Holy Spirit would exercise through the spiritual gifts they had received at Pentecost.

The disciples spoke in tongues at Pentecost when they were baptized with the Holy Spirit. The term *speaking in tongues* is only used in Acts 2:2-4. Two significant events happened at Pentecost:

- The disciples received the power Jesus had promised them when the Holy Spirit came upon and empowered them through His spiritual gifts.
- The Christian church was born, and all the spiritual gifts discussed in the previous chapter on spiritual gifts became operational within the church.

God gave the disciples the gifts of the Holy Spirit at Pentecost. The sign He used to validate this was speaking in tongues. They spoke in languages the people who were there understood as their own native languages.

Other experiences associated with speaking in tongues are recorded in Acts 8:12-17, Acts 10:44-48 and Acts 19:4-7. Jesus told the disciples to begin in Jerusalem, go to Judea and Samaria, and go to the rest of the world. The disciples started with converted Jews, and then they went to the Samaritans and gentiles.

The sign of speaking in tongues recorded in Acts represented major transitions in the growth of the early Christian church.

- Acts 8:12-17 describe Peter and John going to Samaria to lay hands on a group of Samaritans so they could "receive the Holy Spirit." Speaking in tongues was not specifically mentioned, but signs and great miracles were observed after the

Samaritans received the Holy Spirit. In the early church, speaking in tongues was normally accepted as evidence of receiving the Holy Spirit. Therefore, it is reasonable to assume this was one of the signs that occurred with the Samaritans.

- Acts 10:44-48 describe what happened in Cornelius' house when the "Holy Spirit fell upon all those who were listening" to Peter. Peter was presenting the message of salvation through Jesus to the gentiles who were assembled. The gentiles who received the word of salvation "spoke in tongues and exalted God." This was a sign to Peter and the other Jews who were present that the gift of the Holy Spirit and, consequently, salvation through Jesus had been extended to the gentiles.

- Acts 19:4-7 is the last recorded event in Acts associated with speaking in tongues. Paul was passing through Ephesus when he came upon some believers who had not "received the Holy Spirit when they believed." Paul laid his hands on these believers and "the Holy Spirit came upon them, and they began speaking in tongues and prophesying." This is the only recorded incident where Paul laid his hands on believers who then received the Holy Spirit. Perhaps this experience validated Paul's ministry to the gentiles even though there is no clear indication of this fact.

POWER OF THE HOLY SPIRIT IN MINISTRY

Jesus did not begin His earthly ministry until He had experienced water baptism and returned to Galilee in the power of the Holy Spirit. He commanded the disciples to wait in Jerusalem and not begin their ministries until they received power from on high and were baptized with the Holy Spirit at Pentecost. The reason for this is explained in Paul's statements:

> "And my message and my preaching were not in persuasive words of wisdom, but in demonstration of the Spirit and of power, that your faith should not rest on the wisdom of men, but on the power of God. For the kingdom of God does not consist in words, but in power." (1 Corinthians 2:4-5, 4:20)

> "For the gospel did not come to you in word only, but also in power and in the Holy Spirit and with full conviction." (1 Thessalonians 1:5)

Paul stated his preaching was not only in words but also in the "demonstration of the Spirit and of power." He continued our "faith should not rest on the wisdom of men, but on the power of God." The Greek word for power in both statements is *dunamis*, implying the power Paul referred to is the power of the Holy Spirit that manifested itself in the working of miracles. Paul stated in Romans 10:17 faith comes from hearing the Word of Christ preached. He did not contradict this in his statements in 1 Corinthians and 1 Thessalonians. However, he implied it was necessary for those to whom he preached to witness faith work through the power of the Holy Spirit by the working of miracles for faith to be implanted and grow in their minds and hearts.

We make the mistake today of believing we can draw people to Jesus only by persuasive words of wisdom. We center our ministries and service to God and others around preaching and teaching. We do not allow the power of the Holy Spirit to work in and through us by His spiritual gifts. Preaching and teaching God's word are important and must never be ignored. These lead to our growing in our knowledge and understanding of God's spiritual principles contained in the Bible. We cannot apply to and use in our lives what we neither know nor understand. Of equal importance, however, is experiencing the power of the Holy Spirit through His spiritual gifts work in and through us and witnessing this power work in and through the lives of those who have received Jesus as their Lord and Savior. We internalize God's word when these occur, and it becomes written on our mind and implanted in our heart.

BAPTISM WITH THE HOLY SPIRIT

The only direct use of the term "baptism with the Holy Spirit" in the Bible is in reference to Pentecost. Pentecost resulted in the disciples speaking with other tongues and signaled they had received the power of the Holy Spirit Jesus promised in Luke 24:45-49 and Acts 1:4-8. The other accounts in Acts associated with speaking in tongues referred "to the Holy Spirit as being received by" or "to the Holy Spirit falling or coming upon" the individuals who spoke in tongues. In the early church, speaking in tongues was a sign, but not the only sign, an individual had received the Holy Spirit. It also appeared to be the sign the Holy Spirit used when He wanted to confirm to the disciples that salvation through Jesus had also been given to the Samaritans and gentiles, two groups the Jews hated.

Today the term *baptism with the Holy Spirit* is used in charismatic and Pentecostal groups to signify receiving the gift of various kinds of tongues. This is a narrow and unfortunate use of this term. It was used by Jesus to refer to the disciples receiving the power of the Holy Spirit associated with all His spiritual gifts. The gift of various kinds of tongues is only one of these spiritual gifts.

MISUNDERSTANDINGS ASSOCIATED WITH THE GIFT OF VARIOUS KINDS OF TONGUES

Speaking in tongues is used as evidence of being "filled with the Holy Spirit" in Pentecostal and charismatic churches groups. They believe individuals have not received the full power of the Holy Spirit in their lives when they do not speak in tongues. The Bible teaches we receive the gift of the Holy Spirit when we accept Jesus as our Lord and Savior and the He takes up residence in us. The Holy Spirit may choose to give to us the gift of various kinds of tongues as we seek to discover our own spiritual gifts and open to us the ministry of various kinds of tongues. On the other hand, He may choose not to give us these spiritual gifts. These specific spiritual gifts or the lack of them should never be used as an indication of the power of the Holy Spirit working in and through our life.

The presence or the lack of the presence of the above specific spiritual gifts in our life should not be used to indicate the level of our spiritual growth and maturity. The good treasures that proceed from our heart referred to by Jesus in Luke 6:45 and the fruit of the Spirit described by Paul in Galatians 5:22-26 are the only legitimate indication of the level of our spiritual growth and maturity. Our lives must clearly demonstrate our love for the Lord by our obeying His commandments and being involved in ministries and service to God and others.

Cults and individuals who participate in occult activities in Bible and modern times have and still do speak in tongues. These tongues are not from the Holy Spirit; they are from demonic sources. Satan can counterfeit speaking in tongues just as he can counterfeit other spiritual gifts. Therefore, we should never use speaking in tongues or other spiritual gifts as evidence of the presence of the Holy Spirit in a person's life.

Pressure is often placed on individuals to receive the gift of speaking in tongues when this spiritual gift is viewed as a necessary sign for the presence of the Holy Spirit in them. Procedures are often established to facilitate speaking in tongues when this is the case. Spiritual gifts are given to us as the Holy Spirit wills, not as we desire or demand. Spiritual gifts must develop and evolve because of an obedient relationship with God through Jesus. Specific spiritual gifts cannot be coerced, manipulated or developed by following prescribed procedures.

Individuals who receive the gift of speaking in tongues sometimes take on a sense of arrogance because this spiritual gift is one of the more demonstrative spiritual gifts. They have something others do not have. Spiritual gifts must never be used to draw attention to ourself or be used in a manner that makes others feel uncomfortable or embarrassed. Spiritual gifts, including speaking in tongues, must be used in a humble and respectful manner that brings people together in unity. This was at the heart of Paul's discourse on spiritual gifts in 1 Corinthians 14.

In groups where speaking in tongues is expected or required, individuals who do not receive this spiritual gift may feel inferior. They may assume they have sin in their lives that prevents them from speaking in tongues or believe they are not doing what is required to receive this spiritual gift. Paul stated in 1 Corinthians 12:29-31:

> "All are not apostles, are they? All are not prophets, are they? All are not teachers, are they? All are not workers of miracles, are they? All do not have gifts of healing, do they? All do not speak with tongues, do they? All do not interpret, do they? But earnestly desire the greater gifts."

No spiritual gift is received by everyone in a local church. If we desire the gift of various kinds of tongues and the Holy Spirit chooses not to give it to us, we should not feel inferior or guilty nor presume we have or are doing something wrong.

Individuals who receive the gift of various kinds of tongues sometimes become too focused on this spiritual gift, and it becomes the only spiritual gift that is important to them. The Bible teaches we should have a balanced emphasis concerning all spiritual gifts and activities related to spiritual gifts within a local church. Our desire should not be focused on receiving and developing specific spiritual gifts. It should be directed at properly developing and using the spiritual gifts we receive to build up our local churches and equip them for ministries and service to God and others.

Some believe and teach speaking in tongues ended with the age of the early church. They indicate the gift of various kinds of tongues was only given for use in the early church. They further teach there is no valid use for speaking in tongues in the church today. The Bible and history do not support this. The Bible does not teach the Holy Spirit has altered the number and types of spiritual gifts He has given to enable and equip local churches for ministries and service to others. The gift of various kinds of tongues is one of the spiritual gifts described by Paul, and its use in local churches today is just as valid and necessary as it was during the time of the early church. Historically, the gift of various kinds of tongues have been present in churches from the days of the early church to the present. The gifts of various kinds and interpretation of tongues, along with the ministry of various kinds of tongues, are used in Pentecostal and charismatic churches, including some non-charismatic churches, to equip them for ministry and service to God and others.

GUIDELINES FOR THE PROPER USE OF THE GIFT OF VARIOUS KINDS OF TONGUES

Speaking in tongues is one of the multiple signs of the presence of the Holy Spirit in our life and the life of a local church. We should never be afraid to desire and seek this spiritual gift, but we must accept the discretion of the Holy Spirit as to whether He will choose to give us this spiritual gift. The gift of various kinds of tongues is used in two ways in a local church. The first is associated with its use in our private prayer life. The second is associated with its use in the ministry of various kinds of tongues.

Use of Speaking in Tongues in our Prayer Life

Paul stated in Romans 8:26-27:

> "And in the same way the Spirit also helps our weakness; for we do not know how to pray as we should, but the Spirit Himself intercedes for us with groanings too deep for words; and He who searches the hearts knows what the mind of the Spirit is, because He intercedes for the saints according to the will of God."

We may not know how or for what to pray when we pray. Paul stated the Holy Spirit will intercede for us when this occurs. The Holy Spirit speaks to God through our human spirit when we pray using the gift of various kinds of tongues. Paul taught in 1 Corinthians 14:2:

> "For one who speaks in a tongue does not speak to men, but to God; for no one understands, but in his spirit he speaks mysteries."

We speak words God desires to hear when we pray to Him using the gift of speaking in tongues, so He can appropriately respond to the situations for which we are praying. This is important in prayers of intercession, healing, authority, deliverance and protection. For these prayers, we may not know precisely how or for what to specifically pray, but the Holy Spirit knows. He conveys the right information to God through our prayers in tongues.

We may be engaged in spiritual conflict with demonic forces when using prayers of authority and deliverance. We can more effectively engage in these conflicts when we pray using the gift of speaking in tongues. The Holy Spirit knows what we must pray to exercise authority Jesus has given to us in the spiritual realm. He is often better able to assist in exercising this authority through our speaking in tongues.

Paul implied in 1 Corinthians 14:2 our spirit prays to God when we pray using the gift of various kinds of tongues. Our intellectual understanding of a particular situation may be inadequate and impede our ability to effectively pray for the situation. The Holy Spirit can pray through our human spirit to God by speaking in tongues when we obediently submit to Him. This assures us we are effectively praying for the needs that have initiated our prayer.

Paul indicated in 1 Corinthians 14:2 we pray in mysteries and do not know nor understand our prayer when we pray using the gift of various kinds of tones. We do not need to know or understand our prayer when we pray under the guidance of the Holy Spirit. He will always give us the right words to speak. However, God does not want us to be uninformed. Paul stated in 1 Corinthians 14:13, "Therefore, let one who speaks in a tongue to pray that he may interpret." We can ask the Holy Spirit for the interpretation of our prayer, and He will give it to us. He can give us the interpretation directly through our mind and spirit, through an encounter with another Christian, or through a revelation associate with a specific scripture in the Bible.

Use of Speaking in Tongues in the Ministry of Various Kinds of Tongues

There are three operations (or manifestations) of the Holy Spirit that are used to supernaturally convey information in public meetings: prophecy, various kinds of tongues and interpretation of tongues. Paul spoke about these spiritual gifts in 1 Corinthians 14. He stated everything done in a public meeting must be for the edification of those who are present and in an orderly fashion. He indicated the preferred method for communicating God's truth in meetings is through the gift of prophecy in a language those who are present understand.

There are times when the Holy Spirit may choose to have someone give a message using the gift of various kinds of tongues. This occurrence is referred to as the ministry of various kinds of tongues. Not everyone who receives the gift of various kinds of tongues is given a ministry of various kinds of tongues. An interpretation must be given by an individual with the gift of interpretation of tongues when a public message is presented by an individual speaking in tongues. The person in charge of the meeting must ensure messages present by speaking in tongues are properly interpreted.

Public messages presented by speaking in tongues normally:

- Address truths that God wants to reveal about His Word;
- Praise and glorify Jesus;
- Confirm or affirm that events that have or are occurring in the life of an individual or a Christian organization are consistent with the will of God; and
- Confirm or affirm that God is or will be with us during specific situations or events.

Messages given by speaking in tongues point us toward and focuses us on God through Jesus as the source of all authority, truth and power.

Messages that give specific details related to future events are rare. God requires us to trust and have faith in Him concerning these events as they unfold in our life. He will usually not tell us about them before they occur. The Holy Spirit usually speaks in a general sense, encouraging us to trust God for the things He plans to give or reveal to us when He does speak about the future through a message given by speaking in tongues.

Information concerning God's word revealed through messages received through speaking in tongues always find their confirmation in the Bible. *God never reveals information relative to His word either through prophecy or speaking in tongues that contradicts His word presented in the Bible.*

Paul did not instruct the believers at Corinth to stop speaking in tongues when he wrote to them. He encouraged them to continue, but he stated in 1 Corinthians 14:15, 18-19:

> "I shall pray with the spirit and I shall pray with the mind also; I shall sing with the spirit and I shall sing with the mind also. ... I thank God, I speak in tongues more than you all; however, in church I desire to speak five words with my mind, that I may instruct others also, rather than ten thousand words in a tongue."

Paul taught everything must assume its proper perspective and place in our Christian experience and in local churches. He stated speaking in tongues is important, and when we pray in tongues, we speak to God, using words He desires and needs to hear. However, Paul also stated speaking and praying in words others understand to instruct, edify and lift up a body of believers are more important.

Paul instructed us to earnestly desire and seek spiritual gifts, but he also taught us not to do this at the expense of love for and sensitivity toward others. He taught, if our attitude and actions toward others are not motivated by love, the gifts of the Holy Spirit gain us nothing in the eyes of God (1 Corinthians 13:1-3). We must maintain a balanced and proper perspective relative to our seeking and using spiritual gifts in ministries and service to others. We must do this regardless of how much we spiritually grow, and the Holy Spirit is able to work through us. We must continually be sensitive to their needs and to where they are in their relationship with God. Our response to them and our use of our spiritual gifts must always be motivated by love.

CHAPTER 18
SPIRITUAL LIFE PRINCIPLES
MANAGEMENT OF OUR WEALTH

"And He sat down opposite the treasury, and began observing how the multitude were putting money into the treasury; and many rich people were putting in large sums. And a poor widow came and put in two small copper coins, which amount to a cent. And calling His disciples to Him, He said to them, 'Truly I say to you, this poor widow put in more than all the contributors to the treasury; for they all put in out of their surplus; but she, out of her poverty, put in all she owned, all she had to live on.'" (Mark 12:41-44)

"Honor the LORD from your wealth, and from the first of all your produce; so your barns will be filled with plenty, and your vats will overflow with new wine." (Proverbs 3:9-10)

SPIRITUAL LIFE PRINCIPLES (Chapters 18 - 22)

This section presents information regarding:

- Principles associated with effective money management;
- Principles associated with loving and forgiving others and resolution of anger;
- Principles associated with suffering;
- Principles associated with spiritual healing; and
- The Christian family, the relationships between husbands and wives and parents and children in the family, role of intimacy and sex in marriage, role of Jesus in the family, and divorce.

OUR WEALTH AND OUR RELATIONSHIP WITH GOD

The Bible teaches more about money than any other topic. Whereas there are around 500 verses on prayer and fewer than 500 verses on faith, there are more than 2,350 verses that address money. Jesus taught more about money than any other subject. How we manage our money resources demonstrates the level of our faith in and commitment to God and Jesus.

We are taught God wants us to prosper when we approach Him through Jesus. We like to believe our prosperity comes with little effort and the wealth associated with our prosperity can be used for anything we desire. However, the wealth associated with our prosperity is obtained because of our faith in God and Jesus and through hard work. God gives us instructions on how He wants us to use this wealth. The wealth we acquire and can enjoy depends on:

- Our understanding God owns everything,
- Our understanding God is the One who facilitates how we obtain our wealth, and
- Our responsible stewardship over the wealth God entrusts to our care.

Jesus addressed His attitude toward our wise stewardship of wealth entrusted to our care in Matthew 25:14-30. Three slaves were given different sums of money in this parable by their master. One was given five talents (1 talent equals between 58-80 lb); the second was given two talents; and the third was given one talent. Each slave was given according to his ability to manage the money given him, and each was expected to use and invest the money wisely, so they could repay their master with interest when he returned.

The master called his slaves to him when he returned and asked for an accounting from each one. The slaves who had been given five and two talents reported they had traded and invested the money given to them and had earned an additional five and two talents, respectively. They were praised and rewarded for their wise stewardship of the money entrusted to them. What they had earned was given back to them. They were told they would be put in charge of many things because they had faithfully managed what had been entrusted them.

The slave who had been given one talent was afraid and buried his money. He did not invest it. Therefore, he was unable to give his master his money with interest when asked for an accounting. The slave was rebuked and judged. His money was taken from him and given to the slave who had ten talents. With this the master said in Matthew 25:29:

> "For to everyone who has shall more be given, and he shall have an abundance; but from the one who does not have, even what he does have shall be taken away."

The lessons Jesus taught in this parable apply to us. God allows us to earn and accumulate wealth, and He expects us to exercise wise stewardship over the wealth we acquire to support ourself, our family and ministries and services to others in our church, community and throughout the world. God allows us to acquire wealth as we exercise wise stewardship over the wealth He entrusts to our care. However, He will not allow us to prosper beyond our ability to properly manage what He entrusts to our care and in ways that will draw us away from Him. God holds us accountable for our wise stewardship of our wealth, and He expects us to return to Him a portion of the wealth He allows us to obtain.

The LORD gave the people of Israel specific instructions and promises concerning how to use the wealth He gave them. He stated in Malachi 3:10-11:

> "'Bring the whole tithe into the storehouse, so that there may be food in My house, and test Me now in this,' says the LORD of host, 'If I will not open for you the windows of heaven, and pour out for you a blessing until it overflows.' 'Then I will rebuke the devourer for you, so that it may not destroy the fruits of the ground; nor will your vine in the field cast its grapes,' says the LORD of host."

The LORD instructed the people of Israel to give back to Him a tithe (ten percent) of the fruits of their labor. He also instructed them in Proverbs 3:9-10:

> "Honor the LORD from your wealth
> And from the first of all your produce;
> So your barns will be filled with plenty
> And your vats will overflow with new wine."

These Old Testament verses indicate God expected the Israelites to give back to Him the first ten percent of what He allowed them to acquire. He promised to open the doors of heaven, pour out on them His blessing until it overflowed, protect their wealth, and prevent others from taking it when they did this.

Jesus stated in Matthew 4:2-4:

> "When you give to the poor, do not sound a trumpet before you, as the hypocrites do in the synagogues and in the streets, so that they may be honored by men. Truly, I say to you, they have their reward in full. But when you give to the poor, do not let your left hand know what your right hand is doing, so that your giving will be in secret; and your Father who sees what is done in secret will reward you."

Jesus taught we are not to give to God to be seen and honored by others. We will receive our full reward when we do this; we will be seen and honored by others. God will mark the transaction complete and give us nothing more. Jesus stated we are to give to God in secret, and God who sees what we give in secret will reward us.

Paul stated in 2 Corinthians 9:6-10:

> "Now this I say, he who sows sparingly shall also reap sparingly; and he who sows bountiful shall also reap bountifully. Let each one do just as he has purposed in his heart; not grudgingly or under compulsion; for God loves a cheerful giver. And God is able to make all grace abound to you, that always having all sufficiency in everything you may have an abundance for every good deed; as it is written, "He scattered abroad, He gave to the poor, His righteousness abides forever. Now He who supplies seed to the sower and bread for food, will supply and multiply your seed for sowing and increase the harvest of your righteousness; you will be enriched in everything for all liberality, which through us is producing thanksgiving to God."

Paul stated we will receive little in return when we give little. However, we will receive abundantly when we give generously. We must be motivated by our love for, trust and faith in, and obedience to Jesus when we financially support ministries initiated by God, Jesus and the Holy Spirit. Paul indicated God will supply us what is needed to support these ministries. He wants us to share and spread His word in the Bible and minister to others in the name of Jesus. He promises to increase our harvest of redeemed and saved souls when we demonstrate our faithful stewardship over the resources He entrusts to our care.

Paul stated in 1 Corinthians 16:1-2:

> "Now concerning the collection for the saints, as I directed the churches of Galatia, so do you also. On the first day of every week let each one of you put aside and save, as he may prosper, that no collections be made when I come."

God expects us to give to support ministries and services to others on a regular basis. Paul addressed two areas associated with their giving in his instructions to the people in the church at Corinth: when they were to give and how much they were to give. He instructed them to lay aside what they had saved to give at the beginning of each week and to give as they had prospered.

Proverbs 3:9-10 states we are to give the first fruits of our labor. Paul states we are to give on a regular basis. Regular giving on a scheduled bases is a disciplined we are expected to develop as those who love God and Jesus. We have little difficulty in finding other things to spend our money on when we do not do this.

Malachi 3:10-11 states we are to give a tithe of our income to the Lord. The Bible defines a tithe as ten percent. Malachi implies we are to give ten percent of our gross income. This may be difficult for many to do. Therefore, Paul instructed us to give as we may prosper. We are to give what we can give when we cannot give a tithe. However, we are to give more than a tithe when our income allows us to do so. Malachi indicated God will give us blessings that overflow and protect us from those who would seek to steal our wealth when we are faithful to give of our wealth to support God's work in our communities and throughout the world.

Paul stated in 1 Corinthians 12:27, "Now you are Christ's body, and individually members of it." Here Paul referred to the church as the body of Christ in which we are members. We must understand why God requires us to financially support activities of the church in our communities and throughout the world. He has facilitated our acquisition of wealth. Therefore, He requires we give back a portion of this wealth to use as He directs to support activities of the body of Christ. Jesus, who examines our motives for giving, requires we give to support activities of the church out of an attitude of love for Him and others and a desire to support activities of His Body throughout the world. God expects us to give out of gratitude for the love, redemption and reconciliation He extends to us through Jesus.

BIBLICAL PRINCIPLES FOR FINANCIAL MANAGEMENT

With respect to the management of our financial resources, God expects us to (*Crown Ministries*, 1986):

- Avoid debt and spend wisely;
- Seek proper counsel with respect to how we should invest and use our money;
- Deal with others honestly;
- Give generously to help those who are less fortunate and need help;
- Work hard to legitimately obtain the wealth God desires to give us;
- Save consistently so we are prepared to address both expected and unexpected situations that require money;
- Train our children regarding proper money management; and
- Be content with the wealth God allows us to obtain.

We are expected to be faithful stewards over the wealth God allows us to obtain (1 Corinthians 4:2) and exercise sound judgement in how we manage our wealth. We are instructed to avoid debt because we become indebted to and a slave to those from whom we borrow. Proverbs 22:7 states, "The rich rules over the poor, and the borrower becomes the lender's slave." Paul stated in Romans 13:8:

> "Owe nothing to anyone except to love one another; for he who loves his neighbor has fulfilled the law."

We should acquire only those things we can afford and need and not covet things others have that we cannot afford. The Bible states we are to repay our debts when we do borrow money (Psalm 37:21, Proverbs 3:27-28).

The following are suggested to help us manage our prosperity. We should not hesitate to seek and receive proper counsel associated with the management of our wealth. The Proverbs teach:

- A wise man always seeks counsel (Proverbs 12:15);
- Presumption often leads to strife and failure (Proverbs 13:10); and
- Our chances for success are enhanced when we seek proper counsel (Proverbs 15:22).

We should seek the guidance of the Holy Spirit through prayer regarding financial decisions we must make.

God requires we deal honestly with others. He instructed the people of Israel in Leviticus 19:36:

> "You shall have just balances, just weights, a just ephah, and a just hin; I am the LORD your God, who brought you out from the land of Egypt."

Proverbs 16:11 states:

> "A just balance and scales belong to the LORD; all the weights of the bag are His concern."

Proverbs 14:2 states:

> "He who walks in uprightness fears the LORD, but he who is devious in his ways despises Him."

Proverbs 12:21-22 states:

> "No harm befalls the righteous, but the wicked are filled with trouble. Lying lips are an abomination to the LORD, but those who deal faithfully are His delight."

We have fewer problems in our life when we are honest in what we do. It is easier for us to enter relationships with God and others. Our potential for succeeding in what we do is enhanced. Dishonesty:

- Hinders our relationship with God and others;
- Increases our potential for failure; and
- Exposes us to unnecessary suffering.

God will not help us or respond to our prayers when we are dishonest and cheat people. He will instead discipline us to return us to a right relationship with Him (Hebrews 12:10-11).

God has created us to work from the beginning. Adam and Eve were placed in the garden of Eden to cultivate and keep it (Genesis 2:15). Paul instructed in 2 Thessalonians 3:10-11:

> "For even when we were with you, we used to give you this order: if anyone will not work, neither let him eat. For we hear that some of you are leading an undisciplined life, doing no work at all, but acting like busy bodies."

Work is necessary to support our needs and gives purpose to life. God has given us skills and abilities, and as we learned in the parable of the talents, He expects us to use them properly and profitably. They will atrophy when we do not use them, and we will lose them. Paul taught in Colossians 3:23-24:

> "Whatever you do, do your work heartily, as for the Lord rather than for men; knowing that from the Lord you will receive the reward of the inheritance. It is the Lord Christ whom you serve."

He instructed us to put effort into whatever we do and to work as if we are serving Jesus. Our work then becomes a ministry to Jesus and a witness to His presence in our lives.

The Bible teaches we are to save during times of prosperity, so:

- During times of drought we will have a reserve on which to live (Genesis 41:34-36);
- We can provide for our family (1 Timothy 5:8); and
- We can provide for future needs and retirement (Proverbs 21:20, Proverbs 30:24-28).

The Bible teaches parents are responsible for training their children. Proverbs 22:6 states:

> "Train up a child in the way he should go,
> Even when he is old he will not depart from it."

Paul stated in Ephesians 6:4:

> "And, fathers, do not provoke your children to anger; but bring them up in the discipline and instruction of the Lord."

Part of the training implied in these two verses includes training associated with the management of financial resources. Some adults practice poor money management because they did not receive proper instruction on money management as children.

Paul stated in 1 Timothy 6:6-11, 17-19:

> "But godliness actually is a means of great gain when accompanied by contentment. For we have brought nothing into the world, so we cannot take anything out of it either. But those who want to get rich fall into temptation and a snare and many foolish and hurtful desires which plunge men into ruin and destruction. For the love of money is a root of all sorts of evil, and some by longing for it have wandered away from the faith and pierced themselves with many griefs. But flee from these things, you man of God, and pursue righteousness, godliness, faith, love, perseverance and gentleness. ... Instruct those who are rich in this present world not to be conceited or to fix their hope on the uncertainty of riches, but on God, who richly supplies us with all things to enjoy. Instruct them to do good, to be rich in good works, to be generous and ready to share, storing up for themselves the treasure of a good foundation for the future, so that they may take hold of that which is life indeed."

We should be content with the wealth God allows us to obtain. Our acquisition of wealth must never be our main motivation even though He allows us to acquire it. Paul taught the possession of wealth is not evil. However, he stated the "love of money" is the root of evil and those who long for it wander away from their faith in God and suffer many griefs as a result. Paul instructed us to "pursue righteousness, godliness, faith, love, perseverance and gentleness" instead of wealth. All other things in our life will assume their proper place when we pursue these, including the accumulation of wealth. We must not fix our hope on the uncertainty of the wealth we acquire. We must fix our hope on God and store up for ourself "the treasure of a good foundation for the future, so that [we] may take hold of that which is life indeed."

WISDOM ON MONEY FROM THE PROVERBS

Charles Swindoll gave the following six principles on money on one of his *Insight for Living* radio programs. We find these principles in the Proverbs.

1. **Those who honor God with their wealth are blessed in return.**

    We are instructed to honor God from the first of the wealth we acquire. God will bless us when we do this. Proverbs 3:9-10 states:

    > "Honor the LORD from your wealth,
    > And from the first of all your produce,
    > So your bars will be filled with plenty
    > And your vats will overflow with new wine."

    Proverbs 10:22 states:

    > "It is the blessing of the LORD that makes rich, and He adds no sorrow to it."

    True wealth proceeds from activities initiated by God. This wealth does not cause problems that are often associated with wealth obtained independent of Him. Proverbs 13:21 teaches:

    > "Adversity pursues sinners, but the righteous will be rewarded with prosperity."

    Our efforts to acquire wealth are often accompanied with problems when we do not honor God in our pursuit of it. He rewards us with prosperity we can manage and enjoy when we fix our eyes on Him as the source of our wealth. We return to God out of the abundance He allows us to acquire when we exercise good stewardship over the wealth He entrusts to our care.

2. **Those who make wealth and prosperity their passion lose more than they gain.**

    Our culture glorifies wealth and prosperity. Proverbs 15:6 states:

    > "Much wealth is in the house of the righteous, but trouble is in the income of the wicked."

Acquiring wealth and prosperity independent of God often brings with it problems. Proverbs 28:22 states:

"A man with an evil eye hastens after wealth
And does not know that want will come upon him."

We give up much when we become obsessed with acquiring wealth. We first lose our integrity and peace of mind. Proverbs 28:6 states:

"Better is the poor who walks in his integrity,
Than he who is crooked though he be rich."

We become insensitive to the needs of others when becoming rich is our passion. Proverbs 22:16 states:

"He who oppresses the poor to make much for himself
Or who gives to the rich, will only come to poverty."

Our loss of sensitivity to the needs of others often leads to poverty in our own life. This poverty may not be associated with a loss of wealth, but it will lead to a loss of meaning and integrity in our life.

Those who trust only in themselves to prosper often become filled with pride and suffer the consequences. God wants us to look to Him as the facilitator of our prosperity and success. We become filled with pride when we ignore Him. Proverbs 16:18-19 teaches:

"Pride goes before destruction,
And a haughty spirit before stumbling.
It is better to be of a humble spirit with the lowly,
Than to divide the spoil with the proud."

Pride separates us from God and results in spiritual death. Sooner or later we will stumble and come upon troubled and difficult times even though our quest for riches independent of God may initially be successful and bring us honor and prestige. Proverbs 11:2 states:

"When pride comes, then comes dishonor,
But with the humble is wisdom."

What initially brings:

- Honor brings dishonor,
- Prestige and position result in the loss of prestige and position, and
- Riches ultimately results in poverty.

This poverty results in the loss of meaningful relationships, personal integrity, peace of mind, self- esteem, respect and good health. Proverbs 23:4-5 instructs us:

> "Do not weary yourself to gain wealth,
> Cease from your consideration of it.
> When you set your eyes on it, it is gone.
> For wealth certainly makes itself wings,
> Like an eagle that flies toward the heavens."

God is Lord of His creation, and He is Lord of the lives of both the righteous and unrighteous. He exercises His sovereign will in both of their lives as He chooses. God allows both the righteous and unrighteous to prosper, and He can take away this prosperity when it has been obtained in unrighteous and unjust ways. Proverbs 16:8 states:

> "Better is a little with righteousness
> Than great income with injustice."

3. **Wisdom gives wealth needed guidance.**

The Bible does not condemn the acquisition of wealth; it condemns making its acquisition the main purpose for our life. The Bible teach we are to love and honor God above all things and seek His counsel, knowledge and wisdom in all we do. We cannot love and honor God and, at the same time, seek to acquire wealth independent of Him. Proverbs 20:15 states:

> "There is gold, and an abundance of jewels;
> But the lips of knowledge are a more precious thing."

Proverbs 16:16 states:

> "How much better it is to get wisdom than gold!
> And to get understanding is to be chosen above silver."

Proverbs 8:10-11 states

> "Take my instruction, and not silver,
> And knowledge rather than choicest gold.
> For wisdom is better than jewels;
> And all desirable things cannot compare with her."

Acquiring wealth brings with it increase responsibility and an expectation from God to use it in a manner that is pleasing and acceptable to Him. We must seek His counsel, knowledge and wisdom to manage wealth responsibly and meet His expectations. Proverbs 8:18-21 state:

> "Riches and honor are with me,
> Enduring wealth and righteousness.
> My fruit is better than gold, even pure gold,
> And my yield better than choicest silver.
> I walk in the way of righteousness,
> In the midst of the paths of justice,
> To endow those who love Me with wealth,
> That I may fill their treasuries."

Those who love the Lord and seek His counsel will be blessed and endowed by Him with wealth.

4. **Increased riches bring increased complications in life.**

God withholds great wealth from individuals who do not have the skills to manage the increased complications in life it brings.

- Great wealth often gives us a false sense of security. Proverbs 10:15 states:

> "The rich man's wealth is his fortress,
> The ruin of the poor is their poverty."

Proverbs 18:11 states:

> "A rich man's wealth is his strong city,
> And like a high wall in his own imagination."

The Bible teaches real security only comes from God."

- Great wealth often creates within us pride and arrogance. These separate us from God and ultimately cause us to stumble. Proverbs 28:11 states:

  "The rich man is wise in his own eyes,
  But the poor who has understanding sees through him."

People with wisdom can see through the pride and arrogance of the rich even though they may be poor.

- Great wealth attracts friends and acquaintances who seek favors and assistance. Proverbs 14:20 states:

  "The poor is hated even by his neighbor,
  But those who love the rich are many."

Proverbs 19:4, 6 states:

  "Wealth adds many friends,
  But a poor man is separated from his friend. ...
  Many will entreat the favor of a generous man,
  And every man is a friend to him who gives gifts "

Friends and acquaintances we have because of our wealth often result in a false sense of popularity and acceptance. We need God's counsel and wisdom to discern true friends when He chooses to bless us with wealth. We need His guidance and counsel to maintain a proper perspective of our relationships within the community where we live and serve Him.

- Great wealth brings with it moral temptations. Proverbs 29:3 states:

  "A man who loves wisdom makes his father glad,

  But he who keeps company with harlots wastes his wealth."

Only an intimate relationship with God through Jesus and the Holy Spirit gives us the ability to effectively address the complications in life great wealth causes and properly manage the wealth He allows us to acquire.

REDEEMED BY GOD - 1

5. **Money cannot buy life's most valuable possessions.**

- Money cannot buy integrity and a good name.

Provers 28:6 states:

> "Better is the poor who walks in integrity
> Then he who is crooked though he be rich."

Proverbs 22:1 states:

> "A good name is to be more desired than great riches,
> Favor is better than silver and gold."

- Money cannot buy peaceful and harmonic relationships.

Proverbs 15:16-17 state:

> "Better a little with the fear of the LORD,
> Than great treasure and turmoil with it.
> Better is a dish of vegetables where love is,
> Than a fattened ox and hatred with it."

- Money cannot buy us a good life, good health and salvation.

Proverbs 11:4 states:

> "Riches do not profit in the day of wrath,
> But righteousness delivers from death."

The *day of wrath* is the judgment of our Lord, and *death* is spiritual death associated with being separated from God. We will only receive life's most valuable possessions when we develop a relationship with God through our faith in Jesus and abide in His word. Proverbs 4:20-22 teach:

> "My son, give attention to my words;
> incline your ear to my sayings.
> Do not let them depart from your sight;

Keep them in the midst of your heart.
For they are life to those who find them,
And health to all their body."

6. **Money can bring great encouragement when managed wisely; it brings great stress when mishandled.**

God will honor us, allow us to prosper, and protect our wealth when we honor Him in acquiring it and use it in a manner that honors Him. He will give us knowledge and wisdom necessary to use our wealth wisely, manage it effectively, and address the complications that come with it. However, we will not find contentment, fulfillment, and peace of mind in our wealth when we acquire it using deceptive methods and use it in ways that dishonor God. He will not give us the knowledge necessary to use our wealth wisely, manage it effectively, and resist the temptations it causes. Our wealth will bring turmoil and stress into our life. Proverbs 11:28 states:

"He who trusts in his riches will fall,
But the righteous will flourish like the green leaf."

Proverbs 28:20 states:

"A faithful man will abound with blessings,
But he who makes haste to be rich will not go unpunished."

God will not allow deception used to acquire wealth to go unpunished.

Proverbs 21:6 states:

"The acquisition of treasures by a lying tongue
Is a fleeting vapor, the pursuit of death."

Following is a seventh principle associated with wealth found in the Proverbs. It is important even though it is not one of the principles given by Charles Swindoll.

7. **Those who give to, honor, and help the poor and those in need are blessed and honored by God.**

God expects those He has blessed with wealth to use a portion of it to help the poor and those in need. The Proverbs teach:

"He who oppresses the poor reproaches his Maker,
But he who is gracious to the needy honors Him." (Proverbs 14:31)

"He who is gracious to a poor man lends to the LORD,
And He will repay him for his good deed." (Proverbs 19:17)

"He who gives to the poor will never want,
But he who shuts his eyes will have many curses." (Proverbs 28:27)

We honor God when we help the poor and those who need help. He will bless and allow us to prosper when we use a portion of our wealth in this manner.

CHAPTER 19
SPIRITUAL LIFE PRINCIPLES
LOVING AND FORGIVING OTHERS

"Then Peter came and said to Him, 'Lord, how often shall my brother sin against me and I forgive him? Up to seven times?' Jesus said to him, 'I do not say to you, up to seven times, but up to seventy times seven. For this reason the kingdom of heaven may be compared to a certain king who wished to settle accounts with his slaves. And when he had begun to settle them, there was brought to him one who owed him ten thousand talents. But since he did not have the means to repay, his lord commanded him to be sold, along with his wife and children and all that he had, and repayment to be made. The slave therefore falling down, prostrated himself before him, saying, 'Have patience with me, and I will repay you everything.' And the lord of that slave felt compassion and released him and forgave him the debt. But that slave went out and found one of his fellow slaves who owed him a hundred denarii; and he seized him and began to choke him, saying, 'Pay back what you owe.' So his fellow slave fell down and began to entreat him, saying, 'Have patience with me and I will repay you.' He was unwilling however, but went and threw him in prison until he should pay back what was owed. So when his fellow slaves saw what had happened, they were deeply grieved and came and reported to their lord all that had happened. Then summoning him, his lord said to him, 'You wicked slave, I forgave you all that debt because you entreated me. Should you not also have had mercy on your fellow slave, even as I had mercy on you?' And his lord, moved with anger, handed him over to the torturers until he should repay all that was owed him. So shall My heavenly Father also do to you, if each of you does not forgive his brother from your heart." (Matthew 18:21-35)

GOD'S LOVE AND FORGIVENESS

God's love for His creation in general and for us is one of the inscrutable characteristics of His nature. It is hard to understand why the Creator of the universe would choose to love hostile and rebellious men and women who continually violate His commandments. Why and how could He love those who participated in the crucifixion of His Son? We were not there when the crowds shouted, "Crucify Him!" However, if we had been there, we would have been shouting with the rest of the crowd, "Crucify Him!" God loves us not because we deserve it but because He chooses to love us. He has forgiven our sins and reconciled us to Himself through Jesus because of His love for us.

Jesus stated an individual can have no greater love then to give his life for a friend. He demonstrated His love for us when He died on a cross. He stood in our place and took upon Himself all sin and the consequences of sin. He did this even though we were hostile and rebellious toward Him. This is part of God's inscrutable nature manifested through His Son that we will never fully understand. Jesus had the same freedom of choice we have. He could have walked away from the cross. However, He chose to be obedient to His Father and die on a cross for us. Jesus chose to love us by dying on a cross even though we are hostile and rebellious and often ignore the words He spoke. We can be reconciled to and reunited with God through His death and resurrection.

God chose to love and forgive us even though we do not deserve His mercy and grace. He sent His Son, Jesus, and Jesus chose to die on a cross so we can be reconciled to His Father. Therefore, God receives us as forgiven when we approach Him through Jesus.

LOVING OTHERS

Most of us love conditionally. We love others with the expectation of receiving something in return. We expect friends to help us in return for us helping them. We have expectations as to how we want our spouse and other family members to love us in return for us loving them. Conditional love expects something in return. It measures the responses of those whom we love or help in terms of what we have given them and expect to receive in return. We are offended and hurt when our expectations are not met. Love that keeps score and expects something in return can never be fully satisfied. The level of our expectation increases as lesser expectations are met.

We need to be loved and appreciated, and it is gratifying when we are loved and appreciated by others. However, being loved and appreciated should never be our primary motivation for loving and helping others. We discover our love for others should be selfless in nature as we grow in our understanding of God's word in the Bible, freely given and expecting nothing in return. God's love for us is a selfless love as is shown by the Father and the Son. It is given to us by means of an infinite sacrifice, the death of Jesus. There are no preconditions for receiving this love. We do not deserve it, and we cannot earn it. God has chosen to love us. Jesus came to demonstrate His love by dying for us and to teach and show us how to love others in a selfless way.

THE GREAT COMMANDMENTS

When Jesus was asked what the great commandment in the Law was, He responded in Mark 12:29-31:

> "The foremost is, 'Hear, O Israel! The LORD our God is one LORD; and you shall love the LORD your God with all your heart, and with all your soul, and with all your mind, and with all your strength.' (Deuteronomy 6:4-5) The second is this, 'You shall love your neighbor as yourself. There is no other commandment greater than these.'" (Leviticus 19:18)

Jesus stated we are to love God with all our heart, mind, soul and strength. Loving God is an action of our soul - of our mind and heart. The reference to our *mind* implies our love for God is to be a conscious and deliberate choice. The reference to our *heart* implies, in so much as we are able, we are to love God from the very core and center of our being. God wants us to love Him simply because we consciously choose to do so independent of anything we expect to receive or experience because of our relationship with Him. We often love God because of what we expect to receive from Him. God rejects this conditional love. He will give us good things and do good things for us through Jesus and the Holy Spirit. However, He does not want the expectation of these to be the reason we love Him. Jesus implied our love for God is to permeate every aspect of our life when He stated we are to love God with *all our strength*. We are to love Him with everything we are and in everything we do.

Jesus taught in John 14 we show our love for God by obeying His commandments. He repeated these three times, signifying its importance in our relationship with God through Him. The Bible teaches God expects us to obey Him. This runs counter to what the world teaches. It teaches we should feel good about ourself; we should be happy, content and fulfilled. We should be free to do whatever is necessary to achieve these. The Bible teaches we can experience contentment, fulfillment and joy only when we are in an obedient relationship with God through Jesus. We will obey God's commandments and do those things that are pleasing and acceptable to Him when we truly love Him.

Jesus promised in John 14 the Father will love us, and He and the Father, along with the Holy Spirit, will dwell in us when we show our love for Him by obeying His commandments and keeping His words. Jesus also stated in John 8:31-32:

> "If you abide in My word, then you are truly disciples of Mine; and you shall know the truth, and the truth shall make you free."

Abiding in Jesus' word means studying and internalizing God's word in the Bible. The Holy Spirit opens our mind and reveals the meaning of God's word to us as we study it in the Bible. He gives us the ability to understand, internalize and apply it to our life. The Holy Spirit continues His transforming process in our life as our mind is renewed by internalizing God's word. He strips away our negative personality and character traits and replaces them with a Christlike character.

We discover we do not have to rely on our own ability to be obedient to and love Jesus when we receive the love and grace God extends to us through Jesus. God through the Holy Spirit calls us to respond to His love and repent, and God through the Holy Spirit empowers us to respond to His call. The Holy Spirit opens our mind to receive and understand God's word in the Bible. He enables us to apply God's word to our life and creates within us the desire and gives us the ability to trust and obey God. We discover true freedom when we live within the boundaries God has established for our life, and He reveals Himself to us. We can then truly know and relate to God as our Father.

Our love for God is demonstrated by our willingness to yield to His control those areas in our life that are the most important to us. We discussed the handling and distribution of our wealth in the preceding chapter. Are we willing to give back to God ten percent or more of our income for spreading His kingdom on earth, for feeding the poor, for ministering to the needs of others, etc.? We discussed in preceding chapters the renewing of our mind and transforming of our heart. Are we willing to invest the time and energy necessary to study, learn and internalize God's word in the Bible, so we can know and understand how He desires us to interact with the world and how He desires us to interact with Him through Jesus and the indwelling presence of the Holy Spirit? Are we willing to allow the Holy Spirit to come into the core area of our life that defines who we are to transform us, recreating us into the person He desires us to be, as our mind is renewed by studying and internalizing God's word? The highest calling we have is to worship God as our Creator, Savior and Father. Are we willing to place Him first in our life, giving Him the worship and premiere place in our life He requests and expects? Are we willing to allow our relationship with God through Jesus to define the nature and character of our other relationships and to set the priorities we establish in everything we do? God gives us the freedom to answer all these questions as we choose. How we answer them defines our relationship with Him, demonstrates the nature and character of our love for Him, and establishes the level of our commitment to Him.

Jesus commanded us to love our neighbor as ourself. This second commandment is sometimes misunderstood. We attempt to divide it into two commandments: love others and love ourself. However, to love our neighbor as ourself is a single commandment. The commandment is to love our neighbor. As we love ourself is how we are to love our neighbor. This gives us a reference to gauge the love God expects us to have for others. We are to desire for them the same good things we desire, and we are to work to help them receive the same good things we expect to receive.

The Bible teaches not to love ourself in a self-centered manner. It teaches us to focus on things beyond ourself. First, we are to look to God as the source of everything we have. Second, we are taught to be sensitive to the spiritual, emotional and physical needs of others and to help them meet these needs when prompted and guided by the Holy Spirit.

We need a healthy sense of self-esteem and self-worth. Jesus implied in His second great commandment we cannot love our neighbor when we do not love ourself. Healthy self-love develops when we first seek God. Self-love that motivates us to reach out to love others develops only when we first experience God's love. Self-love that gives us the ability to rise above and transcend a world filled with bitterness and hatred toward others develops naturally as our mind is renewed and our heart is transformed by the Holy Spirit into the person God has created us to be.

Some of us may not initially possess a high level of self-esteem and self-worth. We may have been emotionally, physically or sexually abused as a child. We may have had a devastating or traumatic life experience or experienced failed relationships that have seriously wounded our spirit and created a brokenness in us. We may be unable to love others because there is no real reference in our own life on which to base this love. We may never have experienced real love and compassion and may not be able or know how to love others as Jesus commanded. Jesus understood this when He gave His disciples a new commandment in John 13:34-35. He stated:

> "A new commandment I give to you, that you love one another, even as I
> have loved you, that you also love one another. By this all men will know
> that you are My disciples, if you have love for one another."

Jesus stated we are to let His love for us be the reference when we have no real reference as to how to love others. We see His love for us is manifested in His compassion and sensitivity toward us as we read and study the New Testament. We see His love in His desire to respond and minister to our needs and to be present when we need Him. His love for us was ultimately demonstrated in His willingness to die for us. Jesus stated in John 15:13,

"Greater love has no one than this, that one lay down his life for his friends." Let Jesus' love for you be the reference when there is no real reference for love in your life until God transforms your heart and gives you the ability to experience His love and to love Him and others in return. By this you will know you can love others because God first loved you.

We must understand who our neighbor is with respect to Jesus' second commandment. Most of us believe our neighbor to be someone we:

- Love and who loves us,
- Trust and who trusts us, and
- Desire to help and who will help us.

Jesus went beyond this belief when He instructed us in Luke 6:27-28, 31-36 to:

> "But I say to you who hear, love your enemies, do good to those who hate you, bless those who curse you, pray for those who mistreat you. ... Treat others the same way you want them to treat you. If you love those who love you, what credit is that to you? For even sinners love those who love them. If you do good to those who do good to you, what credit is that to you? For even sinners do the same. If you lend to those from whom you expect to receive, what credit is that to you? Even sinners lend to sinners in order to receive back the same amount. But love your enemies, and do good, and lend, expecting nothing in return; and your reward will be great, and you will be sons of the Most High; for He Himself is kind to ungrateful and evil men. Be merciful, just as your Father is merciful."

Jesus stated our reward will be great when we do these things`, and we will be children of God. He expanded the definition of neighbor to include not only those whom we love and who love us, but also to include our enemies and those who hate, curse and mistreat us. Jesus instructed us with respect to these persons to be merciful to and forgive them and not to judge or condemn them. He expected us to love them with the same selfless love with which He loves us. Jesus presented a promise with this expectation. He stated in Luke 6:38:

> "Give, and it will be given to you; good measure, pressed down, shaken together, running over, they will pour into your lap. For by your standard of measure it will be measured to you in return."

Regarding an inquiry from a lawyer who was attempting to justify himself to Jesus in Luke 10:30-37:

> "Jesus replied and said, 'A certain man was going down from Jerusalem to Jericho; and he fell among robbers, and they stripped him and beat him, and went off leaving him half dead. And by chance a certain priest was going down on that road, and when he saw him, he passed by on the other side. And likewise a Levite also, when he came to the place and saw him, passed by on the other side. But a certain Samaritan, who was on a journey, came upon him; and when he saw him, he felt compassion, and came to him, and bandaged up his wounds, pouring oil and wine on them; and he put him on his own beast, and brought him to an inn, and took care of him. And on the next day he took out two denarii and gave them to the innkeeper and said, 'Take care of him; and whatever more you spend, when I return, I will repay you." Which of these three do you think proved to be a neighbor to the man who fell into the robbers' hands?'And he said, 'The one who showed mercy toward him.' And Jesus said to him, 'Go and do the same.'"

Jesus set forth important principles in this story concerning the definition of and how we should respond to a neighbor. The priest, Levite and Samaritan had the resources to assist the man who had been robbed and beaten. We must understand God will never ask or expect us to do anything or to respond to a request for assistance without first giving us the required resources. The priest and Levite were not bad individuals. The priest may have officiated at a worship service in the synagogue in Jericho, and the Levite may have assisted the priest. They were individuals who had significant responsibilities to their congregation that in their minds prevented them from helping the man who was a stranger. They both may had been to the Temple in Jerusalem to be ceremonially cleansed so they could perform their priestly functions in the synagogue in Jericho on the next day. To stop and assist the man who had been robbed and beaten, because he was bleeding, would have made them unclean. They would have had to return to the Temple in Jerusalem to be cleansed again before they could return to Jericho to perform their priestly duties. They both determined they did not want to do this, so they passed by the man without rendering assistance. Therefore, they believed this action was justified. Are we any different today? We are not priest or Levites. Many of us often have opportunities to assist others in need, but because we are too busy or have other more important things to do, we pass these opportunities by, hoping someone else will respond.

Jesus had a way of making a point. The man who had been robbed and beaten needed help. Two individuals who were highly respected in the culture of their day passed by the man, refusing to help him. Who should Jesus select to help the man in His story - a man who was from an area that was despised by the Jews of His day, a Samaritan. Imagine your most hated and despised enemy; this is what the Samaritan was to the Jew in Jesus' day. We are not told this in the story, but possibly the man who had been robbed and beaten was a Jew. Jesus made His point in illustrating who a neighbor is by selecting a Samaritan, who was hated and despised by the Jews, to be the individual who stopped and rendered aid to the man who had been robbed and beaten. The story indicated the Samaritan went beyond just helping the man to be on his way. He bound the man's wounds and provided for his needs until he was able to fully take care of himself.

God gives us resources, and He expects us to use them to minister to the needs of others. He calls us to transcend ethnic and cultural boundaries to assist those who need help. Anyone in need whom we have the resources to help is our neighbor. God not only expects us to love those who love us, He also expects us to love those who do not and are incapable of loving us. He asks us to give what He gives to us without expecting anything in return when we are led by the Holy Spirit to do so. Jesus commanded us in Matthew 25:35-40 to:

- Feed the hungry,
- Give drink to the thirsty,
- Invite in strangers,
- Clothe the naked,
- Care for the sick, and
- Visit those who are in prison.

Our love must be manifested in our obedience to His commandments, and it must be manifested in ministries and service to others under the guidance of the Holy Spirit. John affirmed this in 1 John 3:17-18:

> "But whoever has the world's goods, and beholds his brother in need and closes his heart against him, how does the love of God abide in him? Little children, let us not love with word or with tongue, but in deed and truth."

Paul stated in Romans 13:8-10:

> "Owe nothing to anyone except to love one another; for he who loves his neighbor has fulfilled the law. For this, 'You shall not commit adultery, you shall not murder, you shall not steal, you shall not covet,' and if there is any

other commandment, it is summed up in this saying, 'you shall love your neighbor as yourself.' Love does no wrong to a neighbor; love therefore is the fulfillment of the law."

Loving others is an act of the soul - of our heart and mind. God expects us to love others as He loves us through Jesus even though they do not deserve our love or are unable to love us in return.

THE CHARACTER OF LOVE

Paul described desired characteristics of love, and he challenged us to understand what motivates us to love and serve others. He states in 1 Corinthians 13:1-7:

> "If I speak with the tongues of men and of angels, but do not have love, I have become a noisy gong or a clanging cymbal. And if I have the gift of prophecy, and know all mysteries and all knowledge; and if I have all faith, so as to remove mountains, but do not have love, I am nothing. And if I give all my possessions to feed the poor, and if I deliver my body to be burned, but do not have love, it profits me nothing. Love is patient, love is kind, and is not jealous; love does not brag and is not arrogant, does not act unbecomingly; it does not seek its own, is not provoked, does not take into account a wrong suffered, does not rejoice in unrighteousness, but rejoices with the truth; bears all things, believes all things, hopes all things, endures all things."

Paul implied there are two primary factors that motivate us to love and serve others:

- A genuine love for God and for others and
- A desire to be seen and appreciated by others.

It would be desirable to separate these two motivating factors when we serve and minister to others. However, this often is not possible. Both are involved to varying degrees in our decisions to use our spiritual gifts, resources and knowledge to us to serve and minister to others.

Paul discussed speaking in tongues, having knowledge and understanding God's mysteries, selling our possessions to feed the poor, and sacrificing ourself in God's service. He stated these mean nothing to God when our primary motivation for doing them is not love. He then describes God's desired characteristics of love:

Love is patient. Love bears pain, annoyance, inconvenience, loss, misfortune, etc. without complaining or showing anger.

Love is kind. Love is benevolent and seeks the best for others.

Love is not jealous. Love is not resentful, fearful, or suspicious of others. It does not envy what others have nor does it fear losing to others what it has.

Love does not brag. Love does not boast or vaunt what it has in front of others.

Love is not arrogant. Love is not presumptuous or superior in its conduct.

Love does not act unbecomingly. Love acts in a positive and favorable manner. It never detracts from nor diminishes the reputation of the individual giving it.

Love does not seek its own. Love is unselfish and selfless in nature.

Love is not provoked. Love is never aroused to anger, nor does it arouse anger in others.

Love does not focus on a wrong suffered. Love forgives and seeks the restoration of broken relationships.

Love does not rejoice in unrighteousness. Love seeks to do those things that are pleasing and acceptable to God and to act within the boundaries God has placed on it.

Love rejoices with the truth. Love seeks the truth contained in God's word.

Love bears all things. *believes all things, hopes all things, endures all things.* Love that proceeds from our relationship with God through Jesus can accomplish all things and overcome any adversity it may encounter.

INTIMATE RELATIONSHIPS

Entering an intimate relationship with God through faith and trust in and obedience to Jesus enhances our ability to enter healthy and meaningful intimate relationships with others. We can only extend love with grace, forgiveness and affection to others in an intimate fashion after we have first received and experienced the love, grace and forgiveness God extends to us through Jesus. We must allow the love of God to enter our life to heal wounded and broken places in our soul before we can experience true intimacy in a relationship. We must allow the Holy Spirit to heal painful memories associated with our spiritual wounds and brokenness. These memories prevent us from experiencing true intimacy in relationships. The Holy Spirit enables us to see the loving and healing presence of Jesus in the events associated with our wounds and brokenness and to forgive those associated with these events when He enters these areas within our soul. The Holy Spirit then transforms us from a person filled with resentment, pain, anger and bitterness to one who can forgive and who is filled with the love and compassion of Jesus. This enables us to love with the heart and mind of Jesus.

Intimate Christian love is bounded by truth and discernment. It is founded on the integrity, trust and faithfulness of those who give and receive it. It never requires us to give to others what we do not have to give, nor does it create within us a desire to receive from others what they do not have to give. Love that is consistent with the principles God reveals to us in the Bible is given and received with an understanding of the consequences of the actions it initiates. This love never leads nor requires us to enter unholy relationships nor does it require us to compromise or abandon the Christian principles, ethics, morals and values the Bible teaches.

FORGIVING OTHERS AND SEEKING FORGIVENESS

God extends His love and grace to us through Jesus. The essence of grace is mercy, and the true expression of mercy is forgiveness. Forgiveness then becomes a visible manifestation of love. The visible manifestation of God's love for us is revealed in His forgiving our sins and reconciling us to Himself through Jesus. We can love others because God first loved us and demonstrated this love through the death and resurrection of His Son. We can forgive others because God first forgave us. Forgiveness is a visible manifestation of our love for others just as it is a visible 8umanifestation of God's love for us.

Jesus stated in Matthew 5:23-24:

> "If therefore you are presenting your offering at the altar, and there remember that your brother has something against you, leave your offering there before the altar, and go your way; first be reconciled to your brother, and then come and present your offering."

He further taught in Mark 22:25-26:

> "And whenever you stand praying, forgive, if you have anything against anyone; so that your Father also who is in heaven may forgive you your transgressions. But if you do not forgive, neither will your Father who is in heaven forgive your transgressions."

Jesus taught the lack of forgiveness on our part is an obstacle to our establishing a relationship with God. God has made an infinite sacrifice, the death and resurrection of His Son, so He can forgive our sins and reconcile us to Himself. We did not deserve to be forgiven nor did we deserve the sacrifice He and Jesus made. They both chose to love and forgive us anyway. God expects us to forgive others and seek the reconciliation of broken relationships because He has forgiven our sins through the death and resurrection of Jesus.

Jesus shared a story with Peter in Matthew 18:21-35. He told of a king who desired to settle accounts with his slaves. One of his slaves owed him ten thousand talents (1 talent equals 6,000 denarii). This was an impossible sum for the slave to repay. The king ordered the slave, along with all his family and possessions, to be sold to repay the debt. The slave begged the king to have mercy on him and to give him time to repay the debt. The king felt compassion for the slave and forgave the entire debt. The slave came upon one of his fellow slaves who owed him one hundred denarii and who was unable to repay the debt when he left the king's presence. He had his fellow slave thrown into prison until the debt could be repaid. The other slaves were grieved by this and reported to the king what had happened. The king, moved with anger, summoned the slave who had been forgiven the large debt and turned him over to torturers until he could repay his entire debt. Jesus ended this story with the statement:

> "So shall My heavenly Father also do to you, if each of you does not forgive
> his brother from your heart."

The king in the story is God, and we are the slave with the impossible debt of sin. God could have allowed us to enter slavery to sin and Satan because of our disobedience. Instead, He chose to pay an infinite ransom, so we could be saved and reconciled to Him. We, like the slave in the story, continue to fight and quarrel with others who have offended or hurt us. We choose to retain anger, hatred and bitterness in our hearts associated with offenses committed against us by others. We are unwilling to forgive these offenses that pale in comparison to the infinite debt of sin in our hearts God has forgiven us through Jesus.

Forgiving others is a choice. God has chosen to forgive us through Jesus. Therefore, He requires us to choose to forgive those who have offended or hurt us. We surrender our right to judge, condemn and seek retribution when we forgive. God also desires us to seek reconciliation of associated broken relationships when possible.

We often do not provoke or deserve offenses that hurt us. Therefore, forgiving those who commit these offenses does not imply we are responsible for instigating them. These offenses may cause serious and painful spiritual, emotional and physical wounds that take a long time to heal. We may never forget these offenses even though we may receive healing for them.

The healing of hurting and broken areas in our life will not begin until we forgive those who have caused our suffering and brokenness. The anger, hatred and bitterness we retain and internalize can become buried deep within our soul when we do not forgive. This exposes us to unnecessary grief, pain and suffering. God wants us to forgive our transgressors for our good, not for their good. We release their offenses along with our associated feelings of anger, hatred and bitterness to God when we forgive them, so He can execute His judgment and bring healing and peace to our spirit and soul. Forgiving others is never easy; it often is difficult. It is hard to give up and release the anger, hatred and bitterness we feel toward those who cause suffering and brokenness in our life. Jesus appeared to make forgiving more difficult when He instructs us in Luke 17:3-4:

> "Be on your guard! If your brother sins, rebuke him; and if he repents, forgive him. And if he sins against you seven times a day, and returns to you seven times, saying, 'I repent,' forgive him."

Jesus instructed us to forgive an individual when he offends and hurts us repeatedly and repents each time.

Jesus instructed us in Matthew 11:29-30 when we experience pain, suffering, anger, hatred, bitterness and brokenness associated with offenses committed against us:

> "Take My yoke upon you, and learn from Me, for I am gentle and humble in heart; and you shall find rest for your souls. For My yoke is easy, and My load is light."

Jesus through the Holy Spirit enables us to do what we cannot do for ourself. We need only to ask Him to heal the hurting and broken areas in our soul spirit and to enable us to forgive those who transgress against us. Jesus stated in Revelations 3:20-21:

> "Behold, I stand at the door and knock; if anyone hears My voice and opens the door, I will come in to him, and will dine with him, and he with Me. He who overcomes, I will grant to him to sit down with Me on My throne, as I also overcame and sat down with My Father on His throne."

Jesus will only come into those areas in our life where He is invited. He will allow us to experience grief, pain and brokenness associated with hurtful offenses committed against us as long as we desire to do so. He will give comfort and peace to our soul and spirit when we open the door to our heart and invite Him into our hurting and broken areas. He will take away our pain and heal our brokenness. He will enable us to rise above and overcome the anger, hatred and bitterness we feel toward those who have hurt us. He, along with the Holy Spirit, will give us the ability to forgive them.

Jesus desires offending parties to be reconciled. Reconciliation occurs when individuals who have hurt each other are willing to forgive each other. They must express true remorse for the pain and brokenness they have caused each other and ask for and receive the forgiveness extended to them. Jesus is the One who facilitates reconciliation. Therefore, they must invite Him into the hurting and broken areas in their lives and relationship to begin their healing process. Jesus will walk with them through this process.

It is desirable to interact with individuals we want to forgive or from whom we desire to seek forgiveness. This facilitates resolution and closure to hurtful events we want to address. The fact we sometimes cannot interact with these individuals does not negate our desire to seek resolution to a hurtful event and begin a healing process. To forgive someone is our choice and does not require the participation of the individual we want to forgive. Seeking forgiveness from someone we have hurt normally requires the participation of that individual. However, there are situations where this is not possible. We can bring hurtful events we desire to resolve to Jesus in prayer when we cannot interact with the individuals we want to forgive or from whom we seek forgiveness. He will respond to our prayer and facilitate the healing process we request.

UNRESOLVED ANGER

The lack of forgiveness associated with unresolved *anger* is an obstacle to receiving spiritual healing of a wounded and broken spirit discussed in Chapter 21. *Anger* is an emotional response to the feelings of *hurt*, *frustration* and *fear*. **Hurt** results when:

- We experience disappointment associated with expected actions or words received from others,
- We experience disappointment associated with expected life experiences, and
- A trusted relationship is betrayed or violated.

Frustration results when we continually:

- Experience unfulfilled expectations,
- Do not receive what we expect from others, and
- Do not receive what we expect from life.

Fear is associated with:

- A dreaded expected response from another person,
- A dreaded expected result from a life experience, and
- The expectation something bad or unpleasant is going to happen.

Our *hurts, frustrations* and *fears* are signs something is wrong, and we need to take corrective actions. We can choose to respond in a positive manner to these signs and initiate steps to correct events causing them, or we can choose to ignore them. These feelings can result in *anger* that becomes a negative filter through which we process future relationships and life experiences when they are not resolved in a healthy manner.

Anger, like love and forgiveness, is a choice we make when responding to others and life experiences. It is a defense mechanism used to shield ourself from future hurts, frustrations and fears. Anger is beneficial and has positive consequences when processed in a healthy manner. Anger:

- Spurs us to act to facilitate needed changes in ourself and life situations,
- Alerts us to relationship issues that must be addressed, and
- Is a way we release emotional and other types of stress.

The causes of anger in our life have the potential to cause pain and suffering in our life and make us negative persons who direct our anger toward others when they are not properly addressed and resolved.

Unresolved anger that results from a lack of forgiveness has consequences. Gary Smalley lists these consequences in his book, *Making Love Last Forever* (1996):

Unresolved anger blocks our ability to give and receive love. Anger prevents us from entering intimate relationships and makes it difficult for us to trust others. We reject others before they have a chance to reject us. We sabotage relationships with negative words and actions and emotionally push others away when they get too close. Anger prevents us from receiving affirming words and actions others extend to us. Unresolved anger that predates a new relationship is added to anger that develops during that relationship.

Unresolved anger separates us from God. Anger causes us to blame God for events that cause our anger, and it impedes our ability to receive the love, forgiveness and healing He extends to us through Jesus. God wants us to love and forgive those who cause our anger. Our inability to love and receive love becomes a barrier between God and us. Jesus taught to remove this barrier we must forgive and be reconciled to those who cause our anger.

Unresolved anger prevents us from accepting ourself as a valued creature of God. Anger associated with the violation of a trusted relationship, particularly in cases of molestation and abuse, causes us to believe our life is of little value. The hurt and fear children of divorced parents experience are turned into anger directed at their parents. Anger that results from these and other situations is turned inward, producing feelings of guilt and shame. We often outwardly become angry and negative to compensate for these feelings. Angry persons are more likely to become involved in addictive behaviors that include, but are not limited to, alcohol, drugs, pornography, sex, abuse and molestation.

Unresolved anger prevents us from emotionally maturing. Anger causes our emotional development to freeze at the level it was at the time we experienced hurtful events. We grow physically but not emotionally. The lack of emotional development results in our inability to effectively address relationship problems and resolve difficult life issues. This often results in our responding to these problems and issues in childish ways and saying and doing immature and hurtful things.

Unresolved anger is passed from one generation to the next. Anger is often passed from one generation to the next when it exists within a family. Much of the anger and violence that exists in our culture has originated from parents who did not realize the effects their anger would have on their children. Anger starts in childhood from actions of parents directed at their children. These actions can:

- Be associated with ethnic and cultural stereotypes passed on to children;
- Take the form of emotional, physical or sexual abuse or a combination of all three;
- Take the form of being unresponsive to and unsupportive of a child's unique spiritual, emotional and physical needs;
- Take the form of aggressively pushing a child to achieve in an area one or both of its parents failed to achieve in when a child; and
- Be associated with anger directed at a parent by one or both of his/her parents when a child.

This anger will continue to be passed from generation to generation, wreaking inter-generational havoc, until it is identified and resolved.

Unresolved anger makes us miserable negative persons. Anger can make and keep us miserable when we let it. How we respond to anger directed at us is a choice. Anger can take the forms of meanness, negativity, insensitivity, aggression, repression, abuse, molestation or any other form. Individuals who direct their anger at us often do not realize its effects on us. We can choose to deal with this in a healthy manner, or we can choose to soak in it. This anger becomes part of us when we choose to soak in it. This anger imprisons, blinds and makes us miserable when left unresolved. We can address and resolve anger when we choose to do so. We may need the assistance of a trained Christian counselor or mature Christian friend to deal with and resolve our anger. We will discuss ways of positively resolving anger in the next section.

Angry individuals are at higher risk of experiencing stress-related physical health problems. Drs. Frank and Mary Alice Minirth, Drs. Brian and Deborah Newman, and Drs. Robert and Susan Hemfelt in their book, *Passages of Marriage* (1991), indicated anger causes damage us in five areas:

Anger suppresses the immune system. Anger alters our body chemistry, which is linked to our immune system. Anger induces chemical changes in our body that reduces our natural resistance to disease.

Anger alters neurotransmitters in the brain. Neurotransmitters are chemicals that help nerves pass information among themselves. Anything that alters these transmitters profoundly affects our emotions. Depression, manic conditions and excessive anxiety result. These conditions can only be addressed by returning our brain chemistry back to normal.

Anger affects our autonomic nervous system. Stress triggers this system into action. Every part of the body is affected negatively when the autonomic nervous system is overloaded with stress. Anger produces stress.

Anger is linked to heart disease. Anger is related to the Type A personality. Statistically, Type A's suffer more cardiac problems and die younger.

Anger affects the hormone system. Anger affects the hypothalamus, which controls the pituitary gland. The pituitary gland controls all the hormones the other endocrine glands produce. Therefore, anger can cause secondary endocrine and hormonal problems.

STEPS TO FORGIVING OTHERS

The Bible teaches the only way to effectively resolve anger and experience spiritual healing related to hurtful life experiences is to forgive those who are responsible for the *hurts*, *frustrations* and *fears* that cause our *anger*. We as Christians often believe all that is necessary to forgive someone is to say the words, "I forgive you." Our words must proceed from our heart and be sincere for them to have meaning and be effective in facilitating our healing process. It may be difficult for us to forgive those who have emotionally hurt us from our heart. This act is a process that often takes a long time and may be painful for us and them.

Gary Smalley gives us seven steps that can be followed to forgive others as a precursor to experiencing spiritual and emotional healing associated with hurtful life events (*Making Love Last Forever*, 1996).

We must identify events that have hurt us in the past. We must identify past events and issues related to our anger before we can forgive those associated with these events. We may need the assistance of a trained Christian counselor to help us identify and address the events and issues associated with our anger. This is often true of hurtful events we have experienced as a young child. We can pray and ask the Holy Spirit to help us remember these events and issues when we are unable to receive this assistance (refer to Chapter 20). Over time He will help us remember these events and issues as we are able to process them. We must then identify what these events have caused us to lose along with their relation to our anger. Hurtful events often cause us to lose something or result in something taken from us we perceive as important. These losses intensify the hurts, frustrations and fears associated with our anger. For example:

- A man who was physically or emotionally abused as a young boy may have lost his self-respect, self-worth and ability to enter trusting adult relationships.

- A woman who was sexually molested or abused as a young girl may have lost her innocence and childhood and her perceived ability to attract a future husband.

- An individual who had a serious personal conflict with a trusted co-worker or supervisor may have been denied a promotion or lost his job.

- A woman who went through a traumatic divorce may have lost her self-esteem and self-confidence and her perceived ability to enter an intimate and trusting relationship with another man.

These and other events cause us to lose something important. These can be actual or perceived losses. We emotionally process both types of losses the same. We must identify past events that have hurt us and what they have caused us to lose to begin our healing process and to eventually be able to forgive those who have hurt us through these events.

We must allow ourself to grieve our losses associated with past hurtful events. We must address the reality of hurtful events in our past that have caused us to lose important things in our life. Anger and grief result when we lose or have important things in our life taken from us. This anger and grief ranges from mild to severe, depending on the importance and severity of our losses. We often do not allow ourself time to properly grieve these losses. Our losses can be associated with the:

- Loss of innocence as a child because of emotional, physical or sexual abuse;
- Lack of parental encouragement and support during childhood;
- Unfair loss of a job because of a conflict in the workplace;
- Denial of a promotion;
- Death of a child, spouse or family member;
- Loss of self-esteem and self-confidence associated with a divorce; etc.

Losses experienced during childhood often become buried and do not surface until we are adults. We must allow ourself to grieve our losses when we are able to address them and work through the emotional issues associated with them. This is necessary for our healing process and for the development of our willingness and ability to forgive those who are responsible for the events that caused our losses.

The grief process proceeds through five steps (*Passages of Marriage*, 1991):

- **Shock and denial.** We cannot accept the fact that what has happened has happened. Shock and denial are often mixed with anger.
- **Depression.** Here we develop feelings of sadness, dejection and gloom with respect to what has happened. We may develop a sense of hopelessness and enter a period where it will take more energy to remain active.
- **Bargaining.** Here we attempt to make deals to undo what has happened or prevent what has happened from ocarina again. Fanciful thinking or entering a fantasy world often becomes part of the bargaining process.
- **Sadness.** Sadness is the stage of grief where we begin to accept the reality of what has happened to us. It is a period of sorrow we must pass through to complete our healing.
- **Forgiving and resolution.** We forgive those who have hurt us and accept the event that has happened to us as we proceed through the healing process. We may not like what has happened. The memories may still be there, and they may still be painful. However, we are ready to move on with our life.

The Lord gave us a wonderful promise in Joel 2:23-26:

> "So rejoice, O sons of Zion, and be glad in the LORD your God; for He has given you the early rain for your vindication. And He has poured down for you the rain, the early and latter rain as before. And the threshing floors will be full of grain, and the vats will overflow with the new wine and oil. Then I will make up to you for the years that the swarming locust has eaten, the creeping locust, the stripping locust, and the gnawing locust, My great army which I sent among you. And you shall have plenty to eat and be satisfied, and praise the name of the LORD your God, who has dealt wondrously with you; then My people will never be put to shame."

In the first part of the Book of Joel, God described the desolation Israel was to experience because of the sins of its people. This desolation was symbolized as an invasion of an army of locusts. There were to be swarming locusts, creeping locusts, stripping locusts and gnawing locusts, all doing their own separate and unique damage. However, God also talked about how Israel was to be delivered and restored from the devastating effects of this invasion. All the things that were to be destroyed by the locusts were to be totally restored by God. The things in our life taken from or denied to us because of hurtful events can be compared to things lost because of an invasion of destructive locusts in our life. We have previously described some of these losses. They are painful and must be grieved. However, The Lord promises to heal us and restore what we have lost as He promised Israel when we invite Him into our life to cleanse and heal our wounds. He will restore our innocence. He will restore our self-esteem, self-worth and self-confidence. He will restore broken relationships. He will create within us the ability to trust and enter healthy relationships. The opportunities in a job to which we go will often exceed those in the job we left when we have lost a job. God will heal our wounds and restore what the locusts of anger, bitterness and resentment have taken when we trust and believe in Him. He will replace them with the ability to love and forgive those who have hurt us.

We must attempt to understand those who have hurt us. This often seems hard to do; sometimes it seems impossible. However, this is an important step in our healing process, and it is an essential step in developing our ability to forgive those who have hurt us. We often discover those who have hurt us are acting out of their own pain when we attempt to understand them. They are reacting in destructive and hurtful ways to hurtful acts committed against them. They are acting out of unresolved anger related to personal losses they have experienced, and this anger is directed at us. This understanding does not justify their actions, nor should it create within us a feeling we deserved or invited these actions.

However, this understanding often results in a change in our attitudes toward those who hurt us, and it results in our ability to respond to them with compassion. These make it easier for us to forgive them.

We must release and forgive those who hurt us. We are emotionally and spiritually tied to those who hurt us as long as we retain our anger toward them. The anger of those who hurt us often becomes our anger when we do not release and forgive them. The only way we can separate our anger from their anger is to release and forgive them. Our anger can consume us with all the destructive consequences we have previously discussed when we do not do this. This is an unnecessary price to pay for hanging onto anger, bitterness and resentment. To forgive those who have hurt us, we must name the hurtful offenses they have committed against us and say the words "I forgive and release you" for each offense. This must be a heartfelt response. We must then invite Jesus and the Holy Spirit into the wounded and hurting areas in our life associated with these offenses to continue our healing process and reclaim and restore these areas to us.

We must look for the good that has resulted from hurtful events that have occurred in our life. Paul stated in Romans 8:28 God causes all things to work for the good of those who love Him. Paul stated good can come from bad things that happen to us. Therefore, we should look for the good that results from hurtful events in our life. Identifying good that comes from adversity helps us to transform our anger, bitterness and resentment into gratitude that gives us an increased sense of self-worth and joy. Sometimes it is difficult to identify the good that can come from bad experiences. However, God will show us through the presence of the Holy Spirit and help us understand when we ask Him. Benefits of adversity can include:

- Greater connectivity with God, Jesus and the Holy Spirit,
- A better understanding of ourself and our values,
- Increased confidence in ourself,
- Increased stamina and wisdom in addressing difficult life issues,
- A better understanding of others,
- A greater sensitivity and compassion toward others,
- Identification of new areas of service and ministry,
- Identification of support networks,
- Development of new relationships, and
- New opportunities.

We must put our feelings in writing. We must put our feelings in writing after we have completed the previous five steps. We can release anger and receive healing by doing this. We must:

- List our hurts, frustrations and fears associated with hurtful events in our life;
- Identify what we have lost or what was taken from us because of these events;
- Identify the pain and grief these events have caused us and state how we plan to live beyond our pain and grief;
- Name the offenders associated with these events and affirm we have forgiven and released them; and
- Indicate how we hope they would respond to us if we were to seek reconciliation with them.

The act of putting our feelings in writing is designed to help us clarify them and our responses to the hurtful events that have occurred in our life. We must commit what we have written to God through Jesus. We must then invite Jesus and the Holy Spirit into the broken and hurting areas of our life we have described and release these areas to Them so they can facilitate our healing process. We must then burn the paper on which everything is written after we have committed and released them to God, Jesus and the Holy Spirit. This symbolizes our complete releasing of the hurtful events in our life to God, Jesus and the Holy Spirit so They can facilitate our healing process. This process will take time, but it works.

We must seek reconciliation with those associated with the hurtful events in our life. The final step in forgiving those associated with hurtful events in our life is to seek reconciliation with them. This step is often extremely difficult, and it requires a high degree of maturity, love and faith on our part. It may also require the assistance of a trained Christian counselor or mature Christian friend. There are two important facts we should remember when we attempt to contact persons who have hurt us.

- Individuals we attempt to contact may not want to be reconciled to us. Facing us to address their hurtful words and actions toward us may be too painful for them. They may deny what they have done to us and hate us for asking them to address areas in their own lives they either do not want to or cannot face.
- Relationships with those who have hurt us are forever changed because of the brokenness we have experienced. Trust has often been violated by their hurtful actions, and these actions have caused us to lose things that were important to us.

Our only desire may be to bring closure to and release from a hurtful experience when we seek to be reconciled. We may not want to reestablish a relationship. A new relationship, if desired, will have to begin with the conditions that exist at the time of reconciliation and follow the principles associated with developing any healthy new relationship.

We must approach individuals with whom we seek reconciliation with sensitivity and compassion. We must seek the guidance of the Holy Spirit and ask Him to prepare the hearts of those with whom we seek reconciliation to receive and accept our requests for reconciliation. This often opens doors in their lives to begin a process that will result in their healing and release of their anger when they accept our requests.

God loves, has forgiven and has reconciled us to Himself through Jesus. He calls us to love, forgive, and be reconciled to those who have hurt us. Loving and forgiving are acts of our soul and of our mind and heart that occur because of choices we make and that involve taking risks and trusting God. God will never disappoint us. He will be there to give us the ability and resources to do what He calls us to do.

CHAPTER 20
SPIRITUAL LIFE PRINCIPLES
SUFFERING

"For what credit is there if, when you sin and are harshly treated, you endure it with patience? But if when you do what is right and suffer for it you patiently endure it, this finds favor with God. For you have been called for this purpose, since Christ also suffered for you, leaving you an example for you to follow in His steps, who committed no sin, nor was any deceit found in Him (Isaiah 53:9), and while being reviled, He did not revile in return; while suffering, He uttered no threats, but kept entrusting Himself to Him who judges righteously; and He Himself bore our sins in His body on the cross, that we might die to sin and live to righteousness; for by His wounds you were healed. ... But even if you should suffer for the sake of righteousness, you are blessed. And do not fear their intimidation and do not be troubled (Isaiah 8:12), but sanctify Christ as Lord in your hearts, always being ready to make a defense to everyone who asks you to give an account for the hope that is in you, yet with gentleness and reverence; and keep a good conscience so that in the thing in which you are slandered, those who revile your good behavior in Christ may be put to shame. For it is better, if God should will it so, that you suffer for doing what is right rather than for doing what is wrong. ... Make sure that none of you suffer as a murderer, or thief, or evildoer, or a troublesome meddler; but if anyone suffers as a Christian, let him not feel ashamed, but is to glorify God in this name. For it is time for judgment to begin with the household of God; and if it begins with us first, what will be the outcome for those who do not obey the gospel of God? And if it is with difficulty that the righteous is saved, what will become of the godless man and the sinner? (Proverbs 11:31) Therefore, those also who suffer according to the will of God shall entrust their souls to a faithful Creator in doing what is right. ... Be of sober spirit, be on the alert. Your adversary, the devil, prowls about like a roaring lion, seeking someone to devour. But resist him, firm in your faith, knowing that the same experiences of suffering are being accomplished by your brethren who are in the world. And after you have suffered for a little while, the God of all grace, who called you to His eternal glory in Christ, will Himself perfect, confirm, strengthen and establish you. To Him be dominion forever and ever. Amen." (1 Peter 2:20-24, 3:14-17, 4:15-19, 5:8-11)

REASON FOR SUFFERING

An image of a loving and caring God who has redeemed and reconciled us through His Son, Jesus, has been presented throughout this book. This image is consistently presented in the Christian church. However, many have difficulty in reconciling the image of a loving and caring God with the suffering He allows His creation in general and individuals to experience. Why does God allow this suffering to occur if He is so loving?

We are often led to believe God will protect us when we receive and accept the grace He extends to us through Jesus. We are told He will shield us from suffering, affliction and persecution. We often become disillusioned when this does not occur in the lives of others and when we personally experience suffering, affliction or persecution ourself. Why does God's creation experience suffering? Why do we personally experience suffering? Why does God allow us to suffer, and how does He use suffering in our life to perfect our relationship with Him?

There were no death, disease, discord and disasters in God's original creation. They came into the world with sin and the fallenness sin caused in the world. Along with sin came suffering, pain, affliction, agony, sorrow and persecution.

When God expelled Adam and Eve from the garden of Eden (Genesis 3:14-19), He:

- Told Eve He would greatly multiply her pain and the pain of all women during childbirth. He stated the desire of women would be for their husbands and their husbands would rule over them.

- Told Adam the ground would become cursed because of him, and it would bring forth thorns and thistles in addition to the abundance He had originally promised. Men and women would have to produce the food they eat through toil and the sweat of their forehead.

- Stated there would be enmity and conflict between mankind and Satan.

- Stated women would experience physical and spiritual death.

These were the consequences of the fallenness that entered the world because of sin, and suffering would occur because of this fallenness.

CAUSES OF SUFFERING

We blame God for suffering. However, He does not maliciously cause suffering. He may cause or allow us to suffer to discipline us or to use it to deepen our relationship with Him and perfect our personality and character.

The Bible teaches suffering occurs because of the fallenness that exists in the world and in our lives because of sin. Sin has caused a deterioration in and a disruption of the harmony, order and perfection that existed in God's original creation. These expose us to suffering. Because of sin, we:

- Have or will experience sickness. With proper medical intervention, most of us will recover. However, sometimes sickness causes significant pain, suffering and even death.

- Directly and indirectly experience suffering and sometimes death because of disasters. These disasters can be associated with major accidents. They can also be related to catastrophic events that are either man-made or events that are related to acts of nature.

- Suffer because of discord. Discord causes animosity and enmity to exist between individuals, cultural and ethnic groups, and nations. These result in conflicts, afflictions, persecutions, murders, wars, etc. cause suffering and death.

- Experience physical death. We will also experience spiritual death without the presence of Jesus in our life.

Hopelessness and despair occur when we attempt to work through major events in our life associated with disease, disasters, discord and death without God's presence through Jesus. God through Jesus and the presence of Holy Spirit in our life enable us to persevere through these events with a faith that transcends our suffering.

Sin has caused the souls of men and women to become darkened and blighted, and it has allowed Satan to become the god of this world. Suffering as a result is often caused by Satan and demonic forces in the spiritual realm and by immoral, evil and wrongful actions of men and women whose souls have become darkened and blighted by sin in the physical realm. These actions are associated with:

- Demonic forces and Satan who attempt to blind us to our need of and separate us from the saving grace we receive from God through Jesus;

- People who attempt to manipulate us and lead us into actions that violate God's laws and into spiritual, emotional and physical bondage;

- People who spiritually, emotionally and physically abuse, assault and molest us;

- People who intentionally instigate actions against us that are directed to victimize and hurt us and destroy our sense of self-esteem and self-worth.

- Imperfect relationships often cause suffering. They may be associated with:

- Parents and other authority figures who are unable to give us the affection, support, affirmation and nurturing we need;

- Marriage, family, friendships and business relationships in which we do not receive the affection, support, affirmation and nurturing we need; and

- Failed relationships that result in rejection by a spouse, other family members, close friends and business associates.

The offending persons in imperfect relationships often may not intentionally desire to hurt anyone. However, they often initiate hurtful actions that cause brokenness and suffering because of their brokenness and inability to enter healthy relationships.

Suffering occurs because of sin in our life. The Bible teaches God has established spiritual life principles and laws that govern our life, and He has place boundaries on acceptable behavior. There are consequences when we sin by disobeying and ignoring these principles and laws and by crossing over the boundaries God has established for acceptable behavior. These consequences often involve suffering and brokenness. The salvation we receive through Jesus frees us from the eternal consequences of sin and reestablishes our broken relationship with God. However, they do not free us from the earthly consequences of our disobedience, nor do they free us from the suffering and brokenness that result from our disobedience. God's grace gives us the ability to endure and work through our suffering and brokenness even though it does not free us from suffering and brokenness caused by our sins.

Both non-Christians and Christians experience suffering. Receiving and accepting God's grace through faith in Jesus does not make us immune from events in life that cause suffering. It often results in an increase in suffering. We come under increased attacks from secular groups who oppose Christian ideals and morals and by demonic spiritual forces who oppose God when we enter a relationship with God through faith in Jesus. We may experience persecution, affliction, loss of job, loss of income, sickness, depression, pain, distress, agony and even death because of our relationship with God through Jesus. We will continue to be exposed to events and forces in the world as Christians that cause suffering. However, we will have the ability to deal with these events and forces in a positive manner through the indwelling presence of the Holy Spirit.

Suffering sometimes appears to randomly occur and is often difficult to explain and understand. It seems there are some who are spared intense suffering while others seem to continually suffer. We may respond to life like Solomon in the book of Ecclesiastes in the Old Testament; life sometimes does not make sense. The unrighteous appear to prosper while the righteous seem to suffer.

There are conditions associated with suffering that do not make sense, we cannot explain, and we are not meant to understand. However, God is present in our suffering. We may not recognize His presence, but He is there. God can turn our suffering around to work to His good, accomplish His purpose in our life, and draw us into a closer relationship with Him when we approach Him through Jesus and the Holy Spirit. This is part of the inscrutable nature of God. We do not understand why He chooses to work in our life through suffering. Moreover, we do not understand how He can take what appears to be total disaster, despair and turmoil and turn these around to give us hope and victory.

GOD'S USE OF SUFFERING

There are many things about suffering we may not understand. However, there are some things we do understand. Suffering in the absence of a relationship with God through Jesus is devastating, and it destroys lives and relationships. It produces hopelessness and despair, and sometimes it takes away our desire to live. Paul stated in Romans 8:28:

> "And we know that God causes all things to work together for good to those
> who love God, to those who are called according to His purpose."

This statement applies only to those "who love God and who are called according to His purpose.", "All things work together for good" for these individuals. This includes suffering. Therefore, suffering must have a purpose if all things work together for good for those who have enter a relationship with God through Jesus.

God uses suffering to bring sorrow into our life that leads to repentance. Paul stated in 2 Corinthians 7:8-10:

> "For though I caused you sorrow by my letter, I do not regret it; though
> I did regret it - for I see that letter caused you sorrow, though only for a

while - I now rejoice, not that you were made sorrowful, but that you were made sorrowful to the point of repentance; for you were made sorrowful according to the will of God, in order that you might not suffer loss in anything through us. For the sorrow that is according to the will of God produces a repentance without regret, leading to salvation; but the sorrow of the world produces death."

Suffering often results in sorrow and "sorrow that is according to the will of God" produces repentance. Repentance, which is a turning from hostility and disobedience to God, is a prerequisite for our entering a relationship with God through faith in Jesus or in reestablishing a relationship with Him. God continually works to bring us into a reconciled relationship with Him through Jesus, and He will use suffering to facilitate this when necessary.

God uses suffering to discipline and restrain us. In Hebrews 12:4-13, the author stated:

"You have not yet resisted to the point of shedding blood in your striving against sin; and you have forgotten the exhortation which is addressed to you as sons, 'My son, do not regard lightly the discipline of the Lord nor faint when you are reproved by Him; For those whom the Lord loves He disciplines, and He scourges every son whom He receives.' Proverbs 3:11-12 It is for discipline that you endure; God deals with you as with sons; for what son is there whom his father does not discipline? But if you are without discipline, of which all have become partakers, then you are illegitimate children and not sons. Furthermore, we had earthly fathers to discipline us, and we respected them; shall we not much rather be subject to the Father of spirits, and live? For they disciplined us for a short time as seemed best to them, but He disciplines us for our good, that we may share His holiness. All discipline for the moment seems not to be joyful, but sorrowful; yet to those who have been trained by it, afterwards it yields the peaceful fruit of righteousness. Therefore, strengthen the hands that are weak and the knees that are feeble, and make straight paths for your feet, so that the limb which is lame may not be put out of joint, but rather be healed."

God generally does not desire to use suffering to get our attention when we are disobedient. He prefers we live within the boundaries He has established for our behavior and to obey His laws without any reproof or discipline on His part. Furthermore, He expects us to listen to and heed the counsel and reproof of those whom He leads to us or places in authority over us when we do disobey His laws. God will discipline us Himself when we are disobedient and refuse to accept the righteous counsel and discipline of those whom He leads to or places in authority over us. He will use suffering to accomplish this when necessary.

God uses suffering to humble us and lead us into a dependent relationship with Him. Paul stated in 2 Corinthians 12:7-10:

> "And because of the surpassing greatness of the revelations, for this reason, to keep me from exalting myself, there was given me a thorn in the flesh, a messenger of Satan to buffet me - to keep me from exalting myself! Concerning this I entreated the Lord three times that it might depart from me. And He has said to me, 'My grace is sufficient for you, for power is perfected in weakness.' Most gladly, therefore, I will rather boast about my weaknesses, that the power of Christ may dwell in me. Therefore I am well content with weaknesses, with insults, with distresses, with persecutions, with difficulties, for Christ's sake; for when I am weak, then I am strong."

God knows we must develop a dependent relationship with Him through Jesus and look to Him through the Holy Spirit as the source of our knowledge and wisdom before we can be in ministry and service to others. Our weakness is how God perfects His power and strength through us. We will often fail when we enter ministries relying on our own abilities. We will run the risk of exalting ourself instead of God in these ministries when we rely on our own abilities to perform them. God uses suffering to break down our stubborn self-will and humble us when necessary. This suffering moves us to fix our eyes on Jesus as the author and perfecter of our faith (Hebrews 12:1-2) and the true source of our authority and power.

God uses suffering to develop our faith and produce within us perseverance and Christlike love. Our faith and relationship with God through Jesus develop through our suffering. They grow and produce endurance when we trust in and draw our strength from God through Jesus and the Holy Spirit. James stated in James 1:2-4:

> "Consider it all joy, my brethren, when you encounter various trials, knowing that the testing of your faith produces endurance. And let endurance have its perfect result, that you may be perfect and complete, lacking in nothing."

Peter continued in 1 Peter 1:5-8:

> "Now for this very reason also, applying all diligence, in your faith supply moral excellence, and in your moral excellence, knowledge; and in your knowledge, self-control, and in your self-control, perseverance, and in your perseverance, godliness; and in your godliness, brotherly kindness, and in your brotherly kindness, love. For if these qualities are yours and are increasing, they render you neither useless nor unfruitful in the true knowledge of our Lord Jesus Christ."

The development of our faith produces endurance. It also results in moral excellence that yields knowledge. Knowledge yields self-control that results in perseverance. Endurance and perseverance work together to produce brotherly kindness that produces love. The ultimate outcome of suffering in the context of our relationship with God through Jesus is to experience His love, so we can love others as He loves us. This love enables us to reach out to others to establish channels of communication. The Holy Spirit then work through these channels to develop saving relationships with Jesus and to bless and heal the broken and wounded areas of their lives. This love renders us "neither useless nor unfruitful," and it becomes "perfect and complete, lacking in nothing."

God uses suffering to demonstrate the power of His word in the Bible and the power of His presence in our life. Suffering that is aligned with God's will demonstrates the power of His word in the Bible and of His presence in our life. Peter indicated we find favor with and are blessed by God when we suffer for doing what is right and patiently endure our suffering. This suffering becomes a testimony to others of the presence of Jesus who suffered before us in our life. This opens opportunities to witness to His presence to others. We are instructed to do so with humility and gentleness when we have an opportunity to share Jesus' presence in our life with others. Peter also stated we are never alone in our suffering that is aligned with God's will for us. He stated in 1 Peter 5:10:

> "And after you have suffered for a little while, the God of all grace, who called you to His eternal glory in Christ, will Himself perfect, confirm, strengthen and establish you."

We grow to truly know God and understand how He desires to work in our life through suffering. We discover He will be with us; He will never leave us. We learn God can be trusted to keep His covenants and promises.

We may sometimes fail to recognize God's presence in our suffering and feel alone. This usually occurs because we may not know Him. We may not know how to approach God or how to recognize His presence in our suffering when we have not previously entered a relationship with Him through Jesus. God gives us calm and stable times in our life to establish a relationship with Him through Jesus and to learn and understand the spiritual life principles and dynamics associated with this relationship. We do this through Christian fellowship, prayer and the study of the Bible. God expects us to use these calm and stable times to learn the spiritual life principles and dynamics associated with our relationship with Him through Jesus. We will learn how to approach God in our pain and suffering, sense His love and presence, and draw our strength from Him when we do this. We will discover God is faithful when bad and difficult times come. He will respond to us with love and compassion, and He will walk with us. He will enable us to persevere and overcome our suffering, and He will heal the wounded and broken areas in our life caused by our suffering.

CHAPTER 21
SPIRITUAL LIFE PRINCIPLES
SPIRITUAL HEALING

"See now that I, I am He, and there is no god besides me; it is I who put to death and give life. I have wounded, and it is I who heal; and there is no one who can deliver from My hand." (Deuteronomy 32:39)

"Behold, how happy is the man whom God reproves, so do not despise the discipline of the Almighty. For He inflicts pain, and gives relief; He wounds, and His hands also heal." (Job 5:17-18)

"O LORD my God, I cried to Thee for help, and Thou didst heal me." (Psalms 30:2)

"Is anyone among you sick? Let him call for the elders of the church, and let them pray over him, anointing him with oil in the name of the Lord; and the prayer offered in faith will restore the one who is sick, and the Lord will raise him up, and if he has committed sins, they will be forgiven him. Therefore, confess your sins to one another, and pray for one another, so that you may be healed. The effective prayer of a righteous man can accomplish much." (James 5:14-16)

SELF-IMAGE AND SPIRITUAL BROKENNESS

Our self-image influences our attitude toward life and how we relate to others. We approach the future with hope and confidence and our life has purpose when we have a positive self-image. We easily process life experiences, work through difficult times, and enter and develop trusting and healthy relationships. We find it difficult to process life experiences and work through difficult times when we have a negative self-image. Our life will often lack purpose. We find it hard to trust others and enter healthy relationships. We may be filled with guilt, resentment and anxiety that cause stress, conflicts and personal problems that at times overwhelm us.

David Seamands indicates there are four sources that influence the development of our self-image (*Healing for Damaged Emotions*, 1991):

The outer world: The outer world includes the external factors that help define who we are. It includes:

- Our experiences during birth, infancy, childhood, teen years, adult years - right up to the present time;
- The important people (parents, family members, relatives, friends, coworkers, etc.) in our life whom we used as role models in the development of our personality and character and of priorities in our life;
- Our perceptions of and reactions to how these important people relate to us; and
- How we have been educated, relate to our work environment, generally get along with others, etc.

We develop an image of ourself formed by our experience associated with these factors as we physically, emotionally and spiritually grow.

The world within us: Our inner world includes our soul, spirit, mind and heart. It is where we:

- Process and assimilate information we receive from the outer world through our five physical senses and the spiritual realm through our spirit;
- Address the fact we have been born into an imperfect world with a sin nature that initially separates us from God;
- Deal with the conflicts and struggles between good and evil, right and wrong, and obedience and disobedience;
- Process our feelings associated with tensions between success and failure, acceptance and rejection, joy and emptiness, fulfillment and frustration, confidence and fear, peace and anxiety, etc.; and
- Attempt to satisfy the yearnings of our soul and deal with the brokenness we experience when these yearnings are not satisfied (refer to Chapter 9).

Satan: Satan is the source of our negative self-image and resulting inner feelings of low self-esteem and self-worth. He uses our inner feelings of inadequacy, inferiority, worthlessness, etc. to blind us to the necessity of receiving the grace, love, forgiveness and redemption

God gives to us through Jesus. Satan works to defeat and prevent us from receiving the healing and blessings God desires to give us when we accept the redemption He extends to us through Jesus. He works to prevent us from developing our full potential as children of God.

God: God removes our negative self-image and related inner feelings of low self-esteem and self-worth and replaces them with His peace, joy and acceptance when He redeems us through Jesus. He works through the Holy Spirit to heal our damaged emotions and wounded spirit. God (Father, Son and Holy Spirit) takes up residence in us. He regenerates our spirit, renews our mind and transforms our heart. He enables and empowers us to be the person He has created us to be and to reach our full potential as one of His children.

We experience events in our outer world that cause brokenness and suffering. Because we live in an imperfect world that has been corrupted by sin, the basic yearnings of our soul sometimes are not met (refer to Chapter 9). Some of us are victimized as we grow from infants to adults, and this victimization often results in damaged emotions and a wounded spirit (refer to Chapter 19 and Chapter 20). We live in a world where, in the absence of God's redemption and reconciliation through Jesus, we are separated from God. Therefore, our spirit and soul (mind and heart) may be unable to properly process many of our hurtful *outer world* experiences as their effects and consequences find their way into our *inner world*. This increases our brokenness and suffering. Satan then enters these experiences to accuse us. He creates within us a negative self-image and related feelings of inadequacy, worthlessness, low self- esteem, low self-worth, etc. He then works to add feelings of guilt, shame, hopelessness and despair and to blind us to the necessity of turning to God to receive the salvation, spiritual healing and inner peace He desires to give us through Jesus.

We usually can work through physical, emotional and spiritual issues associated with events that cause grief, pain and suffering with reasonable effort. Major traumatic events, on the other hand, can cause serious emotional and spiritual wounds that result in damaged emotions and a wounded spirit. These damaged emotions and wounded spirit result in feelings of guilt, resentment and anxiety that lead to personal conflicts with others when left untreated and unresolved. These then turn into anger that produces within us emotional and stress-related problems when mixed with an unforgiving heart. This results in a negative self-image and related feelings of hopelessness and despair.

Anger that results from guilt, resentment and anxiety and from related personal conflicts often originates from an inability to forgive persons who have caused our brokenness and suffering or to receive forgiveness from others whom we have victimized and hurt. David Seamands indicated in his book, *Healing for Damage Emotions* (1991), there are three questions we can ask to determine whether there are unresolved anger and a lack of forgiveness in our life. They are:

Are there individuals in your life whom you hate or resent? Are there persons who have wronged you, used you, taken advantage of you, emotionally or physically abused you, sexually abused or molested you, etc. that you have not forgiven?

Do you transfer responsibility for your mistakes, misfortunes, problems, etc. to other persons? Do you accept responsibility for your own faults, failures, problems, etc., or do you always attempt to transfer blame to others? This is often a sign of unresolved anger resulting from a lack of forgiveness on your part. This anger is directed at others because they have victimized and hurt you, thereby causing you to become who you are.

Do you often (or perhaps not so often) respond negatively or with resentment toward other persons because they remind you of someone else that you know? Perhaps this person reminds you of a parent, family member, friend, co-worker, etc. who has victimized and hurt you and whom you have not forgiven.

We will not experience healing for damaged emotions and a wounded spirit until we work through our anger and forgive those persons who have victimized, hurt and caused us to suffer (refer to Chapter 19). Individuals who have damaged emotions and a wounded spirit often have a low self-image and related inner feelings of low self-esteem and self-worth. David Seamands indicated low self-esteem has four negative characteristics (*Healing for Damaged Emotions*, 1991). They are:

Low self-esteem makes us feel inferior. It results in a low self-image and causes us to work way below our potential. We sometimes believe we are incapable of meeting realistic expectations and performing routine tasks. Low self-esteem can prevent us from receiving love, support and forgiveness from others. Satan uses our feelings of low self-esteem to hinder our entering a reconciled relationship with God through Jesus. He deceives us into believing we are unworthy of God's love and forgiveness. This often keeps us in spiritual bondage.

Low self-esteem inhibits our ability to develop a vision for our future. We must be able to look to the future with a sense of hope, purpose and direction to live a satisfying life. Proverbs 29:18 states, "Where there is no vision, the people are unrestrained, but happy is he who keeps the law." Without a vision for the future, there will be no hope, purpose and direction for our life. We will move through life with no real agenda for the future.

We may often let others establish our agenda. We must be able to dream bold visions and then work to make them a reality to have healthy feelings of self-esteem and self-worth.

Low self-esteem hinders healthy relationships. Jesus implied in His two great commandments (Mark 12:29-31) we can only love others to the extent we love ourself. We often see others through the same emotional eyes that we see ourself. We often find it difficult to love and trust others and enter healthy relationships when we have feelings of low self-esteem and a low self-image.

Low self-esteem inhibits our ability to enter Christian service. Satan attempts to prevent us from entering a reconciled relationship with God through Jesus. He then works to prevent us from entering Christian ministries and service when he fails. He uses low self-esteem in both efforts. Low self-esteem causes us to feel inferior and believe we are incapable of participating in ministries and service to which God may call us. Low self-esteem often makes us afraid to discover and develop the talents and spiritual gifts given to us by God.

We must have or develop a positive self-image to receive and experience spiritual healing and develop healthy feelings of self-esteem and self-worth. A positive self-image is at the heart of developing a healthy personality. Dr. Maurice Wagner indicated in his book, *The Sensation of Being Somebody* (1985), there are three essential elements to developing a positive self-image.

We must have inner feelings of belonging. We must perceive we are loved. We must sense others want us, accept us, care for us, enjoy being with us, want to do things with us, want to work with us, etc. Many believe our sense of belonging and being loved begins before birth while we are in our mother's womb. It is difficult to develop a sense of belonging when we sense we are unwanted.

We must have inner feelings of worth and value. We must believe we have something of worth and value to offer others. Proverbs 29:18 implies our inner feelings of worth and value are related to our ability to live within boundaries of acceptable behavior established by God.

We must believe we are competent. We must believe we can cope with difficult life situations and with life in general. We must develop a vision for life, along with related goals, and then work toward making our vision a reality and accomplishing the goals we have established. We must believe we can successfully perform tasks assigned to us by others.

SPIRITUAL HEALING

We may not initially experience the healing of spiritual wounds and brokenness we have experienced during our life when we accept and receive the grace God extends to us through Jesus. We may be unable to experience the peace and joy we expect in our relationship with God through Jesus. There sometimes remains an emptiness and sense of hopelessness and despair we cannot overcome even though the Holy Spirit is present in our life.

Spiritual healing occurs through our relationship with God through Jesus and often require the assistance of a trained Christian counselor, pastor, or spiritually mature Christian friend. It is a process that often takes place over an extended period and occurs in a nurturing and supporting Christian environment that includes our family, our church, and a group of trusted Christian friends. God works in this environment through the Holy Spirit to bring us the spiritual healing we seek.

Following are guidelines based on biblical principles that can help facilitate the healing of spiritual wounds and brokenness in your life.

You must face and address your problems. We tend to run from or ignore our problems. We believe they will go away when we ignore them. This never occurs. Our problems remain until we face and address them. God requires you to do this. It is the only way to resolve them. God will assist you when you seek Him in this effort.

You must accept responsibility for your problems and their consequences in your life. Some of your problems and related brokenness may be because of bad choices you have made and others you have offended and hurt as a result. You must accept responsibility for your choices and identify the individuals you have offended and hurt by these choices. You also must accept responsibility for the related consequences. Other problems may be associated with how others have acted toward you. You chose how you would respond to these actions even though you did not provoke them nor deserve their related brokenness. You cannot assume responsibility for how others have treated you. However, you must accept responsibility for how you chose to respond to them and the related consequences associated with your response.

You must decide whether you want to receive spiritual healing. Surprisingly, there are individuals who do not want to receive spiritual healing. There is nothing anyone can do to help you when you do not want to address your problems and receive spiritual healing for their related brokenness. You will not receive spiritual healing unless you want to be healed and you actively enter the process that will result in your healing.

The above three steps relate to your attitude toward your brokenness and desire to receive spiritual healing. Proceed to the following steps when you want to receive spiritual healing. It may be necessary for you to seek the assistance of a pastor, trained Christian counselor, or spiritually mature Christian friend who has the spiritual gift of healing as you proceed through these steps.

Establish or reestablish a right relationship with God through Jesus. The following procedures are designed for those who have received and accepted the grace God extends to them through Jesus. You must accept Jesus as your Lord and Savior if you have not already done so. Then you must ask the Holy Spirit to reveal to you areas of sin in your life that must be addressed. James stated in James 5:15, "Therefore, confess your sins to one another, and pray for one another, so you may be healed." You must first confess your sins and seek Jesus' forgiveness before He will facilitate your healing through the Holy Spirit. God will always forgive your sins. Uncontested sins give Satan a foothold in your life that will hinder your spiritual healing. This foothold is destroyed when you confess your sins and receive forgiveness. Use the ten commandments listed in Chapter 2 to assist you in identifying areas of sin in your life you must confess. You must bring your involvement in a cult or occult activities to God through Jesus for His forgiveness and ask the Holy Spirit to destroy the demonic spiritual bondage in your life this involvement has caused.

Forgive individuals who are responsible for your wounded spirit and brokenness. Jesus taught in Matthew 5:23-24 you must forgive those who have hurt and victimized you before you can enter a right relationship with God through Him. Forgiving others is necessary for you to resolve and be free of anger and bitterness you have experienced because of your brokenness. Chapter 18 presents steps you can use to forgive others. Some hurtful acts committed against you may be easy to forgive; others may be extremely difficult. The more difficult issues may take time and the assistance of a trained Christian counselor.

Seek forgiveness from individuals whom you have victimized. We often experience anger when we internalize brokenness and hurt. We can act out this anger in aggressive, subtle or both ways. We often victimize and hurt them when we do this. Victimizing and hurting someone can cause feelings of remorse and guilt. You must address the hurt and brokenness you have caused others to effectively deal with this guilt and receive spiritual healing. You should contact individuals you have victimized and hurt to seek their forgiveness when possible and make restitution when necessary. Sometimes this is not possible. Bring the issues for which you are seeking forgiveness to God through Jesus to seek and receive His forgiveness when this is the case. He will forgive and give you peace.

Forgive yourself. We sometimes harbor guilt related to our victimization and related responses. It is usually easy to receive the forgiveness God and others give us. However, it is sometimes difficult to forgive ourself. For you to receive healing for your wounded spirit and brokenness, you need to forgive yourself when it is necessary. In this act, you assume responsibility for your contributions to your problems and seek God's assistance in dealing with them. Forgiving yourself may be the most difficult step in your healing process. This is where you surrender your pride and anger to God and seek His assistance in dealing with problems and related areas in your life you cannot effectively address yourself.

Ask the Holy Spirit to come into your life to heal your wounded and broken areas. Some spiritual wounds and areas of brokenness in your life may be easy to identify and address. Others may be buried deep within your soul and may be more difficult to identify and address. Ask the Holy Spirit to bring to your conscious mind the memories of hurtful and traumatic events in your life. Ask Jesus to enter these events at the age they were experienced to heal the pain and suffering associated with their memories as they are remembered. Then ask Him to cover and cleanse these memories with His blood. Jesus must heal the young child within you who was victimized and hurt when you experienced a hurtful or traumatic event as a young child. Often the child within you must be healed before you can be spiritually healed as an adult. You can address painful memories in two ways. You can begin with less hurtful memories that are easy to address and work toward addressing the more difficult and painful memories. You can also address your memories as they chronologically occurred in your life, beginning with memories associated with your infancy and childhood and working your way forward to the present time. You often may not be able to address all your painful memories in a single healing session. This process may take several sessions that will occur over an extended period, depending on the severity of your spiritual brokenness. You will gradually and systematically move to deeper and more painful memories as you successfully address less painful memories and related areas of brokenness. Ask the Holy Spirit to reclaim and restore to you areas of your life that the locusts of victimization, pain and suffering have damaged or destroyed as you proceed through your healing process (Joel 2:23-26). You may tend to be or become angry with God for causing or allowing hurtful and traumatic events to occur as you address these events in your life. Remember you live in a world that has been corrupted by sin. Remember we all experience the painful effects of sinful acts directed against us, as well as, of acts in our lives associated with our own sinful natures. God can use suffering in your life to draw you closer to Himself, and He will give you ultimate victory over your pain and suffering.

Invite the Holy Spirit to come into your life to begin or continue the renewing of your mind and transforming of your heart. Spiritual healing is a process that often takes a long time. The healing you will experience following the preceding steps is just the beginning of your overall healing process. Victimization at a young age can have a profound effect on our emotional and spiritual growth and on the development of our personality and character. Hurtful and traumatic events we experience as a child can result in our becoming a negative and hurtful person who intentionally or unintentionally reach out to hurt others. Your mind must be renewed so you can be transformed into a new person who can relate and respond to others with love and compassion as you progress through your healing process. You must give the Holy Spirit permission to transform your heart so He can transform you into the person God desires you to be as your mind is renewed.

Become part of a nurturing Christian community. You must be part of a nurturing Christian community for your mind to be renewed and your heart to be transformed. This community will accept and give you the nurturing and support you need as you work through your healing process. It will be a community where you can enter mentoring and discipling relationships with mature Christians. Men must mentor and disciple men, and women must mentor and disciple women. These relationships are necessary for you to learn and internalize the spiritual principles contained in the Bible. They are essential for your continued spiritual and emotional growth and for your learning how to live a triumphant and spirit-filled life.

JESUS - OUR PHYSICIAN AND HEALER

Jesus stated in John 15:5-8:

> "I am the vine, you are the branches; he who abides in Me, and I in him, he bears much fruit; for apart from Me you can do nothing. If anyone does not abide in Me, he is thrown away as a branch, and dries up; and they gather them, and cast them into the fire, and they are burned. If you abide in Me, and My words abide in you, ask whatever you wish, and it shall be done for you. By this is My Father glorified, that you bear much fruit, and so prove to be My disciples."

Jesus indicated He is the One through whom our life yields fruit. Apart from Him we can do nothing. However, we can ask whatever we desire, and it will be done for us when we abide in Him, and His words abide in us. Jesus is the vine through whom we spiritually grow and draw our strength, knowledge and wisdom. At the end of the Sermon on the Mount in

Matthew 5-7, Jesus stated an individual who hears His words and incorporates them into his life will be like a person who builds his house upon *the rock*. The storms and floods of life will come and beat against the house, and it will not fall because it has been built upon a solid foundation. Jesus is *the rock*, the solid foundation, upon which God desires us to build our life, so we can address life's challenges and withstand its adversities.

Paul stated in Colossians 1:16-20:

> "For by Him all things were created, both in the heavens and on earth, visible and invisible, whether thrones or dominions or rulers or authorities - all things have been created by Him and for Him. And He is before all things, and in Him all things hold together. He is also head of the body, the church; and He is the beginning, the firstborn from the dead; so that He Himself might come to have first place in everything. For it was the Father's good pleasure for all the fullness to dwell in Him, and through Him to reconcile all things to Himself, having made peace through the blood of His cross; through Him, I say, whether things on earth or things in heaven."

All things in heaven and earth, visible and invisible, have been created by and for Jesus. We have all been created for the glory of God, and Paul stated in Philippians 2:12-13 God through Jesus continually works in and through our life to work His will and His good pleasure.

All things are held together by Jesus. This includes our individual life. We are continually exposed to conflicts, tragedies, persecutions and other adversities that, if we choose to stand alone, can cause serious problems in our life. Jesus undergirds and holds our life together when we receive and accepts God's grace through Him. He promised in Matthew 16:18 the gates of Hades shall not be able to overpower His Church. The gates of hell will not be able to overpower us when we are in fellowship with Jesus within a local church.

We have been or will be exposed to events in our life that can cause spiritual and emotional wounds. These wounds can cause spiritual brokenness in our life that can prevent us from entering healthy relationships with others when they are serious enough.

This chapter shows us how we can experience healing of our wounded spirit and brokenness. We may need to seek and receive help from a trained Christian counselor to work through some of the issues associated with the hurting and broken areas in our life. However, we must ultimately turn to Jesus to receive lasting healing in these areas. He is our ultimate physician and healer. We must seek His forgiveness when necessary as we yield ourself to His authority over our life and ask Him to heal us. He comes into our life to cover our hurting and broken areas with His blood to heal, cleanse and redeem them when we do this. Jesus may not take away the memories of the events associated with our spiritual wounds and brokenness, and He may not heal related physical wounds or infirmities in a manner we would like. However, He will do the following:

- Heal our memories of the events associated with our spiritual wounds and brokenness. He removes the hurting and emotional suffering and pain these wounds and brokenness have caused.

- Creates the desire within and empowers us to work through problems related to our spiritual wounds and brokenness. His Spirit unites with our spirit to give us the strength and ability to work through those issues that are difficult for us to work through alone or with the help of others.

- Removes the anger, hatred and fear associated with the persons and events that caused our spiritual wounds and brokenness. He cleanses, redeems and heals the related hurting and broken areas in our life.

- Replaces our anger, hatred and fear with His liberating love and compassion. He creates within us the desire and enables us to forgive those individuals who have caused our spiritual wounds and brokenness.

- Removes our feelings of shame, guilt, loneliness, despair, hopelessness, etc. that are associated with our spiritual wounds and brokenness. He replaces these negative feelings with joy and hope rooted in His transforming presence in our life. He enables us to move forward in our life with a heart He has transformed to the better times that lie ahead.

- Redeems and restores to a healthy state those areas in our life that have been corrupted and lost because of our spiritual wounds and brokenness. He returns to us our dignity, innocence, feelings of value and confidence, self-esteem, self-worth, etc. He replaces our negative self-image with a positive self-image fashioned in His likeness.

The healing Jesus gives us and how He does it is a mystery. However, His healing is a complete healing that enables us to move forward in our life with love, joy, peace, patience, kindness, goodness, faithfulness, gentleness and self-control (Galatians 5:22-23).

Jesus is our physician and healer. He undergirds and holds our life together. He enters our life to heal our broken and hurting areas and take away our guilt, shame, loneliness, despair and emptiness when we give Him permission. He enables us to accept and positively respond to and deal with whatever life brings our way. God hears and works with us to bring healing, meaning and purpose to our life when we bring our needs and the broken and hurting areas of our life to Him through Jesus in prayer.

Paul stated in 2 Corinthians 4:6-11:

> "For God, who said, 'Light shall shine out of darkness,' is the One who has shone in our hearts to give the light of the knowledge of the glory of God in the face of Christ. But we have this treasure in earthen vessels, that the surpassing greatness of the power may be of God and not from ourselves; we are afflicted in every way, but not crushed; perplexed, but not despairing; persecuted, but not forsaken; struck down, but not destroyed; always carrying about in the body the dying of Jesus, that the life of Jesus also may be manifested in our body. For we who live are constantly being delivered over to death for Jesus' sake, that the life of Jesus also may be manifested in our mortal flesh."

Jesus is the light that shines in our hearts to make known to us the knowledge of the glory of God. Jesus, along with the Holy Spirit, reveals God's word to us, so we will always have sufficient knowledge to deal with both good experiences and crises that occur in our life. The power of God works through Jesus so even though we may be afflicted, perplexed, persecuted, or struck down, we will never be crushed; we will never despair; we will never be forsaken; nor will we ever be destroyed. Jesus will always walk with us to give us the ability to deal with the good and overcome the bad that come our way.

CHAPTER 22
SPIRITUAL LIFE PRINCIPLES
THE CHRISTIAN FAMILY

"God created man in His own image, in the image of God He created him; male and female He created them. God blessed them; and God said to them, 'Be fruitful and multiply, and fill the earth, and subdue it; and rule over the fish of the sea and over the birds of the sky and over every living thing that moves on the earth.'" (Genesis 1:27_28)

"And [Jesus] answered and said, 'Have you not read, that He who created them from the beginning made them male and female, and said, 'For this cause a man shall leave his father and mother, and shall cleave to his wife; and the two shall become one flesh?' Consequently they are no longer two, but one flesh. What therefore God has joined together, let no man separate.'" (Matthew 19:4-6)

"Wives, be subject to your own husbands, as to the Lord. For the husband is the head of the wife, as Christ also is the head of the church, He Himself being the Savior of the body. But as the church is subject to Christ, so also the wives ought to be to their husbands in everything. Husbands love your wives, just as Christ also loved the church and gave Himself up for her; that He might sanctify her, having cleansed her by the washing of water with the word, that He might present to Himself the church in all her glory, having no spot or wrinkle or any such thing; but that she should be holy and blameless. So husbands ought also to love their own wives as their own bodies. He who loves his own wife loves himself; for no one ever hated his own flesh, but nourishes and cherishes it, just as Christ also does the church, because we are members of His body. For this cause a man shall leave his father and mother, and shall cleave to his wife; and the two shall become one flesh. This mystery is great; but I am speaking with reference to Christ and the church. Nevertheless let each individual among you also love his own wife even as himself; and let the wife see to it that she respects her husband." (Ephesians 5:22-33)

THE FAMILY

The Bible teaches God has established two divine institutions: the family and the Church. God established the family during creation to perpetuate and preserve mankind. He established the Church to be the vehicle through which men and women can come to know Him and learn about and receive the redemption from sin He offers them through faith in Jesus. Issues associated with the family will be discussed in this chapter, and issues associated with the Church will be discussed in the Chapter 23.

Moses states in Genesis 2:18-24:

> "Then the LORD God said, 'It is not good for the man to be alone; I will make him a helper suitable for him.' And out of the ground the LORD God formed every beast of the field and every bird of the sky, and brought them to the man to see what he would call them; and whatever the man called a living creature, that was its name. And the man gave names to all the cattle, and to the birds of the sky, and to every beast of the field, but for Adam there was not found a helper suitable for him. So the LORD God caused a deep sleep to fall upon the man, and he slept; then He took one of his ribs, and closed up the flesh at that place. And the LORD God fashioned into a woman the rib which He had taken from the man, and brought her to the man. And the man said, 'This is now bone of my bones, and flesh of my flesh; she shall be called woman, because she was taken out of Man.' For this cause a man shall leave his father and his mother, and shall cleave to his wife; and they shall become one flesh."

God established the family so a man and woman as husband and wife can find completeness in each other and provide a nurturing and safe environment to conceive, bear and raise children. He determined Adam should not be or work alone. Therefore, He created Eve to be a suitable helper who was to assist Adam in exercising the dominion over the earth he had been given. There is significant symbolism in the creation story of Adam and Eve. Matthew Henry's Commentary indicates Eve was not made from Adam's head to rule over him, nor out of his feet to be trampled upon by him. She was made from his side to be equal with him, under his arm to be protected by him, and near his heart to be loved by him. Paul indicated in 1 Corinthians 11:7:

> "For a man ought not to have his head covered, since he is the image and glory of God; but the woman is the glory of man."

Adam or man was the crown of God's creation. Eve or woman was the jewel in the crown to be given special honor.

The creation story in Genesis 1 indicates *man* was created male and female, and as such, were to jointly exercise dominion over God's creation. However, there was an implied order in God's creation of man and woman in Genesis 2. Adam who was created first was the head of his relationship with Eve and was directly accountable to God. God questioned Adam first when Adam and Eve disobeyed Him and sinned (Genesis 3:8-12). Eve who was created to be a suitable helper to Adam respected and submitted to the position God had given to him in their relationship. Adam in return honored Eve as part of his own body and loved, cherished and provided for her as the helper God had given him.

God commanded Adam and Eve to exercise dominion over His creation, bear children and subdue the earth (Genesis 1:26-28). He established the family to accomplish this. The family consisted of a husband and wife joined together for life and their children. The special position of bearing children was given to Eve. God placed His image and Spirit in Adam and Eve, and He wanted them to be passed on to their children, to their children's children, and so on. His will and spiritual principles were to be perpetuated in this manner throughout His creation, and men and women were to populate and subdue the earth.

God established two holy ordinances during creation: the Sabbath and marriage. The Sabbath was instituted as a holy day of rest from work and of worship and remembrance of their Creator. The Sabbath pointed to the future Church He was to establish through His Son, Jesus. Marriage was initiated to perpetuate and preserve mankind. It was to be a covenant relationship where husband and wife are joined together for life. There initially is no stronger relationship than the one we have with our parents as we grow from infancy to adulthood. However, God calls the son to leave his parents, the daughter to leave her parents, and the two to come together to be joined and cleave to each other as husband and wife in marriage. As a result, marriage is to be the strongest of all human unions.

Marriage was a relationship of innocence and purity before sin entered the world where there were no shame and guilt. God's likeness and Spirit dwelt in Adam and Eve, and they were obedient to the relationships they had with each other and God. Eve accepted and submitted to the headship God had given Adam over her even though they were coequal in exercising the dominion God had given them over the earth. Adam honored, loved and provided for the helper God had given him.

God had not established a formal hierarchy within Adam's and Eve's relationship before they sinned. This all changed when sin entered the world through their disobedience. God spoke to the most sacred parts of Adam's and Eve's relationship with each other and the positions He had given them in His creation when He placed His curse on them and consequently on all men and women. Eve was the most honored and was given the special function of bearing children. Women were still to bear children. However, instead of childbirth being painless as originally created, pain in childbirth was multiplied. Eve, who was created to be coequal with Adam in God's creation, was placed under his authority in marriage, and one of her most basic desires was to be with her husband (Genesis 3:16). God set up a hierarchy within the family because of sin. Paul stated in 1 Corinthians 11:3:

> "But I want you to understand that Christ is the head of every man, and the man is the head of a woman, and God is the head of Christ."

An important observation must be made here. The authority men have been given over women applies only to marriage. Paul's statement that "the man is the head of a woman" refers only to his relationship with his wife. This authority men were given by God does not extend to positions women can assume in the social structures of the cultures where they lived. Many cultures have assigned women a subservient role to men. The Bible does not support this. Paul stated in Galatians 3:26-28:

> "For you are all sons of God through faith in Christ Jesus. For all of you who were baptized into Christ have clothed yourselves with Christ. There is neither Jew nor Greek, there is neither slave nor free man, there is neither male nor female; for you are all one in Christ Jesus."

He affirms men and women are equal in the eyes of God, and outside of marriage women have the same rights as men to assume positions of responsibility, authority and leadership.

God gave Adam dominion over His creation and assigned him the task of caring and providing for Eve and his family. God originally created everything perfect, and everything in God's creation was in perfect harmony. God provided Adam with an environment where he could easily care and provide for Eve and his family. He placed them in a paradise where there were no shame, guilt, pain, suffering, death, disease, discord and disasters.

Adam's and Eve's paradise became a wilderness where there was barrenness, and which contained thorns and thistles when they sinned (Genesis 3:17-19). Instead of the innocence, peace and joy they experienced in God's original creation, they now experienced shame and guilt. The wilderness where they lived contained pain, suffering, death, disease, discord and disasters. Adam had to care and provide for his family by the sweat of his own face and protect them from the hostile and dangerous environment where they lived instead of God providing him with the means to care and provide for his family.

Satan took from Adam and Eve the dominion God had given them over the earth when He withdrew His Spirit from them. This condition exists today. The family unit became how men, women and their children could find refuge, safety and rest in a hostile and dangerous environment.

God established the family to be a divine illustration of Christ's union with His Church. Paul instructed wives to submit and be subject to their husbands because the husband is the head of the wife "as Christ is the head of the church (Ephesians 5:22-24)." Likewise, he instructed husbands to love their wives" just as Christ also loved the Church and gave Himself up for Her (Ephesians 5:25-30)."

Jesus is also the head of the husband in the family just as He is the head of the Church. God has demonstrated His selfless love to us through the mercy, grace and forgiveness He extends to us through Jesus. The family with Jesus as its head is to be a place of mercy, grace and selfless love. It is to be a place where family members are supported and nurtured by the selfless love within the family.

God's image and spiritual life principles were to be passed from generation to generation through the family before sin entered the world. The family today nurtured by the Holy Spirit and with the assistance of the Church is to pass the spiritual life principles of God's word in the Bible from generation to generation. Each new generation comes to know and accept the grace and salvation extended to them through faith in Jesus by means of their relationships within their families and the Church.

MARRIAGE

Marriage as a Covenant Established by God

Marriage is a covenant relationship between a husband and wife established by God. He stated in Genesis 2:18, "It is not good for the man to be alone; I will make him a helper suitable for him." Upon receiving the woman God created for him, Adam exclaimed in Genesis 2:23:

> "This is now bone of my bones, and flesh of my flesh; she shall be called woman, because she was taken out of man."

God then stated in Genesis 2:24:

> "For this cause a man shall leave his father and his mother, and shall cleave to his wife; and they shall become one flesh."

He reaffirmed the marriage union is a covenant relationship in His statement in Malachi in Malachi 2:14:

> "Yet you say, 'For what reason?' Because there has been a witness between you and the wife of your youth, against whom you have dealt treacherously, though she is your companion and your wife by covenant."

Jesus reaffirmed the marriage covenant God established in Matthew 19:4-6:

> "And He answered and said, 'Have you not read, that He who created them from the beginning made them male and female, and said, 'For this reason a man shall leave his father and mother and be joined to his wife, and the two shall become one flesh? (Genesis 2:7, 22, 24-25) So they are no longer two, but one flesh. What therefore God has joined together, let no man separate."

The Bible teaches the marriage covenant is a binding agreement established by God that defines a prescribed relationship between the husband and wife entering the covenant. This covenant relationship is more than a simple contractual relationship. A contract usually has specific beginning and ending dates and only involves specific terms to which individuals agree to honor. The contract also has means by which it can be terminated if any of its terms are violated. However, the marriage covenant is a permanent agreement established by God that can only be terminated by God or the death of the husband or wife who enter the covenant. It is a covenant that requires the total commitment of the husband and wife. This is the basis for Jesus' statement with respect to the marriage covenant, "What therefore God has joined together, let no man separate." Paul taught concerning marriage in 1 Corinthians 7:39:

> "A wife is bound as long as her husband lives; but if her husband is dead, she is free to be married to whom she wishes, only in the Lord."

Even though Paul's reference is for a wife to be bound to her husband as long as he lives, the marriage covenant between husband and wife is for life and can only be ended in a manner established by God.

God established two divinely ordained institutions: the Church and the family. Paul stated in concerning the Church Ephesians 1:19-23:

> "These are in accordance with the working of the strength of His might which He brought about in Christ, when He raised Him from the dead, and

SPIRITUAL LIFE PRINCIPLES – THE CHRISTIAN FAMILY

seated Him at His right hand in the heavenly places, far above all rule and authority and power and dominion, and every name that is named, not only in this age, but also in the one to come. And He put all things in subjection under His feet, and gave Him as head over all things to the church, which is His body, the fullness of Him who fills all in all."

Paul further stated in Ephesians 5:24, "he church is subject to Christ." He indicated in 1 Corinthians 11:3 and Ephesians 6:1-3 God is the head of Christ; Christ is head of the husband; the husband is head of his wife; and the husband and wife as parents are the head of their children. God has made Jesus head over the Church and the family because Jesus has redeemed us and established a new covenant between God and us that has been sealed with His blood. God established the Church and redeemed the family through the shedding of His Son's blood.

Covenants in the Old Testament were a means through which blessings or curses were passed onto those who had entered covenant relationships established by God. God made covenants with Abraham, Isaac, Jacob, Moses, David and other Old Testament leaders in Israel. These were normally covenanting of Law where the individuals with whom God had entered a covenant relationship were expected to honor their covenant promises. They received the promised blessings from God when they were faithful and obedient. God withheld His blessings, meted out punishment, and visited the iniquity of the covenant or law breakers onto their children to the third and fourth generations when they were unfaithful and disobedient. God in his covenant with Moses stated in Exodus 34:6-7:

> "The LORD, the LORD God, compassionate and gracious, slow to anger, and abounding in lovingkindness and truth; who keeps lovingkindness for thousands, who forgives iniquity, transgression and sin; yet He will by no means leave the guilty unpunished, visiting the iniquity of fathers on the children and on the grandchildren to the third and fourth generations."

We still see this today in the absence of the redemption God extends to us through Jesus. Suffering associated with the sins of parents are passed on to their children, grandchildren and so on. Children whose parents are alcoholics often become alcoholics. Children who are abused by their parents often abuse their children. Children whose parents are divorced often get divorced when they get married. The marriage covenant is a covenant of Law where a husband and wife commit to honor when they enter their relationships with each other and their children. Both husband and wife are blessed when they faithfully honor this commitment, and the blessings they receive from God are often passed onto their children.

However, children suffer the most when parents violate their covenant vows. Both parents and children are blessed when they honor their covenant commitments. Both suffer losses when either or both violate their covenant commitments.

Marriage as a covenant relationship should only be entered with a Christian partner. Paul instructed in 2 Corinthians 6:14-17:

> "Do not be bound together with unbelievers; for what partnership have righteousness and lawlessness, or what fellowship has light with darkness? Or what harmony has Christ with Belial, or what has a believer in common with an unbeliever? Or what agreement has the temple of God with idols? For we are the temple of the living God; just as God said, 'I will dwell in them and walk among them; and I will be their God, and they shall be My people.' 'Therefore, come out from their midst and be separate,' says the Almighty.'"

Christians should not be bound together in binding relationships with non-Christians. This includes marriage. Paul indicated sooner or later our Christian values and ideals will come into conflict with the values of the non-Christian partner, and the Christian partner will often compromise or ignore his/ her values to maintain harmony within the relationship. A marriage covenant with a non-Christian spouse often results in disappointment and emotional suffering for the Christian spouse.

Marriage as a Contractual Relationship

Individuals who get married today often consider marriage to be a contractual relationship that can be terminated when either partner wants to end the relationship. There are consequences when marriage partners are divorced because divorce is a violation of a covenant relationship established by God. They will experience these consequences that often result in significant pain and suffering even though one or both may have received the redemption God extends to them through Jesus. Children suffer more when their parents are divorced.

GOD'S ORDER FOR THE FAMILY

Covenants have divinely established rules. God has established specific relationships He expects to exist between husband and wife and between parents and children with respect to the marriage covenant.

Husbands and Wives

God has established hierarchies of authority in His creation to maintain harmony and order. James stated in James 4:7, "Submits therefore to God. Resist the devil and he will flee from you." Paul taught in Romans 13:1:

> "Every person is to be in subjection to the governing authorities. For there is no authority except from God."

He indicated in Titus 3:1-2:

> "Remind then to be subject to rulers, to authorities, to be obedient, to be ready for every good deed, to malign no one, to be peaceable, gentle, showing every consideration for all men."

Peter stated in 1 Peter 2:13-14:

> "Submit yourselves for the Lord's sake to every human institution, whether to a king as the one in authority, or to governors as sent by him for the punishment of evildoers and the praise of those who do right."

He further taught in 1 Peter 5:5 young men are to be subject to their elders. In Hebrews 13:17, the author stated:

> "Obey your leaders, and submit to them; for they keep watch over your souls, as those who will give an account. Let them do this with joy and not with grief, for this would be unprofitable for you."

God's chain of authority also extends to the family through Jesus as the head of the family, the husband as the head of his wife, and the parents as the head of their children.

Marriage is to be a relationship where husband and wife support and nurture each other and where each finds his/her completeness in the other. Paul stated in 1 Corinthians 11:11-12:

> "However, in the Lord, neither is woman independent of man, nor is man independent of woman. For as the woman originates from the man, so also the man has his birth through the woman; and all things originate from God."

Paul implied a husband and wife are not independent of each other in the marriage relationship. However, as in other areas, God has established lines of authority for the family. Figure 13 illustrates the lines of authority and relationships God has established within the family.

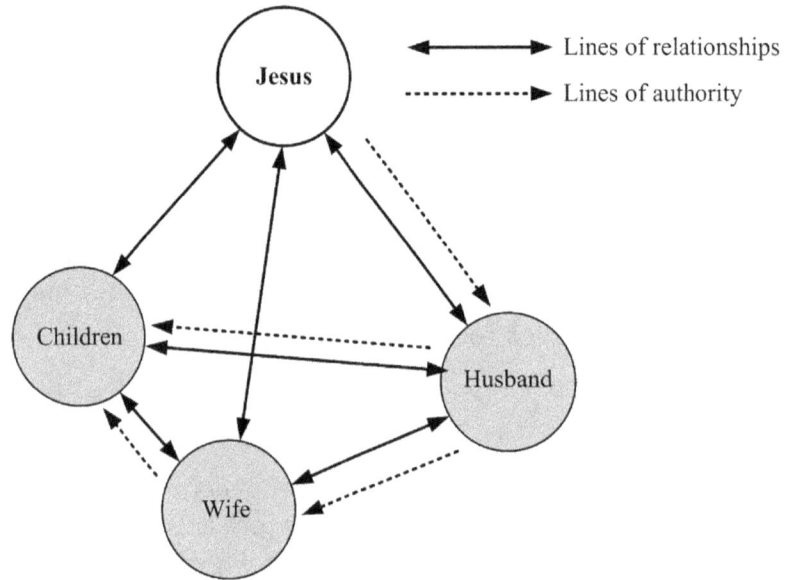

Figure 13

Paul taught in Ephesians 5:22-33:

> "Wives, be subject to your own husbands, as to the Lord. For the husband is the head of the wife, as Christ also is the head of the church, He himself shall be joined to his wife, and the two shall become on flesh. (Genesis 2:22, 24-25) This mystery is great; but I am speaking with reference to Christ and the church. Nevertheless, each individual among you also is to love his own wife even as himself, and the wife must see to it that she respects her husband."

Paul instructed wives to be subject to their husbands and husbands to love their wives as they love themselves.

Jesus taught those who are in positions of authority are to be servants to those over whom they have been given authority. The husband as head of his wife and family is to be a servant to them. He is to love and give himself to them as Jesus loved and gave Himself to the Church. The husband's position of head of his family is not a position of power; it is a position of responsibility and accountability to God. Peter instructed husbands in 1 Peter 3:7:

> "You husbands likewise, live with your wives in an understanding way, as with a weaker vessel, since she is a woman; and grant her honor as a fellow heir of the grace of life, so that your prayers may not be hindered."

Husbands are to honor their wives, so their prayers will not be hindered.

A foolish husband makes important family decisions without seeking his wife's counsel. He deprives himself of the knowledge, wisdom and insight his wife can contribute to these decisions when he does this. This often results in making bad decisions. A wise husband seeks the counsel of his wife before making important family decisions.

The husband and wife should agree when making important family decisions. Jesus stated in Matthew 18:19-20:

> "Again I say to you, that if two of you agree on earth about anything that they may ask, it shall be done for them by My Father who is in heaven. For where two or three have gathered together in My name, there I am in their midst."

The principle of agreement is important in the family who recognizes Jesus as its head. Husband and wife should always give each other the freedom to disagree when discussing important family issues. They will make decisions that are in line with the will of God for their family when they come to points of agreement on these issues. They can then move forward with confidence and act on these decisions with the knowledge God will support them in their actions.

Paul instructed wives to be subject to and respect their husbands. Peter instructed wives in 1 Peter 3:1-6:

> "In the same way, you wives, be submissive to your own husbands so that even if any of them are disobedient to the word, they may be won without a word by the behavior of their wives, as they observe your chaste and respectful behavior. And let not your adornment be merely external - braiding the hair, and wearing gold jewelry, or putting on dresses; but let it be the hidden person of the heart, with the imperishable quality of a gentle and quiet spirit, which is precious in the sight of God. For in this way in former times the holy women also, who hoped in God, used to adorn themselves, being submissive to their own husbands. Therefore Sarah obeyed Abraham, calling him lord, and you have become her children if you do what is right without being frightened by any fear."

Wives being submissive to their husbands have negative connotations in our modern cultures. Submission is a positive act when viewed from a Biblical perspective. The wife makes a deliberate and conscious choice when she yields herself to her husband as the head of their family.

The Bible teaches husband and wife are to commit themselves to grow and persevere in their marriage relationship. The husband is to give himself to the support and nurture of his wife just as she is to yield herself to the headship of her husband. The marriage relationship thrives and grows when both husband and wife are committed to serving and supporting each other.

Role of the Husband in the Family

God has set Jesus as head of the husband and the husband as the head of his wife. Paul set the standard for the relationship of the husband with his wife in Ephesians 5:25-30:

> "Husbands, love your wives, just as Christ also loved the church and gave Himself up for her; that He might sanctify her, having cleansed her by the washing of water with the word, that He might present to Himself the church in all her glory, having no spot or wrinkle or any such thing; but that she should be holy and blameless. So husbands ought also to love their own wives as their own bodies. He who loves his own wife loves himself; for no one ever hated his own flesh, but nourishes and cherishes it, just as Christ also does the church, because we are members of His body."

God has created a paradox in the husband's relationship with his wife. He is not to act as boss even though he is the head of his family. The husband as a servant leader is to love and give himself to and serve his wife as Christ loved and gave Himself to the Church. How much did He love the Church? He loved it enough to become its servant and savior; He loved it enough to die for it. The husband is to nurture and cherish his wife as he would nurture and cherish his own body. Paul instructed husbands in Colossians 3:19, "Husbands, love your wives and do not be embittered against them." Peter admonished husbands in 1 Peter 3:7:

> "You husbands in the same way, live with your wives in an understanding way, as with someone weaker, since she is a woman; and show her honor as a fellow heir of the grace of life, so that your prayers will not be hindered."

The husband is instructed by Paul and Peter to love, cherish, nurture and honor his wife. These all focus on meeting her greatest emotional needs.

The Bible teaches the husband is to relate to his wife as the helper and partner God created her to be. He is to interact with his wife as an equal partner and heir of Jesus even though he has been given the responsibility and authority as head of his family. God created the husband incomplete and intended him to find his completeness in his wife. This has significant implications with respect to the family. Neither the husband nor wife independently possesses all the attributes and skills necessary to effectively manage family affairs. Therefore, God established the family where the husband and wife jointly exercise their unique attributes and skills as they carry out their respective roles within the family.

The husband is expected to sacrifice himself for his wife as Christ sacrificed Himself for the Church. He is to love her with the same selfless love with which Jesus loves all of us. This love is not a jealous, possessing and demanding love. Rather it is a giving and sacrificing love that enables the wife to individually grow and mature within her relationships with her husband and family. This love is not a love that traps the wife into a singular dependent relationship with and controlled by her husband. Rather it is a love that not only enables her to freely develop a caring and dependent relationship with her husband, but it also frees her to develop relationships with others independent of her husband. This love is not a love that makes the wife a dependent extension of her husband in marriage. Rather it is a love that enables her to grow and develop in areas independent of him as she grows in her relationship with her husband. God intends a husband and wife to develop their individual personalities within the context of a marriage relationship even though He has created them to become one flesh within their marriage. A husband and wife will only be able to enter a mutually fulfilling relationship to the extent they are each free to grow and mature within their marriage while maintaining their own unique identities.

A husband is to give priority to meeting the spiritual needs of his wife and children. He is the spiritual leader and priest of his family. He is instructed to feed on, grow and mature in God's word in the Bible. He accomplishes this by studying the Bible, entering fellowship with other mature Christians in a local church, and developing a closer relationship with God through prayer. He is to teach the Bible's spiritual life principles to his wife and children as he grows in his understanding of them. God will be glorified as the husband, wife and children individually and corporately grow in their understanding of these principles and incorporate them into their lives.

God gave the husband the task of providing for and protecting his family as part of the curse He placed on His creation when sin entered the world. This does not prevent his wife and children from assisting when necessary. However, they do so under his leadership when they do assist. The husband is responsible for being the primary provider for the material and physical needs of his family and to establish guidelines with the assistance of his wife as to how she and their children are to assist when required. Both husbands and wives often must work to meet the material and physical needs of their families because of the financial burdens placed on them. They must be honest in their discerning what are legitimate needs and what are desires based on greed when this is necessary.

The husband is responsible for protecting his wife and children from physical, emotional and spiritual assaults from within and outside his family. The husband's role in protecting his family from physical assaults has been universally accepted and documented throughout history. However, his role in protecting his wife and children from emotional and spiritual assaults is often not well understood. We often come under emotional and spiritual attacks from secular and spiritual forces that stand against God and us as Christians. The Bible teaches the husband is the spiritual covering for his wife, and the husband and wife are the spiritual covering for their children. A wife is protected from emotional and spiritual assaults when the husband properly performs his responsibilities as head of his family, and she accepts and submits to the authority he has been given over her. In a like manner, children are protected from emotional and spiritual assaults when the parents properly assume their responsibilities within the family, and they accept and submit to the authority their parents have been given over them.

The husband is responsible for protecting his wife from physical, emotional and spiritual assaults from their children. He is responsible for developing an atmosphere of respect and honor for his wife within the family. He does this by the love, respect and honor he gives her in the presence of their children and by interacting with their children in a manner that inspires them to love, respect and honor their mother. The husband should intercede on behalf of his wife and support her in the presence of their children when there are conflicts between his wife and children and when the children refuse to obey their mother. The husband and wife should resolve disagreements in private when they disagree on how to relate to their children relative to a specific issue.

The husband is the primary peacemaker within the family when there are conflicts. Paul taught in Ephesians 4:26-27:

> "Be angry, and yet do not sin; do not let the sun go down on your anger, and
> do not give the devil an opportunity."

It is okay for husband and wife or parents and children to be angry with each other. Anger is a normal response to life events that upset us when addressed in a proper manner. However, Paul instructed husbands, wives and children not to sin in their anger by acting in destructive and hurtful ways. He further encouraged them to resolve issues associated with their anger as soon as possible, so Satan will not be able to drive a wedge between a husband and wife and parents and children and create other problems within the family. Someone must initiate the move toward resolution and reconciliation when conflicts occur within a family. The husband is responsible for initiating this move in the absence of a move by other family members.

The husband should exercise authority over his wife and children with compassion and humility. He should cherish and honor his wife and not exasperate his children. Proverbs 31:10-12 states:

> "An excellent wife, who can find? For her worth is far above jewels. The heart of her husband trusts in her, and he will have no lack of gain. She does him good and not evil all the days of her life."

The husband should consider his wife as a treasure given to him by God. He should love her, honor her, recognize her talents, appreciate her efforts, and be considerate of her needs and feelings. He should encourage and help his wife to further develop her talents when he recognizes them.

Paul instructed the husband not to treat his wife harshly or with embitterment. Harshness and embitterment undermine their relationship and deprive his wife of her self-esteem and self-worth. The husband often develops his self-esteem and self-worth outside his family in the context of his relationship with his occupation. However, his wife often develops her self-esteem and self-worth in the context of her relationship with her family. Therefore, the husband is expected to nurture his wife and treat her with humility, tenderness, compassion and sincerity. He aids her in the development of her self-esteem and self-worth when he does this.

Paul instructed fathers in Colossians 3:21, "Fathers, do not exasperate your children, that they may not lose heart." The father has a significant impact on the development of self-esteem and self-worth in his children. He is to exercise love and compassion toward his children even though he is expected to interact with and discipline them with wisdom and decisiveness. More will be said about this later. The authority the husband is given in the family is derived from God. God through Jesus has developed the model of the servant leader. The husband is to approach and seek council from the Holy Spirit when there is rebellion from his wife and children with respect to his authority. Rebellion usually occurs when he has not died to self, accepted and properly performed his responsibilities within the family, and assumed the role of servant leader. The husband must repent and seek forgiveness first from God and then from his wife and children to restore order and harmony within his marriage and family. He must die to his own ego and assume the role of servant to his wife and children with the help of the Holy Spirit. He then sets the stage for the Holy Spirit to work with them to follow his lead. The husband must understand he will be called on to die to self and suffer for the needs and wellbeing of his family as Jesus was called to suffer and die for the Church.

Role of the Wife in the Family

Wives are instructed to be subject to their husbands in the family. Paul stated in Ephesians 5:22, 33:

> "Wives, be subject to your own husbands, as to the Lord. Nevertheless, each individual among you also is to love his own wife even as himself, and let the wife see to it that she respects her husband."

He stated again in Colossians 3:18, "Wives, be subject to your husbands, as is fitting in the Lord." Peter instructed wives in 1 Peter 3:1-2:

> "In the same way, you wives, be submissive to your own husbands so that even if any of them are disobedient to the word, they may be won without a word by the behavior of their wives, as they observe your chaste and respectful behavior."

Peter further instructed wives to possess an imperishable inner beauty of the heart, which is characterized by a gentle and quiet spirit. He indicates this inner beauty is precious to God.

Our modern culture has placed a negative connotation on the submission of the wife to her husband. There is a perception this places her in a demeaning and subservient role. This is not the intent of God, nor is this taught in the Bible. God has created a paradox in the wife's relationship with her husband. She has been given the position of honor in creation and marriage by being given the task of conceiving and bearing children. On the other hand, God has made the wife her husband's helper (Genesis 2:18). He has decreed her desires are to be for her husband, and he is to have authority over her (Genesis 3:16).

God has made the husband and wife to be equal but incomplete partners in marriage. The husband is instructed to love, cherish, nurture and honor his wife. These focus on meeting her greatest emotional needs. The wife is instructed to accept and submit to her husband's authority, and in so doing, to respect, support and obey him. These focus on meeting his greatest emotional needs. The basic emotional needs of both husband and wife relate to the roles and responsibilities God has assigned them in supporting and nurturing each other and their children within their family. The Bible teaches the husband and wife will both find completeness and fulfillment within their marriage and will be blessed when they accept their roles and are obedient to the order of authority God has established in their family.

The wife is instructed to be her husband's helper. This is not intended to be a subservient or passive role. The wife is to be active and aggressive in the pursuit of her responsibilities within the family. Who and what is a good wife and what are her rewards? The Proverbs answers these questions in Proverbs 31:10-31:

> "An excellent wife, who can find?
> For her worth is far above jewels.
> The heart of her husband trusts in her,
> And he will have no lack of gain.
> She does him good and not evil
> All the days of her life.
> She looks for wool and flax,
> And works with her hands in delight.
> She is like merchant ships;
> She brings her food from afar.
> She rises also while it is still night,
> And gives food to her household
> And portions to her maidens.
> She considers a field and buys it;
> From her earnings she plants a vineyard.
> She girds herself with strength,
> And makes her arms strong.
> She senses that her gain is good;
> Her lamp does not go out at night.
> She stretches out her hands to the distaff,
> And her hands grasp the spindle.
> She extends her hand to the poor;
> And she stretches out her hands to the needy.
> She is not afraid of the snow for her household,
> For all her household are clothed with scarlet.
> She makes coverings for herself;
> Her clothing is fine linen and purple.
> Her husband is known in the gates,
> When he sits among the elders of the land.
> She makes linen garments and sells them,
> And supplies belts to the tradesmen.
> Strength and dignity are her clothing,
> And she smiles at the future.

She opens her mouth in wisdom,
And the teaching of kindness is on her tongue.
She looks well to the ways of her household,
And does not eat the bread of idleness.
Her children rise up and bless her;
Her husband also, and he praises her, saying:
'Many daughters have done nobly,
But you excel them all.'
Charm is deceitful and beauty is vain,
But a woman who fears the LORD,
She shall be praised.
Give her the product of her hands,
And let her works praise her in the gates."

The husband as the provider, protector and spiritual covering for his wife nurtures, encourages and enables her to become the person she desires to be. The wife who supports and is obedient to her husband brings him honor and respect within their community. She is active in the management of the business affairs of her family, in meeting the needs of the poor and needy, and in business and commerce outside her family. She works to meet the ordinary everyday needs of her family. She is a teacher of wisdom and kindness both inside and outside her family. She has inner qualities of strength and dignity that give her the ability to look to the future with hope and a positive and supportive attitude. She brings trust, praise and blessings to herself while she brings honor and respect to her husband and family.

Paul stated in Titus 2:1-8:

"But as for you, speak the things which are fitting for sound doctrine. Older men are to be temperate, dignified, sensible, sound in faith, in love, in perseverance. Older women likewise are to be reverent in their behavior, not malicious gossips, nor enslaved to much wine, teaching what is good, that they may encourage the young women to love their husbands, to love their children, to be sensible, pure, workers at home, kind, being subject to their own husbands, that the word of God may not be dishonored. Likewise urge the young men to be sensible; in all things show yourself to be an example of good deeds, with purity in doctrine, dignified, sound in speech which is beyond reproach, in order that the opponent may be put to shame, having nothing bad to say about us."

Paul instructed young men to be sensible and show themselves to be doers of good deeds, pure in doctrine, dignified and sound in speech. These all point to the leadership roles young men were expected to assume within their communities and families. Paul instructed young women to love and be obedient to their husbands, love their children, be workers at home, and be sensible, pure and kind. These all point to the roles young women were expected to assume in supporting their husbands and working within their homes. The husband's responsibilities in business and within the family often take him away from the home. Chaos results without someone to effectively manage the affairs of the home and be the caregiver to the children when the husband is absent. Perhaps the most important and significant roles the wife has been given within her family are to support her husband, care for her children, and manage the affairs of her household. This does not mean she cannot be involved in charitable, business and other activities outside her family. Quite often she will be. However, these outside activities must be undertaken considering her responsibilities to support her husband, care for her children, and manage her household. These are the three most important and most fulfilling activities the wife can undertake.

Parents and Children

Role of Children in the Family

One of the most important functions of the family is to provide a nurturing and safe environment for conceiving, bearing and raising children. Both husband and wife share responsibilities associated with this function. God has established an order of authority between parents and children just as He has established an order of authority between husband and wife. Paul stated in Colossians 3:20-21:

> "Children, be obedient to your parents in all things, for this is well-pleasing to the Lord. Fathers, do not exasperate your children, that they may not lose heart."

He also states in Ephesians 6:1-3:

> "Children, obey your parents in the Lord, for this is right. Honor your father and mother (which is the first commandment with a promise), that it may be well with you, and that you may live long on the earth."

The Bible teaches parents are to exercise authority over their children, and children are to obey their parents. Children who honor and obey their parents are promised it will be well with them, and they will live long lives.

Role of Parents in the Family

The role of parents in raising their children is summarized in Paul's statement in Ephesians 6:4 where he stated, "And fathers, do not provoke your children to anger; but bring them up in the discipline and instruction of the Lord." Paul's statement also applies to mothers even though it is made relative to fathers. Parents are to *teach*, *discipline*, *love* and *pray* for their children. These are consistent with the model God as our Father has developed with us. He has redeemed us through the death and resurrection of His Son because of His love for us. He calls us to repent and accept His gifts of grace and salvation. Peter instructed us in 1 Peter 2:2:

> "Like newborn babies, long for the pure milk of the word, so that by it you may grow in respect to salvation, if you have tasted the kindness of the Lord."

God teaches us His word through evangelists, pastors and teachers. He expects us to grow in His word to spiritual adults, so we can live disciplined lives and be involved in ministry and service to others. Paul stated in Ephesians 4:15, "but speaking the truth in love, we are to grow up in all aspects into Him, who is the head, even Christ." God will discipline us when after receiving His word we choose to disobey Him. In Hebrews 12:5-6, the author stated:

> "My son, do not regard lightly the discipline of the Lord, nor faint when you are reproved by Him; For those whom the Lord loves He disciplines, and He scourges every son whom He receives."

The Bible teaches parents to use this same model (love, teach and discipline) in their relationship with their children.

Parents are to teach their children. Proverbs 22:6 states:

> "Train up a child in the way he should go,
> Even when he is old he will not depart from it."

Parents are to teach their children life, functional and relationship skills and spiritual principles from the Bible. These include, but are not limited to, how to learn and master functional and life skills, enter healthy relationships with other children and adults, and enter a relationship of grace with God through faith in His Son, Jesus. Before parents can teach their children, they must know and understand what they will teach and how to relate to the unique needs, desires and skill levels of their children. These require the development of support networks that are normally centralized within local churches and that are made up of other parents and older adults. Paul stated in Titus 2:1-8 that within local churches older men are to teach younger men how to be husbands and fathers and older women are to teach younger women how to be wives and mothers. Parents in so doing are trained in how to teach and care for their children in ways that are pleasing and acceptable to God.

Parents are responsible for passing on moral, ethical, work and cultural values to their children. They do this through instruction, discipline, and modeling these values in their lives. What parents teach must be consistent with how they live and what they do to increase the probability children will accept and internalize these values. Parents are to pass their moral, ethical, work and cultural values onto their children in a manner that does not infringe upon their children's right to choose to reject them. Parents, by making many of the choices for their children during younger years, determine the values by which they initially live. However, as their children mature and assume responsibility for their own lives, they must be free to choose their own values. This means they have the right to reject their parent's values if they choose to do so.

Moses commanded the Israelites before they entered the land the Lord had promised them:

> "And these words, which I am commanding you today, shall be on your heart; and you shall teach them diligently to your sons and shall talk of them when you sit in your house and when you walk by the way and when you lie down and when you rise up. And you shall bind them as a sign on your hand and they shall be as frontals on your forehead. And you shall write them on the doorposts of your house and on your gates." (Deuteronomy 6:6-9)

Paul stated in 1 Thessalonians 2:11-12:

> "Just as you know how we were exhorting and encouraging and imploring each one of you as a father would his own children, so that you may walk in a manner worthy of the God who calls you into His own kingdom and glory."

The Bible teaches parents are responsible for teaching their children God's word. All children are born into this world with a sin nature that separates them from God. Most of us have come into a saving relationship with God through Jesus because someone shared the gospel of Jesus with us and was the vessel through whom the Holy Spirit reached out to call us to repent and invite Jesus into our life. The Bible teaches fathers are responsible for sharing the gospel of Jesus with their children and being the vessels through whom the Holy Spirit reaches out to call them to repent and invite Jesus into their lives. However, both parents should share this responsibility.

Parents are responsible for teaching their children the spiritual life principles contained in the Bible when they have entered a redeemed and reconciled relationship with God thorough Jesus. They are responsible for feeding children the pure milk of God's word so they can grow to spiritual maturity. Parents are to work with their children to help them identify their spiritual gifts and then, along with their local church, help them develop and perfect these gifts to where they can be used in ministry.

Parents are to discipline their children. God expects us to obey His word and live within the boundaries He has established for acceptable behavior as we develop our relationship with Him through Jesus. God disciplines us when we transgress these boundaries. Parents are expected to relate to their children in the same manner. God has placed the care and wellbeing of children in the hands of parents who are to establish boundaries of acceptable behavior to ensure the safety and wellbeing of their children. These boundaries should be based on God's word. They give children an increased sense of security rather than being restrictive. Children need to know these boundaries are there even though they may disobey and cross over them.

The Bible teaches parents to discipline their children when they transgress boundaries of acceptable behavior. Properly administered discipline results in the development of self-esteem and self-worth within children. The Proverbs yield significant insights into the importance of accepting discipline. Proverbs 22:15 states:

> "Foolishness is bound up in the heart of a child;
> The rod of discipline will remove it far from him."

Proverbs 13:1 states:

> "A wise son accepts his father's discipline,
> But a scoffer does not listen to rebuke."

Proverbs 12:1 states:

"Whoever loves discipline loves knowledge,
But he who hates reproof is stupid."

Proverbs 15:5 states:

"A fool rejects his father's discipline,
But he who regards reproof is sensible."

Proverbs 15:32 states:

"He whose ear listens to the life-giving reproof
Will dwell among the wise."

Proverbs 19:20 states:

"Listen to counsel and accept discipline,
That you may be wise the rest of your days."

Only the foolish child rejects discipline (Proverbs 15:5). Proverbs 13:18 states:

"Poverty and shame will come to him who neglects discipline,
But he who regards reproof will be honored."

Parents are jointly responsible for disciplining their children. However, the father, as head of the family, has the primary responsibility for this. He, in consultation with his wife, is responsible for establishing and setting the standards for discipline within the family. This is implied in Paul's statements in Ephesians 6:4 and Colossians 3:21 where he instructed fathers not to provoke children to anger or to exasperate them.

A mother derives her authority to discipline her children from her husband. Children must know he stands behind her authority, and they will have to answer to him when they challenge her authority. This is particularly important when children pass through puberty. They will often challenge the authority of and the respect they have for their mother during this time. The husband is responsible for assuring they respect and honor their mother, establishing her authority within the family. He must support her in administering her authority. The self-esteem young girls develop concerning future relationships with men and the respect young boys develop concerning future relationships with women are significantly affected by how the husband and wife, as father and mother, resolve issues of authority and discipline within the family.

Parents are to love their children. Love must motivate everything we do. This is most important in teaching and disciplining children. Parents must be sensitive to their children's needs and desires, what frustrates and causes them pain, and what motivates them as they raise their children. Every child is unique, and parents must respond to each child in ways that address his/her uniqueness.

Children must know their parents love and care for them. Teaching and discipline must be administered with love and compassion for children to develop self-esteem and self-worth. This is the reason Paul instructed fathers not to provoke children to anger or exasperate them to the point where they lose hope. Growing up is hard and often painful. There must be a place where children can go and individuals to whom they can turn to find comfort, support and safety when they experience difficulties in life. This place should be their home, and the individuals should be their parents. The principles discussed in Chapter 18 apply to parent-child relationships. Parents should discipline their children in ways that build them up in the Lord and give them a view of their future that is filled with hope.

Parents are to pray for their children. The most important function of parents is to continually pray for their children. Parents should pray for everything in their children's lives. The importance of parents praying for their children overshadows the importance of parents teaching, disciplining and loving them. Parents should pray for all aspects related to teaching, disciplining and loving their children. They need to continually seek God's knowledge, wisdom and guidance in all areas of their relationship with their children. One way to do this is through prayer. There may be situations where parents may feel inadequate to meet the specific needs of their children. God can meet these needs even though they may not be able to. Parents enable and give God permission through prayer to work on their behalf in those situations where they feel inadequate. There are times and events in children's lives when they will be in crises. God is in control even though parents may feel they are not. They can enlist His support through prayer to be with them and their children in these crises and to bring order to their children's lives.

Summary

Figure 14 summarizes the relationships between a husband and wife and between parents and children that have been discussed in this section. These relationships form the base of the pyramid shown in Figure 13.

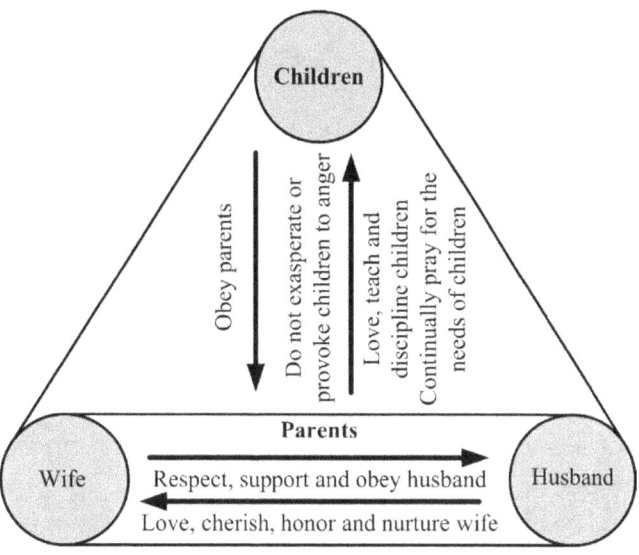

Figure 14

SEX WITHIN THE FRAMEWORK OF MARRIAGE

Role of Sex in Marriage

Sex plays a central role in marriage. Both God and Jesus taught the husband and wife become one flesh in marriage (Genesis 2:24, Mark 10:6-9). Paul affirmed this in 1 Corinthians 6:16 where he stated:

> "Or do you not know that the one who joins himself to a harlot is one body with her? For He says, 'The two will become one flesh.'"

Paul's meaning is clear even though he discussed an inappropriate use of sex in this verse. The husband and wife become one flesh through sexual union. They become physically, emotionally and spiritually united in sexual intercourse. This is a mystery created by God. The amount of time spent in sexual activity is small within married couples. However, this time properly spent has a powerful influence on the quality and health of their marriage. Marriage without sexual union is not real.

God has created sex within marriage to:

- Consummate the marriage covenant between husband and wife,
- Ensure the procreation of humanity, and

- Provide a means for a husband and wife to experience physical and emotional intimacy and pleasure within their marriage.

Only men and women have been created with the desire and ability to engage in sexual union within marriage for purposes other than conceiving and bearing children. Healthy sexual relations enable a husband and wife to experience physical and emotional intimacy and pleasure. Sexual intercourse merges husband and wife into one flesh. Solomon described God's desire for a husband and wife to enjoy each other in sexual union in the Song of Solomon 7:3-13:

> "Your two breasts are like two fawns, twins of a gazelle. Your neck is like a tower of ivory, your eyes like the pools in Heshbon by the gate of Bath-rabbim; your nose is like the tower of Lebanon, which faces toward Damascus. Your head crowns you like Carmel, and the flowing locks of your head are like purple threads; the king is captivated by your tresses. How beautiful and how delightful you are, My love, with all your charms! Your stature is like a palm tree, and your breasts are like its clusters. I said, 'I will climb the palm tree, I will take hold of its fruit stalks.' Oh, may your breasts be like clusters of the vine, and the fragrance of your breath like apples, And your mouth like the best wine! It goes down smoothly for my beloved, flowing gently through the lips of those who fall asleep. I am my beloved's, and his desire is for me. Come, my beloved, let us go out into the country, let us spend the night in the villages. Let us rise early and go to the vineyards; let us see whether the vine has budded and its blossoms have opened, and whether the pomegranates have bloomed. There I will give you my love. The mandrakes have given forth fragrance; and over our doors are all choice fruits, both new and old, which I have saved up for you, my beloved."

A husband and wife experience true physical and emotional intimacy and pleasure in their sexual relationship when they experience companionship and real intimacy in the nonsexual areas of their marriage. Likewise, problems regarding sexual relations are often symptoms of problems in other areas of their marriage.

A successful and healthy marriage requires a significant commitment of time and energy. This is particularly true with their sexual relationship. A husband and wife often enter marriage with misgivings, misunderstandings and unrealistic expectations. They may have experienced serious emotional and spiritual wounds that affect their attitudes toward and abilities to experience intimate sexual relations. It takes time, commitment and perseverance to work through and receive healing for these wounds to experience true emotional and physical intimacy. Neither husband nor wife should presume knowledge on the part of each other concerning these wounds. They must communicate with each other on an intimate level and work through hurting areas where there are wounds that need to be healed. Additionally, they must explore sexual activities that result in mutual pleasure and fulfillment and work together to identify and enter mutually enjoyable activities while avoiding activities that are unpleasant and hurtful. Each must consider the needs, desires and feelings of the other, so their sexual relationship is mutually satisfying and enjoyable.

Serious functional problems and unresolved emotional and physical issues may require the help of a trained Christian counselor. A husband and wife must never forget the Holy Spirit will give them the understanding and healing they seek while working through problem areas. God will heal their wounds and give them the ability to successfully work through their problems when they trust Him and are faithful to obey His word.

Paul taught in 1 Corinthian 7:1-5 concerning sex between a husband and wife:

> "Now concerning the things about which you wrote, it is good for a man not to touch a woman. But because of immoralities, let each man have his own wife, and let each woman have her own husband. Let the husband fulfill his duty to his wife, and likewise also the wife to her husband. The wife does not have authority over her own body, but the husband does; and likewise also the husband does not have authority over his own body, but the wife does. Stop depriving one another, except by agreement for a time that you may devote yourselves to prayer, and come together again lest Satan tempt you because of your lack of self-control."

Husband and wife are to be faithful to each other and honor their marriage covenant. They should not deny each other's need for sex except by mutual consent. Giving or withholding sex should never be used to reward desired behavior or punish undesired behavior within a marriage. Husband and wife have mutual authority over each regarding sexual relations within their marriage. They must work together to satisfy each other's sexual needs, so Satan will not be able to tempt either of them to enter sexual activities that are forbidden by God.

Sex Outside of Marriage

Sex outside of marriage is forbidden by God. He addressed sex outside of marriage in the Old Testament moral law, which is an extension of the commandment on adultery in the ten commandments discussed in Chapter 2. Old Testament scriptures associated with the moral law are listed in Table 9.

Table 9

Sexual Sins	Scripture References
Adultery	Leviticus 20:10; Deuteronomy 22:13-22
Fornication	Exodus 22:16-17; Deuteronomy 22:20-30
Homosexuality	Leviticus 18:22, 20:13
Incest	Leviticus 20:11-12, 14; Deuteronomy 27:20, 22-23
Bestiality	Deuteronomy 27:21
The Exposing of Nakedness	Leviticus 18:8-17, 20:17

The moral law defined the sexual sins of adultery, fornication, homosexuality, incest, bestiality and exposing of nakedness. Discretions of sexual sins associated with the moral law are:

- **Adultery** was defined as sexual contact between a man and woman, one or both who are married, but not to each other.

- **Fornication** was defined as sexual contact between a man and woman neither of whom is married or engaged to be married. A young couple engaged to be married was treated as if they were married. However, they were to refrain from engaging in sexual contact until after they were married.

- A young man and woman who were discovered having sexual intercourse and who were not married were required to marry and were not allowed to divorce. Exodus 22:20; Leviticus 18:23, 20:15-16;

- **Incest** was defined as sexual contact between parents and children of opposite gender, between brothers and sisters, and between aunts, uncles, nieces, nephews and cousins of opposite gender.

- **Homosexuality** was defined as sexual contact between men and women of the same gender.

- **Bestiality** was defined as men or women engaging in sexual contact with an animal.

- **The exposure of nakedness** was defined as members of a family looking at the nakedness of family members of the opposite gender. This did not apply to a husband and wife seeing their nakedness. Individuals were not to look at the nakedness of other relatives and in-laws of the opposite gender (parents, grandparents, aunts, uncles, nieces, nephews and cousins). This also includes the viewing of modern-day pornography.

God created sex to ensure the procreation of the human race, be a sign of the covenant relationship of marriage, and be a means in which husband and wife can enter intimate and pleasure-filled sexual relations as they become one flesh. Therefore, He made sexual drives and desires to be very strong. He knew the hurtful and destructive effects of uncontrolled and undisciplined sexual desires, immorality and perverse sexual behavior upon individuals, families and nations. Therefore, God treated sexual sins seriously and established boundaries for acceptable sexual behavior to ensure the potential for healthy sexual relations between husbands and wives within marriage. In addition, He prescribed harsh penalties, including death, for those who crossed these boundaries.

The theme of sexual purity is continued in the New Testament. Paul stated in 1 Thessalonians 4:3-5:

> "For this is the will of God, your sanctification; that is, that you abstain from sexual immorality; that each of you know how to possess his own vessel in sanctification and honor, not in lustful passion, like the Gentiles who do not know God."

He further instructs us in 1 Corinthians 6:9-10, 18:

> "Or do you not know that the unrighteous shall not inherit the kingdom of God? Do not be deceived; neither fornicators, nor idolaters, nor adulterers, nor effeminate, nor homosexuals, nor thieves, or the covetous, nor drunkards, nor revilers, nor swindlers, shall inherit the kingdom of God. ... Flee immorality. Every other sin that a man commits is outside the body, but the immoral man sins against his own body."

Hollywood and the media portray promiscuous recreational sex between unmarried heterosexual and homosexual partners as without adverse consequences. We are told individuals can participate in safe sex by using condoms. They will not have to worry about contracting sexually transmitted diseases. Women will not have to worry about getting pregnant. We are led to believe there are no adverse emotional and spiritual consequences associated with sex outside of marriage. Unfortunately, many are buying into these lies. Some statistics associated with the consequences of sex outside of marriage include:

- An epidemic explosion of sexually transmitted diseases has occurred in the United States. Depending on what numbers you look at, there are over 110,000,000 individuals in the US infected by sexually transmitted diseases. These diseases include, but are not limited to, gonorrhea, syphilis, chlamydia, genital herpes, human papilloma virus, genital warts, HIV virus and full-blown AIDS. Some of these sexually transmitted diseases can be cured with proper medical treatment. However, many of them, such as genital herpes and AIDS, are incurable.

- Nearly 1 out of every 3 babies is born to an unwed mother. Many of these mothers are single parents living on welfare at or below the poverty level.

- Around 640,000 abortions are performed per year in the US.

There are major consequences associated with promiscuous sex outside of marriage. Lives and families are devastated by the effects of incurable sexually transmitted diseases. Infected individuals often experience significant physical and emotional suffering. Medical expenses for incurable sexually transmitted diseases can be exorbitant. There are significant medical and welfare expenses for single women who have babies outside of marriage. Most medical and welfare expenses are paid by local, state and federal governmental agencies with tax dollars. The media do not discuss the suffering associated with killing unborn babies, botched abortions, or the large number of women who experience post abortion syndrome.

Easy access to pornography results in distorted perceptions of normal and healthy sexual relationships. Children exposed to pornography before they are mature enough to process the highly explicit images they watch develop unhealthy and distorted views of sex. This impedes their abilities to enter healthy and normal sexual relationships as adults when they are married. Those who become severely addicted to pornography develop deviant sexual behaviors as they grow older and progress to harder forms of pornography. Husbands addicted to pornography often develop unrealistic fantasies and expectations associated with sexual relations with their wives that destroy their marriages.

Spiritual consequences associated with promiscuous sexual activities are often overlooked. Paul indicated in 1 Corinthians 6:16 a man who sexually joins himself with a harlot becomes one body with her in the sexual union. Sexual intercourse between a man and women results in a physical, emotional and spiritual union between them. This is true whether they have sex within or outside of marriage. This is the way God has created sex. Emotional and spiritual bonds continue even though the physical bond between a man and women may end after they have ended their promiscuous sexual union. We emotionally and spiritually leave a part of ourself with a person when we have sexual intercourse. Sexual intercourse with multiple partners results in a fracturing and depositing of pieces of our soul with those with whom we have sexual intercourse. Our sexual sins allow Satan and those with whom we have had sexual intercourse to place spiritual hooks into our soul. This enables them to reach from our past into our present and future to torment us. These hooks impair our ability to enter a healthy monogamous sexual relationship with our spouse when we are married.

Paul stated immoral men and women sin against their own bodies with the implication there will be suffering associated with these sins. We do not have to look far to see this suffering. God will not spare us from this suffering even though He forgives our sins through Jesus and will be with and give us the ability to deal with and endure the suffering our sins cause. The Bible teaches men and women to abstain from sexual relationships outside of marriage. The only safe sex is sex that is experienced within the guidelines and boundaries established by God. This is sex between a husband and wife within a monogamous marriage relationship.

Some of you who are reading this may feel it is too late. You have been sexually active outside of marriage and are dealing with the consequences of your actions. You may feel guilt associated with your actions and sense you are separated from God. He is a loving and forgiving God. He has not abandoned you when you feel separated from Him. Your actions have caused you to move away from Him. You must approach God and repent to seek and receive His forgiveness through Jesus. He will forgive you; He already has. Then, refrain from further sexual activities outside of marriage. Be faithful to your spouse and family when you are married. Ask Jesus to come into your marriage and to heal the broken and hurting areas in your life. It will take time, and there will be pain associated with the healing process. However, Jesus will honor your request.

Intimacy and Sex

The casual portrayal of recreational sex and pornography has had devastating effects on the ability of a husbands and wives to develop sexual intimacy in their marriage. A man and woman are often portrayed as racing to a bedroom or other secluded place to engage in sexual activities when they fall in love in a movie, creating the illusion this is normal and okay. Pornography portrays men and women as using each other to gratify sexual desires. The relationship between a man and woman who sexually mimic these stereotypes often ends before marriage with damaging results. Seeds will have been planted that will prevent them from developing true sexual intimacy in their marriage when they get married. These seeds may eventually destroy their marriage.

Men and women seek companionship and intimacy when they enter a serious dating or courting relationship. There is a basic difference between men and women that, when not properly understood, will cause serious difficulties. This difference is:

> A man will often use companionship and intimacy as a means to obtain sex, whereas a woman will often use sex as a means to obtain companionship and intimacy.

This difference can result in exploitation when a man and woman enter a relationship with wounded and broken areas in their lives and have low self-esteem. The couple must commit to a process where they develop companionship and intimacy in a manner that maintains their dignity and affirms their value and worth at the beginning of their relationship to prevent this from occurring.

Dr. James Dobson, the founder and former president of Focus on the Family, identifies twelve steps to establishing true intimacy between a husband and wife in two of his books: *Love Must Be Tough* (1996) and *Life on the Edge* (1995). These steps are taken from the book, *Intimate Behavior* (1971), by Dr. Desmond Morris. They represent a progression in physical intimacy from which a permanent, healthy relationship can evolve. The twelve steps are:

- Eye-to-body
- Eye-to-eye
- Voice-to-voice
- Hand-to-hand
- Hand-to-shoulder
- Hand-to-waist
- Face-to-face
- Hand-to-head
- Hand-to-body
- Mouth-to-breast
- Touching below the waist
- Sexual intercourse

Eye-to-body: This is the beginning of a relationship when we first notice another person of opposite gender. We determine whether the person we are watching is physically attractive. We evaluate things like gender, size, shape, age, the way the person is dressed, the way the person handles himself/ herself in a group, and the way others perceive and relate to the person we are watching. How we evaluate these characteristics determines whether we are attracted to the person we are watching.

Eye-to-eye: This is when the person we are watching notices we are watching. The normal tendency is to look away when the other person is a stranger. This person on the other hand may smile or return some other jester that indicates a possible desire to become better acquainted when his/her eyes meet our eyes. Eye-to-body and eye-to-eye contact can occur over a prolonged period where two individuals observe each other in several different settings, or it can occur in a single setting.

Voice-to-voice: This is a contact between two individuals when they enter dialog and conversation. The initial conversations are generally small talk where trivial questions are often asked and non-sensitive issues are discussed. The voice-to-voice phase of developing intimacy is a time of probing and evaluation. This is the phase where each person in the relationship gets to know each other, and they learn about each other's opinions, desires, hobbies, habits, future plans, etc. This phase of the relationship should never be rushed. It is a time when two individuals evaluate their likes and dislikes and their potential for compatibility and determine whether or not they want to become friends.

Hand-to-hand: This is the first physical contact between a man and woman who may be exploring the possibility of entering a more serious relationship. The first contact is usually of a non-romantic nature where, for example, the man clasps the woman's hand to help her ascend or descend a high step. Either person at this point can withdraw from the relationship without rejecting the other. However, hand-to-hand contact usually indicates the development of a more serious and possibly romantic relationship when it continues.

Hand-to-shoulder: This is the first physical contact between a man and woman that indicates affection. It indicates the relationship has progressed to more than just a close friendship. However, it does not necessarily mean the man and woman are in love. They are usually still more concerned about the world outside their relationship than they are about their relationship.

Hand-to-waist: This is the first physical contact between a man and woman that is clearly romantic in nature. It indicates the relationship is progressing into a more serious and possible romantic stage. The couple at this point are generally sharing more personal information and secrets with each other and developing more intimate verbal and nonverbal communication skills. The phases of intimacy associated with hand-to-hand, hand-to-shoulder and hand-to-waist should not be rushed. They should be allowed to progress slowly. These are probing and evaluation phases where the couple get to know each other on a more intimate level and determine whether they want to enter a more serious romantic relationship.

Face-to-face: This phase involves the couple looking into each other's eyes, hugging and kissing. The couple by this phase have decided they want to risk making a commitment to begin the process of entering a lifelong relationship. They have developed the ability to engage in deep verbal and nonverbal communication when they have properly and slowly proceeded through the previous six phases of intimacy. Sexual desires start to become an important issue during the face-to-face phase of intimacy. These desires must be positively addressed with restraint.

Hand-to-head: This is a continuation of the previous phase to a more intimate level. It involves the man and woman cradling and stroking each other's head while talking or kissing. The touching of someone's head in many cultures is not done unless they are either romantically involved or are family members. Hand-to-head is the final phase of intimacy before the couple are married.

Final phases: The final four phases of intimacy are distinctly sexual in nature, and from a biblical and Christian perspective, they are to be reserved for marriage. *Hand-to-body* involves the husband and wife touching each other's body above the waist. It includes the husband touching and caressing his wife's breasts and both the husband and wife touching and caressing other erogenous zones on their bodies above the waist. *Mouth-to-breast* involves the husband kissing his wife's breasts. *Touching below the waist* involves the husband and wife touching and fondling each other's genitals with the intent of sexually stimulating and arousing each other and preparing each other for *sexual intercourse*. Sexual intercourse is the final act of intimacy where the husband and wife become one flesh when they are united in spirit, soul and body. The final four phases of intimacy normally, but not always, result in the husband and wife engaging in sexual intercourse. They should normally proceed in the order listed.

There are fundamental differences in how a husband and wife sexually relate. The husband's greatest pleasure often occurs at the time of his orgasm during intercourse. The husband can usually proceed directly to intercourse when he and his wife initiates sexual activities and be satisfied. However, his wife will normally feel cheated when he does this. She may feel she is being sexually manipulated and used by her husband and begin to sexually withdraw from him when this persists. The wife usually receives her greatest pleasure in the time of verbal and physical intimacy spent together leading up to intercourse and the quality of time spent together after intercourse.

The order of the last four phases of intimacy gives a natural progression of emotional, sensual and sexual activities through which both husband and wife should proceed, usually at a leisurely pace, to the point where they mutually choose to engage in intercourse. This progression gives them an opportunity to talk about deep personal and emotional issues that affirm their commitment, affection and love for each other. This time of verbal communication is important to the wife and is essential for her enjoyment of sexual activities with her husband.

The progression of the last four steps gives both husband and wife time to enjoy close, intimate physical contact and to touch, caress and explore each other's body before intercourse. This physical contact can be sensuous and arousing, while at the same time allowing both the opportunity to affirm each other's value and worth.

Dr. Dobson indicated the twelve steps leading to intimacy must proceed and develop slowly in the sequence listed. Something precious is lost and the potential for emotional wounds and brokenness is developed within their relationship when a man and woman proceed too rapidly through the twelve steps, skip over steps in the sequence, or enter sexual relations (one or all the final four steps) before they are married.

Sexual Purity and Innocence

The greatest gift a husband and wife can give each other when entering marriage is sexual purity and innocence. Both the Old and New Testaments speak to the importance of maintaining sexual purity before marriage and abstaining from any type of sexual relations or activity outside of marriage. The entertainment and pornography industries attempt to create the illusion that sexual purity and innocence are unimportant.

There are many ways men and women lose their sexual purity and innocence. The first is sexual abuse and molestation, which include rape and incest. Sexual abuse and molestation cause immeasurable damage to the emotional and spiritual development of children, particularly when they are abused or molested by someone they initially trust. It normally takes a trained therapist to help an individual who has been sexually abused or molested to work through the pain and brokenness associated with this experience. Sexually abused and molested individuals often bury the memories of their experiences deep within their mind and do not deal with them until they encounter intimate sexual relations with their spouse in marriage.

A second way men and women lose their sexual purity and innocence is by believing the myth that sexual purity and innocence are unimportant. Individuals who engage in casual sexual activities often experience a loss of self-esteem and self-worth that progress to feelings of guilt and shame. The emotional and spiritual wounds and brokenness associated with these feelings are often buried. It is normally difficult for individuals who have engaged in sexual activities outside of marriage to experience true physical, emotional and spiritual intimacy within marriage until these wounds and brokenness have been identified, addressed and healed.

A third way men and women lose their sexual purity and innocence is by skipping ahead in the twelve steps to establish true intimacy to the final four phases of intimacy before they are married. This particularly applies to young men and women who are virgins and who would never consider entering any type of sexual activity outside of a serious commitment to a relationship that will ultimately result in marriage.

Sexual desires between men and women considering marriage are strong. As a result, engaging in premarital sexual activities will overshadow all other aspects associated with developing an intimate relationship. This is true even when these activities do not lead to sexual intercourse. Time that should be spent developing communication skills, getting to know each other's likes and dislikes, assessing areas of compatibility and incompatibility, etc. is circumvented by these activities.

Premarital sexual activities damage a couple's relationship. They can destroy it. Emotional wounds and brokenness caused by these activities will interfere with the couple's ability to develop true physical, emotional and spiritual intimacy within their marriage. This will persist until they address these wounds and brokenness, forgive each other, and receive true healing.

Understand God loves you and will forgive and provide you with a means to receive healing for your emotional wounds and brokenness when you are a couple experiencing problems with intimacy in your marriage. You must sincerely approach Him, repent and seek His forgiveness. He will forgive you. You then must forgive your spouse and seek your spouse's forgiveness for the premarital sexual activities that have caused your wounds and brokenness. Ask the Holy Spirit to come into your and your spouse's lives to facilitate the healing process. He will honor your request. Also, seek the help of a trained Christian counselor when necessary. Slowly work through the twelve steps for developing intimacy in your marriage in the order presented. Touch each other, hold hands, talk, gaze into each other's eyes, and create memories essential for building and maintaining an intimate relationship as you work through the steps. You will be pleased with the results.

DIVORCE

God states in Malachi 2:16 He hates divorce. It was not part of His original plan during creation. However, He established guidelines in which husbands and wives can be released from their marriage covenant when sin entered the world and affected the structure of the family. For Christians, the Bible provides three valid reasons a husband and wife may be divorced.

Sexual Infidelity of One of the Marriage Partners

Jesus had the following discussion with the Pharisees relative to Jewish Law in Matthew 19:7-9:

> "They said to Him, 'Why then did Moses command to give her a certificate of divorce and send her away?' He said to them, 'Because of your hardness of heart, Moses permitted you to divorce your wives; but from the beginning it has not been this way. And I say to you, whoever divorces his wife, except for immorality, and marries another woman commits adultery.'"

Divorce was not originally part of God's plan. However, God allows divorce for sexual infidelity. The offended spouse can seek and be granted a divorce and be free to remarry when one of the marriage partners is unfaithful and enters sexual relations with someone other than his/her spouse.

Abandonment by the Non-Christian Spouse when a Christian and Non-Christian Are Married

Paul stated in 2 Corinthians 6:14-18 Christians should not be bound to non-Christians. This included marriage. Christians were married to non-Christians in Paul's day, and the same is true today. Sometimes a Christian marries a non-Christian or one of the spouses (both non-Christians when married) becomes a Christian after marriage. Paul gave specific instructions for this situation in 1 Corinthians 7:13-16. The marriage covenant is to be honored in the hope the non-Christian spouse can be saved through the witness of the Christian spouse while the non-Christian spouse consents to live in harmony with the Christian spouse. The marriage covenant is nullified when the non-Christian spouse chooses to leave (abandon) the Christian spouse. The Christian spouse is free to remarry when this occurs.

One of the Spouses Who as a Christian Is Living an Intentional Unrepentant Sinful Life

Paul taught in Romans 7:2-3 and 1 Corinthians 7:39 a husband and wife are bound together in marriage and are not free to remarry until one of them dies. At issue here is how death is defined. It is easy to understand the definition of death when one of the spouses physically dies. However, the Bible mentions spiritual death, which is associated with living an unrepentant sinful life. This is the state of all of us until we accept Jesus as our Lord and Savior. Paul addressed the situation where one who professes to be a Christian lives an unrepentant sinful life. He taught in 1 Corinthians 5:9-13:

> "I wrote you in my letter not to associate with immoral people; I did not at all mean with the immoral people of this world, or with the covetous and swindlers, or with idolaters; for then you would have to go out of the world.

But actually, I wrote to you not to associate with any so-called brother if he should be an immoral person, or covetous, or an idolater, or a reviler, or a drunkard, or a swindler - not even to eat with such a one. For what have I to do with judging outsiders? Do you not judge those who are within the church? But those who are outside, God judges. Remove the wicked man from among yourselves."

The Bible teaches and Paul reaffirmed we are not to judge non-Christians. This is clearly God's responsibility. However, we voluntarily agree to live according to God's word in the Bible when we become a Christian and join a local Christian church. We commit to enter fellowship and disciplining relationships with other mature Christians, study the Bible so our minds can be renewed with God's word, and allow the Holy Spirit to come into our life and begin the process of transforming us into the persons God desires us to be. The local church where we belong is responsible for assisting in and holding us accountable for doing these things. Paul indicated the elders of a local Christian church with love and compassion are to ask us to give an accounting of our actions when we continue to live an intentional unrepentant sinful life after we have accepted Jesus as our Lord and Savior and joined the church. Paul indicated the elders of the church have the responsibility to judge us and remove us from fellowship in the church when we refuse to repent and stop participating in our sinful activities. We are considered to be spiritually dead when this occurs until we stop our sinful activities, repent, and seek forgiveness and are reinstated into fellowship of the church. When:

- We intentionally and persistently sin against our spouse and family without any intent of repenting and seeking forgiveness;
- Our sins cause our spouse and family pain and suffering and place them in danger;
- We have by action of the elders of our church been removed from fellowship in the church; and
- We are declared spiritually dead by the church; and our spouse desires, he/she is free to seek a divorce and remarry.

The role of the elders of a local Christian church in judging its members in cases of intentional unrepentant sinful living is to be taken seriously. Jesus stated:

"Do not judge lest you be judged. For in the way you judge, you will be judged; and by your standard of measure, it will be measured to you."
(Matthew 7:1-2)

"Do not judge according to appearance, but judge with righteous judgement."
(John 7:24)

Judgments are to be administered with compassion and love by elders who are the most knowledgeable of God's word in the Bible and who by their conduct live righteous lives. Elders who judge will ultimately be judged by God and possibly others in the same manner they have judged.

Conclusion

One of the most common reasons for getting divorced today is irreconcilable differences. The Bible cannot be used to justify divorce in marriages between Christian couples even though the culture allows divorce between non-Christian couples. Paul stated in 1 Corinthians 7:10-11:

> "But to the married I give instructions, not I, but the Lord, that the wife should not leave her husband (but if she does leave, let her remain unmarried, or else be reconciled to her husband), and that the husband should not send his wife away."

A Christian couple is expected to work through their marital problems and be reconciled to each other when they have marital problems and cannot get divorced for one of the three previously discussed reasons. They can separate but not remarry when they cannot resolve their differences.

Divorce is a difficult and emotional topic. It touches many lives today and represents failure in a major area of the lives of those who have experienced it. Divorce results in pain and suffering for husbands, wives and children who must work through the difficult and troubled times it causes. It would be nice if the causes of divorce were black and white and blame could be easily assessed. However, issues surrounding divorce are often complex, and in many situations, it is not possible to sort them out.

God hates divorce because of the devastating effects it has on families who experience it. He, however, loves those whose lives are devastated by divorce. His grace, mercy and forgiveness apply to divorce just as they apply to other areas of our lives where we have sinned and transgressed His laws and have experienced failure. God clearly prefers a couple to work through their differences whenever possible and to be reconciled to each other. However, He also recognizes this sometimes is not possible. There is comfort in the Proverbs whether a couple considering divorce can work through their difference and become reconciled to each other. Proverbs 16:9 states:

"The mind of man plans his way,
But the LORD directs his steps."

This verse teaches God will walk with those considering a divorce irrespective of the choice they make. There will be pain, suffering and troubled times associated with their choice regardless of what it is. However, God will direct their steps whether they stay together or get divorced, and He will give them the ability to deal with and work through their difficult times.

CHAPTER 23
THE BODY OF CHRIST
MINISTERING TO OTHERS THROUGH THE CHURCH

"For we are His workmanship, created in Christ Jesus for good works, which God prepared beforehand, that we should walk in them." (Ephesians 2:10)

THE BODY OF CHRIST (Chapter 23 - 24)

Topics in this section include:

- The relationship God wants us to have with the Body of Christ, the Church, and how we can minister to and serve others through local churches.

- Promises Jesus makes to all Christians.

GO INTO THE WORLD

Redemption and reconciliation with God come only through our faith in Jesus. He is God's only provision for sin. Paul stated in Romans 10:12-15:

"For there is no distinction between Jew and Greek; for the same Lord is Lord of all, abounding in riches for all who call on Him for 'Whoever will call on the name of the Lord will be saved. [Psalm 55:16]' How then shall they call upon Him in whom they have not believed? And how shall they believe in Him whom they have not heard? And how shall they hear without a preacher? And how shall they preach unless they are sent? Just as it is written, 'How beautiful are the feet of those who bring glad tidings of good things!'"

Paul indicates everyone who calls on the name of Jesus will be saved. However, many have not heard about Jesus and the redemption and reconciliation with God they can receive through faith in Him. They may not have the opportunity to receive this redemption and reconciliation unless we who have received it are willing to go into the world to share Jesus with them.

We are reconciled to God and receive spiritual life through faith in Jesus. We are God's workmanship created in Jesus for good works (Ephesians 2:10). Jesus instructed His disciples to spread His word in the Bible throughout the world and minister to the needs of others. He instructs us to do the same. We must examine what Jesus said to His disciples in the Gospels of Matthew, Mark and Luke to understand the full extent of His instructions to His disciples. He stated in Matthew 28:18-20:

> "All authority has been given to Me in heaven and on earth. Go therefore and make disciples of all nations, baptizing them in the name of the Father and the Son and the Holy Spirit, teaching them to observe all that I command you; and lo, I am with you always, even to the end of the age."

Jesus stated in Mark 16:15-18:

> "Go into all the world and preach the gospel to all creation. He who has believed and has been baptized shall be saved; but he who has disbelieved shall be condemned. And these signs will accompany those who have believed: in My name they will cast out demons, they will speak with new tongues; they will pick up serpents, and if they drink any deadly poison, it shall not hurt them; they will lay hands on the sick, and they will recover."

Luke stated in Luke 24:45-49 and in Acts 1:7-8:

> "Then [Jesus] opened [the] minds [of the disciples] to understand the Scriptures, and He said to them, 'Thus it is written, that the Christ should suffer and rise again from the dead the third day; and that repentance for forgiveness of sins should be proclaimed in His name to all the nations, beginning from Jerusalem. You are witnesses of these things. And behold, I am sending forth the promise of My Father upon you; but you are to stay in the city until you are clothed with power from on high.' ... He said to them, 'It is not for you to know times or epochs which the Father has fixed by His own authority; but you shall receive power when the Holy Spirit has come upon you; and you shall be My witnesses both in Jerusalem and in all Judea and Samaria, and even to the remotest part of the earth '"

Jesus gave His disciples a six-part commission in the Gospels of Matthew, Mark and Luke. He instructed them to:

Proclaim repentance for sins in the name of Jesus. They were to call people to repent, turn from their life of sin, and return to God by receiving the salvation He offered them through Jesus.

Baptize people in the name of the Father, Son and Holy Spirit. They were to baptize people. This baptism was a public identification with the death and resurrection of Jesus.

Preach the gospel of Jesus. They were to proclaim God's word as revealed to them by Jesus.

Instruct people to observe the teachings of Jesus. They were to teach others how to observe all that Jesus had taught them and how to live Christian lives.

Be witness to the presence of Jesus in their lives. They had lived with Jesus. They were to be witnesses to all the things they had observed and to the presence of the Holy Spirit in their lives.

Make disciples of all people. They were to call others to discipleship and teach them how to be followers of Jesus.

Jesus told His disciples those who believed in Him and were baptized would be redeemed and reconciled to God while those who did not believe in and rejected Him would experience God's judgement. He stated four signs would characterize those who believed. They would:

Cast out demons in the name of Jesus. Believers would have authority over Satan and demons in the name of Jesus, and they would have to obey.

Speak with new tongues. Believers would receive the gift of various kinds of tongues. The sign of speaking in tongues was possibly more important in the early church as confirmation of receiving the gift of the Holy Spirit than it is today. We believe today we receive the Holy Spirit when we profess with our mouth Jesus is Lord and believe in our heart He was raised from the dead.

Pick up serpents and drink poison without harm. The word *serpents* can refer to real serpents or Satan and the spiritual forces who follow him (Luke 10:18-19). The word *poison* can refer to actual poison that one might drink or poison that is contained on the lips of those who direct assaults against Christians (Psalms 58, 140). The implication is Christians would prevail against any spiritual force that came against them. They were given authority in the name of Jesus to tread upon serpents and scorpions and prevail "over all the power of the enemy."

Heal the sick. Believers would have the authority to lay their hands on the sick and pray for healing, and they would be healed. Prayer today may not result in instantaneous physical healing. However, it does aid in physical halting.

MINISTER THROUGH THE CHURCH

Jesus instructed His disciples to wait in Jerusalem until after the Church had been born at Pentecost before they began the ministries to which He had called them. He expected them to spread His gospel of salvation and minister to others through the Church. He expects us to do the same today. Local Christian churches provide nurturing and caring environments where:

- We are taught and learn the spiritual life principles contained in the Bible;
- We enter discipling and mentoring relationships with mature Christians;
- We identify and develop our spiritual gifts;
- Our faith develops and grows;
- We receive support and help when we need them; and
- We develop networks to minister to the needs of others and to the needs of the communities where we live and the world.

The following experience associated with our relationship with God through Jesus and our spiritual development are designed by God to occur in and under the direction and authority of local Christian churches:

- Spiritual rebirth, forgiveness, and reconciliation;
- Regeneration of our spirits, renewal of our minds, and transformation of our hearts; and
- Prayer, healing, and loving and serving others.

Local Christian churches are spiritual fortresses where we can take refuge from the assaults of the spiritual forces arrayed against us. They are places where we can effectively engage in spiritual warfare and reach out to minister to the needs of and serve others. Jesus promised in Matthew 16:18, "And upon this rock I will build My church; and the gates of Hades shall not overpower it." Jesus is the rock on which the church is built, and nothing in all creation can prevail against it.

Dr. Howard Hendricks, who was a distinguished professor and lecturer at the Dallas Theological Seminary in Dallas, Texas, has visited local churches of all kinds and denominations throughout his ministry. He has observed vibrant and growing local churches possess nine basic characteristics. He indicated it is not necessary for a church to possess all nine characteristics. However, the more of them a church possesses, the greater the probability it is or will become a vibrant and growing church. A vibrant and growing church:

Has clear cut objectives. It has a clear understanding of what the Bible states a church should be and is able to distinguish between Biblical and cultural objectives.

Has an effective means of community penetration. The church is a Bible training facility that effectively equips its members for evangelism and ministry outreach. It has a good understanding of the needs of the community it serves and can adapt its evangelism and outreach programs to meet these needs.

Has discovered a practical means of mobilizing and equipping its laity. The church recognizes it is not the responsibility of nor is it desirable for pastors to do everything. Programs are established to help laity identify their spiritual gifts and assist them in developing and employing their spiritual gifts for building up their church.

Has a high commitment to the family. It understands there are only two divine relationships discussed in the Bible: our relationship with the church and our relationship with our family. The church clearly understands the responsibilities that are associated with each relationship. It equips parents to perform their responsibilities within their families. It further recognizes the needs of pastors relative to their families and structures their responsibilities, so they have sufficient time to address these needs.

Has intensified interpersonal relationships. It recognizes the greatest problem today is loneliness. It establishes small group ministries where people feel they belong and perceive they are valued and needed. It understands the friendliness of a church is determined by how church members relate to people who walk in off the street. It uses interpersonal relationships to help its members identify community, regional and worldwide needs and then motivates them to initiate or become involved in ministries directed toward meeting these needs.

Is willing to innovate and change. It must be willing to take risks and change to respond to the changing needs of the community it serves. It must be willing to get involved in processes associated with ministries without first having answers to all the questions related to these ministries.

Has strong Bible teaching ministries. The Bible is preached from the pulpit. It has Bible teaching programs at all age levels. Bible teaching is related to equipping people for ministry and relates to real-life issues.

Has an emphasis on discipleship. It knows discipleship is not optional; it is mandated by the Bible. The church makes discipleship one of its most prized ministries. It understands one-on-one discipleship is one of the most effective ways of entering meaningful interpersonal relationships and preparing people for ministry.

Is concerned with cultivating the faith of its members. It emphasizes Jesus' greatest discipleship activities with His disciples were to develop in them trust and belief in Him and assist them in becoming wholly dependent on and obedient to Him. It cultivates and develops within its members the ability to have faith in God and trust Him to do those things only He can do. It teaches where prayer is focused the power of God is released.

Charles Colson, who was the founder of Prison Fellowship, stated in one of his *Break Point* radio programs a true church:

- Always gives evidence of the presence of Jesus;
- Is established by the grace of Jesus;
- Is built up by the power of Jesus; and
- Is sealed with the Spirit of Jesus. He continued a true church:
- Preaches God's word contained in the Bible;
- Administers the sacraments;
- Calls people to discipleship and disciplined living; and
- Gives evidence of the presence of the fruit of the Holy Spirit (love, joy, peace, patience, kindness, goodness, faithfulness, gentleness and self-control).

MINISTER TO THE WHOLE PERSON

Jesus instructed us in Matthew 25:31-46 to respond to the emotional, physical, material and spiritual needs of individuals to whom we minister. James stated in James 2:15-16:

> "If a brother or sister is without clothing and in need of daily food, and one of you says to them, 'Go in peace, be warmed and be filled," and yet you do not give them what is necessary for their body, what use is that?'"

John stated in 1 John 3:17-18:

> "But whoever has the world's goods, and beholds his brother in need and closes his heart against him, how does the love of God abide in him? Little children, let us not love with word or with tongue, but in deed and truth."

Jesus ministered to the spirit, soul and body of individuals, and He calls us to do the same. We must often minister to the emotional, material and physical needs of individuals before they will hear and respond to our invitation to enter a relationship with God through Jesus. We may believe we express the love of Jesus when we witness to His presence in our life by the words we speak. However, Jesus, James and John indicated we must express our love for those to whom we minister by helping them meet their physical and emotional needs before they will allow us to help them meet their spiritual needs. This often requires our sharing our material resources to help meet their needs.

General Eva Burrows who was the international head of the Salvation Army from 1986 to 1993 presented the following principles associated with sharing the gospel of Jesus with others at the Seventeenth World Methodist Conference in Rio de Janeiro, Brazil, in August 1996 (*Proceedings of the Seventeenth World Methodist Conference,* 1996).

We communicate the gospel best when we lift Jesus up first. Jesus instructed His disciples and He instructed us to go "make disciples of all nations" and to go "into the world and preach the gospel." We are to share a two-part message. First, we are to share John's message in John 3:16:

> "For God so loved the world, that He gave His only begotten Son, that whoever believes in Him should not perish, but have eternal life."

God loves us, and He demonstrated this love by sending His Son, Jesus, to die on a cross so we can have life. Second, we are to share Paul's message in Ephesians 2:8-9:

"For by grace you have been saved through faith; and that not of yourselves,
it is the gift of God; not as a result of works, that no one should boast."

The redemption and reconciliation God extends to us through our faith and trust in and obedience to Jesus is a gift. It is not based on anything we can do to earn it. We enter a reconciled relationship with God through His grace extended to us through our faith in Jesus. Our church and church programs often become the focus of our presentation when we share this gospel message. Jesus, not the church nor its programs, must be the focus of the message even though the church is the vehicle through which we share the message of salvation and its programs are the methods we employ to share this message.

We must communicate the gospel of Jesus with a sensitivity of the environment and culture where we share it. We must learn about and understand the environment and culture where we share the gospel. We must learn its customs and language. Definitions and meanings of words continually change. We must be aware of these changes and speak to those with whom we share the gospel with words they understand. The gospel of Jesus must be relevant to the environment and culture where it is presented. It must be presented in a manner that does not place obstacles in the way of those who are being invited to enter a reconciled relationship with God through Jesus. The gospel must be presented using media through which it will be received and accepted and in ways in which it will be understood while still being true to its message as revealed in the Bible.

We must enter the environment and culture where people live to share the gospel of Jesus with them. We must identify with the individuals we seek to evangelize. We must step out of our comfort zone into the danger zones where people live. We must seek to understand their joys and sorrows, what excites and turns them on and what discourages and turns them off. We must live where people live and identify with and understand conditions where they live to be able to effectively share the gospel with them.

We must be willing to enter difficulties and heartaches of people with whom we share the gospel of Jesus. Satan attempts to make us indifferent to needs and problems of others and deceive us into believing what happens in their lives is not our responsibility. The Bible calls us to love people, care about them, and be willing to get involved in and with their lives when we are invited or led by the Holy Spirit to do so. We must be sensitive to the leading of the Holy Spirit when we get personally involved with the lives of people to whom we witness the gospel. We must often minister to their material, physical and emotional needs before they will give us permission to minister to their spiritual needs. They often give us permission to share the gospel of Jesus with them and are willing to receive it when we enter their environments and minister to these needs.

We must call people to repentance, conversion and discipleship when we share the gospel of Jesus. The Holy Spirit convicts us of sin and calls us to repent and return to God when we enter a relationship with God through faith in Jesus. The Holy Spirit regenerates our spirit and breathes spiritual life back into our soul when we repent and enter a relationship with God through Jesus. We must share these actions of the Holy Spirit with others so He can use us to reach out to draw them to Jesus when we present the gospel of Jesus to them. We must call them to repent and return to God by accepting Jesus as their Lord and Savior. We must enter discipling relationships with them or lead them to others who will disciple them after they have received Jesus as their Lord and Savior. The Holy Spirit then begins a process with them to renew their minds and transform their hearts, transforming them into the persons God desires them to be.

CHAPTER 24
THE BODY OF CHRIST
JESUS – OUR HOPE FOR THE FUTURE

"For God so loved the world, that he gave his only begotten Son, that whoever believes in him shall not perish, but have eternal life. For God did not send the Son into the world to judge the world, but that the world might be saved through him. He who believes in him is not judged; he who does not believe has been judged already; because he has not believed in the name of the only begotten Son of God. This is the judgment, that the Light has come into the world, and men loved the darkness rather than the Light, for their deeds were evil. For everyone who does evil hates the Light, and does not come to the Light for fear that his deeds will be exposed. But he who practices the truth comes to the Light, so that his deeds may be manifested as having been wrought in God. ... He who believes in the Son has eternal life; but he who does not obey the Son will not see life, but the wrath of God abides on him." (John 3:16-21, 36)

THE SECURITY OF GOD AND SUPREMACY OF JESUS

We are secure in our relationship with God through our faith and trust in and obedience to Jesus. Nothing can separate us from God and Jesus in this relationship. Jesus stated in John 10:27-30:

"My sheep hear My voice, and I know them, and they follow Me; and I give eternal life to them, and they will never perish; and no one will snatch them out of My hand. My Father, who has given them to Me, is greater than all; and no one is able to snatch them out of the Father's hand. I and the Father are one."

Paul described the relationship we have with God through Jesus in Romans 8:15-17:

> "For you have not received a spirit of slavery leading to fear again, but you have received a spirit of adoption as sons by which we cry out, 'Abba! Father!' The Spirit Himself testifies with our spirit that we are children of God, and if children, heirs also, heirs of God and fellow heirs with Christ, if indeed we suffer with Him so we may also be glorified with Him."

We become adopted children of God through our relationship with Jesus and joint heirs with Jesus of God with all the privileges of being an heir of God.

Paul implied our relationship with Jesus will result in difficult life challenges and suffering. Jesus affirmed in Matthew 28:19, "All authority has been given to Me in heaven and on earth." He has authority in our relationship with Him to equip us through the presence of the Holy Spirit in our life with the means to persevere through and triumph over difficult life challenges and suffering in our life that may appear to overwhelm us.

THE PROMISES OF JESUS IN REVELATION 2 AND 3

God's righteousness and justice will ultimately prevail in the conflict between good and evil. He instructed us to have faith and trust Him in difficult and troubled times. David stated in Psalm 37:38-40:

> "But transgressors will be altogether destroyed; the posterity of the wicked will be cut off. But the salvation of the righteous is from the LORD; He is their strength in time of trouble. And the LORD helps them, and delivers them; He delivers them from the wicked, and saves them, because they take refuge in Him."

Jesus delivered messages to seven churches in Asia in Chapters 2 and 3 of Revelation. These were actual churches during John's day. Some Bible scholars today indicate these churches represented churches with different cultural, sociological and theological characteristics that have existed down through the ages and that exist today. Others indicate they represented different church ages from the days of the apostles to the present day.

Jesus' promises at the end of each message can be interpreted to be specific to the people of each church or church age. He prefaced each promise with the statement, "He who has an ear, let him hear what the Spirit says to the churches." The promises were made to those who would remain faithful and obedient to Him in each church or church age. We can argue that all seven promises apply equally to all who have been and will remain faithful and obedient to Jesus throughout the ages.

Jesus prefaced each promise with the phrase, "to him who overcomes." He will grant what He has promised to those who persevere through difficult times, hardships and trials that result from their faith and trust in and obedience to Him. Jesus promised those who overcome:

Promise 1:

> "To him who overcomes, I will grant to eat of the tree of life, which is in the Paradise of God." (Revelation 2:7)

Adam and Eve were driven from the garden of Eden when they disobeyed God and sinned, so they would not be able to eat the fruit of the tree of life and be eternally separated from God (Genesis 3:22-24). The tree of life then disappeared from the earth. The tree of life will be present in the new Jerusalem, and all whose names are written in the book of life will be allowed to eat its fruit. Access to the tree of life was the first thing that was denied Adam and Eve after they had sinned; it is the first thing Jesus promised to return to the righteous in his eternal kingdom.

Promise 2:

> "He who overcomes will not be hurt by the second death." (Revelation 2:11)

All whose names are written in the book of life will not experience the second death that is eternal separation from God.

Promise 3:

> "To him who overcomes, and to him I will give some of the hidden manna, and I will give him a white stone, and a new name written on the stone which no one knows but he who receives it." (Revelation 2:17)

The manna that was given to the Israelites during their forty-year journey in the wilderness was enough to satisfy the needs of their physical hunger (Exodus 16:3-18). The hidden manna can refer to the sufficiency of God's grace that is extended to the righteous through Jesus to satisfy their spiritual hunger (John 6:47-51). A white stone during John's day was used to vote for the acquittal of an accused person. This statement indicates the righteous will be acquitted before God and given new names in His eternal kingdom.

Promise 4:

> "And he who overcomes, and he who keeps My deeds until the end, to him I will give authority over the nations; and he shall rule them with a rod of iron, as the vessels of the potter are broken to pieces, as I also have received authority from my Father; and I will give him the morning star." (Revelation 2:26-28)

This is the only one of Jesus' seven promises with a condition in addition to remaining faithful and obedient to Him. This condition is a possible reference to Jesus' statement in His parable of the talents (Matthew 25:14- 30). He indicated those who are faithful to perform the good works God prepares for them during their lives will be given the authority to exercise leadership in His eternal kingdom. Lucifer was called the star of the morning in Isaiah 14:12 before he sinned and rebelled against God. This was a reference to the special position he had in God's kingdom before he was cast out of heaven. To be given the morning star can imply those who meet the special condition of this promise will be given special positions in God's eternal kingdom.

Promise 5:

> "He who overcomes will be thus clothed in white garments; and I will not erase his name from the book of life, and I will confess his name before My Father and before His angels." (Revelation 3:5)

The righteous will be given bodies without sin and that will not be corrupted by sin. Their names will never be removed once they have been written in the book of life.

Promise 6:

> "He who overcomes, I will make him a pillar in the temple of My God, and he will not go out from it anymore; and I will write upon him the name of My God, and the name of the city of My God, the new Jerusalem, which comes down out of heaven from My God, and My new name." (Revelation 3:12)

Jesus promised in John 14:2-3 He was going to prepare a place for us. This place is in the kingdom of heaven, and more specifically, in the city of God, the new Jerusalem. The righteous will be allowed to enter the temple of God and His very presence. The names of God, the new Jerusalem, and the new name of Jesus will be written on the righteous.

Promise 7:

> "Behold, I stand at the door and knock; if anyone hears My voice and opens
> the door, I will come in to him, and will dine with him, and he with Me."
> (Revelation 3:20)

Jesus has extended this promise to everyone down through the ages. It is an invitation that requires a response. We must open the door of our heart and invite Him into our life. We can keep the door shut, or we can open it and invite Jesus in. The choice is ours, and He will honor the choice we make. Jesus promised to enter, commune and fellowship with us when we open the door to our heart and invite Him in. He will allow those who open the doors of their hearts to Him to sit with Him on His throne throughout eternity.

JESUS IS OUR HOPE FOR THE FUTURE

God will at a time of His choosing direct His judgments against men and women and the earth, and He will bring this present age to an end. He will destroy the existing heaven and earth and create a new heaven and earth where there will be no sin or suffering. This can occur at any time in the future. Therefore, we must be prepared by accepting the redemption and reconciliation God extends to us by means of His grace through our faith and trust in and obedience to Jesus

Solomon and other writers present sound and practical advice and wisdom in Proverbs regarding life's challenges and choices. Solomon stated in Proverbs 3:1-12:

> "My son do not forget my teaching,
> But let your heart keep my commandments;
> For length of days and years of life,
> And peace they will add to you.
> Do not let kindness and truth leave you;
> Bind them around your neck,
> Write them on the tablet of your heart.
> So you will find favor and good repute
> In the sight of God and man.
> Trust in the LORD with all your heart,
> And do not lean on your own understanding.
> In all your ways acknowledge Him,
> And He will make your paths straight.

Do not be wise in your own eyes;
Fear the LORD and turn away from evil.
It will be healing to your body
And refreshment to your bones.
Honor the LORD from your wealth,
And from the first of all your produce;
So your barns will be filled with plenty,
And your vats will overflow with new wine.
My son, do not reject the discipline of the LORD,
Or loathe His reproof,
For whom the LORD loves He reproves,
Even as a father, the son in whom he delights."

When we incorporate the wisdom that Solomon and others give to us in Proverbs, we will:

- Find peace in our soul,

- Experience a long life,

- Find favor with God and man,

- Receive health and refreshment for our body,

- Be prosperous, and

- Accept discipline from the LORD with a right attitude.

Solomon encouraged us to turn away from evil, fear God, develop a personal relationship with and be in fellowship with Him, and trust and lean on Him. God will guide and make the paths of our life straight when we do these.

Solomon addressed many important life issues and the futility of things in life that we often incorrectly believe are important in Ecclesiastes. He encouraged us to enjoy life to the fullest and recognize it as God's gift to us. He admonished us to avoid the futility of pursuing things in life that do not have eternal value and direct us away from God. Solomon indicated God has given us life to enjoy while He expects us to live it in obedience to Him. Solomon concluded in Ecclesiastes 12:13-14:

> "The conclusion, when all has been heard, is: fear God and keep His commandments, because this applies to every person. For God will bring every act to judgment, everything which is hidden, whether it is good or evil."

We must enter a redeemed and reconciled relationship with God through faith and trust in and obedience to Jesus to enjoy meaning and purpose in our life. We can find true meaning, purpose and joy only when we enter this relationship and allow the Holy Spirit to transform us into the person God has created us to be. Paul stated in Galatians 2:20:

> "I have been crucified with Christ; and it is no longer I who live, but Christ lives in me; and the life which I now live in the flesh I live by faith in the Son of God, who loved me, and delivered Himself up for me."

We have been redeemed by God's grace through our faith and trust in and obedience to Jesus. God freely extends His gift of redemption to us because of His love, mercy and grace. He promises to place His Spirit in us through Jesus and the Holy Spirit and walk with us as we encounter life's challenges, disappointments and joys. He will prepare our way and enable and equip us to persevere. Jesus is our hope for the future.

EPILOGUE

WHAT JESUS SAID

I asked the Holy Spirit in 1982 to help me better understand God's word in the Bible as it relates to our relationship with Him through Jesus when I agreed to His request to write my initial *REDEEMED BY GOD* book. His assistance over a span of 39 years has given me an understanding of God's word in the Bible necessary to write my series of four *REDEEMED BY GOD* books. I will use words Jesus spoke in the Gospels of Matthew and John to summarize my understanding of the basis for our relationship with God and the redemption He extends to us through our faith and trust in and obedience to Jesus.

I begin with Jesus' statement in John 3:16-17:

> "For God so loved the world, that He gave His only begotten Son, that whoever believes in Him shall not perish, but have eternal life. For God did not send the Son into the world to judge the world, but that the world might be saved through Him."

Jesus indicated God, His Father, made the conscious decision to redeem the world through Him, and this redemption results in eternal life for those who are redeemed. Jesus, as the Son of God, is our Lord who God sent into the world to be our Savior. Jesus stated in John 4:34:

> "My food is to do the will of Him who sent Me and to accomplish His work."

Jesus affirmed His agreement with His Father's decisions to redeem the world through Him even though He knew this decision would ultimately result in His sacrificial death on a cross. Jesus stated in John 8:10:

> "I am the Light of the world; he who follows Me will not walk in the darkness, but will have the Light of life."

Jesus came into the world to show us how to live in a manner pleasing to God and that will result in our receiving eternal life.

Paul indicated in Ephesians 2:8 we are saved by God's grace through faith. He indicated God's grace is offered to us as a gift, and he referred to this gift as being free in Romans 5:15-17. God offers us His grace with no cost to us because we can do nothing independent of His love to obtain it.

Jesus stated in Matthew 5:17-18:

> "Do not think that I came to abolish the Law or the Prophets; I did not come to abolish but to fulfill. For truly I say to you, until heaven and earth pass away, not the smallest letter or stroke shall pass from the Law until all is accomplished."

Jesus confirmed He came to fulfill the Law and the Profits, not to do away with them. Therefore, the Ten Commandments and their extension in the moral law remain to define and convict us of sin.

Jesus stated in John 12:47-50:

> "If anyone hears My sayings and does not keep them, I do not judge him; for I did not come to judge the world, but to save the world. He who rejects Me and does not receive My sayings, has one who judges him; the word I spoke is what will judge him at the last day. For I did not speak on My own initiative, but the Father Himself who sent Me has given Me a commandment as to what to say and what to speak. I know that His commandment is eternal life; therefore the things I speak, I speak just as the Father has told Me."

Jesus reaffirmed He did not come to judge the world, but to save it. He indicated God, His Father, instructed Him to speak the words He spoke, and it is these words that will judge us at the last day. Jesus' words are recorded in the four Gospels of the New Testament. Therefore, we will do well to read, study and internalize them.

Jesus stated in John 10:27-30:

> "My sheep hear My voice, and I know them, and they follow Me; and I give eternal life to them, and they will never perish; and no one will snatch them out of My hand. My Father, who has given them to Me, is greater than all; and no one is able to snatch them out of the Father's hand. I and the Father are One."

Jesus affirmed we know Him and hear his voice when we enter a relationship with Him. He reaffirmed He gives us eternal life, and He stated no one will be able to separate us from our relationship with Him because God, His Father, sustains this relationship.

Jesus stated in John 14:15, 21, 23:

> "If you love Me, you will keep my commandments. ... He who has my commandments and keeps them is the one who loves Me, and he who loves Me will be loved by My Father; and I will love him and will disclose Myself to him. ... If anyone loves Me, he will keep My word, and My Father will love him, and We will come to him and make Our abode with him."

Jesus indicated we demonstrate our love for Him by keeping His commandments and the word He spoke. He stated He will reveal Himself to us, and He and His Father will love and take up residence in us when we do this.

Jesus stated in Matthew 10:37-39:

> "He who loves father or mother more than Me is not worthy of Me, and he who loves son or daughter more than Me is not worthy of Me. And he who does not take his cross and follow after Me is not worthy of Me. He who has found his life will lose it, and he who has lost his life for My sake will find it."

Jesus indicated our love for Him must be greater than our love for anyone or anything that may become an object of our love. Our love for Him must motivate us to obey His words in the Gospels. We risk losing our eternal life when anyone or anything other than Jesus becomes the primary object of our love. We will receive eternal life when we lose our life because of our faith and trust in and obedience to Jesus.

Jesus stated in John 14:1-3, 6-7:

> "Do not let your heart be troubled; believe in God, believe also in Me. In My Father's house are many dwelling places; if it were not so, I would have told you; for I go to prepare a place for you. If I go and prepare a place for you, I will come again and receive you to Myself, that where I am, there you may be also. ... I am the way, and the truth, and the life; no one comes to the Father but through Me. If you had known Me, you would have known My Father also; from now on you know Him and have seen Him."

These are words Jesus spoke to His disciples. He stated He is going to prepare a place for us in God, His Father's, house in heaven, and He will return to receive us to Himself so we can be where He is. Jesus stated we can come to God, His Father, only through Him, and we come to know God as our Father when we know Him.

Jesus stated in John 15:1-6:

> "I am the true vine, and My Father is the vinedresser. Every branch in Me
> that does not bear fruit, He takes away; and every branch that bears fruit,
> He prunes it so that it may bear more fruit. You are already clean because
> of the word which I have spoken to you. Abide in Me, and I in you. As the
> branch cannot bear fruit of itself unless it abides in the vine, so neither can
> you unless you abide in Me. I am the vine, you are the branches, he who
> abides in Me and I in him he bears much fruit, for apart from Me you can
> do nothing. If anyone does not abide in Me, he is thrown away as a branch
> and dries up; and they gather them, and cast them into the fire and they
> are burned."

These are words Jesus spoke to His disciples. He stated He is the true vine, and God, His Father, is the vinedresser who will remove branches from the vine that do not bear fruit. Jesus' statement indicated we are to bear fruit in our relationship with Him, and God, His Father, will remove us from this relationship when we do not bear fruit in it. Knowing God will remove us from our relationship with Jesus when we do not bear fruit in this relationship is distressing and a shock. However, God can do as He wills. Jesus indicated we can bear fruit only when we abide in Him, and He abides in us. He emphasized we can do nothing independent of our relationship with Him. Jesus continued in John 15:7:

> "If you abide in Me, and My words abide in you, ask whatever you wish, and
> it will be done for you."

Jesus indicated we can request anything from Him in prayer when we abide in Him, and His words abide in us. We have His assurance our requests will be granted. Our requests must be compatible with the nature and character of God.

Paul stated in Romans 10:8-10 we enter a relationship with Jesus when we profess with our mouth He is Lord and believe in our heart God raised Him from the dead. The Bible teaches we are to grow and mature in this relationship after we enter it. Peter instructed us in 1 Peter 2:1-3 to long for the pure milk of the word so we can grow in respect to salvation. Paul instructed us in Philippians 2:12-13 to work out our salvation with fear and trembling so God can will and work His good pleasure through us. He also instructed us in 1 Corinthians 3:10-15 to build our life on the foundation of Jesus. These actions prepare and equip us to do the good works referred to by Paul in Ephesians 2:10 that God prepares for us to perform.

Paul indicated in Romans 12:4-8, 1 Corinthians 12:3-11, 28, and Ephesians 4:11-13 the Holy Spirit gives us supernatural spiritual gifts that uniquely equip and enable us to perform our good works. Our good works are the fruit on Jesus' vine that God prunes so we can bear more fruit. Jesus instructed us in Matthew 5:16 to let our light shine before men so they can see our good works. Our good works are performed to glorify God, and they are proof of the presence of Jesus and the Holy Spirit in our life.

James indicated we demonstrate our faith by our works in James 2:14-24. He indicated faith that does not result in works is useless; it is dead. Our faith must motivate us to do the good works God has prepared for us to perform as it grows and matures.

Jesus stated in Matthew 7:13-14:

> "Enter through the narrow gate; for the gate is wide and the way is broad that leads to destruction, and there are many who enter through it. For the gate is small and the way is narrow that leads to life, and there are few who find it."

Jesus' parable of the Sower in Matthew 13:1-9 helps us understand His statement. Jesus indicated in this parable that sharing His words with others is like a sower who spreads seeds over the ground. Some seeds fall beside a road and are immediately eaten by birds. Some seeds fall on rocky places where there is little soil. They initially grow, and then they dry up when the sun shines on them because they do not have deep roots. Some seeds fall among thorns, and the thorns grow and chock them when they grow. Some seeds fall on good soil, and they grow and produce fruit. Jesus identified those represented by the Sower's seeds in Mathew 13:18-22:

- **Seeds that fall beside a road** represented individuals who hear Jesus' words and do not understand them. Therefore, Satan deccives and snatches them from Jesus.

- **Seeds that fall on rocky places where there is little soil** represented individuals who eagerly receive Jesus' words with joy, but they fail to learn what His words mean. They fall away from Jesus when afflictions or persecutions arise. This occurs because Jesus' words do not form the foundation of their lives.

- **Seeds that fall among thorns** represented individuals who receive and understand Jesus' words, but the worries of life and the deceitfulness of wealth overshadow and obscure His words. As a result, they do not produce fruit in their relationship with Jesus. Therefore, God removes them from the relationship.

- **Seeds that fall on good soil represented** individuals who receive, understand, and build their lives on the foundation of Jesus' words. As a result, they produce fruit in their relationship with Jesus. Therefore, they are among the few who Jesus indicated find life.

There are individuals who enter a relationship with Jesus who do not grow and mature in this relationship and perform good works God has prepared for them to do in this relationship. Therefore, they do not bear fruit in this relationship. This normally occurs because they are not motivated to grow and mature in their relationship with Jesus and perform good works God has prepared for them to do in the relationship. They may also do nothing after receiving God's gift of grace through Jesus because they believe this gift is free, and therefore, they do nothing after receiving it.

There is no acceptable reason for our light not to shine before men as proof of our bearing fruit through our good works in our relationship with Jesus. Therefore, individuals who do not bear fruit in this relationship will be removed from the relationship by God. This will occur when their failure to bear fruit through their good works has not been addressed and corrected before they stand in judgement before God after they die (Hebrews 9:27-28).

I want to return to God's love for us demonstrated by sending His Son, Jesus, into the world so we can receive eternal life after we die. Jesus' sacrificial death on a cross enables God to redeem and reconcile us to Himself by means of His gift of grace.

God gives us the freedom to choose to either accept or reject His gift of grace and receive His redemption, and He gives us to the end of our life to make this choice. Ignoring or avoiding this choice has the result of our rejecting God's gift of grace and redemption. The Bible teaches we will be judged by God when we stand before Him after we die, and we will be separated from God, Jesus and the Holy Spirit forever when we have not received His gift of grace and redemption. We will initially be in Hades after we die and then in the lake of fire after the great white throne judgement. The Bible also teaches we enter a redeemed and reconciled relationship with God through Jesus after we accept His gift of grace and receive His redemption, and we will be with God, Jesus and the Holy Spirit in the kingdom of heaven forever after we die.

Some individuals do not believe or recognize there are requirements when they enter a reconciled relationship with God through Jesus because Paul referred to God's gift of grace as being free. Christian denominations also teach the salvation we receive through Jesus is free. This creates a false perception we do not need to do anything before and after we receive our salvation. However, previous paragraphs indicate, and the Bible teaches there are requirements when we enter a reconciled relationship with God after we have been redeemed by His grace through Jesus.

The Bible teaches God and Jesus bless and reward us when we do what is required of us after we are redeemed by God and have entered a reconciled relationship with Him through our faith and trust in and obedience to Jesus. These blessings and rewards begin while we are alive and continue after we die. The Bible also teaches we will experience God's judgement when we stand before Him after we die, and we have done none of these requirements while we were alive.

CLOSING COMMENTS

Moses gave us the Law that established the moral code God expects us to live by. The Law defined sin that separates us from God when it is present in our life. The Law convicts us of sins in our life. It cannot redeem us from these sins and reconcile us to God. Therefore, God extended His love and grace to us by sending us a Savior, Jesus, to redeem us from the consequences of our sins and reconcile us to Himself. Jesus stated in Matthew 5:17-19 that nothing shall be removed from the Law until heaven and earth pass away. This will not occur until the great white throne judgement.

Joshua stated in Joshua 1:8:

> "This book of the law shall not depart from your mouth, but you shall meditate on it day and night, so that you may be careful to do according to all that is written in it; for then you will make your way prosperous, and then you will have success."

It is impossible for us to live a life without sin. Therefore, God sent Jesus into the world to be a sacrifice for and to save us from the consequences of our sins. God forgives and redeems us from our sins through Jesus when we repent of our sins and seek and receive His forgiveness and redemption through our faith in Jesus.

God gives us freedom to choose to or not to seek His forgiveness, redemption and reconciliation through Jesus. We are separated from Him, Jesus and the Holy Spirit forever when we die, and we did not repent of our sins and seek God's forgiveness and receive His redemption and reconciliation through Jesus while we were alive. We will be sent to Hades (hell) after we die and then to the lake of fire after the great white throne judgement. We are redeemed by God and reconciled to Him when we repent of our sins and receive Jesus as our Savior and Lord of our life. We then enter a bilateral relationship with Him, Jesus and the Holy Spirit in the kingdom of God on earth.

God, Jesus, the Holy Spirit and we have obligations in this bilateral relationship. God and Jesus will honor their covenants and promises that are presented in the Bible. We are to spiritually grow and mature as we grow in our faith and trust in and obedience to Jesus.

This is a lifelong process. The Holy Spirit facilitates our ability to spiritually grow and mature in our relationship with God through Jesus though our faithful and disciplined study of the Bible. He then equips us to perform good works in Jesus' name that God prepares for us to perform. We secure our entrance into the kingdom of heaven after we die by performing our good works in service and ministry to others for God's glory because we love Jesus and obey His words (1 Timothy 4:14-16, 2 Peter 1:5-11). God then acts through the Holy Spirit in our relationship with Him through Jesus to make our "way prosperous" and enable us to "have success" during our life.

REFERENCES

1. Blackaby, H.T. and King, C.V., *Experiencing God*, Life Way Press, 1990.

2. Dobson, J. C., *Life on the Edge*, Word Publishing, 1995.

3. Dobson, J. C., *Love Must Be Tough*, Word Publishing, 1996.

4. Faid, R. W., *A Scientific Approach to Christianity*, New Leaf Press, 1990.

5. Faid, R. W., *A Scientific Approach to Biblical Mysteries*, New Leaf Press, 1993.

6. Foster, R. J., *Celebration of Discipline*, Harper San Francisco, 1988.

7. Foster, R., J., *Prayer, Finding the Heart's True Home*, Harper San Francisco, 1992.

8. Gangel, K. O. and Wilhoit, J. C., *The Christians Educator's Handbook on Spiritual Formation*, Victor Books, 1994.

9. Hale, J. (Ed.), *Proceedings of the Seventeenth World Methodist Conference*, Rio De Janeiro, Brazil, The World Methodist Council Press, August 7-15, 1996.

10. Hendricks, H. G. and Hendricks, W. D., *Living By The Book*, Moody Press, 1991.

11. Grant, R. D. and Wells Miller, A., *Recovering Connections*, Harper San Francisco, 1993.

12. Heeren, Fred, *Show Me God*, Day Star Publications, 1997.

13. Kinghorn, K. C. and Gustafson, G., *Discovering and Using Your Spiritual Gifts*, Bristol Books, 1987.

14. McDowell, J., *Evidence That Demands A Verdict*, Campus Crusade for Christ International, 1972.

15. McDowell, J., *A Ready Defense*, Here's Life Publishers, 1990.

16. Miller, J. K., *The Secret Life of the Soul*, Broadman & Holman Publishers, 1997.

17. Minirth, F., Minirth, M.A., Newman, B., Newman, D., Hemfelt, R., and Hemfelt, S., *Passages of Marriage*, Thomas Nelson Publishers, 1991.

18. Morris, D., *Initimate Behavior*, Random House, 1971.

19. Reynolds, Douglas D., *Redeemed by God - Our Relationship with God through His Son, Jesus Christ*, Trafford Publishing, 2006.

20. Rhodes, R., *Angels Among Us*, Harvest House Publishers, 1994.

21. Ross, H., *The Fingerprint of God*, Promise Publishing Co., 1989.

22. Sandford, J. and Sandford, P., *Healing the Wounded Spirit*, Bridge Publishing, 1985

23. Seamands, David A., *Healing for Damaged Emotions*, Chariot Victor Publishing, 1991.

24. Smalley, Gary, *Making Love Last Forever*, Word Publishing, 1996.

25. Stoner, Peter W., *Science Speaks: An Evaluation of Certain Christian Evidences*, Chicago: Moody, 1963.

26. Strobel, Lee, *The Case for Christ*, Zondervan Publishing House, 1998.

27. Strobel, Lee, *The Case for Faith*, Zondervan Publishing House, 2000.

28. Tenney, M.C, (ed.), *Pictorial Bible Dictionary*, The Southwestern Company, 1971.

29. Wagner, Maurice, *The Sensation of Being Somebody*, Zondervan, 1985.

30. Warren, Rick, *The Purpose Driven Church*, Zondervan, 1995.

31. Webb, Chris, *The Fire of the Word - Meeting God on Holy Ground*, IVP Books, 2011.

32. Wilkinson, Bruce H., *The Prayer of Jabez*, Multnomah Publishers, 2000.

33. Wilmington, H. L., *Willmington's Guide to the Bible*, Tyndale House Publishers, 1981.

34. Crown Ministries, Small Group Financial Study, 1986.

35. *Matthew Henry's Commentary, PC Study Bible*, Biblesoft, 1993-94.

36. *Nelson's Illustrated Bible Dictionary*, Thomas Nelson Publishers, 1986.

Internet References

37. Manning, Scott, "Process of copying the Old Testament by Jewish Scribes," March 17, 2007; http://www.scottmanning.com/archives/scribeswritingoldtestament.php.

38. Century - One Bookstore, "Fascinating Facts about the Discovery at Qumen," http://www. centuryone.com/25dssfacts.html.

39. Walker, D. B., "First Century Manuscript? Clarification statement about the discovery of several New Testament papyri," https://voice.dts.edu/article/wallace-new-testament-manscript-first-century/

APPENDIX A
CANONIZATION, ACCURACY AND TRANSLATIONS OF THE BIBLE

INTRODUCTION

Christians throughout history have claimed and still claim that the Bible is the inspired word of God. Paul states in 2 Timothy 3:16-17:

> "All Scripture is inspired by God and profitable for teaching, for reproof, for correction, for training in righteousness; that the man of God may be adequate, equipped for every good work."

Peter states in 2 Peter 1:20-21:

> "But know this first of all, that no prophecy of Scripture is a matter of one's own interpretation, for no prophecy was ever made by an act of human will, but men moved by the Holy Spirit spoke from God."

We must answer two questions when these statements are true:

- How did the Bible as we know it today come into existence?
- How has it been transmitted to us down through history?

CANONIZATION OF THE BIBLE

The Bible came into existence through a process by which the people of God accepted certain writings as being divinely inspired by God and authoritative. This process resulted in what are referred to as the Old and New Testament canons. The term **canon** refers to the closed collection of biblical literature that is regarded as divinely inspired by God. There were three main criteria that had to be met for a writing to be considered divinely inspired by God and authoritative:

- The contents of the writing had to be theologically consistent with other writings judged to be divinely inspired by God.

- The writing had to be judged to be authoritative and from God. For the Old Testament, it had to carry the connotation of "thus saith the Lord," or be consistent with commandments, instructions, and/or teachings that were directly ascribed to God. For the New Testament, it had to be directly related to the teachings of Jesus.

- The writing had to have a history of continuous and widespread approval and use among the people of God for whom it was written. For the Old Testament, this was the Jewish community in the nation of Israel. For the New Testament, these were the Christian communities that were formed during the first four centuries after the death and resurrection of Jesus. For most of the early life of Israel, the Tabernacle or the Temple in Jerusalem served as the storehouse for the Old Testament scrolls. Many of the writings for the New Testament were letters written to early Christian churches that were circulated between cities.

- The writing had to be written by a person in a position of authority to speak for God. For the Old Testament, this person had to be a prophet, king, judge, scribe, or someone intimately connected with one of these persons. This person had to be an original apostle or someone intimately connected with one of the original apostles for the New Testament. The contents of the writing had to be theologically consistent with other writings judged to be divinely inspired by God.

- The contents of the writing had to be theologically consistent with other writings judged to be divinely inspired by God.

The canonization process for the Hebrew Old Testament occurred over a period of around 470 years. The Hebrew Old Testament canon consisted of three parts: the Torah (also referred to as the Law), the Prophets, and the Writings. The Torah contained the primary foundational doctrines and laws of the Jewish community. The Prophets were the practical outworking of these fundamental doctrines and laws. The Writings were the reflective and liturgical dimensions of the Jewish tradition. The books of the Hebrew Old Testament canon are listed in Table A1.

The canon of the Torah (Law) and the Prophets was closed after the writing of Malachi sometime during the fourth century B.C. Jewish literature indicates that a collection of the Writings existed as early as the second century B.C. The Writings contained five books of poetry (Psalms, Proverbs, Job, Song of Solomon, and Ecclesiastes). The remaining books were included in the Writings because the persons who were inspired by God to write them were not recognized as prophets. The books of the Hebrew Old Testament appeared to be completely intact by around 250 B.C.

Torah (or Law)	Prophets	Writings
Genesis	**Former**	Psalms
Exodus	Prophets	Proverbs
Leviticus	Joshua	Job
Numbers	Judges	Song of Songs
Deuteronomy	1-2 Samuel	(Solomon)
	1-2 Kings	Lamentations
	Later Prophets	Ruth
	Isaiah	Esther
	Jeremiah	Daniel
	Ezekiel	Ezra
	Hosea	Nehemiah
	Joel	1-2 Chronicles
	Amos	Obadiah
		Jonah
		Micah
		Nahum
		Habakkuk
		Zephaniah
		Haggai
		Zechariah
		Malachi

The early Christian communities accepted the Old Testament canon established by Jewish authorities. Even though the books of the Hebrew Old Testament and the Christian Old Testament were the same, their organization was different. The Christian Old Testament is listed in Table A2.

Initially, Scripture to Christians of the early Church meant the Old Testament. Irenaeus (120-202) was one of the first bishops to equate the authority of the New Testament to that of the Old Testament. Apostolic writings were accorded authority, but initially not on the same level as the Old Testament. The apostolic writings were gradually gathered together into the New Testament. By the time of Irenaeus, the New Testament was close to what it is today. The four Gospels, Acts, and Paul's letters were universally accepted. The writings in the New Testament from Hebrews through Revelation were generally accepted in most

Christian communities, but initially they were not universally accepted. The books of the New Testament are listed in Table A3.

Table A2

Pentateuch	Historical Books	Poetic Books	Prophets
Genesis	Joshua	Job	Isaiah
Exodus	Judges	Psalms	Jeremiah
Leviticus	Ruth	Proverbs	Lamentations
Numbers	1-2 Samuel	Ecclesiastes	Ezekiel
Deuteronomy	1-2 Kings	Song of Solomon	Daniel
	1-2 Chronicles		Hosea
	Ezra		Joel
	Nehemiah		Amos
	Ester		Obadiah
			Jonah
			Micah
			Nahum
			Habakkuk
			Zephaniah
			Haggai
			Zechariah
			Malachi

The canonization process for the New Testament occurred over a period of 400 years. Three factors led to the adoption of the New Testament canon. The first was the rise and spread of Gnosticism. Gnosticism, which began to spread about the time of Irenaeus, threatened the existence of Christianity. It was an esoteric system of mystical religious and philosophical doctrines that stressed a secret and superior knowledge of spiritual ideology as essential to salvation, viewed all matter as evil, and variously combined ideas derived from mythology, ancient Greek philosophy, ancient religions, and Christianity. The second was the development and spread of false writings. These came out of a desire to know more about the childhood of Jesus and to have more information about New Testament characters. Most of these writings centered on unproven mythical legends. The third reason for the development of the New Testament canon was the rise in the persecution of Christians. The Edict of Diocletian in 303 A.D. declared that all Christian books were to be destroyed. This forced the Church to identify those books that were authoritative and inspired by God and the ones that could be destroyed. The Council of Athenasius (367 A.D.) and the Council of Carthage (397 A.D.) accepted all 27 books of the New Testament as being inspired by God and authoritative.

Table A3

Gospels & Acts	Letters	Prophecy
Matthew	Romans	Revelation
Mark	1 Corinthians	
Luke	2 Corinthians	
John	Galatians	
Acts	Ephesians	
	Philippians	
	Colossians	
	1 Thessalonians	
	2 Thessalonians	
	1 Timothy	
	2 Timothy	
	Titus	
	Philemon	
	Hebrews	
	James	
	1 Peter	
	2 Peter	
	1 John	
	2 John	
	3 John	
	Jude	

After Jewish captives were allowed to return to Jerusalem from their Babylonian exile around 516 B.C. (see Ezra in the Old Testament), Jewish scribes adopted the following process for copying the books of the Torah and eventually the other books in the Old Testament:

- They could only use clean animal skins, both to write on, and even to bind manuscripts.

- Each column of writing could have no less than forty-eight, and no more than sixty lines.

- The ink must be black, and of a special recipe.

- They must verbalize each word aloud while they were writing.

- They must wipe the pen and wash their entire bodies before writing the word "Jehovah," every time they wrote it.

- There must be a review within thirty days, and the entire manuscript had to be redone if there was one mistake in the manuscript. The manuscript with the mistake was to be buried.

- The letters, words, and paragraphs had to be counted, and the document became invalid if two letters touched each other. The middle paragraph, word and letter must correspond to those of the original document.

- The documents could be stored only in sacred places (synagogues, etc.).

- Since no document containing God's word could be destroyed, they were stored, or buried, in a genizah - a Hebrew term meaning "hiding place." These were usually kept in a synagogue or sometimes in a Jewish cemetery.

ACCURACY OF THE BIBLE

Information for this section was obtained from the article: "Process of copying the Old Testament by Jewish Scribes," by Scott Manning, March 17, 2007 (http://www.scottmanning.com/archives/ scribeswritingoldtestament.php) and "Fascinating Facts about the Discovery at Qumen," Century- One Bookdstore (http://www.centuryone.com/25dssfacts.html).

After Jerusalem was sacked by Rome in A.D. 70, this process was lost. However, Hebrew copies of the Old Testament continued to be developed. Beginning in the 6th century and continuing until the 10th century, some European Jewish scribes used a similar method to copy manuscripts of the Old Testament. Until the discovery of the Dead Sea Scrolls in 1947, the oldest manuscript of the Old Testament only dated back to 895 A.D.

Palestinian herdsmen near the ruins of the former ancient village of Qumran discovered the Dead Sea Scrolls between 1947 and 1956. The scrolls were discovered in elevated caves west of the village. They are thought to have been written by a group referred to as the Essenes during the period of around 200 B.C. to 68 A.D. The scrolls are primarily written in Hebrew with some being written in Aramaic. Around 15,000 fragments from more than 500 manuscripts have been found. Scholars have identified the remains of about 825 to 870 separate scrolls. Fragments from all books of the Hebrew Old Testament, except Ester, have been found. Identified among the scrolls are 19 copies of Isaiah, 25 copies of Deuteronomy and 30 copies of the Psalms. Old Testament manuscripts dating back to the 10th century have few discrepancies relative to related manuscripts and fragments found at Qumran.

The New Testament has far more early manuscript evidence from a much earlier period than all other classical works of antiquity. Around one-hundred papyri Greek manuscripts that contain various parts of the New Testament have been discovered that date back to the second through eight centuries. (Wikipedia) According to Dr. Daniel B. Wallace, "… we have as many as eighteen New Testament manuscripts from the second century and one from the first. Altogether, more than 43 percent of all New Testament verses are found in these manuscripts." ("First Century Manuscript? Clarification statement about the discovery of several New Testament papyri;" http://www.dts.edu/read/wallace-new-testament-manscript-first-century/) Today the number of ancient New Testament manuscripts and fragments in various languages number well over 5,000.

TRANSLATIONS OF THE BIBLE

The Bible was not originally written in English. The Old Testament was written in Hebrew, with a few portions being written in Aramaic. The New Testament was written in Greek. The Bible that people normally read today is not written in these original languages. It is translations of the texts of these languages.

No translation of the Bible is 100 percent perfect, and none is 100 percent identical to the original texts. There is no best translation. All have some advantages and some drawbacks. Newer Bible translations developed within the last 45 years are better than the older ones.

Some early translations of the Bible include:

- The Septuagint (Greek translation of the Old Testament), 250-150 B.C.
- Latin Vulgate, 4th century A.D.
- John Wycliffe Translation, 1380
- William Tyndale Translation, 1525
- Coverdale Bible, 1535
- The Great Bible, 1539
- The Tavernier's Bible, 1539

- The Geneva Bible, 1560
- The Bishop's Bible, 1568
- The Rheims-Douai Bible, 1582
- The King James Version, 1611.

Listed below are modern Bible translations:

Other Translations	Updated Translations
American Standard Version (ASV), 1901 1971, Updated 1995	New American Standard Bible (NASB)
Revised Standard Version (RSV), 1952	New Revised Standard Version (NRSV), 1989
New American (Roman Catholic Bible), 1953	
New English Bible (NEB), 1961	Revised English Bible (REB), 1992
Today's English Version (TEV), 1966 (aka Good News Bible (GNT))	Contemporary English Version (CEB), 1995
Jerusalem Bible (JB), 1966	New Jerusalem Bible (NJB), 1985 (only the NT & Psalms updated), 1987
New Living Translation, 1966	
The Living Bible, 1971	
New International Version (NIV), 1978	
New King James Version (NKJV), 1982	
Amplified Bible (AB), 1987	
Tree of Live Version of the Holy Scriptures (TLV), 2014	

The Bible app presents multiple Bible versions for use on cell phones and computers.

APPENDIX B
PROPHESIES CONCERING JESUS

PROPHESIES CONCERNING EVENTS IN
THE LIFE OF JESUS

Events in Jesus' Life	Old Testament Prophesies	Fulfilled in the New Testament
1. Born of a woman	Genesis 3:15	Galatians 4:4 Matthew 1:20
2. Born of a virgin	Isaiah 7:14	Matthew 1:18, 24, 25 Luke 1:26-35
3. Son of God	Psalm 2:7 1 Chronicles 17:11-14 2 Samuel 7:12-16	Matthew 3:17 Matthew 16:16 John 1:34, 49
4. Seed of Abraham	Genesis 22:18 Genesis 12:2-3	Matthew 1:1 Galatians 3:16
5. Son of Isaac	Genesis 21:12	Luke 3:23, 34 Matthew 1:2
6. Son of Jacob	Numbers 24:17	Luke 3:23, 34 Matthew 1:2 Luke 1:33
7. Tribe of Judah	Genesis 49:10	Luke 3:23, 33 Matthew 1:2 Hebrews 7:14
8. Family line of Jesse	Isaiah 11:1, 10	Luke 3:23, 32 Matthew 1:6

9.	House of David	Jeremiah 23:5 2 Samuel 7:12-16	Luke 3:23, 31 Matthew 1:1
10.	Born in Bethlehem	Micah 5:2	Matthew 2:1 Luke 2:4-7
11.	Presented with gifts	Psalm 72:10 Isaiah 60:6	Matthew 2:1, 11
12.	Herod Kills Children	Jeremiah 31:15	Matthew 2:16
13.	Jesus' pre-existence	Micah 5:2 Isaiah 9:6, 7 Isaiah 41:4; 44:6; 48:12 Psalm 102:25	Colossians 1:17 John 1:1-2; 8:58 John 17:5.24 Revelation 1:17, 2:8 Revelation 22:13
14.	He shall be called Lord	Psalm 110:1 Jeremiah 23:6	Luke 2:11 Luke 20:41-44
15.	He shall be Emmanuel	Isaiah 7:14	Matthew 1:23 Luke 7:16
16.	He shall be a prophet	Deuteronomy 18:18	Matthew 21:11 Luke 7:16 John 4:19, 6:14, 7:40
17.	He shall be a priest	Psalm 110:4	Hebrews 3:1, 5:5-6
18.	He shall be a judge	Isaiah 33:22	John 5:30 2 Timothy 4:1
19.	He shall be a king	Psalms 2:6	Matthew 21:5, 27:37 John 18:33-38
20.	He shall be anointed by the Holy Spirit	Isaiah 11:2 Isaiah 42:1, 61:1-2	Matthew 3:16-17 Mark 1:10 Luke 4:15-21, 43 John 1:32
21.	He shall have a zeal for God	Psalm 69:9	John 2:15-17

22.	He shall be preceded by a messenger	Isaiah 40:3 Malachi 3:1	Matthew 3:1-2 John 1:23 Luke 1:17
23.	Jesus' ministry was to begin in Galilee.	Isaiah 9:1	Matthew 4:12-13, 17
24.	Jesus was to have a ministry of miracles	Isaiah 35:5-6	Matthew 9:32-35 Matthew 11:4-6 Mark 7:33-35 John 5:5-9, 9:6-11 John 11:43-47
25.	Jesus was to teach in parables	Psalm 78:2	Matthew 13:34
26.	Jesus was to enter the temple	Malachi 3:1	Matthew 21:12
27.	Jesus was to enter Jerusalem on a donkey	Zechariah 9:9	Luke 19:35-37 Matthew 21:6-11
28.	Jesus was to be a "stone of stumbling" to the Jews	Psalm 118:22 Isaiah 8:14, 28:16	1 Peter 2:7 Romans 9:32-33
29.	Jesus was to be a light to the Gentiles	Isaiah 60:3 Isaiah 49:6	Acts 13:47-48 Acts 28:28
30.	Jesus' resurrection	Psalm 16:10, 30:3 Psalm 41:10 Hosea 6:2	Acts 2:31 Luke 24:46 Mark 16:6 Matthew 28:6
31.	Jesus' ascension	Psalm 68:18	Acts 1:9
32.	Jesus to sit at the right hand of God	Psalm 110:1	Hebrews 1:3 Mark 16:19 Acts 2:34-35
33.	Jesus to be betrayed by a friend	Psalms 41:9, 55:12-14	Matthew 10:4 Matthew 26:49-50 John 13:21

34.	Jesus sold for 30 pieces of silver	Zechariah 11:12	Matthew 26:15, 27:3
35.	Money to be thrown in God's house	Zechariah 11:13	Matthew 27:5
36.	Silver to be used to buy Potter's Field	Zechariah 11:13	Matthew 27:7
37.	Jesus to be forsaken by disciples	Zechariah 13:7	Mark 14:27, 14:50 Matthew 26:31
38.	Jesus to be accused by by false witnesses	Psalm 35:11	Matthew 26:59-61
39.	Jesus to be dumb before accusers	Isaiah 53:7	Matthew 27:12-19
40.	Jesus to be wounded and bruised	Isaiah 53:5 Zechariah 13:6	Matthew 27:26
41.	Jesus to be smitten and spit upon	Isaiah 50:6 Micah 5:1	Matthew 26:27 Luke 22:63
42.	Jesus to be mocked	Psalm 22:7-8	Matthew 27:31
43.	Jesus to fall under His cross	Psalm 109:24-25	John 19:17 Luke 23:26 Matthew 27:31-32
44.	Jesus' hands and feet to be pierced	Psalms 22:16 Zechariah 12:10	Luke 23:33 John 20:25
45.	Jesus to be crucified with thieves	Isaiah 53:12	Matthew 27:38 Mark 15:27-28
46.	Jesus made intercession for His persecutors	Isaiah 53;12	Luke 23:34
47.	Jesus was rejected by His own people	Isaiah 53:3 Psalm 69:8, 118:22	John 1:11, 7:5, 48 Matthew 21:42-43
48.	Jesus was hated without a cause	Psalm 69:4 Isaiah 49:7	John 15:25

49.	Friends stood far off when He was crucified	Psalm 38:11	Luke 23:49 Mark 15:40 Matthew 27:55-56
50.	People shook their heads at Jesus when He was crucified	Psalm 22:7, 109:25	Matthew 27:39
51.	Jesus was stared upon when He was crucified	Psalm 22:17	Luke 23:35
52.	Jesus' garments were parted and lots were cast for them when He was crucified	Psalm 22:18	John 19:23-34
53.	Jesus was to suffer thirst when He was crucified	Psalm 22:15, 69:21	John 19:28
54.	Gall and vinegar were to be offered to Jesus when He was crucified	Psalm 69:21	Matthew 27:34 John 19:28-29
55.	Jesus was to feel forsaken by God when He was crucified	Psalm 21:1	Matthew 27:46
56.	Jesus was to commit Himself to God when He was crucified	Psalm 31:5	Luke 23:46
57.	None of Jesus' bones were to be broken when He was crucified	Psalm 34:20	John 19:23
58.	Jesus' heart was to be broken when He was crucified	Psalm 22:14	John 19:34
59.	Jesus' side was to be pierced	Zechariah 12;10	John 19:34
60.	Darkness was to come over the land when Jesus was crucified	Amos 8:9	Matthew 27:45
61.	Jesus was to be buried in a rich man's tomb	Isaiah 53:9	Matthew 27:57-60

PROPHESIES CONCERNING THE
SECOND COMING OF JESUS [1]

	Bible Verse	Prophesy
1.	Psalm 50:3-6	Jesus will return to execute judgment and to gather His people, Israel, to Himself. Refers to the return of Jesus at the end of the Tribulation.
2.	Isaiah 9:6-7	Jesus will return to rule during His millennial kingdom.
3.	Isaiah 66:18	Jesus will return to gather the nations of the world to Himself. Refers to Jesus setting up His millennial kingdom.
4.	Daniel 7:7-8	Ten-kingdom federation will be formed with the Antichrist as its head.
5.	Daniel 7:13-14	Jesus will be given dominion to set up His kingdom on earth during the middle of the tribulation.
6.	Daniel 7:26-27	The Antichrist will be judged and dominion o of the earth will be given to the followers of Jesus.
7.	Daniel 8:23-25	The Antichrist's power will be derived from Satan. The Antichrist will make war against Jesus, who will defeat him.
8.	Daniel 9:24-27	Tribulation will be seven years. The Antichrist will commit abomination of desolation and break 7-year covenant with Israel during the middle of the tribulation.
9.	Daniel 11:31, 12:11	The Antichrist commits abomination of desolation.
10.	Ezekiel 38-39	Israel will be invaded by the king of the north (Russia) and the king of the south (Egypt).

11.	Zechariah 12:10	Israel will recognize Jesus as her Messiah and will acknowledge with deep contrition that He was the One whom their forefathers had nailed to a cross when He returns to set up His millennial kingdom.
12.	Zechariah 14:1-9	Jesus will return with the armies of heaven to battle the Antichrist and the armies of the kings of the ten-kingdom federation at the battle of Armageddon. He will return by way of the Mount of Olives.
13.	Matthew 24:15-18 Mark 13:5-13 Luke 21:8-9	Prophesies by Jesus concerning the first half of the Tribulation.
14.	Matthew 24:15-18 Mark 13:14-16	Prophesies by Jesus concerning the abomination of desolation during the middle of the Tribulation.
15.	Matthew 24:19-25 Mark 13:17-23 Luke 17:22-37	Prophesies by Jesus concerning the great Tribulation (last three and one-half years of the Tribulation).
16.	Matthew 24:26-41 Mark 13:24-29 Luke 17:22-37	Prophesies by Jesus concerning the rapture.
17.	Acts 1:9-11	Jesus will return in the same way that He ascended to heaven. He ascended from the Mount of Olives to the east of Jerusalem and He will return by way of the Mount of Olives.
18.	1 Corinthians 15:51-52	Jesus will return to gather Christians to Himself at the rapture at the sound of the last trumpet.
19.	1 Thessalonians 1:10	Jesus will rescue us from the wrath of God duringthe great tribulation.
20.	1 Thessalonians 4:13-17	The dead in Christ will rise first, after whichthose who are alive will be caught up with Jesus at the rapture.

21. 1 Thessalonians 5:9-10   Jesus will rescue Christians from the wrath of God during the great tribulation by gathering them to Himself at the rapture.

22. 2 Thessalonians 2:1-4   Jesus will return to gather Christians to Himself at the rapture after the abomination of desolation by the Antichrist.

---

[1]   Does not include prophesies in the Revelation of John

APPENDIX C
SPIRITUAL GIFTS INVENTORY

**Developed from the spiritual gifts inventory in
Kinghorn and Gustafson, *Discovering and
Using Your Spiritual Gifts*, 1987**

INSTRUCTIONS FOR COMPLETING THE SPIRITUAL GIFTS INVENTORY

The spiritual gifts inventory consists of three components:

- Instructions for completing the inventory,
- 130 questions that make up the inventory plus a response sheet, and
- Instructions on how to interpret the results of the inventory.

This inventory of spiritual gifts provides you with an opportunity to identify your clusters of motivational gifts and ministries and to determine the level of the operations of the Holy Spirit in the performance of your ministries. Do not respond to the questions on the bases of how you think you ought to respond. Respond on the bases of your experiences and perceived interests. Do not be modest in answering the questions. However, answer the questions honestly. There are no right or wrong responses to the questions.

Rate your answers to the questions on a scale that ranges from 0 to 5:

0. I have no interest in and/or have had no experiences relative to the question.

1. I only have a very slight interest in and/or have had very minor or no experiences relative to the question.

2. I have a little interest in and/or have had some relatively minor experiences relative to the question.

3. I have an average interest in and/or have had some moderate experiences relative to the question.

4. I have above average interest in and/or have had some significant experiences relative to the question.

5. I have a strong interest in and/or have had substantial experiences relative to the question.

Mark a "0" to the right of the question when it is not relevant to your experiences and/or you have no interest in the question. Mark a "5" to the right of the question when you have a strong interest in the question and/or if you have had substantial experiences relative to the question. Mark your response to the question accordingly when your response is somewhere in between these two extremes. You may also copy the response sheet and then mark your responses directly on the response sheet.

SPIRITUAL GIFTS INVENTORY

1. I can verbalize biblical truths in a clear, concise, and direct manner.

2. I have a strong desire to meet the practical needs of others or of groups or programs within my church.

3. I enjoy researching spiritual principles contained in the Bible and then presenting these principles in a systematic way to others.

4. I am more interested in emphasizing how to make Christianity a practical means of meeting our daily needs then on focusing on the theoretical aspects of Christianity. I am interested in showing how biblical principles can be directly applied to daily living.

5. I have a significant ability to make money and accumulate assets, and I enjoy using my money and assets to spread the Gospel of Jesus Christ and to meet the physical needs of others who need help.

6. I am generally a person of action who often works to immediately get things done. I will usually step forward and assume the responsibility to lead a particular activity if no structured leadership exists.

7. I am a very sensitive person, and I can understand and emphasize with the feelings and needs of others. I am generally attracted to persons who are experiencing trouble and difficulties in their lives.

8. At times God gives me a wisdom that is clearly beyond my natural abilities.

9. I sometimes become aware of an event or situation apart from any verbal or other type of communication from other persons.

10. I easily see God's hand at work in many events in my life.

11. I have prayed for the healing of persons who have been miraculously healed by the Holy Spirit through my prayers.

12. God sometimes miraculously changes circumstances when I pray for specific situations.

13. I sometimes receive a revelation from the Holy Spirit concerning an understanding of a biblical principle that is clearly beyond my ability to comprehend using my own intellectual capabilities.

14. I can discern whether a prophecy and/or other utterance is inspired by the Holy Spirit or by a demonic spirit.

15. I often pray or speak in tongues with a language that I do not know or understand.

16. I sometimes interpret messages given in tongues.

17. I can adapt to different cultures and lifestyles to bring the gospel of Jesus Christ to people in foreign lands.

18. will not compromise the truth contained in the Bible even though I may appear to be stubborn and hard-headed.

19. I find it easy to invite persons to accept Jesus Christ as their Lord and Savior.

20. I like to help other persons grow as Christians.

21. I enjoy showing others how biblical principles apply to their daily lives.

22. When I have prayed for the healing of a person, he/she has been healed even though medical doctors have said healing was impossible.

23. I am often led to pray for the spiritual, emotional, and/or physical healing of other persons.

24. I enjoy helping others so they may be free to perform their ministries.

25. People often ask me for guidance and help in organizing and managing activities and/ or programs.

26. I am sometimes led by the Holy Spirit to give a message in tongues to a group of Christians during a prayer or other type of meeting or during a worship experience.

27. I have high standards for my own conduct, and I present the truths of God in a straightforward manner without compromise.

28. Without trying I can recognize the practical needs of others or of groups or programs within my church when others do not recognize these needs.

29. I can present the truths contained in the Bible to other persons in a manner that makes them easy to learn and memorize.

30. I am not only able to see and understand the nature of a person's problem, but I can also see how God can use this problem to enable the person to grow in His grace and to be perfected in His sanctifying love.

31. I am usually able to discern beforehand whether ministries I am asked to financially support will succeed or fail.

32. I can see the overall picture associated with a project and then to establish clearly defined long-range goals to meet the objectives of the project. I am then willing to delegate responsibility and authority to others to meet these goals and objectives.

33. I am usually concerned about the emotional or "inner" feelings of persons to whom I minister. As a result, I often spend time with these persons, and I spend time in prayer for them.

34. I sometimes receive an insight from the Holy Spirit into how to apply a particular biblical principle or a particular piece of knowledge to develop a specific course of action or to solve a specific problem.

35. During counselling I sometime discern information about something that has happened in the life of the individual I am counselling that was not communicated to me by that individual nor by anyone else.

36. I trust God when approaching difficult and/or dangerous assignments or tasks I feel led by Him to do.

37. I often have a strong sense that God desires to heal a particular person.

38. The Holy Spirit sometimes causes things to happen that clearly transcend the normal laws of physics and nature when I pray.

39. I sometimes feel led by the Holy Spirit to share a specific biblical truth to a group that is beyond my normal understanding of the truth at the time I share it.

40. I can sense the presence of evil and/or evil spirits.

41. I often pray to God in tongues.

42. Sometimes when I pray in tongues, I ask the Holy Spirit to give me an understanding or interpretation of what I pray.

43. I would enjoy learning a new language to start and grow a new church in a foreign country.

44. I do not mind being ridiculed and/or criticized for sticking to God's Word as I understand it.

45. I enjoy speaking to persons about what Christ has done in my life and for me.

46. I am patient with persons who are making slow progress in developing Christian character.

47. I enjoy studying biblical principles and then presenting them in an orderly fashion to others.

48. God has abruptly changed circumstances because of my prayers.

49. The Holy Spirit sometimes gives me a sense that a person needs deliverance from spiritual bondage and that he/she may also need emotional and spiritual healing.

50. I do not mind working in situations where I am required to perform menial tasks.

51. I can effectively organize persons and use available resources to participate in ministry and/or service to others.

52. I am sometimes led by the Holy Spirit to give an interpretation of a message in tongues that has been given to a group of Christians during a prayer or other type of meeting or during a worship experience.

53. I have a very good understanding of the Bible, and I often quote scriptures to validate biblical truths that I proclaim.

54. When working to meet the needs of others, I often neglect opportunities to get involved in activities that are important to my own spiritual growth.

55. I feel the spiritual principles and truths contained in the Bible must fit together in a systematic and consistent manner throughout the entire Bible. Furthermore, I feel it is important to use words and terms accurately and correctly when presenting the truths contained in the Bible.

56. I can share ways with other to help them deal with daily problems and overcome weaknesses.

57. I often use the giving of my financial support to motivate others to give to and support ministries I feel are important.

58. I am a good organizer, and I can get people moving in the same direction to achieve specified goals and objectives.

59. I am usually very tolerant of persons who are experiencing troubles and difficulties in their lives, and I am careful not to hurt their feelings. As a result, I sometimes fail to present the truth to them when they need it.

60. I am often able to bring illumination and clarification to situations where persons are confused with respect to a specific course of action or with respect to the understanding of a particular biblical principle.

61. I sometimes become aware during a conversation with a person of a significant need within that person that he/she is careful to hide.

62. I have seen the hand of God working in devastating tragedies that have occurred in my life and in the lives of others.

63. I have a sense that the Holy Spirit has given me the gift of healing.

64. Persons are sometimes miraculously healed when I pray for them.

65. Sometimes I am given an understanding of a particular biblical principle before I have read and studied the specific Bible verses that validate and substantiate the principle.

66. I can easily discern spiritual truth and spiritual error.

67. Praying in tongues has significantly added to my personal prayer life.

68. Sometimes when I hear a person giving an interpretation of a message in tongues, I sense he is not giving the correct interpretation.

69. I am fascinated with the idea of moving into a new culture and learning their ways so I can bring the gospel of Jesus Christ to them.

70. When it is necessary, I do not mind speaking the truth contained in the Bible when I confront those who are in places of authority.

71. I often conclude my witness for Christ to others with an appeal to them to accept Jesus Christ as their Lord and Savior.

72. I like to disciple individual Christians or groups of Christians.

73. I feel God wants me to participate in a teaching ministry.

74. I have sometimes been used by God to effect supernatural changes in circumstances or in lives.

75. I feel led by the Holy Spirit to participate in healing ministries.

76. I do not mind helping others even though they may take advantage of me.

77. I am effective in leading church committees and other church groups in decision making.

78. When someone gives a message in tongues to a group in which I am present, I can usually sense whether he/she is being led by the Holy Spirit to give the message.

79. I have a burning desire to break the stubborn self-will of others and to bring them into a relationship with God through Jesus Christ.

80. I do not mind working in the background to meet specific needs of my church or of others.

81. I tend to focus more on the theoretical aspects of Christianity than on the practical aspects.

82. I can persevere with others as long as they listen to me and keep on working to resolve their problems. However, when they lose interest in listening to me and/or when they give up on working through their problems, I tend to move on to others who need help.

83. When I give large sums of money to support specific ministries, I often do so quietly and anonymously.

84. I can discern the personnel and material resources that are available to accomplish a specific task or project and then to effectively use these resources to successfully complete the task or project.

85. I have an almost compulsory need to assist persons who need help. However, I usually can discern the sincerity or insincerity of persons who request help.

86. Sometimes I have special insights into proper courses of action a person ought to take in resolving a problem.

87. Sometimes during a meeting I suddenly understand the options associated with the solution to a difficult problem or situation that others do not perceive.

88. I trust and follow the leading of the Lord when dealing with difficult and painful family problems.

89. I have an insight into the fact that when God heals us, He wants to heal our spirit, soul, and body, often in that order.

90. God sometimes directly intervenes in seemingly hopeless situations when I pray for these situations.

91. Sometimes I receive a special revelation concerning my understanding of a specific biblical principle that is essential for determining a specific course of action or solving a problem.

92. I can discern whether a message given in tongues is from the Holy Spirit or from a demonic spirit.

93. Sometimes during my personal prayer time I feel overwhelmed by what I am praying and cannot find the words with which to express myself. When this happens, I pray in tongues.

94. I sometimes feel led by the Holy Spirit to give an interpretation of a message when I hear the message given by another person in tongues.

95. I would enjoy the challenge of being a missionary.

96. I often feel led to call persons to be accountable for their actions and to repent when their actions violate the commandments of God.

97. I like to go where non-Christians congregate to lead them to Christ.

98. I feel led to help protect baby and/or weak Christians from influences that would undermine their faith in Jesus Christ.

99. It bothers me when I hear a Christian testimony from a person that contains some false teachings or unsound advice.

100. God has worked miracles in my life.

101. I enjoy praying for those who are physically and/or emotionally ill.

102. I do not mind working at tasks for which I get little or no recognition.

103. I easily recognize the talents and spiritual gifts of others, and I can help them find ways of using their talents and gifts in the life of the church.

104. I am usually able to sense whether a group of Christians will receive and accept a message given to them by the Holy Spirit in tongues.

105. I am more concerned with presenting the Gospel of Christ to bring about repentance and transformation in the lives of others than I am in establishing personal relationships with others.

106. I tend to be more job oriented than people oriented within the church.

107. I insist on knowing the authoritative basis of a spiritual principle or biblical truth before I accept it as being from God.

108.   I tend to thrive on the success of others whom I have helped, while I have a difficult time in dealing with and accepting those who fail.

109. It is important that my decision to financially support a particular program or ministry be confirmed and supported by my church and by my spouse. It is particularly gratifying when I sense my decision to financially support a particular program or ministry is an answer to prayer.

110. I am willing to listen while others discuss the issues associated with a specific task or project. I am then usually able to use the results of their discussion to clearly define the goals and objectives associated with the task or project and then to specify ways in which these goals and objectives can be achieved.

111. I do not mind spending long periods of time with persons who have significant needs or who just need someone to talk to.

112. I can often sense several sides of a specific issue and discern which way God is leading a group relative to an issue.

113. I sometimes receive direct knowledge from the Holy Spirit concerning my understanding of a specific biblical principle or of a particular event, problem or situation before it is known to others.

114. I undergird everything I do with respect to my involvement in ministry, to my family, and to my profession with prayer.

115. The Holy Spirit has often led me to pray for the physical and emotional healing of a particular person.

116. Impossible things are often accomplished through my prayers.

117. Sometimes I feel led by the Holy Spirit to bring a special message, warning, exhortation or revelation from God to a group. The message, warning, exhortation or revelation is in a language that is understood by the group.

118. I can sense when a person is being inspired by the Holy Spirit, by a demonic spirit or by his/ her own human spirit.

119. Often when I am involved in intercessory prayer or in spiritual conflict I do not know how or for what to pray. When this happens, I pray in tongues.

120. When I give a message in tongues and there is no one present to interpret my message, I am led by the Holy Spirit to give an interpretation of my own message.

121. I am confident that I can stand alone to bring the gospel of Jesus Christ to a hostile, non- Christian culture.

122. I like to tell others about God's judgment and about the gift of salvation He gives to us through Jesus Christ.

123. I would rather evangelize a person than teach him/her about biblical truths.

124. I am interested in the details of a person's life so I can help nurture him/her in becoming a stronger Christian.

125. I like to organize and arrange biblical material in a way that makes it easier for others to learn and memorize.

126. The Holy Spirit sometimes inspires my prayers so that impossible things are accomplished.

127. I enjoy helping persons work though emotional and spiritual problems.

128. I like to work to relieve the physical and emotional burdens of others.

129. I usually work well under pressure, and I have little difficulty in making decisive decisions when necessary.

130. When I give or interpret a message in tongues, I am sensitive to the leadership of the Holy Spirit and to the mood of the group to whom the message is given.

RESPONSE SHEET

Total Spiritual Gift

1. ___	27. ___	53. ___	79. ___	105. ___	A. ___ _____
2. ___	28. ___	54. ___	80. ___	106. ___	B. ___ _____
3. ___	29. ___	55. ___	81. ___	107. ___	C. ___ _____
4. ___	30. ___	56. ___	82. ___	108. ___	D. ___ _____
5. ___	31. ___	57. ___	83. ___	109. ___	E. ___ _____
6. ___	32. ___	58. ___	84. ___	110. ___	F. ___ _____
7. ___	33. ___	59. ___	85. ___	111. ___	G. ___ _____
8. ___	34. ___	60. ___	86. ___	112. ___	H. ___ _____
9. ___	35. ___	61. ___	87. ___	113. ___	I. ___ _____
10. ___	36. ___	62. ___	88. ___	114. ___	J. ___ _____
11. ___	37. ___	63. ___	89. ___	115. ___	K. ___ _____
12. ___	38. ___	64. ___	90. ___	116. ___	L. ___ _____
13. ___	39. ___	65. ___	91. ___	117. ___	M. ___ _____
14. ___	40. ___	66. ___	92. ___	118. ___	N. ___ _____
15. ___	41. ___	67. ___	93. ___	119. ___	O. ___ _____
16. ___	42. ___	68. ___	94. ___	120. ___	P. ___ _____
17. ___	43. ___	69. ___	95. ___	121. ___	Q. ___ _____
18. ___	44. ___	70. ___	96. ___	122. ___	R. ___ _____
19. ___	45. ___	71. ___	97. ___	123. ___	S. ___ _____
20. ___	46. ___	72. ___	98. ___	124. ___	T. ___ _____
21. ___	47. ___	73. ___	99. ___	125. ___	U. ___ _____
22. ___	48. ___	74. ___	100. ___	126. ___	V. ___ _____
23. ___	49. ___	75. ___	101. ___	127. ___	W. ___ _____
24. ___	50. ___	76. ___	102. ___	128. ___	X. ___ _____
25. ___	51. ___	77. ___	103. ___	129. ___	Y. ___ _____
26. ___	52. ___	78. ___	104. ___	130. ___	Z. ___ _____

INSTRUCTIONS ON HOW TO INTERPRET THE RESULTS OF THE SPIRITUAL GIFTS INVENTORY

After you have marked your numerical response to each question to the right of the question, transfer your responses to the corresponding question number locations on the response sheet. Add the values of your responses horizontally across each line of the response sheet and place the total at the letter located at the end of each line. For example, add the responses for questions 1, 27, 53, 79, and 105 and place the total at letter A. Complete this process for all twenty-six lines for letters A through Z. Each line (A through Z) corresponds to a spiritual gift that is listed in Table 7 on page 151 in Chapter 15, Spiritual Gifts.

Lines A through G correspond to your motivational gifts. The key is given below:

A - prophecy
B - service
C -teaching
D - exhortation
E - giving
F - leading (administration)
G - showing mercy

Each of you is given a cluster of typically two to three motivational gifts. This cluster in general will not change as you spiritually grow and mature as a Christian. Some persons tend to respond more conservatively than others to the questions. Also, persons who are more mature as Christians tend to respond higher to those questions that relate to their cluster of motivational gifts. Thus, there is no standard score that qualifies a particular gift as one that may be in your cluster of motivational gifts. Generally, the gifts with the top two to three totals represent your cluster of motivational gifts.

Lines H through P correspond to the supernatural operations (or manifestations) of the Holy Spirit in your life. The key is given below:

H - word of wisdom
I - word of knowledge
J - faith
K - gifts of healing
L - effecting miracles
M - prophecy

N - distinguishing of spirits
O - various kinds of tongues
P - interpretation of tongues

These gifts are used in conjunction with your cluster of motivational gifts to better equip you for ministry. Totals at the end of each line associated with the operations of the Holy Spirit are influenced by your Christian maturity and by whether you have received the *baptism with the Holy Spirit* described in Chapter 16, Baptism with the Holy Spirit and Speaking in Tongues, and you speak in *tongues*. Those persons who are more mature in their Christian faith and/or who have received the *baptism with the Holy Spirit* tend to have higher response values on the questions associated with the operations of the Holy Spirit. There is no standard method for interpreting the responses to the questions associated with the operations of the Holy Spirit in your life. Also, there is no cluster of operations of the Holy Spirit that is predominant in your life. The Holy Spirit uses these operations as He wills and as He determines you need them when you are involved in ministry. Higher response values tend to indicate a greater sensitivity to the presence of the Holy Spirit and a greater reliance on the leading of the Holy Spirit in your ministries. Values greater than 20 tend to indicate a significant sensitivity to the Holy Spirit; values between 10 and 20 tend to indicate a moderate sensitivity to the Holy Spirit; and values less than 10 tend to indicate a minor sensitivity to the Holy Spirit. The numerical values of your responses to these questions will generally increase as you become a more mature Christian and particularly if you receive the *baptism with the Holy Spirit* and speak in *tongues*.

Lines Q through Z correspond to the ministries to which God is calling you. The key is given below:

Q - apostles (missionaries)
R - prophets
S - evangelists
T - pastors
U - teachers
V - ministries of miracles
W - ministries of healing
X - ministries of helps (service)
Y - ministries of administration
Z - ministries of various kinds of tongues

Mature Christians tend to respond higher to those questions that relate to their cluster of gifts of ministry. As before, there is no standard score that qualifies a particular gift as one that may be in your cluster of gifts of ministry. Generally, the gifts with the top two to three totals represent your cluster of gifts of ministry. It should be noted that God sometimes calls us into different areas of ministry as we grow in our relationship with Him through Jesus Christ. Thus, your responses to the questions that relate to your gifts of ministry may change with time.

www.ingramcontent.com/pod-product-compliance
Lightning Source LLC
Chambersburg PA
CBHW080944120626

46546CB00010B/2834